Penal Practice and Culture, 1500–1900

Penal Practice and Culture, 1500–1900

Punishing the English

Edited by

Simon Devereaux

and

Paul Griffiths

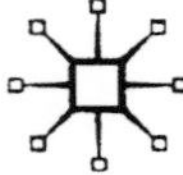

First published 2004 by
PALGRAVE MACMILLAN
Houndmills, Basingstoke, Hampshire RG21 6XS and
175 Fifth Avenue, New York, N.Y. 10010
Companies and representatives throughout the world

PALGRAVE MACMILLAN is the global academic imprint of the Palgrave Macmillan division of St. Martin's Press, LLC and of Palgrave Macmillan Ltd. Macmillan® is a registered trademark in the United States, United Kingdom and other countries. Palgrave is a registered trademark in the European Union and other countries.

ISBN-13: 978-0-333-99740-6
ISBN-10: 0-333-99740-9

This book is printed on paper suitable for recycling and made from fully managed and sustained forest sources. Logging, pulping and manufacturing processes are expected to conform to the environmental regulations of the country of origin.

A catalogue record for this book is available from the British Library.

Library of Congress Cataloging in Publication Data
Penal practice and culture, 1500–1900: punishing the English/edited by Simon Devereaux and Paul Griffiths.
p. cm.
Includes bibliographical references and index.
ISBN 0–333–99740–9 (cloth)
1. Corrections – England – History. 2. Punishment – England – History. 3. Violence – England – History. 4. Social control – England – History. I. Devereaux, Simon, 1966– II. Griffiths, Paul, 1960–
HV9649.E5P45 2003
365′.942′0903 – dc21 2003056400

10 9 8 7 6 5 4 3 2 1
13 12 11 10 09 08 07 06 05 04

Printed and bound in Great Britain by
CPI Antony Rowe, Chippenham and Eastbourne

Contents

List of Plates and Tables

Plates

Tables

Notes on the Contributors

Simon Devereaux is Lecturer in History at the University of Queensland, Australia. He is the co-editor of *Criminal Justice in the Old World and the New* (Toronto University Press, 1998), and his monograph *Convicts and the State: Criminal Justice and English Governance, 1750–1810,* is forthcoming from Palgrave.

J.R. Dickinson took his BA and PhD in History at the University of Liverpool. He has worked on a number of research projects, including two major projects with J.A. Sharpe, the first on crime, litigation and the courts in the Isle of Man c. 1580–1700, and the second on a regional study of violence in England, 1600–1800. He has published articles on the history of the early modern Isle of Man, and is the author of *The Lordship of Man under the Stanleys: Government and Economy in the Isle of Man, 1580–1704* (Cheetham Society, 1996). His future projects include acting as a volume editor for the New History of the Isle of Man.

Paul Griffiths is an Assistant Professor at Iowa State University and was a fellow at The National Humanities Centre, North Carolina, 2002–03. He is the author of *Youth and Authority: Formative Experiences in England, 1560–1640* (Oxford University Press, 1996), and co-editor of *The Experience of Authority in Early Modern England* (Macmillan, 1996) and *Londinopolis: Essays in the Cultural and Social History of Early Modern London* (Manchester University Press, 2000). He is currently preparing *Lost Londons: Crime, Control, and Change in the Capital City, 1545–1660* for publication.

Cynthia Herrup is Professor of History and Law at Duke University. She is the former editor of the *Journal of British Studies* as well as the author of *The Common Peace: Participation and the Criminal Law in Seventeenth-Century England* (Cambridge, 1987), and of *A House in Gross Disorder: Sex, Law and the 2nd Earl of Castlehaven* (Oxford University Press, 1999). She is currently completing a study of pardoning in seventeenth-century England.

Martin Ingram is a Fellow, Tutor and University Lecturer in Modern History at Brasenose College, Oxford. His publications include *Church Courts, Sex and Marriage in England, 1570–1640* (Cambridge University Press, 1987), and numerous articles on crime and the law, sex and marriage, religion and popular customs. He has also published on the history of climate.

Randall McGowen is Professor of History at the University of Oregon. He is co-author with Donna Andrew of *The Perreaus and Mrs. Rudd: Forgery and*

Betrayal in Eighteenth-Century England (California University Press, 2002), and he has written many articles on the death penalty and the criminal law in eighteenth- and nineteenth-century England.

Mark Rigstad received his PhD from Johns Hopkins University in 2001, and he is currently Assistant Professor of Philosophy at Oakland University. He is currently completing a book about natural law theory in seventeenth- and eighteenth-century British political thought.

Philippe Rosenberg teaches in the programme in Cultures, Civilizations and Ideas at Bilkent University in Ankara. He was a postdoctoral fellow at the Center for Humanistic Inquiry at Emory University, Atlanta, GA, 2002–03 and a Visiting Assistant Professor in the Department of History, 2000–02. He is completing a book entitled *Negative Enlightenment: Cruelty, Polemics, and Restraint in the British Isles, 1640–1700.*

Katherine Royer is an Assistant Professor of History at California State University, Stanislaus. She is currently working on a book on capital punishment in late medieval and early modern England. She has also written on the rhetorical construction of disease, published an article in the *Archives of Internal Medicine* on renal disease, and practiced medicine for over a decade.

J.A. Sharpe is Professor of History at the University of York. He has published extensively on the history of crime and punishment and, more recently, on the history of witchcraft in early modern England. His current research interests include further work on these topics, on the legal history of the Isle of Man in the early modern period, and the Dick Turpin legend. He is also author of *Early Modern England: A Social History, 1550–1760* (Edward Arnold, 2nd edn, 1997).

R.S. Shoemaker is Reader in History at the University of Sheffield. He is the author of *Prosecution and Punishment: Petty Crime and the Law in London and Rural Middlesex, c.1660–1725* (Cambridge University Press, 1991), and *Gender in English Society, 1650–1850: The Emergence of Separate Spheres?* (Longman, 1998), and is currently working on a study of public conflict in eighteenth-century London, *The Rise and Fall of the London Mob.* He is also co-director of the Old Bailey Proceedings Online project <http://www.oldbaileyonline.org>.

Greg T. Smith is an Assistant Professor of History at the University of Manitoba. He completed graduate studies at the University of Toronto, after which he held a SSHRC Postdoctoral Fellowship at the University of Guelph. He is the co-editor of *Criminal Justice in the Old World and the New* (Toronto University Press, 1998), and is currently completing a monograph entitled *Violence and the London Metropolis, 1760–1830.*

List of Abbreviations

AHR	*American Historical Review*
BIHR	Borthwick Institute of Historical Research, York
BL	British Library
BODL	Bodleian Library, Oxford
C&C	*Continuity and Change*
CJH	*Criminal Justice History*
CLRO	Corporation of London Record Office
DRO	Devon Record Office, Exeter
HER	*English Historical Review*
GL	Guildhall Library, London
HJ	*The Historical Journal*
HL	Huntington Library, San Marino
JBS	*Journal of British Studies*
LMA	London Metropolitan Archive
P&P	*Past and Present*
PRO	Public Record Office, London
SH	*Social History*
SP	State Papers
STC	Short Title Catalogue
TRHS	*Transactions of the Royal Historical Society*

Introduction: Punishing the English

Paul Griffiths

No other part of our penal past can match the emotional force of the gallows. No other moment was as dreadful as the speaking of death sentences by judges, except for the time it took for a hangman to slip a noose over an unlucky felon's head and to open the hatch to leave bodies dangling, legs kicking, and chests buckling. There was no other scene like this one, no matter how many lashes it took to make backs 'bloody' in markets, or cuts to sever an ear on the pillory. Executions were the most violent face of the state, taking lives for lives or for a piece of stolen property. The general public looked on, adding hisses, jeers and sometimes cheers from the moment convicts left their cell for the last time to the instant when they were 'launched into eternity'. This gallows ceremony, so familiar now from a string of histories of penal culture since 1500, publicly expressed authority, morality and sound religion in displays, sermons and speeches from the gallows. Might was right. If all went well, according to the authorities' script, doomed felons lectured the crowd, urging them to stay on the right side of the law and to live life like good christians ought to do. It was now too late for felons on the gallows who, however, hoped to be up in Heaven in the next hour or so, but not for people in the crowd, so long as they listened and learned from the bad examples on the gallows. Not long after the last breath was sucked from swinging felons, the whole event and its ideological moorings were written down in pamphlets that were distributed far and wide to reach readers as well as the spectators on the day.[1]

Nearly all interpretations of the historical development of punishment lead back to the gallows. Public execution hogs the historiography of punishment and the cultural shifts that follow on from penal change. No other question is asked as often as this one: How did society get from the grisly gallows to the 'well-ordered' prisons that were springing up all over Victorian England?[2] This is *the* question, and it is asked all the time. We zoom in on the gallows and ask why fewer felons were hanged over time, and why it was felt that there was a need to come up with other ways to punish them, through transportation overseas and imprisonment. These are questions that will never go away because penal cultures speak so much about emotions and the exercise of political power. It must have meant something for humanity when the English were no longer punished in public, or had bits and pieces of their bodies chopped off or pulled out with sizzling tools. A prison cell was a chilling prospect, but at least it offered a glimmer of hope that people may one day change for the better with the right sort of moral coaching and discipline. The story of the gallows is one of life and death, and even redemption. Small wonder, then, that it is the one that we return to again and again to explain punishment over time.

In what follows I will reaffirm the huge importance of the gallows and the other 'secondary' penalties that were suggested as more workable and efficient alternatives to hanging days – transportation and imprisonment. But this introduction is divided more or less equally into discussions of punishing petty crime and more serious felonies. This is because the overwhelming prominence of the gallows in work so far means that our understandings of how penal cultures and practices have developed since 1500 are based on probably less than 5 per cent of all the penalties that were dished out in the time covered by this book. I would like to try and strike a better balance between the punishment of these two major categories of crime, and so a considerable chunk of this Introduction will make a case for the significance of punishing petty crime whenever our ancestors thought about the nature of criminality, penal culture and penal practice. This is in no shape or form a counter argument to the one based on capital crime. There was a single line of explanation that linked the first 'lesser' penalty to the one at the end on the gallows. So, the first task of this Introduction is to draw attention to these connections once again, and to give more time and space to the conceptual significance of petty crime than we have usually seen in other work up to now. The second main task is to introduce the chapters that follow. I want to start by running through some of the principal themes and turns in work about punishing felony over the last six decades or so, and to introduce the chapters that are mostly concerned with capital crimes. The rest of the Introduction turns to punishing petty crime, and the need to combine its various significances for past penal cultures and practices with what we know now about the course of punishing capital crime through time. No claim is made that this is a coherent collection with a single purpose that follows on from what I have to say in my review of the field. The leading link, of course, is that each essay is on punishment and sheds new light on past penal cultures and practices.

I

'There is nothing we can learn from the penal code' of the later eighteenth century, one observer noted in 1974, 'except that we are well rid of it'.[3] Getting rid of executions was a high-water mark for humanity. Ever since executions disappeared behind tall prison walls once and for all in 1868, the story of punishing felony has been portrayed as a brash forward movement from the 'enlightened sunshine' of the eighteenth century on. It is a good story, with a good ending: the removal of a sadistic sight from public gaze. We as a society are said to be better for it, and the fact that it could happen at all was a proof of human kindness and sympathy to the agony on the gallows.[4] Even the words that we use for this bygone brutality are emotive ones, based in blood: the capital code that was extended around 1700 to protect property in the main was called the 'Bloody Code'.[5] This code along with felony and the 'long' eighteenth century (stretching from c.1680–1830, also the lifetime of the 'Bloody Code') are the principal reference points for how we have come to understand past penal cultures and practices.

This is true of Sir Leon Radzinowicz's mammoth five-volume *History of English Criminal Law* (1948–86),[6] as well as the work that followed by John Beattie, Vic Gatrell, Douglas Hay, and Peter King, to name only the most prominent people in a packed field. Radzinowicz's work was a work of its time that was driven by cultural assumptions that went with him to the archives. He was a beaver there, and all after him have benefited from his mighty labours in the Public Record Office, and his close combing of printed books, Parliamentary papers, and a mixed bag of ephemera (all copiously noted and listed in appendices and bibliographies that run on for many pages). Radzinowicz's argument over several thousand pages boils down to a single sentence of Whig wisdom in which the rise of reason smoothly unseats irrationality, and a new humanity softens once nasty and mean-spirited emotions. He writes in the opening pages of his first volume that 'Lord Macauley's generalization that the history of England is the history of progress is as true of the law of the country as of the other social institutions of which it is a part'. This glowing story of modernity after 1780 or so ends with a tribute to 'the forces of morality, of philosophical thought and social consciousness'; that were the leading lights in the move towards modern methods of punishment and policing.[7] And like the first historians to write about the coming of modern administrative systems, Radzinowicz gives the accolade of principal protagonist to the ubiquitous Jeremy Bentham (1748–1832): 'the greatest legal philosopher [of his time], the inspiring architect of a new jurisprudence', and an astounding author whose collected works on penology were 'the first attempts to combat delinquency by enlightened preventive measures rather than by extreme punishments'.[8]

Yet Whigs like Radzinowicz never had the stage entirely to themselves. There was never just one version of the story, and even before Radzinowicz put pen to paper to start his first volume, two leading figures in the Frankfurt sociology school – Georg Rusche and Otto Kirchheimer – had published *Punishment and Social Structure* (1939), a landmark work that is not mentioned once in Radzinowicz's flood of footnotes in his first volume, or in the

50-page bibliography at the end of the book (four decades later it only turned up once in the last of the five volumes). The two German sociologists were fishing for the origins of the prison, and they looked towards contexts rather than the texts of a polymath like Bentham. In vigorous prose they wrote that the prisons' preeminence was rooted in capitalism and the proliferation of factories where wage-earners worked in walled spaces. Prisons even looked like factories and most of their inmates were the sort of working men who also filled factories, and who needed heavy-handed discipline to make them toe the line.[9] Whatever we may think about these causes and effects today, *Punishment and Social Structure* is still a topical book, not least because it was the first to draw a sequence of steps leading from the houses of correction of four centuries ago to the penitentiaries that followed 200 years later.[10] But it is also the last major book on the roots of prisons to give so little space to the gallows, except as a crudely characterized tool of discipline to keep the working classes in dumbstruck awe.

Maybe it was this skirting of the gallows that led to this book staying largely unread until its reissue three decades after it first appeared. By then, however, a brand-new story of the shift from gallows to cells was leading debate in other directions. Michel Foucault published *Surveilleur et Punir* in 1975, and an English translation – *Discipline and Punish* – followed in the next year. Put as simply as possible, Foucault sees the 'Enlightenment' shift from penalties that were meant to harm bodies in public to new penal cultures that nursed and reformed offenders' souls inside prisons, as a shift in the exercise of power. But far from being an outcome of reason and compassion, the new-fangled penitentiary was a darker and more insidious way of ordering inmates lives (and minds). Behind its tall walls where the public could not see, it was hoped that solitary confinement, continuous surveillance and heavy doses of religious guidance and work discipline might lead prisoners to think long and hard about their flaws and change their ways.[11] Bentham was again a leading light in the story. Although unlike Radzinowicz – who spent longer working with Bentham's juridical and penal ideas – Foucault's main concern was with Bentham's closely explicated model for imprisonment: his panopticon plan (from the Greek meaning 'all-seeing').[12] Foucault does not credit Bentham with being the inventor or philosopher of the prison, but sees the panopticon plan as a good example of the ambition that lay behind the new penal regime. With its clever uses of space, light and glass, the panopticon enabled round-the-clock surveillance (though inmates would never know when the guards' gaze fell on them), what Foucault calls 'inspection [that] functions ceaselessly', and its 'strict spatial partitioning', made sure that prisoners were kept apart to 'let them think and feel remorse alone'. The prison was part of a penal order that aimed at the creation of the 'modern soul'.[13] The irony, of course, is that despite hawking his plans around the Home Office for a couple of decades, Bentham's panopticon was never built in his lifetime, though it did have a heavy influence on the leading penitentiary of the day – Pentonville – which received its first prisoners in 1842.

Discipline and Punish was read everywhere, though its influence has been softer on historians who write about punishing the English. The reasons for this are not always apparent, though other interpretations were making an impact on the questions we asked about penal changes and the ways in which we thought through the answers. Foucault had (has) followers and admirers among historians, but no matter how vital his voice, it was only one in a field that was filling up rapidly. Michael Ignatieff published *A Just Measure of Pain* two years after *Discipline and Punish* had first appeared in English. He did not slam Foucault's ideas as others have after him for their thin sense of past societies and loose use of sources. In matter of fact, his book is as near as they have yet come to entering the mainstream of English penal histories. Like Foucault Ignatieff began with the panopticon plan, and he traced it through to Pentonville, a place which is as dark in his pages as it was in *Discipline and Punish*, with a moral mission to get prisoners to change for the better that is every bit as cold and calculating as it was in Foucault's hands. The major difference is that Ignatieff situates the main impetus for penal planning not in Bentham's design-sheets for a make-believe prison, but in the fevered inward-looking spirituality of prison-reform lobbyists like John Howard and Jonas Hanway.[14]

He also looks more deeply into the part played by the sweeping industrial changes around 1800, and with his interest in the common characteristics of prisons, workhouses and asylums, Ignatieff is on much the same ground as Rusche and Kirchheimer before him, and also as David Rothman in his pathbreaking work on penal cultures in the early American republic.[15] But the social control potential of the penitentiaries to subdue workers and to make them meek and mild for factory-work was an important matter for Ignatieff, as it had been for Foucault. Strange, then, that a little less than three years later Ignatieff had turned full circle and was now taking himself (and others) to task for simplifying the complex narratives of penal change which had many twists and turns, and for following a simple binary polarity of domination/submission to sum up life within prison walls.[16] Other reasons were now being proposed for prison reform, and prison life no longer seemed as harsh and bleak as it once had been. The fullest study of English prisons so far, Margaret DeLacy's painstaking work on Lancashire prisons from 1700–1850, makes a strong case that concern for the care of prisoners was a driving force for reform, though she does not exclude coercion and control. In other words, overcrowding was seen to be a breeding ground for sickness and other sufferings, so that compassion counted when it came to debating the state of prisons, along with control and discipline.[17]

As already mentioned, this balance between emotions and cold control is one of the thorniest topics in all the questions we ask about past penal cultures. As with Foucault, we need to look across the English Channel to find the most all-encompassing account of the emotions (or civility) in bringing about the end of public executions. Pieter Spierenburg published *The Spectacle of Suffering* in 1984. This was the first full-blown attempt to apply Norbert Elias's influential idea that a 'civilizing process' changed 'the behaviour and affective life of Western peoples' once and for all after the Middle Ages to the fall of the gallows. People – or at least upper-class and middling people – were softer skinned after 1700, more touchy about the suffering of others, and more squeamish about seeing grisly miseries.[18] Elias mentions punishment in the first page of his book, but nowhere else in its 576 pages. It was Spierenburg who spotted the ties between Elias, emotions and executions. The moment when the gallows were reduced to rubble was a civilizing one.[19] Spierenburg believes that an accelerating emphasis upon public-physical punishments around 1500 and after was an offshoot of the expansion of the power of the state and of sudden bursts of urban growth. Their decline over the next three centuries or so was a result of the more humane and enlightened nation-state whose population (straight from Elias's pages) was now much more sensitive 'to the sufferings of convicts' as a 'critical threshold of sensibility was reached' after 1800.[20]

Like Foucault before him, there is no camp of historians in the English-speaking world who follow Spierenburg's lead to the letter. His project to couple civility and penal change has not been rejected out of hand, but few historians would go as far back in time as 1500 to look for a framework for the study of the emotions. Neither Randall McGowen or V.A.C. Gatrell, who both give a prominent place to emotional responses to sufferings on the gallows, spend much time looking at the period running up to the so-called 'era of reform' (c.1770–1830).[21] They have this in common, but they differ about the substance of the 'sympathy' that was softening reactions to pain and gory public displays, and was a leading argument for the reform/repeal of the capital code. They also disagree about how much this 'sympathy' contributed to the dismantling of the 'Bloody Code' (1820s) and to the later abolition of public execution (1868). McGowen is more willing to believe in the sincerity of this 'sympathy' and its pulling power for advocates of penal reform, helping them to come behind this great human cause. For these reformers, the agony on the gallows made the older arguments, according to which the larger good of society – that is the body politic as opposed to the individual body that was made to suffer so horribly – was well-served by these state spectacles, seem hollow and shallow. Nor was this agony the doomed felon's alone, for it was also felt by soft-skinned reformers and people in the crowd as an assault on their own well-being. 'Society', McGowen notes, 'was [now] composed of separate bodies, of individuals who might be connected by interest and feeling rather than by a shared ceremonial life. The life of the individual [he adds] was uniquely important, and sacrifice of the physical body would injure rather than heal the social body.'[22] McGowen asks us to take seriously the claim to sympathy, but also urges us to examine what reformers meant when they used it in their books and speeches. This sympathy went beyond simple fellow-feeling for the suffering of others. It also concealed both an anxiety about social distance and the use of violence to correct the faults of others, and it imagined brand-new forms of discipline and control that could appear to be non-coercive.

Gatrell, on the other hand, is sceptical about what he reads in the pages of penal reformers. He doubts that 'sympathy' was ever sincere, and suspects that the 'civilized' critics of the capital code never truly felt the agony on the gallows as they said they did in prose that dripped with emotion. Another word was needed to characterize their reactions and Gatrell came up with squeamishness: an immersion in the real (if only imagined) anguish on the gallows, that went hand-in-hand with a self-congratulatory opposition to (and distance from) these bloodthirsty displays. Nor were these expressions of sympathy as regular as we once believed. Gatrell seems sure that they were in fact more intermittent and selective. Feeling dying pains on the gallows was not a spur for reform. What made reformers speak against the gallows was squeamishness; their deep-seated unease with the show of so much suffering. Their discomfort led them to write sweeping simplified characterizations of the gallows crowd, calling them all depraved and itching for gore. Although Gatrell sees a role for the emotions in the disappearance of hanging days, it is altogether different to the one imagined by McGowen or, indeed, Radzinowicz.[23]

John Beattie is another historian who has invoked Elias to explain penal changes, and he was also one of the first scholars of 'sympathy' and punishment to go outside the 'era of reform' to take the story back to the late seventeenth century.[24] In a series of pioneering articles, Beattie had worked with assize and quarter sessions records to pick out the patterns of crime and to make us all aware of the difficulties raised by the 'dark figure' of unreported and unrecorded crimes.[25] It may therefore have come as a surprise to some that his first major monograph on crime – *Crime and the Courts in England, 1660–1800* (1986) – ended up spending so much time on changing penal cultures and practices. The cornerstone of Beattie's interpretation is the Transportation Act (1718), not because sending convicts overseas was new then, but because of the scope of the Act and its widespread implementation. It was also the first time that the central government took the leading role in guiding a penal measure of such importance through Parliament. By covering the costs of putting convicts from London and its nearby counties on ships across the Atlantic (more than half the national annual total of transportees), as well as countering moves by colonial leaders to block their passage in the first place, the central government turned a punishment that had once been vulnerable to swings in colonial needs and the will of merchants, into one that was imposed as a matter of routine. Nor was this an overnight change. The Transportation Act was the eventual outcome of three or four decades of searching by leaders in Whitehall and the (London) Guildhall to come up with a reliable and credible alternative (or 'secondary punishment') to the gallows. The efficacy and brutality of the gallows had long been a concern in some circles that fretted about the number of people being put to death for pinching something worth no more than a couple of shillings. The other alternative to the gallows that grabbed a great deal of attention was imprisonment with hard labour. Bills were brought to Parliament towards the close of the seventeenth century that never made it onto the statute book. But, finally, in 1706, a law was passed that gave judges the option of putting felons in prison in houses of correction for up to two years. Like the Transportation Act, this law was a milestone, even though it was little used after 1718. By that date, judges had never before had so many choices about how best to make felons pay for their crimes.[26]

The recent work of Beattie and McGowen, in particular, argues that there was some uneasiness with the failings of penal practices in the seventeenth century and a larger measure of experimentation with penal practises than we once previously suspected. This is also an argument about the status of 'secondary' penalties. Beattie believes that it is wrong to think of transportation as merely a more merciful alternative to the loss of life on the gallows. It was a dreadful penalty in its own right, and the worst one for felons next to the noose.[27] Taking debate to new ground, Beattie makes the point that the 'real revolution' happened in the treatment given to petty criminals or to thieves who had the gravity of their offence lessened to petty larceny. More than half of all guilty thieves in Surrey were branded and left free to go home up until 1715, but about the same ratio were sent across the sea from 1722–50. More revealing still, by far the highest number of thieves who were sent to North America were not felons with the luck of a pardon, but first-time offenders who had stolen a pittance.[28] Beattie takes this to mean that the burst of transportation (and prison) sentences after 1720 was not a simple matter of humanity and rationality, but in some ways the opposite: a harsher attitude towards small-time thieves who had once had a better than even chance of leaving prison with a whipping and/or branding. The main aim of the criminal law, Beattie comments, was to make sure 'that the consequences of conviction [became] more serious', and 'to bring the greatest unhappiness to the greatest number of convicts'.[29]

Beattie began his overhaul of the history of penal practice nearly two decades ago in *Crime and the Courts*, and his most recent book – *Policing and Punishment in London, 1660–1750* (2001) – continues to push deep concern about the limits and lasting cruelty of the gallows further back in time.[30] In this body of work he has also shown how the option of transportation completely changed criminal justice procedure from 1718 on, not least by streamlining the pardoning process. Since transportation quickly became the only acceptable alternative for nearly all capital convicts – apart from a few who were able to show that 'special circumstances' had a bearing on their case – it was used time and time again, and led to a loosening in the review of judges' recommendations by royal officials. It was now standard practice for judges to list the names and offences of offenders who were convicted on their last circuit in a letter that also put down how long they should be sent overseas. In nearly all cases the royal authorities simply rubber-stamped the judge's recommendation, and a pardon followed, as asked.[31] In the long run, the switch from whipping/branding to transportation to clear packed prisons meant that swings in the availability of transportation shifted attention towards prison conditions and the possibility that time spent in a cell might become more purposeful and productive.[32] We have almost certainly downplayed the place of pragmatism and even common sense in bringing about penal changes. At any rate, the collapse of transportation to America after 1775, and the lag in getting an alternative in New South Wales up and running, had a large impact on imprisonment, including the passing of the Penitentiary Act (1779).[33]

One last point which matters for us because it is at the core of Simon Devereaux's chapter in this book, is that we have not yet taken enough notice of the points of contact between the development of punishment and policing over time. The two affected each other, and in ways that mattered. Beattie has made us aware of how the same steps that led to the sudden increase in transportation after the statute also gave a boost to policing criminal gangs and crooked thief-takers – Jonathan Wild more than any other – with the bait of princely rewards to grass on ringleaders.[34] Evidence is now coming to light that the perception of the connection between policing and punishing was a driving force behind the major measures of police reform in London in the last two decades of the eighteenth century.[35] Devereaux argues later in this book that this connection is a key to understanding Home Secretary Robert Peel's approaches to the conundrums raised by the capital code over the 1820s. As objections to it reached fever-pitch, Peel pinned his hopes on reducing and preventing crime on the Metropolitan Police Act (1829).

There is almost a small cottage-industry pumping out books and essays on the capital code. The largest number of chapters in this collection continues this examination of punishing the English felon. It is not a shock that the Transportation Act (1718) is the focal point of most work on sending convicts over oceans. So far major books and essays on transporting felons before 1660 can be counted on the fingers of one hand.[36] Cynthia Herrup adds another chapter to this small pool in her contribution to this collection. One of her main aims is to remind us that transportation was treated on the whole as a form of pardon rather than as the first-instance penalty it was to become after 1718. She goes back to the medieval period to trace how the pardoning process softened the letter of a rigid royal law code, and it continued to exert this moderating influence up until the seventeenth century. Herrup breaks new ground when she pinpoints the Interregnum

(1649–60) as a turning point in how pardons were used. There was enough coverage of conditions in the colonies by this time to suggest that transportation to one of them was a tough penalty, and not a golden opportunity for warmer weather and a nice fresh start in life. By this time, too, the pardon was nothing else except an alternative punishment for capital felons. It was now no longer simply linked to a reprieve which put an original death sentence on hold for a while. Transportation became instead a condition of pardon on its own, and for the first time the primary purpose of law to put felons to death was set aside. What Herrup show us, is that from now on transportation was first and foremost a punishment, rather than a mere alternative to the noose.[37]

Randall McGowen picks up some of the threads of this story after 1660 in his chapter on 'the problem of punishment'. He has combed through shelves of printed books to look for the words in which contemporaries wrote down their unease about the agony on the gallows. Their words expressed the 'good' reasons for coming up with alternatives to killing felons. In the four decades after 1690 this concern did not usually appear as an out-and-out lambasting of hanging by its avid opponents, but more gently as apologetic rhetoric from its backers. From the 1730s on, however, when debating punishment became more passionate and widespread through mainstream magazines like *The London Magazine* or *The Gentleman's Magazine*, it more directly aimed at getting rid of hanging days. By the 1750s, reformers were narrowing their case to lobby for imprisonment at hard labour as an alternative to executing and transporting felons. There are few watersheds in the long history of penal change. But some scholars point to 1770 and after as the period when criminal law reform became an extremely serious matter as England's chattering classes absorbed the arguments of Cesare de Beccaria's classic work of reform, *Of Crimes and Punishments* (English translation, 1767).[38] But McGowen, like Beattie, dates the upsurge in earnest debate about the criminal code to before 1700. This is not the first time that historians have tinkered with this chronology. Tudor and Stuart historians have long been aware of people who pressed the case for penal reform before 1660 with passion.[39] But both Beattie and McGowen are better known as historians of the eighteenth-century penal code, and with their recent work we can now see a long line linking reform calls over more than two centuries. At any rate, the ground for the storm about penal reform in the middle of the eighteenth century and after had been well-prepared beforehand, in seventeenth-century books, Parliamentary bills, and in the Hard Labour Act (1706).

Three other chapters look more closely at a question that must have hovered over all hanging days: on what grounds did the state (or any legal philosopher for that matter) give itself the right to put felons to death? Mark Rigstad rereads English receptions of Hugo Grotius's keynote book, *The Laws of War and Peace* (1625), to seek some such justifications. He puts a spotlight on the less well-known sections of this book that put the case for the natural right of individuals not only to question wrongdoing by people over them in authority, but also to punish it when it was serious enough. Grotius wrote that long ago the duty of dishing out punishments for the good of society had rested with individuals, however humble. But today that obligation had been turned into 'the judicial authority of sovereign states and princes'. Yet even now, he continued, in grave moments when lives were at risk from the abuse of authority, the 'first duty' of people to punish a bully came before anything else.[40] Rigstad follows this line of argument through the trial of the king and his execution (1649), the steady spread of Machiavellian ideas in English intellectual circles, and the tense times of the Exclusion Crisis and Glorious Revolution.

Katherine Royer also revisits another major text – John Foxe's *Actes and Monuments* (1571) – with some new questions about perceptions of differences between Catholic and Protestant martyrs/martyrdom in a work that was second only to the Bible on the early modern bestsellers list. She notes that protestants suffered more willingly (and actively) for their cause at the stake, and that their courage in the wave of flames was said to reveal the power of the true word of God. Catholic martyrs, on the other hand, were said to be more spare and submissive, and to give up their lives almost passively. The moral of the story, as we might expect in an inspirational Protestant text, was that protestants were spirited and steadfast even at the very end, while lily-livered catholics died like lemmings. Royer reads Foxe as a penal text that told execution stories like a cheap pamphlet, except that *Acts and Monuments* chronicled many deaths. Philippe Rosenberg counts penal texts as well as reading them. He runs through the Short Title Catalogue from 1550–1750 adding up the texts with one or more keywords in their title (including 'execution', 'punish[ment]', and 'justice'), and finds that more of them were printed over the five decades after 1625. The apparent bloodthirstiness of the capital code made a difference, for the most part because the number of executions reached its highest point around 1600, and dropped off over the next two centuries.[41] Rosenberg makes the point that his authors were writing to give good reasons for the terrifying letter of English law. They had murder most in mind, but the violence of crimes excused the violent end on the gallows. A robber with a knife deserved to lose his life. Rosenberg cleverly switches attention to contemporary outrage at crime, and picks out some overlooked concerns that help us to understand why educated men could argue ardently for public killings.

Like McGowen, Simon Devereaux takes as his subject the feverish debates about the efficacy of the gallows, although he pushes forward in time to look at the part played by Home Secretary Robert Peel in bringing the 'Bloody Code' to an end in the 1820s. The use of the gallows slowed down all the way through Peel's time at the head of the Home Office, though doubt has been cast on his zeal for reform and whether or not he did much to alter the letter of the law or the practice on the gallows. Some scholars suspect that the legislation consolidating criminal laws (1827) had little impact on cutting back the number of hangings.[42] Some recent work on Parliamentary statistics shows that only one decade before the capital code was stripped down to putting only murderers to death (1837), Peel had been putting his signature to the killing of far more felons than most home secretaries before him, and the Whig ministers who followed after him from 1830 on.[43] Devereaux, however, still wants to suggest that Peel's time at the Home Office led to long-lasting changes. He has looked very closely at hanging days in London (by far the largest criminal jurisdiction in the land), and counted a fall in the number of gallows deaths after 1822 (when Peel took over at the Home Office). It was not just a matter of numbers, however, as there was fuller and more thoughtful discussion of each death sentence in Peel's Home Office. Peel may have had few qualms about hanging felons, but there were a smaller number of executions in the time when he was home secretary, and he is said to have been more prepared to listen to the mounting loathing for the capital code in London and elsewhere.

Murderers continued to be hung before an audience up until 1868, and behind prison walls after that. Already, in 1840, William Ewart had made his first Parliamentary bid to get capital punishment abolished across-the-board, and he was the leading light in the abolitionist lobby until the day he died in 1869.[44] The movement of execution indoors may or may not have been planned as a stepping stone to the ending of the death penalty altogether, not enough is known about the abolitionist movements in the decades after 1870 to speak with confidence about this. Ewart's death was a blow to them, and only a tiny fraction of MPs backed his out-and-out hostility to capital punishment.[45] Gatrell and others believe that Victorians continued to visit 'hanging trees' in their mind's eye after 1868: 'tucked away in distant clubs and drawing-rooms, consuming images in safety'.[46] A vivid newspaper story of an execution appeared now and then, otherwise there was not much in print at the time that might be called gallows pornography. But nowhere is the gallows lasting 'appeal' better revealed than in the letters for the job of hangman in 1883 that are the core of Greg Smith's chapter. There was not even a formal job vacancy. The rumour rushed around that William Marwood (the hangman) had just died, and the flood of letters – 1,400 in less than one month – shows hard-core support for the death penalty and a dark hankering for the details of death. These were uncivil letters and moments in a culture that others call 'civilized' and 'enlightened'. Some letters were jokes, others were fakes or pranks putting the name of a friend forward who had no inkling of what was going on. But others were serious and earnest applications, from 'morbid' men, Arthur Griffiths said in 1883, with the same spite and lack of care for suffering that made 'cruel children' 'spin cockchasers or torture flies'.[47] But from that year on the government clarified the position of 'public hangman' and not long after was hiring a pair of hangmen to go round the country dispensing death until the second half of the twentieth century.

There is some agreement about the timing of key changes in the punishment of serious crimes, though there is also some disagreement about the influences of political power, the emotions, and pragamatic evaluations of how a particular penalty is working. The balance can tilt from one explanation to another according to whose book we are reading. I want now to move beyond these debates in another direction, and to spend some time looking at the punishment of petty crime.

II

We will never know the exact balance between punishing felonies and punishing petty crimes, not least because so many misdemeanours were handled quickly in petty sessions in the seventeenth century (constituted with summary powers) which have left few traces of their activities before 1700. All we can say at this point is that it will tip heavily towards punishing the 'lesser' crimes. Misdemeanours were petty crimes, little lapses like being idle, begging, vagrancy, or stealing something that was worth only a few pennies. Bob Shoemaker guesses that one-in-ten cases that came before the Middlesex Quarter Sessions from 1660–1725 involved a felony.[48] The overall figure in all courts up and down the land will be smaller than this, because it would need to include the thousands of urban and manor courts that punished minor troublemakers week-in-and-week-out.[49] The following figures from Norwich are not completely compatible, but they will establish a rough sense of the balance there between punishing capital and non-capital crimes. There are 2,264 *recorded* punishments of minor offenders jotted down in the books of the Mayor's Court from 1580–1645 (the cases of other 'ordinary' offenders were heard at the quarter sessions); while 151 death sentences were handed out in the half-decade after 1570 at the City Quarter Sessions (we can be sure that some of these sentences were not carried out). These imperfect measures give us proportions of 6.25 per cent for punishing felons, and 93.75 per cent for disciplining petty offenders, though the actual ratios are likely to have tipped even more towards the 'lesser' crimes.[50] The 'dark figure' of non-capital penalties that were never noted down by a clerk is likely to be huge, mainly because so many petty criminals were punished 'off the record', either on the spot by a constable who made the arrest, or later in petty sessions of about which we know so little. But unlike capital crimes they were punished day after day with whips, stocks, cages, spells in houses of correction, duckings in rivers, cartings around bustling market-squares and, more often than any of these more elaborate 'shows', with fines.[51]

These 'lesser punishments' were 'commonplace' and ordinary.[52] London had an upper limit of eight hanging days each year (though not all of them saw an execution), and there were a couple of hanging days in selected Assize towns across the land. An argument could be made that the punishment of petty crime was much more visible and that it therefore had a considerable impact on the onlookers. There would have been something to see in most major marketplaces every weekend or midweek market, and 'open' punishments were usually timed for the peak hour of buying and selling to catch the eye (and mind) of as many shoppers as possible. Yet this may be one area of the cultures of the past where the 'numbers-game' makes little sense. The gruesome gallows must surely have had a more awesome and spellbinding impact on bystanders than a humdrum public whipping, no matter how many more whipping-days there were each year. And the different scales of these outdoor events would seem to bear little if any comparison: the execution of a celebrity criminal could draw many thousands of rapt spectators. On top of this, because they were more serious and shocking crimes, felonies were more written about at the time (and now). There was not much mileage or colour in the life story of a scold who was ducked in water or a wanderer who was whipped at a post, unless these minor offences were stepping stones to a stomach-churning felony. Contemporary pamphleteers made money from knowing what people would most like to read and chatter about, and they put out scores of cheap pamphlets that told the cradle-to-gallows tale of murderers, witches, notorious highway robbers and others who committed sickening crimes.[53] The shock-value of the execution and the pamphlet that followed is not in doubt. Nor is the potential to use both the performance and the printed word to spread advice about living obediently and virtuously. It is crystal-clear that the gallows loomed large in contemporary thinking about crime and its punishment. Everybody old enough to know would have been able to say what the gallows looked like and exactly what they were used for.

Nevertheless, our understanding of past penal cultures is far from complete. Nor could it be, as we nearly always imagine the course of punishment over time without considering somewhere in the region of 95 per cent of inflicted penalties. As we shall see, this oversight would have seemed strange to contemporaries who did not imagine the punishment of petty crime and felony apart from each other. Nor has enough been said so far about the importance of 'lesser' penalties for formulations of order three or four centuries ago. Like executions, they were 'public' examples to learn by, but they were more than a visual cue to better behaviour. Their significance is also a matter of their ordinariness and almost monotonous use. Misdemeanours were the sort of run-of-the-mill or momentary slip-ups that on another day might easily have passed by unrewarded and unpunished. Felonies were far more out-of-the-ordinary offences. Unlike hard-up beggars or thieves who were trying to keep hunger at bay, or vagrants who took to the road to find work, witches, murderers and even some thieves could seem ghoulish, shockingly scandalous and far from ordinary, no matter how often the gallows literatures represented doomed felons as wicked wrongdoers who had once been as ordinary as anybody who came along to watch them hang. It was this remoteness from routine that could make the gallows message matter less than we might think from its visual nastiness. Misdemeanours, on the other hand, were the commonplace excesses and eruptions of streets, markets, households and bodies. There was a nearness to little lapses, not least because the small-time thief or work-shy breadwinner came back to the community. It was for this reason that some contemporaries believed that their quick and effective punishment was of more value than another gallows corpse. And this is also why the standard description of the fall to the gallows began with a small slip-up, and proceeded through a sequence of progressively greater offences to the last day. This was a view that was aired all the way through the sixteenth and seventeenth centuries, and it was also continued afterwards in the work of the most influential legal author of the eighteenth century – the Italian Cesare de Beccaria – who was persuaded that short, sharp, shock penalties left a longer lasting mark in the minds of onlookers:

> Since men are not induced on the spur of the moment to commit the gravest crime [Beccaria commented], public punishment of a great misdeed will be regarded by the majority as something very remote and of improbable occurrence; but public punishment of lesser crimes, which are closer to men's hearts, will make an impression which, while deterring them from these, deters them even further from graver crimes.

This view of 'minor' punishments was a cornerstone of the religion-heavy pamphlets of the seventeenth century and the enlightenment psychology that was at the root of de Beccaria's penal thought. 'Lesser crimes' are 'closer to mens hearts', he wrote, to their habits, and to their moods. In a nutshell, they are more intuitive.[54] At the root of numerous misdemeanours were questions about crooked lifestyles or trying to scrape a living. What de Beccaria means it that it is much more probable that a day-labourer or shopkeeper could imagine themselves in the shoes of a tramping vagrant or a needy thief who only wanted to put food on the table. A murderer or condemned robber could seem like a stranger, somebody to boo at from a distance, and in any case they were only punished in public every now and then, and horrifically.

There would be no felonies without misdemeanours. This is what people said at the time. The 'graver crimes' followed on from little lapses, like a line of tumbling cards, one misdemeanour after another, until the final fatal felony. The standard accounts of criminality all pointed to this downward spiral to the gallows. They were little life-stories that described a descent from the first small breach of the law in a misspent youth. And the moral of the story was that the eventual execution was *bound to happen*. It was just a matter of time, because once the slide started it quickly became uncontrollable. Greed, green envy, lust, and habit made sure of that. This was why the first punishment mattered to people at the time. If the first warning did not 'deter' offenders and onlookers – if it was an outdoor event – then nothing else could come after, no crime, no criminal, and certainly no execution. It was of the utmost importance for the individual, for society, and for humanity, to nip crime in the bud before it got out if hand. The evidence that this did not always happen was real enough, and it is not only a perception. It was apparent whenever a recidivist stepped back into a courtroom through its 'revolving doors'. Each brand on a hand, back, or arm was a mark of a fall from grace toward the gallows.[55] The capable and effective punishment of petty crime could stop this plunge, but only if it was applied early on. But nearly all our existing work is on the end. It is about the exit of felons, not their ominous entry. Our larger narratives of punishment in time are felony stories. The reasons for this are to do with the awfulness of executions and their undoubted political role in broadcasting the dictates of church and state, but also the methods and sources that we bring to the study of past penalties.

In matter of fact, much has been written about 'lesser' penalties already, but with a limited impact on how we have seen the historical development of penal cultures and practices up to the nineteenth century. The full scope of legal practices began with efforts by justices and others to seek compromise and accommodation within their communities without having to impose penalties. Much has been written about the significance of mediation and arbitration in settling disputes. The better way to keep peace and quiet was often not to wage law but to calm antagonisms with a warning, third-party arbitration, or another form of pressure that kept cases within the community. Constables often made choices about whether or not to enforce the law, and they frequently felt that it was a better idea to settle spats with words rather than warrants.[56] And even when offences were taken to court, magistrates might still encourage victims and offenders to reach an agreement without a full-blown court case. Bob Shoemaker has uncovered a large amount of informal mediation by justices in Middlesex over the period 1660–1725.[57] Punishment, therefore, might indicate a break down in social relations and a failure to reach a compromise. There were indeed many times when this was the case. Yet it is also important to bear in mind that the aims of punishing petty crime in public included not only humbling offenders, but also – ultimately – to try and bring them back into the fold of the community. A link has been made between the decline of public punishment after 1700 and a dwindling sense of community in large cities, like London.[58]

We also have some first-rate work on particular offences and penalties. A rare example of a piece of work that follows a penalty through time for nearly three centuries is Joanna Innes's study of houses of correction (bridewells), that traces a line of descent to the prison-penitentiary.[59] We also have a few studies of bridewells that leave us in no doubt of their role in combatting crime, spreading sound religion, and putting people to work, though we know much more about London Bridewell – the first Bridewell, that was chartered in 1553 – than about any other one anywhere else in the land.[60] There is also a growing body of work on whipping, that seems to be mainly concerned with matters of the emotions, with civility, feelings and pain. Like hanging, whipping is a window on emotions, and the rate of its use (or otherwise) is treated as some sort of statement about what the culture is, and where it is currently situated on the long shift from a dark coarse past to a society of sentiment in the age of Enlightenment. There is a connection (implicit or explicit) in this work between the public exposure and pain of a marketplace whipping to a hanging day. It might be an outcome of this conceptual link that, as with the gallows, the turning points in practice and culture are all located in the 'enlightened' eighteenth century or even after. Like the drop in hangings, the fall in the number of public whippings in the long run after 1700 (though there were spurts when their number suddenly soared) is matched with a 'politer' society and a middling class (especially) who were now compassionate and full of empathy for the suffering of others. And, like the story of the gallows, the story of whipping through time can make the early modern past seem very different and distant: an additional version of the cold-hearted centuries when a gallows crowd could have filled one of our football grounds today, and still left people outside on the streets, trying to get in.[61]

Whipping was only one possible public reprimand for small-time offenders in the past, and it is not alone in attracting attention from historians over the last decade or so (and before). The cucking stool has been at the centre of an academic spat since 1985 when David Underdown first told us that this stool was a gauge of gender stresses: the more often women were dipped in water strapped in one, the argument runs, the hotter the concern about badly-behaved women amongst male magistrates.[62] Martin Ingram has been the leading sceptic casting doubt on Underdown's understanding of the cucking stool. He wonders whether or not these dippings were more markedly urban punishments, and there is very good reason to believe that this may indeed have been the case: more and more women moved to the towns over the seventeenth century, as can be counted in sex-ratios or observed in judicial records as the number of female vagrants and thieves shoots up.[63] Ingram also wonders if there is not a better word or way to describe the nature of gender relations at this time than 'crisis'.[64] Inevitably, it seems, we always return to numbers: how many scolds were ducked, and when and where? Little counting has been done in these fields. Whipping has been counted, but only after 1700 and mainly in London. We measure scolding rates for example, but we are never sure that a ducking followed a court case. We are almost completely in the dark about rates of punishing petty crime before 1700, though this does not stop scholars from commenting on the newness of what they see after

1700. It is possible to follow execution rates all the way through from 1500–1900, and we now feel that we have a sound sense of their dips, falls and pauses. But this is not the case with whipping, or with ducking, carting or locking people in stocks. All that we can say is that, apart from military floggings, they were no longer used at some point in the eighteenth or nineteenth centuries (depending on which one of them we are looking at and where).[65] So, it seems that public punishment falls away completely towards the end of the centuries covered in this book, though it may be that it was accelerating at the start of the sixteenth century. A recent book about misbehaviour from 1370 to 1600 notices a rise in the use of these public performances around 1500.[66]

But there are still big gaps in our coverage of the time in-between the start- and finish-dates of this book. A number of the chapters to come continue the task of filling them, though there is still a long way to go. We have written much more so far about the functions and forms of penal performances, about how they were showcases for law and order. Whippings went on in markets in a neat blend of ethics and economics, and there was always a guaranteed crowd to tease and jeer at culprits sitting in stocks or strapped to whipping posts, and also to learn from their sad 'example'. None of these choices were random: the manner of punishing was calculated to get maximum publicity. The full force of 'example' hinged on getting these things right. The full force of shaming, however, depended on embarrassed offenders being known to the people who looked on as they squirmed in the stocks or stool. Humiliation also meant submission and sorrow, as when Robert Jorden was spared punishment after scoffing at his master 'upon his humiliacion' to him.[67] What could be worse, the idea ran, than to sit helpless in ignominy as the people you mixed with day-after-day poked fun, sniggered and chided you for your misdemeanours. And the shame could stick long after the day of disgrace: I 'hath heard divers strange men saie' that my master's wife 'hath rode on a carte', George Fletcher tipped off London Bridewell Court in 1576. 'My mother is an honester woman than thine', Sebastian Coney snapped in 1614 when he was locked in a war of words with a constable, 'for my mother never was drawen to the cucking stooll and so was thine, which old Baker will say as well as I'. The smarting constable later lodged a complaint against Coney at Hertford Quarter Sessions.[68] The memory of a stint in the stool a or ride round a market in a cart still stained a character and reputation months or years later.

At some point after the sixteenth century the authorities started to drop penalties that depended on the sight of the offender and the sound of the critical crowd for others that were more straightforward physical punishments that doubled as deterrents. Martin Ingram's chapter in this book looks at 'themes and variations' in punishing petty crimes under the Tudors. His title might even seem a little bit strange to a few people. We hardly ever talk about *changing* penal practices before 1600. But 'variations' there were, no matter how many times we have looked to the decades after 1700 for the first glimmers of far-reaching change. Ingram spots a switch towards using pain more often to deter offenders and onlookers. His story is largely a metropolitan one, but it has important implications for other places. Around 1500, London's leaders worked with church, civil and criminal jurisdictions to hand out penalties that were in the main planned to shame guilty offenders. Penance was at the core of each one of these rites. Contrite wrongdoers were expected to seek forgiveness in marketplaces, churches or on the spots where they offended to get back into the fold of the community and/or church. The performance was every bit as scripted as a hanging day, and offenders were required to play by the book. There was kneeling, pleas for pity, sorrow, tears from time to time, and papers listing the details of offences in big capital letters. And it was hoped that shamed offenders would be sincerely repentant, like Sara Shaw of Westminster, who showed 'hearty repentance' for her 'fault' in 1611, or John Hodgetts who ended up in court in 1560 after being found with a 'naughty woman', and who 'penytent[ly] and humbl[y]' confessed his 'synne' with much wailing and weeping, and fell to his knees, 'beseching forgivenes'.[69] These were textbook performances. The visual validation of order – what Paul Griffiths calls 'the optic order'[70] – was also much in evidence in outdoor punishments, in clothes, wands, gestures and parades that went hand-in-hand with scores of penal displays. But Ingram does not believe that their use was constant. Vagrancy was on the rise all over England around 1600, and nowhere was more swamped with people on the move than London.[71] Vagrancy and its offshoots – chief among them begging and theft – were dealt with for the most part with a whip. And Ingram notices a surge in the use of more outright physical penalties, like whipping, towards the end of the sixteenth century. Pain and shame were merged in these thrashings, though there was not much point in punishing vagrants before a market-day crowd in a place where they were not known. In his updated edition of John Stow's *Survey of London* (1720), John Strype wrote about the 'customary punishment in the city of shame or pain or both', listing riding, carting, the stocks and the pillory.[72]

There was no overnight disappearance of shaming displays, but a coexistence with the infliction of pain as there always had been, except that whipping was now the more usual correction for the street-crimes that proliferated all over England. Offenders were still carted, paraded, ducked and put in stocks all the way through the seventeenth century, and into the next one, but in far fewer numbers as time passed. There were also still ridings or 'walkings' around market-squares. Thomas Carpenter was punished as follows in Northampton market in 1673. He was ordered

> on Saturday next betweene ye howers of one and two of the clock [to] walke round the mket place with a paper on his breast written wth capitall letters to this effect that he hath bene convict of an assault and

> attempt to ravishe Ann ye wife of Thomas Andrew. And [he was told to] stand still in ye 4 most eminent places where most concourse of people is for the space of a quarter of an hower for people to read his fact.

These market displays could still be seen late around 1700, but again in fewer numbers.[73] Whipping continued, however, and still in the market rush-hour, and still at times with offenders walking behind a cart or standing in one. Shoppers had to clear a path in Nottingham's busy Saturday market in 1733 when James Rawson was whipped for pinching pears 'in a cart' that rolled back and forth between the weekday cross and the malt cross at noon.[74] Petty larceny was by far the most common crime of offenders who were 'publickly whipped' in and around market-squares after 1700.[75] While the pillory was still wheeled out from time to time (if it was not a permanent structure) for forgerers, cheats, thieves, and people with loose tongues who spoke 'seditious words'.[76]

Hanging after 1827 was cut back to punish particular offences in narrower ways than before. Much the same thing happened with 'lesser' penalties a century or so earlier. Whipping survived into the eighteenth century, but it was no longer a broad-brush penalty for whatever misdemeanour came before the courts, as it once had been. Nor is there a single history *of* whipping or, to put it another way, there is no *national* history of whipping, and surely the same is true of the ducking stool, for example, or the gallows. We have histories *about* whipping or hanging in certain cities or counties, and one day we might even have enough of them covered to write a history of whipping the English, but it will result in a patchwork of local differences. The timing of changes in penal practice will not be the same across the land. Different towns might well have had their own particular penalties or variations on the well-established penal themes and practices. A word that was used a lot was 'accustomyd': as when a pair of 'coen harlotts' were 'droppyd in [the] Theamys' in 1550, or when Anne Walker taunted Andrew Shaw in 1614, calling him a 'cuckoe', and was 'runge through ye towne of Wakefield with basins before her, as is accustomed for common scowldes'.[77] It is a word that more often than not referred to local practices that were thought to have existed for a long while, whether or not they were in line with customs elsewhere.

There are also punishments that crop up so rarely in records that if they were not particular to a place, they were only ordered by a tiny fraction of English courts. Only now and then do we come across a scold wearing a bridle (iron mask) with a bolt that pinned her tongue to the roof of her mouth: Martha Farrant of Salford was ordered to 'put' on 'the bridle' and to 'beare it for one whole houre' in 1655, after showering a constable with 'most un-civell language'. Another rare punishment was dished out to Maudlin Tichon of Westminster after she was caught scorning her neighbours for the second time in 1611: 'according to the ancient custome of the city', she was 'fastened to a boats tayle' and 'drawn through the water to the other side of the Thames' (a similar sounding 'water punishment' took place in the sea off Peeltown in The Isle of Man in 1714).[78] Diversity is a rule of thumb in stories of punishing the English: different penalties, different locations, different formats, and different chronologies. The same penalty was even spelled differently: there was a 'cook stool' in Liverpool, a 'cucking stoole' in Southwell, a 'cocynstole' in Maidstone, a 'coucstole' in Manchester, and a 'kucstole' in Prescot (Lancashire), as well as a 'ducking stoole' in Oxford, and a 'ducking chair', also in Manchester.[79] Punishments and their sites were even built into local topographies: Henry Newcome mentions 'Hanging Ditch' in his part of Lancashire, and we could add many more examples to this one.[80]

This is all to say that there is nearly always a local dimension to penal practices and cultures, and that once overall patterns (chronologies) are established they will be jagged, moving first one way and then another. This is clear from Paul Griffith's chapter on Norwich in this book, which maps the patterns of punishing petty crime in England's second city up to the end of the seventeenth century. He can only count recorded punishments, and we must always be aware of the limitations of these measurements, but this is the first time that we have a rough outline of the twists and turns in punishing petty crime in a single place for more than a century. What Norwich's records reveal is a slump in the use of public punishment long before the eighteenth century. This fall was across the board, and had an effect on carting, ducking, whipping and putting people in stocks. It is suggestive and noteworthy, but the curves and changes on the chart come from one city only. There is also a good chance that whipping rates might have bounced back after 1700, as they did in other places at various points. But the Norwich numbers caution against inevitable and straightforward progresses through time, and also against pinpointing the 'long' eighteenth century as *the* sole century of critical change. A major turning point in the city can be tracked back to the moment when the Bridewell first opened its doors in 1571. From then on small-time crooks, drifters, domestic pests, and the workshy could all be sentenced to backbreaking hard work.[81] The timing of penal change at this level depends to a great extent on when and where bridewells were first opened. A brand-new bridewell could lead to sudden and striking changes, causing the use of outdoor penalties to plummet at an earlier date then we might expect if we were working with felony cases alone. Norwich's magistrates used their bridewell continually to discipline and edify the rowdy poor, and its imposing image in many minds was a warning to others not to fall foul of the law.

Norwich had its own penal paths that were shaped by its particular predicaments, political circumstances, and by the implementation of by-laws and statutes. We go back to London in Robert Shoemaker's chapter, which tracks the falling use of public, physical punishments there from the start of the eighteenth century on. The number of people put on pillories tumbled, and only perjurers stood in disgrace on one after 1816 – the pillory was got rid of altogether in 1837, the same year in which the bulk of the 'Bloody Code' was scrapped. The number of public whippings also slumped, and the option of whipping through the streets was cut back, so that most offenders were now whipped standing still at a post. The few outdoor whippings after 1780 nearly always took place outside the Old Bailey or the Middlesex sessions house. Whippings were not just fewer in number, they were also now rooted to a couple of spots. Mounting unease about street disorders in a more genteel, civilized, and commercial capital city made some sort of a difference. Just like the move from rowdy Tyburn to hanging felons in front of Newgate,[82] whipping at fixed posts was a crowd-control measure. But there was another factor that was of more importance than crowd-control, and this was the changing complexion of the crowd itself. Shoemaker argues that public penal displays were less relevant by now; that Londoners were less interested in seeing strangers flogged or that they no longer understood shame as being public in character. He has made the point with force in another essay that the neighbourliness which was an active aspect of penal displays was crumbling after 1700 as people poured into the city in large numbers.[83] On top of this, a more urban/urbane polite print culture encouraged people to interiorize shame rather than express it in public as before.

If we should ever need reminding of the hefty influence of local circumstances and characteristics on penal practice, then we need only turn to Roger Dickinson and Jim Sharpe's chapter on the public punishments dished out by the Isle of Man church courts in the seventeenth and eighteenth centuries. Their main argument dovetails nicely with others made in this book. The island's population was little more than 10,000 around 1700, and it was still possible for neighbours to share common traits and to look out for each other for good or bad. Unlike the mainland's bulging towns (some scholars say), where neighbours no longer mixed as before, and were more distant and cool with each other, neighbourliness was still a force to be reckoned with, and this helps to explain why shaming punishments lasted longer on the island. The Manx authorities backed off from inflicting 'purely' physical pain as time passed. There were only two hanging days in the last two decades of the seventeenth century, and the pillory was only wheeled out once. There were more whippings than this, but even so their numbers were low, and whipping was usually used in tandem with the stocks rather than alone as a separate punishment. What did last well after 1700, however, were scripted ritualized displays of public penance handed out by the church courts. There are jurisdictional and procedural matters to bear in mind here, but what mattered more, it seems, were the points of intersection between a still strong spirit of neighbourliness and the main goals of ecclesiastical discipline.

The Isle of Man seems different from London which in turn looks different from Norwich. The timing and pattern of penal changes in which all places could one day share, were never the same everywhere. There is no ultimate chronology, no definitive sequence of causes and effects. It is no longer possible, for example, to argue that changing offenders for the better was a brand-new goal late in the eighteenth century when one prison was built after another, unless we stick to felony-cases alone, and even then to a limited reading of the purposes of previous prisons, hanging days, and transportation overseas. There is no doubt that starting with London Bridewell in the mid-1550s, it was hoped that inmates in Britain's bridewells would profit from sound religion and work discipline. Words of reformation, repentance, and renewal were spoken all the time in the chapel and workrooms, and also in London Bridewell's courtroom. Heavy-drinking Francis Taylor was not alone in 1639 when he gave his word that he would 'become a new man' after causing trouble for his master, his mother, and her family day-after-day.[84] Other courts up and down the land also spoke of amendment and saving small-time offenders from sliding down the slippery slope to the gallows. This reforming language and intention can be found all the way through the records of the Norwich courts that are the principal sources for Paul Griffith's chapter in this book. The bridewell made a real difference in Norwich and elsewhere; the one in Acle, not far from Norwich, was called 'the house of reformation'. The plan at the Clerkenwell 'house' was that surly servants would be 'humbled' and 'reformed', and that vagrants would be 'reduced to goodnes'.[85] Legislation passed by Parliament in 1576 and 1610 asked authorities to open houses of correction all across the land. The last Act was an order rather than a piece of advice, and soon after it became law town and county magistrates took steps to open a 'house' in their jurisdictions, though it usually took them five years or so to get it ready for the first intake, as happened in Clerkenwell, Leicester, and Northampton. This was the second of several bursts of setting up houses of correction (and workhouses) all over England.[86]

Not enough work has been done as yet on reforming rogues, idle layabouts, and other 'lesser' offenders before 1700. A 'bloody' back is sometimes seen to be evidence of cruelty and little else. Yet whipping posts in London were called 'postes of reformacon'. A loudmouth apprentice landed in trouble in 1583 for chatting 'undutifull[y]' about the conduit in Fleet Street, and he was 'stripped naked from hys gyrdle upward' and given 'twelve strypes with a rodd at the poste of reformacon' next to the conduit.[87] Martin Ingram twins pain and shame, and we should never forget that physical punishment (along with hard work) was a mental correction in this culture. Whip-sting was supposed to prompt remorse and renewal long after it had cooled. Esther Cohen has taught us that sensations of pain were always a matter of the mind as well as of the body. Each sting, however hot, was intended to train thoughts and behaviour; to turn troublemakers into better citizens and christians. Pain was an active and effective teacher and preacher.[88] Women who were ducked in rivers or pools felt the chill and the uncomfortable dampness and wetness of water. Offenders were often locked in stocks and the pillory for an hour or more, and were lucky to leave with only a few bruises and sores. Shame was at the root of all public penalties, and it was not meant to be momentary or to last as long as the time it took for a cart to roll around a market-square. Like pain, shame was a no-nonsense catalyst to change people for the better. The mortification of public blame, scorn and glee was meant to be healing. It patched up neighbourly clashes and mended minds. Part of the 'problem' for us is that we have been encouraged for a long while now to think of the body and the soul singly and apart from each other. This is not what early modern men and women were told by their magistrates, ministers, medical guides or by each other. This is what Ralph Josselin wrote in his diary one day in 1645: 'Jone my mayd came to us the Lord make me faithfull to her and blesse her for soule and body under mee.' And again in the next year: 'This weeke was good to mee and mine in our health, peace, plenty, in outward mercies, [and] in goodness to soule and body.'[89] Josselin thought of the body and soul in the same sentence and second. There was no separation, no action that did not touch the soul. This is what most people believed and acted on whether they ordered a punishment or if they were on the receiving end of one. A whip may seem nothing other than a cruel tool to us today, but not to the people who thought of it first and foremost as blending convalescent pain with thought-provoking shame in the early modern period.

The punishment of petty crime through time also gives us a different impression of the balance between indoor and outdoor penalties. Imprisonment did not emerge out of the blue as a widespread option in the eighteenth century. Petty offenders were being sentenced to spells in bridewells from as early as the middle of the sixteenth century. The length of these custodial sentences was hardly ever spelled out, but they stretched from as short as a single week to several months, and some prisoners stayed in a bridewell for more than a year. Magistrates all over the country now had a handy indoor alternative to public pain and shame from 1610 on. Punishments were moving inside but these were not civilizing moments. Paul Griffiths reveals a relationship between the opening of the bridewell in Norwich and the subsequent slump in outdoor punishments there, and there seems little reason to think that this is an odd case. He also shows that whipping was moving away from the market-square over the seventeenth century (in an 1868 moment) and that more and more offenders were getting their 'stripes' behind the walls of the Guildhall or the bridewell. In a later ironic twist, the balance tipped back towards public whipping after 1700 when the whip was nearly always used to make petty thieves toe the line and no longer to punish a fuller range of misdemeanours.

To reiterate, some of the most creative thinking on penal matters at this time lingered on first or early/petty offences. Bridewells were new, there had been nothing like the one in London before 1550 in this country or, for that matter, in mainland Europe.[90] The magistrates who sat in courtrooms to hear petty crime cases had a range of indoor and outdoor punishments to choose from, not to mention common fines. They had more flexibility than judges or justices. This broad scope was the deliberate outcome of first-hand experience, measured penal planning, and careful testing of penalties to find the best ones to meet the needs not of the country, but of individual towns, counties, or even villages. The bridewell laws were the major juncture, not just because they extended flexibility still further, but because magistrates now had a nearby place to lock up people for offences that could be stretched to cover nearly every occasion when the poor broke the law: 'loose idle, and disorderly' were all written down in statute law in the 1610 Act.[91] Bridewells have also been talked about as 'proto-prisons', paving the way for the later spurts in building penitentiaries.[92] Any developments along these lines would not have been smooth or plain-sailing. But there is good reason to see bridewells/houses of correction (anachronistically maybe, as this was not why they were opened in the first place) as stepping-stones to lock-ups for felons, not least because felons were put in them after the 1706 Act and even before it. Nor should we forget that the other key secondary penalty – transportation overseas – was also most commonly used at first to punish petty offenders, small-time crooks, vagrants and the like.[93] Some creativity and skill went into 'lesser' penalties before 1700. It can almost seem that these 'lesser' punishments were almost practice-grounds or trial-runs for the changes that came afterwards in punishing the most serious crimes.

And maybe more than anything else, we should always keep in mind how much punishing petty crime mattered to contemporaries. They believed that 'lesser' penalties were integral to thinking about law and order problems, and that trouble would always follow if a community was without a whipping post, a pair of stocks or a cucking stool, for however short a span of time. The constable and concerned people of Southwell moaned in 1654 that their cucking stool had been 'broken and destroyed' in 'the tyme of the late warres', and that its loss was a spur for scolds: it 'hath emboldened and encouregd many lewd and turbulent women to continue in their unquiett and unpeaceble behaviour', they grumbled, and now the friendly and well-mannered neighbours were at their wits end. Please give us 'a new cucking stoole', they asked the Nottinghamshire justices.[94] In Southwell, and all over England, the power of the 'lesser' penalties to deter and reform people was almost a byword for peace and quiet, year-after-year. To be sure, their problems were real enough and they did not always work as magistrates wished. There were countless recidivists everywhere. But sometimes just having a cucking stool or a pair of stocks on show in a community was enough of a visual deterrent to stop someone from falling on the wrong side of the law. This is why warning signs like whipping posts were located in markets, so that they were seen by as many shoppers as possible, even when they were not in use. Penal iconographies from the gallows all the way to the stocks were important aspects of the visual validation of order. They could be marks of reassurance as well as deterrence. If we do not give the same amount of attention to punishing petty crime as people did who lived through these times, our histories of penal practice, penal culture and optic order will never be complete.

III

The history of punishing petty crime is not an alternative story to the one on the gallows. They are two sides of the same coin, and their stories cannot be told apart. They merge and affect each other too often for that to happen. These overlaps are where we now need to position the work to come. Nearly all contemporary theories of the sliding scale of penalties and the fall into crime start with petty crimes and end with capital ones: hanging days follow on from whippings, grand larcenies follow petty larcenies, unless there is an intervention – a 'lesser' penalty – to make offenders quake and change, and stop the slide. True enough there are differences in the directions taken by the punishment of misdemeanours and felonies through time. And they are as important as each similarity and connection, so long as we remember that they all occurred on a plane of convergence. If we stick for one moment to the misdemeanour side of things, we will see that the 'privatization' of penalties or character-reform (working with souls) were not the 'enlightened' gifts of the eighteenth century and after. Their dawn was at an earlier time, and muddles a few long-established chronologies. It is of the utmost importance to know what happened to the gallows over time, so long as we understand that this is not *the* history *of* punishment, but the history of punishing felony. Again, this invalidates nothing that has been written to date from the angles and records of serious crime. All parts of the country were moving along the same path towards the ending of public penal displays, but not at the same time. And once we mingle misdemeanours and felonies in a single story the contingent character of change will be plain to see.

Notes

1 The most important contributions include V.A.C. Gatrell, *The Hanging Tree: Executions and the English People, 1770–1868* (Oxford, 1994), chaps 1–5; Douglas Hay, 'Property, ideology, and the criminal law', in Hay *et al.*, eds, *Albion's Fatal Tree: Crime and Society in Eighteenth-Century England* (1975), 17–63; Peter King, *Crime, Justice, and Discretion in England, 1740–1820* (Oxford, 2000), chap. 10; Thomas Laquer, 'Crowds, carnivals and the state in English executions, 1604–1868', in A.L. Beier *et al.*, eds, *The First Modern Society* (1989), 305–55; Peter Linebaugh, 'The ordinary of Newgate and his account', in J.S. Cockburn ed., *Crime in England, 1500–1800* (1977), 246–69; J.A. Sharpe, *Judicial Punishment in England* (1990), chap. 2; *id.*, '"Last dying speeches": religion, ideology, and public execution in

seventeenth-century England', *Past and Present*, 107 (1985), 147–65. A forthcoming book by Andrea McKenzie looks at the cultures and practices of Tyburn: *Tyburn's Martyrs: Execution in England, 1675–1775* (Hambledon and London Books). For the forms and symbolism of rituals elsewhere see R.A. Bosco, 'Lecturers at the pillory: the early American execution sermon', *American Quarterly*, 30 (1978), 156–76; A. Blok, 'The symbolic vocabulary of public executions', in J. Starr and J.F. Collier eds, *History and Power in the Study of Law: New Directions in Legal Anthropology* (1989), 31–54; Esther Cohen, '"To die a criminal for the public good": the execution ritual in late medieval Paris', in B.S. Bachrach and D. Nicholas eds, *Law, Custom, and the Social Fabric in Medieval Europe* (1990), 285–304; R.J. Evans, *Rituals of Retribution: Capital Punishment in Germany, 1600–1987* (Oxford, 1996), chaps 2–5; Pieter Spierenburg, *The Spectacle of Suffering: Executions and the Evolution of Repression, from a Preindustrial Metropolis to the European Experience* (Cambridge, 1984); chaps 2–4; Richard van Dumen, *Theatre of Horror: Crime and Punishment in Early Modern Germany*, trans. Elizabeth Neu (Oxford, 1990), chaps 5–6.

2 Randall McGowen, 'The well-ordered prison: England, 1780–1865', in N. Morris and D.J. Rothman eds, *The Oxford History of the Prison* (Oxford, 1996), 78–109.

3 Brian Hogan, 'Crime and the Criminal Law', in *Then and Now: Commemorating 175 Years of Law Bookselling and Publishing* (1974), 116; quoted (and paraphrased) in Greg T. Smith, '"Civilized people don't want to see that kind of thing: the decline of public physical punishment in London, 1760–1840', in Carolyn Strange ed., *Qualities of Mercy: Justice, Punishment, and Discretion* (Vancouver, 1996), 48, n.1. This section contains some materials and ideas which Simon Devereaux was kind enough to let me use, and which will appear in revised form in his forthcoming essay, 'New directions in the history of crime and punishment in England.'

4 See the first-rate discussion of the abolition of public execution in Randall McGowen, 'Civilizing punishment: the end of public execution in England', *JBS*, 3 (1994), 257–82.

5 John Beattie has provided us with the best accounts of the origins, development, and implementation of the 'bloody code'. See his *Policing and Punishment in London, 1660–1750: Urban Crime and the Limits of Terror* (Oxford, 2001) chaps 7 and 9; *Crime and the Courts*, chap. 10; and 'London crime and the making of the "bloody code", 1689–1718', in L. Davison *et al.*, eds, *Stilling the Grumbling Hive: The Response to Social and Economic Problems in England, 1689–1750* (1992), 49–76. See also Julian Hoppit, 'Patterns of Parliamentary legislation, 1660–1800', *HJ* (1990), 109–31.

6 Sir Leon Radzinowicz, *History of English Criminal Law and its Administration from 1750–1850* (5 vols.; 1948–86). It should, of course, be pointed out that Radzinowicz co-authored the fifth volume with Roger Hood.

7 Sir Leon Radzinowicz, *History of English Criminal Law and its Administration From 1750: Volume 1, The Movement for Reform* (1948), ix. There is a more detailed discussion of the Whig line in David Philips, '"A just measure of crime, authority, hunters and blue locusts": the "revisionist" social history of the law in Britain, 1780–1850', in Stanley Cohen and Andrew Scull eds., *Social Control and the State: Historical and Comparative Essays* (Oxford, 1983), 50–74, esp. 51–2.

8 Radzinowicz, *History of English Criminal Law and its Administration From 1750: Volume 1*, 358, 396. The precise role of Bentham in the emergence of the Victorian administrative state generated a large literature from the late 1950s on. For a recent review, see Stephen Conway, 'Bentham and the nineteenth-century revolution in government', in Richard Bellamy ed., *Victorian Liberalism: Nineteenth-Century Political Thought and Practice* (1990), 71–90.

9 For a recent evaluation of the place of *Punishment and Social Structure* in the history of the prison, see David Garland, *Punishment and Modern Society: A Study in Social Theory* (Oxford, 1990), chap. 4.

10 We now almost take these connections for granted, in large part because of an excellent essay by Joanna Innes, 'Prisons for the poor: English bridewells, 1555–1800', in Francis Snyder and Douglas Hay eds, *Labour, Law, and Crime: An Historical Perspective* (1987), 42–122, esp. 43–9.

11 Michel Foucault, *Discipline and Punish: The Birth of the Prison*, trans. Alan Sheridan (New York, 1976). The best introductions to Foucault's work for historians include Peter Burke ed., *Critical Essays on Michel Foucault* (1992); Martin Dinges, 'Michel Foucault's impact on the German historiography of criminal justice, social discipline, and medicalization', in N. Finzch and R. Jutte eds, *Institutions of Confinement: Hospitals, Asylums, and Prisons in Western Europe and North America, 1500–1950* (Cambridge, 1996), 155–74; Richard J. Evans, *Rituals of Retribution: Capital Punishment in Germany, 1600–1987* (Oxford, 1996), 27–56; Garland, *Punishment and Modern Society*, chaps 6–7 and Randall McGowen, 'Power and humanity, or Foucault among the historians', in Colin Jones and Roy Porter eds, *Reassessing Foucault: Power, Medicine and the Body* (1994), 91–112.

12 The story of Bentham's planned panopticon is told by Janet Semple, *Bentham's Prison: A Study of the Panopticon Penitentiary* (Oxford, 1993).

13 Foucault, *Discipline and Punish*, 195. Almost a decade before the publication of *Discipline and Punish*, Gertrude Himmelfarb questioned the humanity of Bentham's Panopticon, tracing his futile efforts to sell the project to the government of Pitt the younger by emphasizing the severity of its internal regime and extolling its financial self-sufficiency by comparison with public institutions of confinement: 'The haunted house of Jeremy Bentham', in her *Victorian Minds* (New York, 1968), 32–81.

14 Michael Ignatieff, *A Just Measure of Pain: The Penitentiary in the Industrial Revolution, 1750–1850* (1978), chap. 3. See also Robin J. Evans, *The Fabrication of Virtue: English Prison Architecture, 1750–1840* (Cambridge, 1982), esp. chap. 5.

15 Ignatieff, *Just Measure of Pain*, chap. 8; David J. Rothman, *The Discovery of the Asylum: Social Order and Disorder in the New Republic* (Boston, 1971; revised edition, 1990).

16 Michael Ignatieff, 'State, civil society and total institutions: a critique of recent social histories of punishment', *Crime and Justice: An Annual Review of Research*, 3 (1981), 153–91.

17 Margaret DeLacy, *Prison Reform in Lancashire, 1700–1850: A Study in Local Administration* (Stanford, 1986). DeLacy's case looks impressive in the context of Lancashire, which by 1800 was one of the most populous of English localities, but the role of more strictly reformative impulses was apparent in other jurisdictions by the 1780s. See E.A.L. Moir, 'Sir George Onesiphorus Paul', in H.P.R. Finberg ed., *Gloucestershire Studies* (Leicester, 1957), 195–224; Robert Alan Cooper, 'Ideas and their execution: English prison reform', *Eighteenth-Century Studies*, 10 (1976), 73–93; Evans, *Fabrication of Virtue*, chaps 2–4; David Eastwood, *Governing Rural England: Tradition and Transformation in Local Government, 1780–1840* (Oxford, 1994), 242–60; McGowen, 'Well-Ordered Prison', 83–92. Other important studies of early penitentiaries and their reform include Roy Porter, 'Howard's beginning: prisons, disease, hygiene', in W.F. Bynum and J. Beam eds, *The Health of Prisoners: Historical Essays* (1995); 5–26; George Fisher, 'The birth of the prison retold', *Yale Law Journal* (1995); Beattie, *Crime and the Courts*, chaps 9–10; Simon Devereaux, 'The making of the penitentiary act, 1775–1779', *HJ*, 42 (1999), 405–33; David Taylor, *Crime, Policing, and Punishment in England, 1750–1914* (1999), chap. 8.

18 Norbert Elias, *The Civilizing Process* (2 vols.; 1939). The best translation by far is by Eric Dunning *et al.*, which was published as *The Civilizing Process*, revd edn (Oxford, 2000), quoting xii. The best introductions to Elias for historians include Garland, *Punishment and Modern Society*, chap. 10; Norbert Finzch, 'Elias, Foucault, Oestreich: on a historical theory of confinement', in Finzsch and Jutte, *Institutions of Confinement*, 3–16; Stephen Mennell, *Norbert Elias: An Introduction* (Oxford, 1992); Robert van Krieken, *Norbert Elias* (1998).

19 Spierenburg, *Spectacle of Suffering; id.*, *The Broken Spell: A Cultural and Anthropological History of Preindustrial Europe* (1991); *id.*, 'The body and the state: early modern Europe', in Morris and Rothman, *Oxford History of the Prison*, 49–77; *id.*, 'Four centuries of prison history: punishment, suffering, the body, and power', in Finzsch and Jutte, *Institutions of Confinement*, 17–35. A similar view of early modern punishment, though more descriptive and less analytical in character, is provided in van Dümen, *Theatre of Horror*. See also Sharpe, Civility, civilizing processes, and the end of public punishment'.

20 Spierenburg, *Spectacle of Suffering*, x. An ambitious new exploration of civility and punishment since the late eighteenth century is John Pratt, *Punishment and Civilization: Penal Tolerance and Intolerance in Civil Society* (2002).

21 In his more recent work on forgery and the capital code, however, McGowen has gone back in time to the late seventeenth century and after. See his 'From pillory to gallows: the punishment of forgery in the age of the financial revolution', *P&P*, 165 (1999) 107–40; and, of course, his chapter in this collection.

22 Randall McGowen, 'The body and punishment in eighteenth-century England', *Journal of Modern History*, 59 (1987), 651–79, quoting 679. See also his 'A powerful sympathy: terror, the prison, and humanitarian reform in early nineteenth-century Britain', *JBS*, 25 (1986), 312–34; 'The changing face of God's justice: the debates over divine and human punishment in eighteenth-century England', *CJH*, 9 (1988), 63–98; 'The image of justice and reform of the criminal law in early nineteenth-century England', *Buffalo Law Review*, 32 (1983) 89–125; 'Punishing violence, sentencing crime', in Nancy Armstrong and Leonard Tennenhouse, eds, *The Violence of Representation: Literature and the History of Violence* (1989), 140–56; and 'Civilizing punishment'; J.A. Sharpe, 'Civility, civilizing processes, and the end of public punishment in England', in Peter Burke *et al.* eds, *Civil Histories: Essay presented to Sir Keith Thomas* (Oxford, 2000), 215–30; Richard R. Follett, *Evangelicalism, Penal Theory and the Politics of Law Reform in England, 1808–30* (Basingstoke, 2001). This last work should be contrasted with Gatrell, *Hanging Tree*, chap. 14.

23 Gatrell, *Hanging Tree*, chaps 7–11.

24 J.M. Beattie, 'Violence and society in early-modern England', in Anthony N. Doob and Edward L. Greenspan eds, *Perspectives in Criminal Law: Essays in Honour of John L.J. Edwards* (Aurora, 1985), 36–60. Lawrence Stone had invoked Elias in seeking to account for the long-term decline in violence. See his 'Interpersonal violence in English society, 1300–1980', *P&P*, 101 (1983), 22–33. In doing so, he was following the lead of Ted Robert Gurr, 'Historical trends in violent crime: a critical review of the evidence', *Crime and Justice: An Annual Review of Research*, 3 (1981), 295–53. But Beattie was the first historian to apply this argument to penal practices in particular. See also J.S. Cockburn, 'Patterns of violence in English society: homicide in Kent, 1560–1985', *P&P*, 130 (1991), 70–106; V.A.C. Gatrell, 'The Decline of theft and violence in Victorian and Edwardian England', in Gatrell *et al.*, eds, *Crime and the Law: A Social History of Crime in Western Europe Since 1500* (1980), 238–370; Peter King, 'Punishing assault: the transformation of attitudes in the English courts', *Journal of Interdisciplinary History*, 27 (1996), 43–74.

25 J.M. Beattie, 'The pattern of crime in England, 1660–1800', *P&P*, 62 (1974), 47–95; *id.*, 'Crime and the courts in Surrey, 1736–1753', in J.S. Cockburn ed., *Crime in England, 1550–1800* (1977), 155–86; *id.*, 'Towards a study of crime in 18th century England: a note on indictments', in Paul Fritz and David Williams eds, *The Triumph of Culture: 18th Century Prespectives* (Toronto, 1972), 299–314; *id.*, 'Judicial records and the measurement of crime in eighteenth-century England', in Louis A. Knafla ed., *Crime and Criminal Justice in Europe and Canada* (Waterloo, 1981; reveised edn, 1985), 127–45. See also Douglas Hay, 'War, dearth and theft in the eighteenth century: the record of the English courts', *P&P*, 95 (1982), 117–60; King, *Crime, Justice, and Discretion*, Part II.

26 Beattie, *Crime and the Courts*, 492–9; *id.*, *Policing and Punishment*, chap. 7. There are handy summaries of Beattie's complex arguments in Joanna Innes and John Styles, 'The crime wave: recent writing on crime and criminal justice in eighteenth-century England', in Adrian Wilson ed., *Rethinking Social History: English Society, 1570–1920 and its Interpretation* (Manchester, 1993), 201–65, esp. 229–40; and in Beattie's own 'Criminal sanctions in England since 1500', in M.L. Friedland ed., *Sanctions and Rewards in the Legal System: A Multidisciplinary Approach* (Toronto, 1989), 14–35. See also King, *Crime, Justice, and Discretion*, Part III; and Randall McGowen's chapter in this volume, which looks closely at the arguments and measures that brought about penal reform after 1660.

27 See also A. Roger Ekirch, *Bound for America: The Transportation of British Convicts to the Colonies, 1718–1775* (Oxford, 1987), chap. 1; Kenneth Morgan, 'English and American attitudes towards convict transportation, 1718–1775', *History*, 72 (1987), 416–31; *id.*, 'Petitions against convict transportation, 1725–1735', *English Historical Review*, 104 (1989). 110–13.

28 Beattie, *Crime and the Courts*, 506–19. See also Ekirch, *Bound for America*, 28–45; and Joanna Innes, 'The role of transportation in seventeenth- and eighteenth-century English penal practice', in Carl Bridge ed., *New Perspectives in Australian History* (1990), 1–24.

29 Beattie, *Crime and the Courts*, 616–17.

30 Beattie, *Policing and Punishment in London*, esp. Part II.

31 Beattie, *Crime and the Courts*, 431–2, 509–13; *id.*, *Policing and Punishment in London*, chap. 9.

32 Beattie, *Crime and the Courts*, 625–6.

33 *Ibid.*, 560–613; David Mackay, *A Place of Exile: The European Settlement of New South Wales* (Melbourne and Oxford, 1985), chap. 2; Wilfrid Oldham, *Britain's Convicts to the Colonies*, ed. W. Hugh Oldham (Sydney, 1990), chap. 3; Devereaux, 'Making of the Penitentiary Act'; *id.*, 'In place of death: transportation, penal practices, and the English State, 1770–1830', in Strange, *Qualities of Mercy*, 52–76.

34 Beattie, *Policing and Punishment in London*, 378–83.

35 This is a key argument in Simon Devereaux's forthcoming book with Palgrave Press, *Convicts and the State: Criminal Justice and English Governance, 1750–1810*, esp. chap. 4. The major studies of police reform at this time include Ruth Paley, 'The Middlesex Justices Act of 1792: Its Origins and Effects' (PhD thesis, University of Reading, 1983); Elaine A. Reynolds, *Before the Bobbies: The Night Watch and Police Reform in Metropolitan London, 1720–1830* (Basingstoke, 1998); and Sir Leon Radzinowicz, *A History of the English Criminal Law and its Administration: Volume 3, Cross-Currents in the Movement for the Reform of the Police* (1956).

36 The major monograph on this topic at this time was written over half-a-century ago: Abbot Emerson Smith, *Colonists in Bondage: White Servitude and Convict Labour in America, 1607–1776* (Chapel Hill, NC, 1947).

37 Krista Kesselring has made a similar point for another period and legal device in her 'Abjuration and its demise: the changing face of royal justice in the Tudor period', *Canadian Journal of History*, 34 (1999), 345–58. Her ideas are more fully set out in her new book *Mercy and Authority in the Tudor State* (Cambridge, 2003).

38 For Beccaria's reception in Britain, see Hugh Dunthorne, 'Beccaria and Britain', in David W. Howell and Kenneth O. Morgan eds, *Crime, Protest and Police in Modern British Society: Essays in Memory of David J.V. Jones* (Cardiff, 1999), 73–96; and Anthony J. Draper, 'Cesare Beccaria's influence on English discussions of punishment, 1764–1789', *History of European Ideas*, 26 (2000) 177–99.

39 See David Dean, *Law-Making and Society in Late Elizabethan England: The Parliament of England, 1584–1601* (Cambridge, 1996), chap. 6; Alan Cromartie, *Sir Matthew Hale, 1609–1676: Law, Religion, and Natural Philosophy* (Cambridge, 1995); Christopher Hill, *The World Turned Upside Down: Radical Ideas During the Puritan Revolution* (1972), chap. 12; Barbara Shapiro, 'Law reform in seventeenth-century England', *American Journal of Legal History* (1975), 280–312; Donald Veall, *The Popular Movement for Law Reform, 1640–1660* (Oxford, 1970), chaps 3–5; G.B. Warden, 'Law reform in England and New England, 1620–1660', *William and Mary Quarterly*, third series, 35 (1978), 668–90; Mary Cotrell, 'Interregnum law reform: the Hale Commission of 1652', *EHR*, 83 (1968), 689–704; G.R. Elton, 'English law in the sixteenth century: reform in an age of change' (Selden Society Lectures, 1979 for 1978).

40 Hugo Grotius, *The Laws of War and Peace* (1625), II, xx, 40; I, ii, 1.

41 Innes and Styles, 'Crime wave', 244–5; Philip Jenkins, 'From gallows to prison? The execution rate in early modern England', *CJH*, 7 (1986), 51–71.

42 Gatrell, *Hanging Tree*, 579–83; K.J.M. Smith, 'Anthony Hammond: "Mr Surface" Peel's persistent codifier', *Legal History*, 20 (1999), 24–44; Radzinowicz, *History of English Criminal Law*, I, chap. 18.

43 Derek Beales, 'Peel, Russell, and reform', *HJ*, 17 (1974), 873–82, 879–80; Gatrell, *Hanging Tree*, 570, 579–82.

44 T.C. Hansard ed., *The Parliamentary Debates, From the Year 1803 to the Present Time*, 3/52 (1840), cols, 914–19.

45 David D. Cooper, *The Lesson of the Scaffold: The Public Execution Controversy in Victorian England* (1974); Radzinowicz, *History of English Criminal Law*, V, 671–6, 685–8; Gatrell, *Hanging Tree*, 22–3, 589–611; McGowen, 'Civilizing punishment'.

46 Gatrell, *Hanging Tree*, 599.

47 Arthur Griffiths, 'Why have a hangman?', *Fortnightly Review*, o.s. 40/n.s., 34 (1883), 581–6, quoting 581.

48 Robert B., Shoemaker, *Prosecution and Punishment: Petty Crime and the Law in London and Rural Middlesex, c. 1660–1725* (Cambridge, 1991), 6.

49 Penalties at the manor courts up to 1600 have been recently described by Marjorie Keniston McIntosh, *Controlling Misbehaviour in England, 1370–1600* (Cambridge, 1998).

50 See my chapter for a fuller discussion of these findings.

51 Jim Sharpe writes that 'it seems likely that, if the records of all courts with a "criminal" jurisdiction were to be consulted, it would be revealed that the most common form of punishment inflicted on criminals in the period in question would be fining: whatever the early modern criminal justice system was doing to the body or soul of offenders, it was certainly damaging their purse': 'Civility, civilizing processes, and the end of public punishment', 223. See also Beattie, *Crime and the Courts*, 456–61; Sharpe, *Judicial Punishment*, 49.

52 Martin Ingram, '"Scolding women cucked or washed": a crisis in gender relations in early modern England?', in Jenny Kermode and Garthine Walker eds, *Women, Crime, and the Courts in Early Modern England* (1994), 48–80, quoting 60.

53 Important work on early modern crime pamphlets includes Lincoln B. Faller, *Turned to Account: The Forms and Functions of Criminal Biography in Late-Seventeenth and Eighteenth-Century England* (Cambridge, 1987); Gatrell, *Hanging Tree*, chaps 4–6; Peter Lake with Michael Questier, *The Antichrist's Lewd Hat: Protestants, Papists, and Players in Post-Reformation England* (New Haven and London, 2002), esp. chaps 1, 9 and 12; Andrea McKenzie, 'Making crime pay: motives, marketing strategies, and the printed literature of crime in England, 1670–1770', in G.T. Smith *et al.*, eds., *Criminal Justice in the Old World and the New* (1998); Philip Rawlings, *Drunks, Whores and Idle Apprentices: Criminal Biographies of the Eighteenth Century* (1992); Sharpe, '"Last dying speeches" '; W. Speck, *Literature and Society in Eighteenth-Century England, 1680–1820* (1998).

54 Cesare de Beccaria, *On Crimes and Punishments*, 1764, ed. Henry Paolucci (New York, 1963), 57.

55 There will be a chapter on these themes in Paul Griffith's forthcoming book, *Lost Londons: Crime, Control, and Change in the Capital City, 1545–1660.*

56 See J.A. Sharpe, '"Such disagreement betwyx neighbours": litigation and human relations in early modern England', in John Bossy ed., *Disputes and Settlements: Law and Human Relations in the West* (Cambridge, 1983), 167–87; *id.*, 'Enforcing the law in the seventeenth-century English Village', in Gatrell *et al.*, eds, *Crime and the Law* 97–119; Keith Wrightson, 'Two concepts of order: justices, constables and jurymen in seventeenth-century England', in John Brewer and John Styles, eds, *An Ungovernable People: The English and Their Law in the Seventeenth and Eighteenth Centuries* (1980), 21–46; Joan Kent, *The English Village Constable 1580–1642: A Social and Administrative Study* (Oxford, 1986), esp. chaps 7–8.

57 Shoemaker, *Prosecution and Punishment*, esp. chaps 4–5.

58 See Bob Shoemaker's chapter in this volume.

59 Innes, 'Prisons for the poor'.

60 Ian W. Archer, *The Pursuit of Stability: Social Relations in Elizabethan London* (Cambridge, 1991), chaps 5–6; A.L. Beier, *Masterless Men: The Problem of Vagrancy in England 1560–1640* (1985), chap. 9; Anthony Fletcher. *Reform in the Provinces: The Government of Stuart England* (New Haven and London, 1986), chap. 7; Paul Griffiths, 'Numbering Norvicians: information, institutions, identities, 1570–1660', in Carole Rawcliffe and Richard Wilson eds, *History of Norwich*, forthcoming; *id.*, 'Contesting London Bridewell, 1576–1580', *JBS*, 43, 3 (2003) 283–315; *id.*, Masterless young people in Norwich, 1560–1645', in Paul Griffiths *et al.*, eds, *The Experience of Authority in Early Modern England* (Basingstoke, 1996), 146–86; Valerie Pearl, 'Puritans and poor relief: the London Workhouse, 1649–1660', in Donald Pennington and Keith Thomas eds, *Puritans and Revolutionaries: Essays in Seventeenth-Century History Presented to Christopher Hill* (Oxford, 1978), 206–32; Paul Slack, *Poverty and Policy in Tudor and Stuart England* (Harlow, 1988), chaps 6–7; *id.*, 'Hospitals, workhouses, and the relief of the poor in early modern London', in O.P. Grell and A. Cunningham eds, *Health Care and Poor Relief in Protestant Europe, 1500–1700* (1997), 234–51; David Underdown, *Fire From Heaven: Life in an English Town in the Seventeenth Century* (1992), chap. 4. London Bridewell will be a corner-stone of Paul Griffith's next book, *Lost Londons*. His essay in this collection looks again at Norwich Bridewell. For the wave of houses of correction in mainland Europe, see P. Spierenburg, *The Prison Experience: Disciplinary Institutions and their Inmates in Early Modern Europe* (1991).

61 For public whipping see Beattie, *Crime and the Courts*, chap. 9; J.S. Cockburn, 'Punishment and brutality in the English Enlightenment', *Law and History Review*, 12 (1994), 155–79; King, *Crime, Justice, and Discretion*, chap. 10; *id*. 'Punishing assault'; Sharpe, 'Civility, civilizing processes, and the end of public punishment'; Smith, 'Civilized people don't want to see that kind of thing'; and Bob Shoemaker's chapter in this collection. For changing sentiments in the eighteenth and nineteenth centuries see N. Fierin, 'Irresistible compassion: an aspect of eighteenth century sympathy and humanitarianism', *Journal of the History of Ideas*, 37 (1976), 195–218; Garland, *Punishment and Modern Society*, chap. 10; Gatrell, *Hanging Tree*, chaps 7–10; T.L. Haskell, 'Capitalism and the origins of humanitarian sensibility', parts 1 and 2 *AHR*, 90, 339–61, 547–66 (1985); L.E. Klein, *Shaftsbury and the Culture of Politeness: Moral Discourse and Cultural Politics in Early Eighteenth-Century England* (Cambridge, 1994); John Mullan, *Sentiment and Sociability: The Language of Feeling in the Eighteenth Century* (Oxford, 1988); M.J. Wiener, *Reconstructing the Criminal: Culture, Law, and Policy in England, 1830–1914* (Cambridge, 1990), chap. 1.

62 David Underdown, 'The taming of the scold: the enforcement of patriarchal authority in early modern England', in A. Fletcher and J. Stevenson eds, *Order and Disorder in Early Modern England* (Cambridge, 1985), 116–36.

63 Martin Ingram, ' "Scolding women cucked or washed": a crisis in gender relations in early modern England?', in Kermode and Walker eds, *Women, Crime, and the Courts*, 48–80. See also Griffiths, 'Masterless young people'; Michael Roberts, 'Women and work in sixteenth-century English towns', in P.J. Corfield and D. Keene eds, *Work in Towns, 850–1850* (Leicester, 1990), 86–102; Laura Gowing, ' "The freedom of the streets": women and social space, 1560–1640', in Paul Griffiths and M.S.R. Jenner eds, *Londinopolis: Essays in the Cultural and Social History of Early Modern London* (Manchester, 2000), 130–51; D.V. Glass, 'Notes on the demography of London at the end of the seventeenth century', in Glass and R. Revelle eds, *Population and Social Change* (1972), 275–85; David Souden, 'Migrants and the population structure of late seventeenth-century provincial cities and market towns', in Peter Clark ed., *The Transformation of English Provincial Towns, 1660–1800* (1984), 133–68. Jim Sharpe writes that carting 'seems to have been most often used in urban areas' (*Judicial Punishment*, 21). David Underdown mentions Ingram's criticisms in a later essay but he does not respond to them at any length: 'Yellow ruffs and poisoned possets: placing women in early Stuart political debate', in Susan Dwyer Amussen and Adele F. Seeff eds, *Attending to Early Modern Women* (Newark, DE, 1998), 230–43.

64 Laura Gowing notes that 'Gender is *always* in contest' and is a scene of 'perpetual conflict': *Domestic Dangers: Words, Women, and Sex in Early Modern England* (Oxford, 1996), 28, 275.

65 As well as works mentioned in n. 58, see Greg T. Smith, 'The state and the culture of violence in London, 1760–1840' (University of Toronto PhD thesis, 1999), 390, table 7.1. On military discipline see John Dinwiddy, 'The early nineteenth-century campaign against flogging in the army', *English Historical, Review*, 97 (1982) 308–31; E. Steiner, 'Separating the soldier from the citizen: ideology of criticism of corporal punishment in the British armies, 1790–1815', *Social History*, 8 (1983), 19–35; David Killingray, 'The "rod of empire": the debate over corporal punishment in the British-African colonial forces, 1888–1946', *Journal of African History*, 35 (1994), 201–16.

66 McIntosh, *Controlling Misbehaviour*, 63–4, 106, 115. Judith Bennett associates the cucking stool with the punishment of alewives in the late medieval period: see

her *Ale, Beer, and Brewsters in England: Women's Work in a Changing World, 1300–1600* (Oxford, New York, 1996), esp. 104–5. The story of cucking stools is told in John Webster Spargo, *Juridical Folklore in England Illustrated by the Cucking Stool* (Durham, NC, 1944).

67 B[ridewell] H[ospital] C[ourtbook] 7, fo. 125v, consulted on microfilm at the Guildhall Library, London. The best studies of the role of shame in recent cultures include John Braithwaite, *Crime, Shame, and Reintegration* (1978); William Ian Miller, *Humiliation, and Other Essays on Honour, Social Discomfort, and Violence* (Ithaca, NY, 1993); Frank Henderson Stuart, *Honour* (1998); and Pierre Bourdieu, *Outline of a Theory of Practice*, trans. R. Nice (Cambridge, 1977).

68 BHC 3, fo. 50; W. Le Hardy ed., *Hertford County Records: Notes and Extracts from the Sessions Rolls 1581 to 1698* (9 vols.; Hertford. 1905–39), I, 42.

69 W[estminster] C[ity] A[chives] WCB/1, fo. 49; BHC 1, fo. 70v. See the important and wonderfully wide-ranging discussion by Dave Postles, 'Penance and the market place: a Reformation dialogue with the medieval church (*c.* 1250–1600)', *Journal of Ecclesiastical History*, 54 (2003), 441–68.

70 See below, chap. 3.

71 See Beier, *Masterless Men*, esp. 40–7; Griffiths, *Lost Londons*, chaps 1–2.

72 *A Survey of the Cities of London and Westminster… by John Stow… Corrected, Improved, and Very Much Enlarged… by John Strype* (1720), 257.

73 N[orthamptonshire] R[ecord] O[ffice] Northamptonshire Quarter Sessions minute book 1668–78, fo. 37.

74 Nott[inghamshire] R[ecord] O[ffice] CA361(B), Nottingham Sessions Minute Book 1732/43, fo. 9.

75 Beattie, *Crime and the Courts*, 461–4 and 485–7; *id.*, *Policing and Punishment in London*, 444–7; King, *Crime, Justice, and Discretion*, 262–6.

76 NOTTRO CA361(B), Nottingham Sessions Minute Book 1732/43, fo. 31; NRO Northamptonshire Quarter Sessions minute book, 1690–1708, fos. 79v, 110; Northamptonshire Quarter Sessions minute book 1708–27, fo. 14v. See also McGowen, 'From pillory to gallows'.

77 C[orporation of] L[ondon] R[ecord] Office Rep[ertories of the Court of Aldermen] 12, fo. 283; John Lister ed., *West Riding Sessions Records. Vol. 2, Orders, 1611–1642, Indictments, 1637–42* (Yorkshire Archeological Society, 54, Leeds, 1915), 18.

78 J.G. de T. Mandley ed., *The Portmote or Court Leet Records of the Borough or Town and Royal Manor of Salford, from the Year 1597 to the Year 1669* (2 vols.; Chetham Society, second series, 46, 48, Manchester, 1902), II, 45–6; WCA WCB/1, fo. 81. The Peeltown punishment is described by Dickinson and Sharpe later on in this book, and they also spend several paragraphs looking at the use of the scold's bridle on the island.

79 Michael Power ed., *Liverpool Town Books, 1649–1671* (The Records Society of Lancashire and Cheshire, 136, Dorchester, 1999), 101; NOTTRO QSM/13, fo. 12; J.P. Earwaker ed., *The Court Leet Records of the Manor of Manchester from 1552 to 1686* (6 vols; Manchester, 1884–90), II, 247; K.S. Martin intro., *Records of Maidstone Being Selections from Documents in the Possession of the Corporation* (Maidstone, 1926), 191; F.A. Bailey ed., *A Selection from the Prescot Court Leet and other Records, 1447–1600* (Lancashire and Cheshire Record Society, 89, Blackpool, 1937), 106; M.G. Hobson and H.E. Salter eds., *Oxford Council Acts, 1626–1665* (Oxford Historical Society, 95, Oxford, 1933), 448; Earwaker, *Court Leet Records of the Manor of Manchester*, VII, 70.

80 *The Diary of the Rev. Henry Newcome, from September 30, 1661, to September 29, 1663*, ed. Thomas Heywood (Chetham Society, 18, Manchester, 1849), 161.

81 See Paul Griffith's chapter in this book, and his 'Numbering Norvicians'. He is also writing a book – *Paper States: Penal Cultures and Surveillance in Early Modern England* – that more fully examines many of the ideas and themes that are raised in this introduction and in his chapter in this collection.

82 See Simon Devereaux's forthcoming essay, 'Recasting the theatre of public justice in London: the end of Tyburn in context'.

83 Robert B. Shoemaker, 'The decline of public insult in London, 1660–1800', *P&P*, 169 (2000), 97–131.

84 BHC 5, fo. 361v.

85 Quoted in Innes, 'Prisons for the poor', 67; L[ondon] M[etropolitan] A[rchives] MJ/SBR/2, fo. 411.

86 LMA MJ/SBR/2, fos 242–3; Leicestershire Record Office Leicester City Hallbooks 3386/24; 3390/69; NRO Northampton City Assembly Book, 1553–1629, fo. 359. See also Innes, 'Prisons for the poor'; Slack, *Poverty and Policy*, chap. 6.

87 CLRO Rep. 21, fo. 4.

88 Esther Cohen, 'The animated pain of the body', *American Historical Review* (2000), 36–68.

89 *The Diary of Ralph Josselin, 1616–1683*, ed. Alan Macfarlane (British Academy Records of Social and Economic History, new series, 3, 1976), 39, 58. See also 114, 438, 600.

90 Beier, *Masterless Men*, 164; and Innes, 'Prisons for the poor', 42, 53; Robert Jutte, *Poverty and Deviance in Early Modern Europe* (Cambridge, 1994), 169.

91 Shoemaker, *Prosecution and Punishment*, esp. 168–78.

92 Rusche and Kirchheimer, *Punishment and Social Structure*; Innes, 'Prisons for the poor'.

93 The best recent history of the first decades of transportation is Innes, 'Role of transportation'. See also Shaw, *Colonists in Bondage*, chaps 1–4; Robert C. Johnson, 'The transportation of vagrant children from London to Virginia, 1618–1622', in Howard S. Reinmuth ed., *Early Stuart Studies: Essays in Honour of David Harris* (Minneapolis, MN, 1970), 137–51. Paul Griffiths will cover the first four decades of transportation from London Bridewell in his next book *Lost Londons*, chap. 7.

94 NOTTRO QSM/13, fo. 12.

1
Shame and Pain: Themes and Variations in Tudor Punishments

Martin Ingram

One of Sir John Harington's epigrams tells the story of a man brought into the Star Chamber, who 'for the greater terrour' was sentenced to be branded on the face and to have his nose slit. His wife begged for him, but the judges 'gravely' told her that he had had mercy enough: his offences really deserved the death penalty. Thereupon she broke out:

> If you disgrace him thus, you quite undo him,
> Good my Lords hang him, pray be good unto him.[1]

This essay is not concerned with the kinds of judicial punishment that spring most readily to mind in the modern world: the death penalty, incarceration or fines; its subject is legal sanctions that touched the bodies of culprits more or less grievously, or at least exposed them to public obloquy, yet without threatening their lives or depriving them of liberty for lengthy periods. When public exhibition was the main object, they may be referred to as shame penalties, while when physical chastisement was the chief emphasis, they fall more naturally under the heading of corporal punishment; but in fact these were ends of a spectrum, and many of the penalties under review combined shame and pain in varying proportions. While there is a long, quasi-folkloric literature on such 'bygone' or 'olden time' punishments,[2] they have received surprisingly little attention, at least in an English context, from recent historians of crime and punishment. The subject has been squeezed out by concentration on capital punishment and the search for alternatives from the seventeenth century onwards; and, secondarily, on the development of houses of correction as a precursor of later reformatory institutions. Hence James Sharpe's otherwise excellent study of judicial punishments devotes only a few pages to stocks, pillory, ducking stools and related topics, and is almost at pains to emphasize the infrequency of their appearance in his principal sources – mainly records of quarter sessions and assizes in the late sixteenth and especially the seventeenth century. He recognizes that whipping was a major form of punishment, yet again his discussion is brief.[3] The following essay gives these subjects much fuller attention, on the basis chiefly of London materials for what is, for English historians of crime and punishment, a relatively neglected period – the century or so before 1570. From this examination, the early to mid-Tudor era emerges as a creative period in the sphere of judicial punishment, marked by a variety of experiments and innovations designed both to deter and, more crucially, to *reform*. In general terms these developments may be explained as a reaction to the social pressures of the period, deriving not only from the stress of population increase, price inflation, growing urban populations and changes in land use, but also from the religious upheavals of the Reformation, as catholics and protestants struggling for the moral high ground ratcheted up the scale of penalties while self-righteously accusing their religious rivals of being soft on sin.[4] Yet they were not an unthinking response, and the precise form of their evolution – more complex than might at first sight appear – is the subject of this chapter.

I

Of pivotal importance, and hence the best starting point for studying these developments, was the practice of ecclesiastical penance. Church courts were unlike secular courts in that their primary object was the health of the soul of the individual sinner, and their penalties were supposed to be medicinal rather than retributive. Characteristically they involved public confession or acknowledgement of the fault. Offenders in pre-Reformation times, penitentially clad in a white sheet and carrying a white rod or wax taper, had to go before the parish procession, kneel or prostrate themselves during the service, and present a candle or other offering to the priest or before the image of a saint as a token of their submission.[5] After the Reformation the ritual was still characteristically performed in penitential garb, but candles and tapers were abandoned. The central act usually took place in church; culprits had to stand within sight of the congregation during part of the service, and sometimes they had to endure a sermon on adultery, drunkenness or whatever theme was appropriate in the particular case. Finally they had to confess their sin, ask the forgiveness of God (and of their neighbours in some versions), and lead the congregation in the Lord's Prayer, thus completing an act of symbolic reintegration with the Christian community.[6]

But the practice of penance was shot through with ambiguities. The medicinal principle looks less benign when it is realized that the church courts could hand over obdurate or relapsed heretics – those who held seriously unorthodox religious doctrines – to the secular power for execution by burning. Such harsh measures, which reached a peak in Mary's reign, became much rarer after the accession of Elizabeth; but a man was burnt for unorthodoxy as late as 1612 and Hobbes feared that he would suffer this fate after the Restoration.[7] Even in cases of immorality, or of other sins of

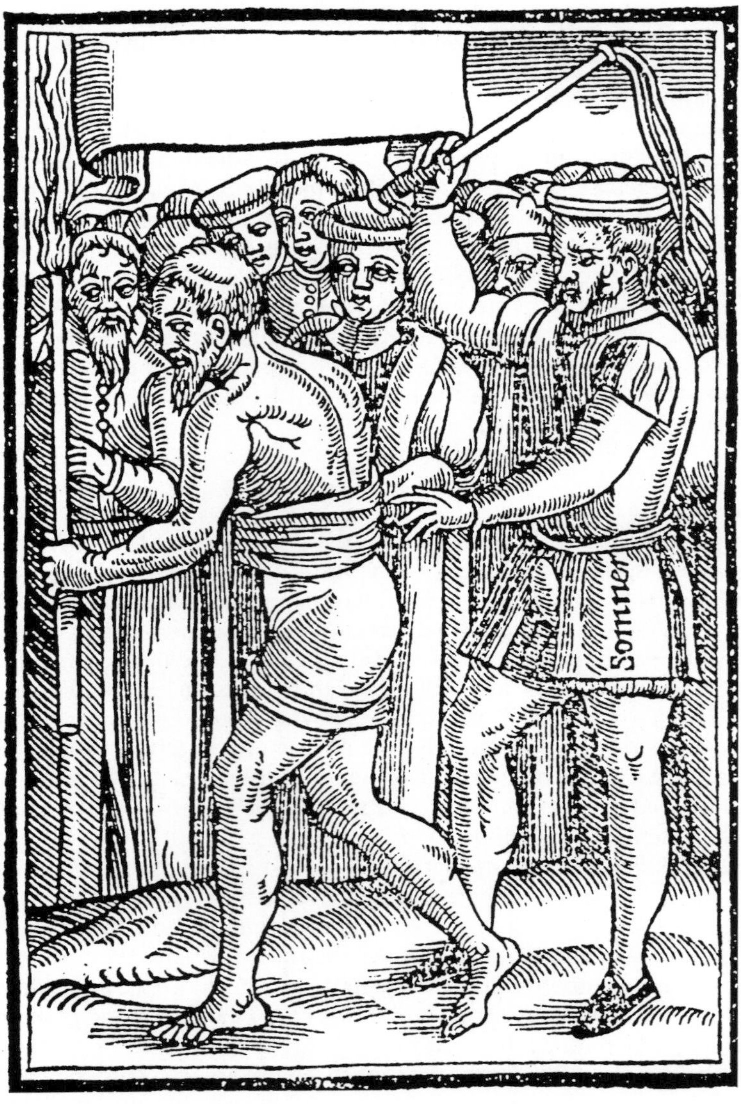

Plate 1.1 Penitential whipping

Source: John Foxe, *Actes and Monuments* (3 vols, 1641 edn), I, 870. By permission of Brasenose College.

commission or omission that were the staple of ecclesiastical court business, proceedings had a harder edge than might at first sight appear. James Morice, sharply criticizing Richard Cosin, the late Elizabethan apologist of the spiritual power, demanded rhetorically:

> shall not penaunce although it bee but the standing in a sheete ... respect of publique shame and reproache (grievous and odious unto all men) [and so] be accompted for a punishment? True it is, all corrections are or should bee medicines for the amendement of man[n]ers. But doeth it therefore follow that the same be no paines or punishments?[8]

Moreover penance was not always 'but the standing in a sheete'. Throughout the period, it was not uncommon for penitents to suffer additional personal indignities, such as going barefoot or bare-legged. It is true that penitential whippings (Plate 1.1) – still common in some areas on the eve of the Reformation – were abandoned by the later sixteenth century, since common lawyers insisted that church court penalties could touch neither life, limb, nor property.[9] But still very much in operation in the later period was the practice of making notorious offenders perform penance not only in church but also in a public, secular space, usually the open market. Often, when that happened, they had to wear papers or placards advertising the offence, and the experience can have been hardly different from a spell in the pillory.[10]

II

In London, which will be the main focus of what follows, secular shame punishments were indeed often referred to as 'penance'. One reason for this is indicated by Thomas Walsingham's account of the genesis of the City of London's ordinances against scolds, bawds and other sexual offenders in the reign of Richard II: claiming that the church courts were letting such sinners get away with commuted penances, the civic authorities took it upon themselves to enact a series of stiffer penalties with real penitential bite.[11] However, the secular appropriation of the notion of 'penance' was not confined to these particular measures but had wider application in the city's penal regime. Thus in 1466 a juryman, having been convicted of receiving bribes to deliver false verdicts, an offence described as 'dampnable afore god & man', was therefore ordered to be punished 'to hys shame & rebuke and to thexample of all other sembleable mysdoers or disposed to effend [*sic*] in like wise'. In 1543, a woman who had abandoned a child was ordered to do 'penaunce ... to thintent that she from hensforwarde & all other warnyd by her may call for grace and be well ware [not] to p[er]petrate or comytt the like offence at any tyme herafter'. There was a similar reference to the call to God for grace in a case from 1561, when an apprentice was punished for spending his master's goods.[12]

A man convicted in 1529 of opprobrious words against the sheriffs was ordered as his 'pen[a]u[n]ce' to be led through the city 'all naked except his shyrte and a shete abowte hym bare leggyd and barefoted'.[13] However, secular shame penalties did not usually mimic quite so closely the procedures of ecclesiastical justice, but had their own characteristic forms. The proceedings ordinarily began with incarceration. In London this might be in the stocks (the most basic form of holding device, consisting of lockable wooden boards, shaped for the accommodation of one or both legs of a variable number of culprits); a cage (a wooden prison in which the offender was exposed to view); one or other of the overnight prisons – the Tun (shaped like a barrel) or one of the Counters; or Newgate or other secure prison.[14] After 1553 it might be Bridewell, the former royal palace adapted to penal use following its grant by Edward VI. There was nothing quite like Bridewell elsewhere in England, though following an act of 1576 houses of correction and workhouses began slowly to be established. In other respects provincial towns and cities had similar, albeit less elaborate and extensive provisions to those of the metropolis.[15]

Offenders characteristically spent only a few days or even hours under lock and key, but in conditions that were evidently harsh enough to subdue all but the most obdurate spirits. At any rate, that was clearly the intention. Equally plainly, punishments involving public shame or exposure were designed to capitalize on this initial shock. The most basic form of such penalties was simply to parade the culprit through the city or town.[16] In London from the later 1550s, this was sometimes done by frogmarching him (occasionally her) between two officers of Bridewell. More elaborate was to 'ride' the culprit round the town, either astride a horse, often 'bare ridged' (that is, without a saddle) or, from the 1520s in London, in a cart or 'car'.[17] A variant, evidently thought to be especially opprobrious and reserved for more serious cases or repeated offenders, was to cause the usually (though not invariably) male offender to ride backwards with his face to the horse's tail, indeed sometimes holding the tail in his hand (Plate 1.2). This was a punishment of great antiquity, found not only in many parts of Europe in medieval and ancient times but in other parts of the world as well. The element of inversion or reversal – found also in 'ridings' or 'skimmington rides' or other charivaresque folk punishments – not only evoked derision but was, more basically, a powerful symbol of shame and obloquy.[18]

In all these cases, the prescribed route encompassed some or all of the most crowded thoroughfares and market places in order to ensure maximum exposure. In 1478, for example, William Campion was ordered to ride from the Counter in Bread Street to Cornhill, thence to Cheap, Paternoster Row, Ludgate, Fleet Bridge, Fleet Street, Temple Bar, and so back to the Counter. More summarily, it was ordered in 1543 that Agnes Oxley should be 'ledde thurrough all the co[mm]en m[ar]kett plac[es] of this cytye, That is to [say] Newgate m[ar]kett, Chepesyde & Graschurche m[ar]kett'. Plainly

Plate 1.2 Riding backwards: the punishment of Dr John London and William Simons, 1543

Source: John Foxe, *Actes and Monuments* (3 vols, 1641 edn), II, between 554 and 555. By permission of Brasenose College.

the length and openness of the route could considerably augment the impact of the punishment.[19] Moreover, means were used to attract the crowds. In London it was standard procedure to order that 'proclamation' should be made of the offence either at the end of the ride or at intervals along the route: indeed the precise text of such proclamation was often entered in the city's records. It was also common in the metropolis and elsewhere for the cause of the punishment to be advertised by means of 'papers' or 'scriptures' on which the nature of the offence was written or painted 'in greate letters'. Sometimes these papers were set mitre-like on the heads of the culprits, sometimes they were pinned to their clothes or exhibited close by.[20] Such placards were already in use in the fifteenth century but may have become more common in the Tudor period in line with the spread of literacy, and some references suggest that a wide audience was envisaged: thus in 1549 it was ordered that a butcher, for adultery aggravated by conspiracy to kill the husband, should ride through the city facing backwards and then be set on the pillory with a 'pap[er] upon his hed and an other pap[er] having the same word[es] lykewyse wrytten therupon to be affyxed to the pyllorye ov[er] hys hed that ev[er]ye p[er]son may easely see & red ye same'.[21]

There was a long and persistent tradition of complementing verbal representations of offences, and at the same time enhancing the spectacle and increasing the opprobium directed at the culprit, by the use of signs and symbols. London ordinances of the late fourteenth century specified that 'common women' or prostitutes should be paraded wearing ray (striped) hoods, with a white wand in their hands; scolds or brawlers should carry a 'dystaf with towen' (flax). (In the case of male offenders, this may have been a deliberate act of symbolic feminization based on the assumption that scolding was quintessentially a female crime.) These and other offenders were to be led through the city by minstrels; that is, to the raucous accompaniment of musical instruments.[22] These provisions continued to be applied, with variations, in Tudor times. Distaffs dressed with 'the worst tow' sporadically made an appearance, while ray hoods were a very regular feature of civic punishments, as was the rough music of metal 'basins' beaten before delinquents or other 'vile minstrelsy'. In 1537 a man who was himself a professional minstrel, condemned for keeping a mistress disguised 'in mannes rayment', was ordered to ride 'on horsebakke w[i]t[h] his face to the horse tayll w[i]t[h] a pap[er] on hys hedde & to play upon hys owne instrument afore her'.[23]

In addition to these inherited usages, symbols could be improvised: indeed magistrates clearly took delight in making the punishment fit the crime. In an unusually spectacular example in 1478, a man convicted of unlawfully tapping a conduit and conveying the water into his own well was ordered to be paraded on horseback 'w[i]t[h] a vessell like unto a conduyt full of water uppon his hede, the same water runnyng by smale pipes oute of the same vessell and that when the water is wasted newe water to be put in the said vessell ageyn'.[24] More routinely, sellers of rotten meat and other dishonest tradespeople (whether male or female) were paraded with some appropriate symbol of their offence: in a typical case in 1517, a man was ordered to ride round the city with two flitches of bacon fastened upon him, two others borne before him, a basin ringing to attract attention and a paper on his head 'ffor puttyng to sale of mesell and stynkyng bacon'. Deceitful wood-sellers were normally ridden with billets of wood slung round their necks; coal merchants who gave false measure were liable to suffer the fate of a pair from Croydon and Edgware in 1553 who were subjected to the backward-facing ride around London 'havynge a sak of their coles hangynge aboute their neck[es] the one ende of the same sakkes w[i]th the one half of the coll[es] hangynge at their bakk[es] & thother ende w[i]th thother half of the coll[es] hangynge at their brest[es]'.[25]

Less usual was the punishment of a Southwark card sharper in 1551, who had to ride backwards with 'his cote prycked full of playing card[es] on ev[er]y syde'; and that of a 'gongfarmer' (latrine cleaner) in 1535, who was ordered to stand 'yn one of hys owne pypes [that is, barrels]...yn fylthe w[i]t[h] a pap[er] upon hys hed for castyng of ordure yn the open stretes'.[26] Another variant was to adorn the culprit with the initial letter of the offence and, sometimes, a picture to evoke it. Thus in 1516 a woman convicted of being a common harlot who walked the city in priest's clothing, and a bawd who had procured a thirteen-year-old girl, were ordered to be paraded with ray hoods and white rods and basins ringing, 'the said Elizabeth Chekyn havyng on her brest a letter of H. of yelowe wollen clothe in sygne and tokyn of a harlot, and on her left shulder a picture of a woman in a preest['s] goun; and the said Elizabeth Knyght havyng upon her shulder a letter of B in signe and tokyn of a bawde'. In 1519 three common strumpets, who had cut their hair like men in order to dress in male garments, were for this 'abhomynacion' sentenced to be paraded with white wands in their hands, ray hoods about their shoulders, and 'mennes bonett[es] on their hed[es] w[i]t[h]out eny kercher, their hed[es] kemte'.[27]

III

Some of these parades, with their embellishments, clearly involved considerable physical discomfort for the culprits, and presumably exposed them also to missiles thrown by bystanders and to other abuse. That there were worse possibilities was often symbolically evoked: many of these punishments involved a stop under the pillory, where the nature of the offence was often formally proclaimed, while by the beginning of Elizabeth's reign the London authorities had a 'lyttle pillorie...openly borne upon a longe pole' to be carried in front of bakers who had broken the assize of bread.[28] The pillory, whereby the offender was exposed on a special scaffold or framework, was evidently considered a more severe and shameful punishment than a simple parade, and was often imposed in addition to the latter in aggravated cases or for repeat offenders. This gradation of punishments emerges clearly from many entries in the records. Thus in November 1560 the London civic authorities punished a butcher of Woodford in Essex by making him ride backwards with pieces of pork hanging on his breast and back. Two months later they punished another butcher, from Theydon in the same county, in much the same way; but since he had already suffered the same penalty a few years before, they ordered that in addition he should 'be sett on the pyllory in Cheapesyde...w[i]t[h] the sayd bacon hanginge aboute him and over his hedde uppon the saide pyllorye, and a paper affyxed to the seyd pyllorie declarynge not only this his sayd offence, but also the lyke offence by him here com[m]ytted in the tyme of the mayraltye of...S[ir] Thomas Leigh'.[29] Even a pillory sentence allowed for degrees of discomfort. The duration of the punishment could vary from a brief spell to several hours, and it could be repeated; it mattered also whether the

Plate 1.3 The pillory: the punishment of Robert Ockham, 1543

Source: John Foxe, *Actes and Monuments* (3 vols, 1641 edn), II, between 554 and 555. By permission of Brasenose College.

punishment occurred in market time, when large numbers of bystanders were invariably present. In London it would seem that offenders were often ordered merely to sit or stand on the pillory; much worse was to be set with head and hands secured within holes in the wooden frame of the pillory, a position both painful and extremely vulnerable (Plate 1.3).

Plainly shame and pain were never altogether distinguished, but the punishments so far described emphasized the former, while the latter was a subsidiary or incidental element. However, these and similar penalties could be associated with features more obviously recognizable as corporal punishments. One that was largely if not entirely confined to women was ducking. In late medieval London there existed a version of the pillory, called the 'thew', apparently designed specifically for female use. At first the thew seems to have been barely distinguishable from the cucking stool: references dating from before about 1500, in London and other towns, suggest that the latter was primarily an instrument for achieving the public exposure of the culprit, not for her immersion. However, in the course of the sixteenth century the cucking stool became a ducking stool. In London the

Court of Aldermen in 1529 ordered seven females, probably prostitutes or 'common women', 'to be had to the cukkyng stole'; whether they were actually ducked is unclear, but in 1535 a group of 'myghty vagabond[es] & wyswomen of theyre bodyes' were sentenced to be taken to Smithfield and 'sett upon the cukkyng stoole & ... wasshed over the eares'. Thereafter references occurred regularly, a practice that explains William Harrison's observation in *The description of England* in 1577 that 'harlots and their mates, by carting, ducking, and dooing of open penance ... are often put to rebuke'. However, as Harrison correctly noted, 'scolds' or quarrelsome women were also 'ducked upon cuckingstooles in the water', and this became the offence most characteristically punished by immersion in the reign of Elizabeth and beyond.[30] Ducking, 'dipping' or 'dopping' must always have been a brutal affair, a danger to health and perhaps even life-threatening when the immersion was prolonged or occurred in winter. But there was also an aggravated version of the penalty, mentioned by Harrison in his discussion of the punishment of sexual offenders: 'the dragging of some of them over the Thames betweene Lambeth and Westminster at the taile of a boat'. He added that 'this is inflicted upon them by none other than the knight marshall, and that within the compasse of his iurisdiction & limits onelie' (that is, within the royal court and its environs). In fact similar penalties were imposed by the Westminster Court of Burgesses in exemplary cases, usually of scolding, after its establishment by statute in 1585, while analogous practices are found in the provinces too.[31]

A less drastic assault on the body of offenders was the cutting or clipping of their hair, a mark of infamy applied to both men and women. The late fourteenth-century ordinances of the City of London laid down that 'if any man shall be found to be a common whoremonger or bawd, ... let all the head and beard be shaved except a fringe on the head, two inches in breadth; and let him be taken unto the pillory, with minstrels, and set thereon for a certain time'. Likewise, 'if any woman shall be found to be a common receiver of courtesans or bawd, ... let her be openly brought, with minstrels, from prison unto the thew, and set thereon for a certain time ..., and there let her hair be cut round about her head'. Common prostitutes were liable, along with other indignities, to have their hair cut round their heads at the third offence.[32] These penalties, or variants on them, were occasionally imposed in later times. Thus in 1510 the London Court of Aldermen dealt with two male bawds by ordering 'their hed[es] to be polled above the eyes and the same day in the markett season [they] to be ledde from thens to the pillorie in Cornhull thervppon to stande by the space of an houre'; in 1549 two 'auncyent co[mm]en harlott[es] of their bodies' were to be carted through the city with ray hoods and white wands, basins and pans ringing before them, and to have 'their here to be cutt of & shavyn above their eares' upon the pillory; while in 1551 it was ordered that an incestuous couple (a man and his half-sister) should be ridden round the city on three market days 'havyng their heare shorne above their eares' – 'for a deformitie', as a contemporary chronicler noted.[33]

Imposing a more painful and permanent stigma was an obvious way of increasing the severity of punishments. It was, moreover, one that was firmly rooted in non-judicial popular practice. Men sometimes threatened to thrust a dagger through their enemies' cheeks, evidently intending to mark them for life; while a threat often made against women was to give them 'the whore's mark', that is, to slit or cut off their noses.[34] But the first of these practices was not taken up into judicial use; while nose slitting, prescribed in an act of 1563 for certain kinds of forgery, and referred to in Harington's epigram, was in practice only rarely inflicted.[35] Branding, a well-established element in the penal repertory of many continental states, was also not commonly used in England save for the routine practice of 'burning in the hand': that is, branding the thumbs of convicts who had successfully pleaded 'benefit of clergy', thus saving them from the gallows, to ensure that they could not 'plead their clergy' on another occasion. An altogether more draconian procedure was recorded by the chronicler and antiquary John Stow in November 1556:

> a man was brought from Westminster Hall riding with his face to the horse tail, and a paper on his head, to the Standard in Cheape, & there set on the pillorie, and then burned with an hote yron on both his cheekes, with two letters *F.* and *A.* for False Accusing one of the court of Com[m]on place [i.e. Pleas] in Westminster of treason.

But such a punishment, though not unique, was very unusual.[36] A notorious act of 1547 did prescribe that sturdy beggars were not only to be enslaved but also 'marked with an whott iron in the brest with the marke of V', but this, like other provisions of the act, proved a dead letter. Only slightly less notorious was the provision of an act of 1572 that vagrants, in addition to other punishments, should be 'burnte through the gristle of the right eare with a hot yron of the compasse of an ynche about'. This measure was sporadically enforced, sometimes upon whole groups of vagrants, before it was repealed in 1593.[37]

Ears were indeed the favoured target of magistrates and judges seeking to impose both pain and stigma, but the branding iron was generally not employed. The usual procedure was to order that one or both ears of the offender should be nailed to the pillory for the duration of the punishment. The culminating and presumably disfiguring indignity was, as stated in a London case in 1552, that the culprit 'shall pluck it [the ear] from the pyllorye hym selfe att his goinge downe w[i]thoute the helpe of eny other or els remayne there styll' (though sometimes the nails were in fact pulled out with pincers). When a group of offenders was subjected to this punishment in 1521, it was ordered that a purpose-built 'new engyne' should be 'sette faste to the Standard in Chepe where as moste confluence of people shall be'.[38] There were other variants. In London in 1530, where two men had planned to steal lead and prepared slings and a pole to carry it off, the Court of Aldermen ordered 'that they shall bere the staff of the said slyng[es] betwene theym upon their sholders and oon of the eres of either of theym [to be] nayled to the said staff w[i]t[h] pap[ers] upon their heddes written w[i]t[h] the scrypture "ffor a false dede"'.[39] The cutting off of one or both ears was the next step up in terms of severity of punishment, which might simply be imposed for more serious offences as well as serving as an additional penalty for those who had not been deterred by having their ears nailed. In London in 1502 a contriver and publisher of seditious tales against the king and his nobles was ordered to have both his ears excised on the pillory; on the same day a notorious cutpurse was ordered to lose his right ear only.[40]

IV

Before exploring further, let us consider the context in which these penalties were administered and the thinking that underlay them. The offences that occasioned them appear at first sight very diverse, ranging from sedition through theft and various forms of deception and sharp practice to notorious sexual offences, especially those which had some connection with the trade in prostitution. What linked them in the contemporary mind was a sense of false dealing, the inverse of what was expected of the 'honest' citizen or those who wished to do business with citizens; and it is evident that the idea of 'honesty' had a broader signification than its modern equivalent, more redolent indeed of notions of 'honour'. These ideas, moreover, were rooted in an intensely communal ethos, that demanded not merely that citizens should themselves avoid misdoing but that they should be vigilant and active in preventing – or, if prevention failed, in correcting – such misdoing in others. In London these expectations were institutionalized in the offices of the Aldermen and the Aldermen's deputies, who exercised extraordinarily wide but highly discretionary powers of local discipline, and in the wardmote inquests which both enabled and required local inhabitants to identify persistent sexual delinquents, quarrellers and other local offenders. Characteristically these were thought of as 'nuisances', as nasty and as worthy of amendment as dunghills or dangerous pavements.[41]

At the apex of the possibilities open to these policing agencies was outright removal from the city. Indeed, many of the ignominious parades so far described did culminate in the exile of offenders: in London they were taken to Aldgate and unceremoniously ejected. At the other end of the spectrum, it is evident that a variety of informal warnings and cajolings were normally the first response to many misdoings, and that these in turn blended imperceptibly into formal admonition. Even simple shame punishments of the type reviewed earlier were not penalties of first resort: they were imposed because offenders 'by no gentle admonyc[ion] or correcc[i]on dyv[er]s and meny tymes ... heretofore gevyn ... wyll in eny wyse be steyd, reforemyd or amendyd'. Likewise more severe penalties were administered to those whom 'no co[mm]en or indyfferent correcc[i]on or punyshem[en]t wyll stey, refo[u]rme or w[i]t[h]drawe from their detestable & devylysshe vice & synfull lyfe'.[42] Alternatively, threat of severe punishment was used as a device to secure submission. It was often this that the court or local officers really wanted, and culprits who were prepared to humble themselves were frequently accorded relatively lenient treatment. Thus in 1552 a wax chandler was sentenced to the pillory on three market days 'for slaunderous rayllyng upon my lord mayer & his brethern thaldermen'. However, even on the pillory he denied his offence, so he was ordered to submit himself publicly on pain of suffering 'hys eares upon the rest of thexecuc[i]on of hys seid iudgem[en]t to be cutt of openly upon the pyllorye'. He duly recanted and was discharged. In a case in 1544 things did not proceed so far: the Lord Mayor forgave the wife of a yeoman of the guard for 'speakyng of lewde word[es] ageynst his lordyship' because both she and her husband 'were very repent[a]unt & sorye for ytt & askyd hym forgevenes'.[43]

When they were punished, offenders were characteristically described as 'not dredyng godd ne the shame of thys worlde', 'not feryng ne dredyng god almyghty, the shame of the worlde nor yet regardynge the othe that he toke when he was fyrst admytted into the lib[er]ties of this citie', or 'not dreding god nor their consciens'.[44] The magistrates appear to have assumed that individuals were capable of experiencing guilt and amending their behaviour accordingly, but that they had wilfully neglected to do so. They were therefore publicly punished, and their misdoings made manifest, for a dual purpose: both 'to their rebuke and shame and to thexample [of] other semblable mysdoers', 'for the terro[u]r, stey and example of others' that they might thereafter be 'well ware of hensforthe neu[er] to com[m]it or practise the like acte or offence'. In some cases the point was driven home by the threat of 'ffurther punysshement which shalbe to theym paynfull & grevous in such wise as such other idyll p[er]sones may haue cause to be ware by theym'.[45] These practices were rooted in contemporary notions of shame, which following Aristotle saw it as an intensely unpleasant emotion – characteristically expressed in reddened cheeks and downcast eyes – that was, however, closely related to virtue in serving both as a bridle on misconduct and a spur to better behaviour in the future.[46]

The impact of these shame punishments no doubt varied according to status and position. Some of those who suffered them were outsiders, coming into the city to trade. Many sexual offenders and others were no doubt poor and already of low social credit. Yet more substantial citizens were targeted on occasion, and contemporary annalists make plain that they 'wolde have gevyne moch to a be scowsyd'.[47] In certain circumstances the effects of public exposure could apparently be devastating. In 1509 six London citizens were punished for perjury and extortion in legal proceedings, repeated after due warnings from the Lord Mayor. Three of them, who 'more haynously have offended in detestable p[er]iurye', were subjected to the backward-facing ride and ordered to be set upon the pillory with 'their hedd[es] in the holys'; then they, together with the other three men who were simply led from prison to stand under the pillory, were to be conveyed round the city 'by the most [public] highwayes'. According to a contemporary city annalist, the three men who were ridden backwards 'died all w[i]t[h]-in VII days aft[er] for sham'. Whether this lethal 'shame' was the gnawing of their own consciences; or whether their sense of self was destroyed by the mortification of public exposure; or whether the brickbats and ordure, which probably assailed them while their heads were through the pillory, had something to do with their demise is unfortunately obscure. But there is certainly other evidence that a sense of shame unaccompanied by physical mistreatment could on occasion lead to death, and there are indications that the prospect of the pillory drove some individuals to suicide.[48]

On the other hand, it is evident that shame penalties were not always taken so seriously, and that their effects could vary considerably from person to person even on the same occasion. Thus in 1519 two perjurers were ordered to stand on two market days under the pillory with papers on their heads. But after they had been punished the first time, they were brought into court again and it was ordered that on the second occasion one of the men should be set *on* the pillory before being banished for seven years and a day, 'for asmoche as he had taken the saide punysshement but in derision and no thyng shewed hym selfe to be repentaunt nor sory for the same'. The other man had merely to stand under the pillory as before, and was banished for only a year and a day, 'for that that ... [he] toke the same punysshement repentauntlike'. In any case, it was apparently possible for the effects to wear off in time; and, in the crowded metropolis, either for the events to fade from the public mind or for the offender to start afresh in another place. 'I haue knowne a man carted, rung with basons, and banished out of Bishopsgate ward,' reported Stow, 'and afterward in Aldgate ward admitted to be a Constable, a grand Iuryman, and foreman of their wardmote inquest'.[49] Reactions even to the more extreme forms of physical stigma were perhaps more varied than might be imagined, to judge by a Wiltshire case in 1560. Faced with prosecution for unjustly seizing and selling a batch of shoes in the marketplace of Lavington, under colour of an Exchequer commission, a man retorted 'th[a]t he cannott losse his lyff for hit he knoweth very well, allthowghe he losse his eares w[hi]ch he wolld cov[e]r w[i]th a nyght cappe if he so dyd'.[50]

The capacity of offenders to make light of punishments, or at least endure them, was presumably influenced partly by the attitudes of other people. Not everyone was in favour of inflicting the punishments in question, particularly the more gruesome versions. In 1545, when a brewer announced to bystanders in Cheapside that 'I have arrested yo[u]r neighbo[u]r Page, for he is a false harlott for he occupyed and kept a false measure. And I wyll cause his eares to be nayled to the pyllorye', a woman protested 'god forbydde you shulde so doo, I wolde rather nev[er] selle meale whiles I levyd than I wolde see my neyghbo[u]r so handled'. Similarly the 1572 act against vagrants aroused protest: in 1581 an East Tilbury husbandman was said to have averred that 'ther is no christian prince that hathe suche crewell lawes as to burne men throwe their eares which are nowe used in this Realme'.[51] It is evident from the context that this man was a catholic sympathizer, and religious commitment could certainly give individuals the courage not merely to endure harsh or humiliating penalties but also to deny their justice or defy the authorities. Stow records the case of a woman who, for hooting at the bishop of London in 1566 during the vestiarian controversy, was 'sett uppon two laddars lyke a cuckengstole'. Far from being repentant, she

> satt [there] the space of one owre, greatly rejoysynge in that her lewde behavowr, and that she was punyshyd for the same, and lyke wyse the beholdars of ye same dyd myche rejoyce ther in and anymatyd the lewde woman to rejoyce and prayse the Lorde for that He had made hir worthy to soffer persecution for ryghtwysnes, and for the truths sake (as they said) and for crienge owt a gaynst supersticion as the[y] termed it.[52]

Yet the evidence does not suggest that religious convictions invariably had the power to undermine the impact of such punishments. On the contrary, it is notable that in Edward VI's reign the authorities had no qualms about using variants of these traditional shame sanctions to punish those who broke the laws against selling meat in Lent: for example, in 1552 a man and a woman responsible for bringing into London two pig carcases to sell were ordered to 'be ledde thurroughe all the m[ar]kett plac[es] of this cytie upon horse back[es] either of theym havynge one of the seid pygges hangynge upon their brest[es] & the petytoes of the same pygges sev[er]ally sett in garlond[es] upon their hedd[es] in example, terro[u]r & stey of other lyke offendo[u]rs'. Similar measures were used in Mary's reign, in the wholly different religious context of her attempt to restore catholic beliefs and practices.[53]

Some historians stress the degree to which public punishments, whether capital or lesser penalties, were not fully within the control of the authorities, with the danger that their meaning would be subverted by offenders or the populace at large.[54] While, as has been seen, there is some truth in this proposition, the point should not be exaggerated. Contemporary diarists and chroniclers noticed very few mishaps. Henry Machyn's detailed diary for the period 1550–63 noted one case in which a woman being paraded round the city was taken out of the cart; but the perpetrator was immediately whipped. The scores of other cases that Machyn recorded appear to have proceeded without a hitch.[55] If offenders did depart from the official 'script', the degree of deviance was likely to be minor in the extreme. Wriothesley's chronicle for 1552 recorded the case of a person, described as a 'gentleman', who had his ear nailed to the pillory in Cheapside for obtaining goods by deceit. If the bystanders were awaiting with relish the moment when he would have to tear himself free, they were doomed to disappointment, for 'when he had stand on the pillory till the clocke was past xii. he would not rent his eare'. It availed him little, however, for a resourceful beadle 'slitted yt upwards with a penknife'.[56]

Far from these shame punishments appearing a risky proposition, they seem to have positively recommended themselves to the higher authorities as a means of bidding for popular support by associating crimes against the state with crimes against the commonweal – that is, common nuisances, infringements of the financial and economic interests of the community, and offences against popular morality. From early in its history the Star Chamber used pillory, cucking-stool and other shame penalties, sometimes with ferocious additions or fanciful embellishments, to demonstrate its authority, and other prerogative courts did the like.[57] The populist political intent was sometimes quite patent. Shortly after Elizabeth's accession,

> one of the takers of freshe fishe for the provision of the Queenes house[hold], was set on the Pillorie in Cheape side in the fishe market over agaynst the kings head, having a baudrike of smeltes hanging about his necke with a paper on his foreheade, written 'for buying smelts for .xij. pens the hundred, and solde them againe for tenne pens the quarter'.

He was pilloried for three hours, an ordeal repeated on two further days, and 'on the last day he should have had one of his eares slitte, if by great suyte made to the Counsayle by the Lorde Mayor of London, he hadde not beene pardoned'. As the chronicler explained,

> this penaunce was assigned to him by the Queenes owne appoyntment, when to hir Grace his trespasse was revealed. Whereby she gave a taste to the people of a zealous minde to have iustice duely ministred, and faults accordingly punished, namely of those which under pretence of hir Graces authoritie shoulde goe aboute to wrong and oppresse hir loving subjects.[58]

This was one of a long sequence of punishments by royal authority, in the course of the sixteenth and early seventeenth centuries, of officials guilty of corruption or malfeasance and of speakers of seditious or slanderous words.[59] It was this tradition on which Parliament was to build in 1621 with the impeachment of Edward Floyd, for slandering James I's daughter and her husband, the Elector Palatine and deposed king of Bohemia; and of the notorious monopolists Sir Giles Mompesson and Sir Francis Michell. Amongst other punishments, Floyd was sentenced to ride 'from Westminster then to the Fleete with his face to the horse tayle and the tayle in his hand, with a paper on his forhead'.[60]

V

While shame punishments and their variants continued to be applied in the early seventeenth century, and there is no indication that they were thought to have lost their efficacy, their role was in fact diminishing rather than widening. The pillory was the statutory penalty for certain types of witchcraft, which meant that this punishment was in regular use in areas, notably the county of Essex, where prosecutions for this offence were common. Otherwise, secular shame punishments were particularly associated with certain offences such as perjury and malfeasance in office, that were characteristically tried by the Star Chamber and other prerogative courts, and with sedition and slander. In London and its suburbs, and in the neighbouring city of Westminster, the carting of bawds and notorious sexual offenders (particularly 'common women' or prostitutes) continued to occur, often to the traditional accompaniment of 'basins ringing' or rough music. Similar usages were found in some provincial towns and cities, despite occasional challenges from the royal courts to justify the legal basis for these local customs. But everywhere by the reign of James I these penalties were of subsidiary importance to (and sometimes combined with) a different form of punishment, namely whipping, which had come to play the leading role in the theatre of lesser penalties.

As a punishment, whipping had very deep cultural roots, especially in domestic and pedagogic settings. The Book of Proverbs stated plainly that 'he that spareth his rod hateth his son' and that 'the rod and reproof give wisdom'.[61] As John Brinsley elaborated the point in 1612, 'God hath sanctified the rod and correction, to cure the evils of their [i.e. children's] conditions, to drive out that folly which is bound up in their hearts, [and] to save their soules from hell'. Early in the sixteenth century, Richard Whitford made the point with 'a pretty lesson, whiche I pray you teche your chylder & every chylde that cometh into your company':

Yf I lye, bacbyte or stele,
Yf I curse, scorne, mocke, or swere,
Yf I chyde, fyght, stryve, or threete,
Than am I worthy to be bete,
God mother or maystres myne,
Yf any of these nyne
I trespace to your knowynge,
With a newe rodde and a fyne,

Erly naked before I dyne,
Amende me with a scourgynge.[62]

Corporal punishment was so integral to the school that a birch rod was the stock symbol of a master's authority, and reflections on whipping naturally presented themselves as the subject of grammatical exercises: 'My felow y-bete w[i]t[h] a byrch yerd, y ham to be bete w[i]t[h] a whyppe.'[63] Strikingly, in the sixteenth century the use of corporal punishment was also introduced in the universities.[64] It is true that Tudor educational reformers advocated 'jentlenes better than beating, to bring up a childe rightlie in learninge', and condemned the unthinking and heartless use of the rod; nonetheless they had no hesitation in urging corporal punishment to correct vice. As Ascham put it, 'God forbid, but all evill touches, wantonnes, lyinge, pickinge [theft], slouthe, will, stubburnnesse, and disobedience, shold be with sharpe chastiseme[n]t, daily cut away'.[65] The same principle applied in household and workshop where masters and mistresses exercised authority *in loco parentis* over apprentices and servants. As is evident from cases that came to court, such magisterial discipline could be on occasion be excessive; and it may be that it always had a tendency to degenerate into disorderly violence, either through adults' lack of restraint when punishing youngsters who were not their children or, contrariwise, because older servants or apprentices might well fight back.[66] Both brawling and unbridled physical abuse ran counter to the ideal view of corporal punishment, which stressed that it should be administered with sober moderation and in such a way as to emphasize the authority of the individual dispensing punishment and the submission of the culprit. Thus Brinsley recommended that in correcting

> any stubborne or unbroken boy, you make sure with him to hold him fast; as they are inforced to do, who are to shooe or to tame an unbroken colt. To this end to appoint 3. or 4. of your schollars ... or moe, if need be, to lay hands upon him together, to hold him fast, over some fourme, so that he cannot stir hand nor foot; or else if no other remedy will serve, to hold him to some post (which is farre the safest and free from inconvenience) so as he cannot any way hurt himselfe or others, be he never so peevish. Neither that he can have hope by any devise or turning, or by his apparell, or any other meanes to escape. Nor yet that any one be left in his stubbornness, to go away murmuring, pouting, or blowing and puffing, untill he shew as much submission as any, and that hee will lie still of himselfe without any holding; yet so as ever a wise moderation be kept.

The crucial thing was 'that all their correction be done with authority'.[67]

Judicial whipping (Plate 1.4) was not an innovation, but the London sources indicate that it was resorted to with both increasing frequency and growing enthusiasm as the sixteenth century progressed. The development

Plate 1.4 Judicial whipping

Source: Raphael Holinshed, *The Chronicles of England, Scotlande, and Irelande* (2 vols, 1577), I, 30. Bodleian Library, Douce H, 240. By permission of the Bodleian Library.

was via two main routes. The first was the whipping of vagrants and beggars, as exasperation at a persistent and growing problem led to hardening attitudes and escalating penalties. In 1510 it was ordered that beggars within the city should be set on work cleansing the town ditches; those who evaded this labour should be 'sett in the stokk[es] ij dayes w[i]t[h] brede and water. And the third day to be beten naked w[i]t[h] whippes from Algate to Newgate' before being banished. In 1524 vagabonds were to be searched out and the able-bodied among them whipped at the cart's tail; and 'rownde colers of iron to be made for ev[er]y of theym havyng the armes of this citie uppon theym & the same colers to be putt aboute their nekk[es]'. In 1528, a list of vagrants whipped in the city catalogued 18 men, one boy and two women. Thereafter references to the whipping of vagrants became commonplace.[68] Indeed national legislation, in the form of the act of 1531 'conc[er]nyng punysshement of beggers & vacabund[es]', laid down that unlicensed beggars were to be stripped to the waist and whipped, while able-bodied vagrants were to 'be tyed to the end of a carte naked and be beten wyth whyppes thoroughe oute the same market towne or other place tyll his body be blody'.[69] In London these provisions were supplemented by the foundation of Bridewell Hospital in a former royal palace in 1553: ostensibly a training establishment, it came to function primarily as a penitentiary where vagrants deemed to be idle, men and women judged to be guilty of sexual immorality (especially 'common women' or prostitutes), and other petty offenders were subjected to whipping, temporary confinement and hard labour.[70]

The second route towards the greater use of judicial whipping was as a deliberately exemplary punishment. In London in the middle decades of the sixteenth century, the offenders were often young people or apprentices, in which case the penalty may be seen as a formalized version of household usage; or there was a connection with vagrancy. But this was not invariably so. In 1545 it was

> orderyd & agreyd by the hole court that Hugh Wever ffyssemong[er] for his grett contumacye, very lewde behav[i]o[ur] & stubburn dysobedyence & contempte used & shewyd to my lorde mayers owne p[er]son opynly att the stall of the sayd Hugh in the ffysshem[ar]kett att the stock[es] shall tomorowe tyed naked at a cart[es] taylle be whipped thurrough both the ffysshe stret[es] & all other the m[ar]kett plac[es] of this cytie for the admonyshem[en]t & example of all other to be well ware to comytt eny lyke offence.

Predictably, given that he had publicly affronted the mayor, he was also imprisoned until he showed 'lowly submyssyon & grett repentaunce'.[71] In this and other cases, it is plain that the use of corporal punishment was not merely an unthinking reaction but a considered response, with careful attention to technique and presentation. In May 1553 Agnes Browne, widow, Anne Richardson, and John Lane, waterbearer, 'who coulde not denye ... but that they were idle loyterers, vacabound[es] and com[m]en harlot[es] of their bodies', were sentenced to be whipped about the city at the cart's tail, while it was further ordered that William Foweler, an ironmonger's apprentice,

> who dide playnely confese hym self to have com[m]ytted fornicac[i]on wythe the saide Agnes Browne shall to morowe be whipped nakede at the Ire[n]mongers hall in the p[rese]ns[e] of a good nu[m]ber of thappreyntesies of the same companye to thintente that they admonyshed by his correcc[i]on may the rather eschue the lyke offence.

Similarly, in May 1555 it was ordered that a pewterer's apprentice

> who boldely & develyshelye movyd & attemptid his m[aste]rs wyf to have com[m]ytted adulterye w[i]th hyme shall furthew[i]th be stryppyd nakyd to the gyrdlestede at the utterdoore of this hall and so be lead frome thence to the poste of reformac[i]on in Cheape syde and there be well beaten till his bodye blede and then to be leade frome thence tyed at a cartes tayle owte of Ludgate in to the Olde Baylye and from thence to the barres in Smythefelde adioyninge to Seynte Johnstrete & there to be dysmyssed.

That the whipping post was referred to as 'the post of reformation' is itself suggestive of the aims of civic punishment.[72]

The examples so far discussed will have given some idea of the variants on whipping. It could take place indoors, before a restricted audience; or it might be administered in the street or market, in a blaze of humiliating publicity. Sometimes the punishment was inflicted with 'rods' of birch, applied to the shoulders or (in the case of young people) to the buttocks and lower back (Plate 1.5). More severe was beating with a whip, generally applied to the shoulders (Plate 1.4). Sometimes the culprit was tied to a post for the infliction of the punishment; a refinement was the provision of a long chain that tethered the offender but allowed a certain amount of movement as the whipping proceeded.[73] Alternatively offenders were tied to the 'tail' or end of a cart and whipped as they were trundled about the city. Culprits were generally ordered to be stripped to the waist, or to be punished 'naked'. Probably this phrase did not imply literal nudity – though in one case the offender was ordered specifically 'to be tied naked his p[ri]vie members onelie coverede'[74] – but neither did it indicate merely that the offender should be scourged on the bare skin; in a society in which clothes

Plate 1.5 Beating with rods: Bishop Bonner whips a protestant suspect, 1558

Source: John Foxe, *Actes and Monuments* (3 vols, 1641 edn), III, 880. By permission of Brasenose College.

were so important as a mark of status and identity, being stripped in public was clearly intended to humiliate. During the mayoralty of Richard Dobbs, there were apparently concerns about protecting the modesty of women: in January 1552 eight common harlots were sentenced to be whipped at the cart's tail 'havynge their brest[es] cov[er]yd [but] their bakk[es] streipyd nakyd to the gyrdelstede'. But such niceties were generally ignored.[75]

The severest whippings, as the 1531 and later acts specified for vagrants, proceeded till the culprit's back was bloodied; and this became the norm for judicial floggings imposed for theft and similar offences. In many London cases the outcome in terms of physical damage was left unclear, but the general intent was evident enough; only occasionally was it specified that culprits should receive a certain number of strokes, such as 'a dossyn good lasshes' or 'xij strypes at the leaste'.[76] For offences deemed to be particularly serious or especially despicable, some truly spectacular floggings were organized. In 1559 a man who had beaten his own mother was ordered to be publicly 'whepped nakyd w[i]th rodd[es] thre sev[er]all tymes, a good pawse beinge takyn bytwene ev[er]y of the same tymes'; while in 1563, according to the account of a contemporary chronicler, a man was

> whipt on a sckaffold at ye Stondard in Chepe, his neke, his hands, and fett made faste to a stake above ye sayd skaffold with kolars of iron by ye bedeles of ye begars; some tym one, som tyme ij, some tym iij att once whipte hym, and they strove who mowght whype hym moste extremlye; it was for that he had betyn a boye with a lethar gurdle havynge a buckle of yron, whiche buckle smate in to ye fleshe of ye boye very sore.

The boy was exhibited 'naked by him upon the said pillorye that the people may evidently see & behold the crueltye' of the offender. This provision – which to the modern mind presents itself as further abuse of the child – was a wholly characteristic contemporary touch, designed to drive home the lesson of the occasion.[77]

The examples discussed here relate to what appears to have been a formative period. As time went on, whipping became more and more embedded in judicial practice. In London in the late sixteenth and early seventeenth centuries, thousands of culprits, male and female, received the 'correction of the house' within the walls of Bridewell; numerous others were openly punished in the street or market by constables and by order of the justices. Apart from the exceptional scale of operations in the London Bridewell, it was much the same in the provinces. The development can be clearly seen in the Court of Great Sessions at Chester. In the early part of Elizabeth's reign, the justices commonly punished cases of petty theft with the pillory, with or without the nailing of ears. Whipping was only one among a repertory of possible penalties. By the end of the sixteenth century, however, whipping had become the standard sentence in cases of misdemeanour.[78] In Wiltshire, to take another example, the very full quarter sessions records show that by James I's reign petty thieves were whipped after every court, while A.L. Beier has calculated that between 1603 and 1638 the constables of this county reported punishing 982 vagrants in this manner.[79] The shift is likewise visible in manuals of instruction for justices of the peace. Tudor commentators such as Anthony Fitzherbert and William Lambard emphasized that the punishment of petty theft was a matter for judicial discretion: they made no further specification. Yet Michael Dalton, writing in 1618, stated plainly that for 'Petie Larcenie … the offendor shalbe imprisoned for some certaine time, and after shall be whipped, or otherwise punished by the discretion of the Justices'.[80]

As Paul Griffiths demonstrates in this volume, the history of whipping in the seventeenth century is an intricate subject that requires full investigation. Yet its prevalence around 1600 is undoubted. This was, as Lawrence Stone averred, 'the great flogging age'.[81] That the penalty, once established, was so widely employed is hardly surprising. It added pain to shame in a way that was predictable and even measurable; it was a persuasive demonstration of authority that nonetheless stopped short of maiming, far less killing the culprit, and at least gestured towards the hope of reform. Certainly the execution of the penalty was in a sense indecorous, and it could be described as 'uncivil' or 'shamefull' if not carried out by rightful authority: thus Bishop Bonner was criticized by Foxe for allegedly scourging protestant suspects in the garden of his palace of Fulham.[82] But as a punishment it was evidently much feared: an Exeter man, threatened with the prospect of being whipped for a second time, averred in 1627 that 'I will goe hange my selfe rather then I will come into their hand[es] againe'.[83] Yet, as always, it is well to be cautious in assessing the efficacy of punishment. It is perhaps fitting to end with a case in which whipping was combined with another of the other penalties discussed in this chapter. Despite the ferocity of what was done to them, the victims were unbowed – sustained by what appears to have been a wholly disinterested loyalty to Catherine of Aragon. In the words of a contemporary London chronicler:

> The xxiij. day of August [1533] wear ij. women betton abowght the Chepe nakyd from ye waste upwarde, w[i]t[h] roddes, & theyr eris naylyd to ye Standard for bycause they sayd quene Katheryn was ye treu quen of England, & not quene Ane: and one of ye wemen was byge w[i]t[h] childe: & whan thes ij. wemen had thus bene punyshed, they forteffyed theyr sayenge styll, to dy in ye quarell for quene Katheryns sake.[84]

Or, as a comment on many less principled recipients of shame and pain punishments in this period, and a counterpoint to Harington's epigram at the head of the chapter, let Robert Burton have the final word. While stressing that 'shame and disgrace cause most violent passions, and bitter pangs', he nonetheless reflected that:

> I know there be many base, impudent, brazen-faced rogues, that will ... be moved with nothing, take no infamy or disgrace to heart, laugh at all; let them be proved perjured, stigmatized, convict rogues, thieves, traitours, lose their ears, be whipped, branded, carted, pointed at, hissed, reviled and derided ... they rejoyce at it; ... what care they?[85]

Notes

1 Sir John Harington, *Epigrams Both Pleasant and Serious* (London, 1615), sigs C3v–4r.

2 George Roberts, *The Social History of the People of the Southern Counties of England in Past Centuries* (1856), 150–70; William Andrews, *Old-Time Punishments* (Hull, 1890); *idem, Bygone Punishments* (1899).

3 J.A. Sharpe, *Judicial Punishment in England* (1990), 18–27.

4 Martin Ingram, 'Regulating Sex in Pre-Reformation London', in G.W. Bernard and S.J. Gunn eds, *Authority and Consent in Tudor England* (Aldershot, 2002), 81–3.

5 Brian L. Woodcock, *Medieval Ecclesiastical Courts in the Diocese of Canterbury* (1952), 97–9; Ralph Houlbrooke, *Church Courts and the People during the English Reformation, 1520–1570* (Oxford, 1979), 46–7; Richard M. Wunderli, *London Church Courts and Society on the Eve of the Reformation* (Cambridge, MA, 1981), 49–53. On the general background, see Thomas N. Tentler, *Sin and Confession on the Eve of the Reformation* (Princeton, NJ, 1977).

6 Martin Ingram, *Church Courts, Sex and Marriage in England, 1570–1640* (Cambridge, 1987), 3, 53–4, 334–6. See also Hubert Hall, 'Some Elizabethan penances in the Diocese of Ely', *Transactions of the Royal Historical Society*, third series, 1 (1907), 263–77; F.G. Emmison, *Elizabethan Life: Morals and the Church Courts* (Chelmsford, 1973), 281–91.

7 Keith Thomas, *Religion and the Decline of Magic: Studies in Popular Beliefs in Sixteenth and Seventeenth Century England* (1971), 171.

8 [James Morice], *A Briefe Treatise of Oathes Exacted by Ordinaries and Ecclesiasticall Judges* (Middleburg, ?1590), 23.

9 Houlbrooke, *Church Courts and the People*, 46; Ingram, *Church Courts, Sex and Marriage*, 52.

10 Ingram, *Church Courts, Sex and Marriage*, 337–8; Hall, 'Some Elizabethan penances', 274–5; Emmison, *Elizabethan Life: Morals and the Church Courts*, 285–7.

11 Thomas Walsingham, *Historia Anglicana*, ed. Henry Thomas Riley (2 vols; Rolls Series, 1863–64), ii. 65.

12 C[orporation of] L[ondon] R[ecord] O[ffice] Journal 7, fos 129v–30. Cf. Journal 9, fo. 226v; Journal 15, fo. 30(31)r–v (dual foliation); Journal 17, fo. 321v.

13 CLRO Journal 13, fo. 153.

14 John Stow, *A Survey of London*, ed. Charles Lethbridge Kingsford (2 vols; Oxford, 1908), i. 64, 188–91, 225, 296, ii. 53, 59, 176, 179. For various references to stocks and cages, see CLRO Repertory 2, fo. 201; Repertory 3, fo. 168; Repertory 11, fo. 41v.

15 A.L. Beier, *Masterless Men: the Vagrancy Problem in England, 1560–1640* (1985), 164–9.

16 For example CLRO Repertory 9, fo. 147.

17 For example CLRO Repertory 10, fo. 323; Repertory 7, fo. 260(278)v (dual foliation).

18 For example CLRO Repertory 3, fos 161v–2r. See Ruth Mellinkoff, 'Riding backwards: theme of humiliation and symbol of Evil', *Viator*, 4 (1973), 153–76;

Klaus Schreiner, 'Gregor VIII, nackt auf einem Esel. Entehrende Entblößung und schandbares Reiten im Spiegel einer Miniatur der "Sächsischen Weltchronik"', in Dieter Berg and Hans-Werner Goetz eds, *Ecclesia et Regnum. Beiträge zur Geschichte von Kirche, Recht und Staat im Mittelalter. Festschrift für Franz-Josef Schmale* (Bochum, 1989), 155–202; Martin Ingram, 'Juridical folklore in England illustrated by rough music', in Christopher W. Brooks and Michael Lobban eds, *Communities and Courts in Britain, 1150–1900* (London and Rio Grande, 1997), 61–82.

19 CLRO Journal 8, fo. 185; Repertory 10, fo. 335. For a provincial example, see PRO STAC 5/C70/2, m. 2.

20 CLRO Journal 17, fo. 148v. For examples of such placards, surviving among the borough archives of Colchester, see Essex RO (Colchester), D/B5 Sr 5, nos 1–4, 8, 46, 48, 55.

21 CLRO, Repertory 12, fo. 55r–v.

22 Henry Thomas Riley ed., *Munimenta Gildhallæ Londoniensis* (3 vols in 4.; Rolls Series, 1859–62), i. 457–60, iii. 179–82 (translation).

23 CLRO Repertory 9, fo. 241.

24 CLRO Journal 8, fo. 185.

25 CLRO Repertory 3, fo. 133v; Repertory 14, fo. 184v; Repertory 13, fo. 18v.

26 CLRO Repertory 12, fo. 302v; Repertory 9, fo. 95v.

27 CLRO Journal 11, fos 264v–5, cf. fo. 327; Journal 12, fo. 10.

28 CLRO Repertory 15, fo. 224v.

29 CLRO Letter Book T, fos 14, 22.

30 CLRO Repertory 8, fo. 43(44)v (dual foliation); Repertory 9, fo. 104; cf. Repertory 9, fos 178, 256v; Repertory 11, fos 305v, 364v–5; Frederick J. Furnivall ed., *Harrison's Description of England in Shakspere's Youth* (New Shakspere Society, sixth series, 1, 5, 8, 1877–81), i, 225, 228; Martin Ingram, '"Scolding women cucked or washed": a crisis in gender relations in early modern England?', in Jenny Kermode and Garthine Walker eds, *Women, Crime and the Courts in Early Modern England* (Manchester, 1994), 58–9; Marjorie Keniston McIntosh, *Controlling Misbehavior in England, 1370–1600* (Cambridge, 1998), 63–4.

31 Furnivall, *Harrison's Description of England*, i, 226; W.H. Manchée, *The Westminster City Fathers (The Burgess Court of Westminster), 1585–1901* (1924), 118–19; Devon RO, Chamber Act Book 4, fo. 94v, cf. fo. 96v.

32 Riley ed., *Munimenta Gildhallæ Londoniensis*, i. 458–90 (French), iii. 180–1 (English).

33 CLRO Journal 11, fo. 112; cf. fo. 114v; Journal 12, fo. 169; Repertory 12, fos 128v–9, 359v; Charles Wriothesley, *A Chronicle of England during the Reigns of the Tudors, from A.D. 1485 to 1559*, ed. William Douglas Hamilton (2 vols; Camden Society, 11, 20, 1875, 1877), ii. 51. Cf. the orders of Bury St Edmunds in 1579: British Library, Lansdowne MS 27/70, fo. 155.

34 Laura Gowing, *Domestic Dangers: Women, Words, and Sex in Early Modern London* (Oxford, 1996), 103–4; Elizabeth Foyster, *Manhood in Early Modern England: Honour, Sex and Marriage* (London and New York, 1999), 78, 182–3. Cf. Valentin Groebner, 'Losing face, saving face: noses, honour and spite in the late medieval town', *History Workshop Journal*, 40 (1995), 1–15.

35 5 Eliz. c. 14. Cf. John Hawarde, *Les Reportes del Cases in Camera Stellata, 1593–1609*, ed. William Paley Baildon (London, 1894), 19, 321.

36 John Stow, *The Annales of England* (1601 edn), 1063. Cf. *ibid.*, 991 and Wriothesley, *Chronicle*, i. 149–51 (in the latter case the culprits suffered not only branding but also loss of ears).

37 *Statutes of the Realm* (11 vols; 1810–24), iv. 5 (1 Edw. VI c. 3), 591 (14 Elizabeth c. 5); J.S. Cockburn ed., *Calendar of Assize Records: Essex Indictments: Elizabeth I* (London, 1978), 200; J.S. Cockburn ed., *Calendar of Assize Records: Surrey Indictments: Elizabeth I* (1980), 136, 164.

38 CLRO Repertory 12, fo. 555. Cf. Wriothesley, *Chronicle*, ed. Hamilton, ii. 100; CLRO Repertory 4, fo. 76v.

39 CLRO Journal 13, fos 190v–1. For a provincial example, see Cameron Louis ed., *Records of Early English Drama: Sussex* (Toronto, 2000), 106.

40 CLRO Journal 10, fo. 250(253)r–v (dual foliation). Cf. Wriothesley, *Chronicle*, i. 149–51.

41 Ingram, 'Regulating sex in pre-Reformation London', 79–95; Frank Rexroth, *Das Milieu der Nacht: Obrigkeit und Randgruppen im Spätmittelalterlichen London* (Göttingen, 1999).

42 CLRO Repertory 13, fo. 321(322)v (dual foliation); Repertory 12, fo. 128v. Cf. fo. 435; Repertory 13, fo. 179. See also Wriothesley, *Chronicle*, ii. 55.

43 CLRO Repertory 12, fos 517v–18 (521v–2) (dual foliation); Repertory 11, fo. 80; for another example, see Repertory 11, fo. 173.

44 CLRO Journal 13, fo. 143v; Journal 13, fo. 153; Journal 9, fo. 226v.

45 CLRO Journal 9, fo. 226v; Journal 17, fo. 321v; Journal 12, fo. 168.

46 Werner L. Gundersheimer, 'Renaissance concepts of shame and Pocaterra's *Dialoghi Della Vergogna*', *Renaissance Quarterly*, 47 (1994), 34–56; see also Ewan Fernie, *Shame in Shakespeare* (London and New York, 2002).

47 John Gough Nichols ed., *Chronicle of the Grey Friars of London* (Camden Society, 53, 1852), 70. Cf. A.H. Thomas and I.D. Thornley ed., *The Great Chronicle of London* (1938), 222.

48 CLRO Journal 11, fos 75r–v; 'A Chronicle, 1413–1536', in R. Dyboski ed., *Songs, Carols, and Other Miscellaneous Poems, from ... Richard Hill's Commonplace-Book* (Early English Text Soc., extra series, 101, 1907), 155; cf. Nichols, *Chronicle of the Grey Friars*, 34; Stow, *Annales*, 758; John Gough Nichols ed., *The Diary of Henry Machyn, Citizen and Merchant-Taylor of London, from A.D. 1550 to A.D. 1563* (Camden Society, 42, 1848), 277.

49 CLRO Journal 11, fos 387v–8; Stow, *Survey of London*, ed. Kingsford, i. 191.

50 B. Howard Cunnington ed., *Some Annals of the Borough of Devizes, Being a Series of Extracts from the Corporation Records, 1555 to 1791*, 2 parts (Devizes, 1925), i. 34. Cf. C.J. Sisson, *Lost Plays of Shakespeare's Age* (Cambridge, 1936), 48.

51 CLRO Journal 15, fo. 160; Cockburn, *Calendar of Assize Records: Essex Indictments: Elizabeth I*, 213. But cf. Steve Hindle, *The State and Social Change in Early Modern England, c. 1550–1640* (Basingstoke, 2000), 92.

52 J. Gairdner ed., *Three Fifteenth-Century Chronicles, with Historical Memoranda by John Stowe* (Camden Society, new series, 28, 1880), 140.

53 CLRO Repertory 12, fo. 460. Cf. *ibid.*, fo. 458; Repertory 13, fo. 126v; Repertory 14, fo. 12v.

54 Thomas W. Laqueur, 'Crowds, carnival and the state in English executions, 1604–1868', in A.L. Beier, David Cannadine and James M. Rosenheim eds, *The First Modern Society: Essays in English History in Honour of Lawrence Stone* (Cambridge, 1989), 305–55.

55 Nichols ed., *Diary of Henry Machyn*, 123 and *passim*.

56 Wriothesley, *Chronicle*, ed. Hamilton, ii. 79–80.

57 John Guy, *The Court of Star Chamber and its Records to the Reign of Elizabeth I* (PRO Handbooks, 21, 1985), 46.

58 Raphael Holinshed, *The Chronicles of England, Scotlande, and Irelande* (2 vols; 1577), ii. 1778 [recte 1798].
59 For example Hawarde, *Reportes del Cases in Camera Stellata*, 177, 248; Norman Egbert McClure ed., *The Letters of John Chamberlain* (2 vols; The American Philosophical Society, Memoirs, 12, Philadelphia, 1939), i. 98, 211.
60 Wallace Notestein, Frances Helen Relf and Hartley Simpson eds., *Commons Debates, 1621* (7 vols; New Haven, CT, 1935), iii. 122–8 (quotation at 128), v. 196–7, 386, vi. 13. Cf. McClure, *Letters of John Chamberlain*, ii, 377. It was perhaps only with the proceedings against Burton, Bastwick and Prynne in 1637 that this policy went seriously awry: on this incident, see Kevin Sharpe, *The Personal Rule of Charles I* (New Haven, CT and London, 1992), 758–65.
61 Proverbs 13.24; Proverbs 29.15.
62 John Brinsley, *Ludus literarius: or, the Grammar Schoole* (1612), 290; Richard Whitford, *A Werke for Housholders* (Southwark, ?1531 edn), sig. D2r.
63 Nicholas Orme, *Education and Society in Medieval and Renaissance England* (London and Ronceverte, 1989), 102, cf. 72 (illustration), 96, 104.
64 Lawrence Stone, *The Family, Sex and Marriage in England, 1500–1800* (1977), 165.
65 Roger Ascham, *The Scholemaster* (1570), fos 4, 12. Cf. Sir Thomas Elyot, *The Book Named The Governor*, ed. S.E. Lehmberg (1962 edn), 27; Richard Mulcaster, *Positions ... Necessarie for the Training Up of Children* (1581), 282–3.
66 For examples, see F.G. Emmison, *Elizabethan Life: Disorder* (Chelmsford, 1970), 155–6; Paul Griffiths, *Youth and Authority: Formative Experiences in England, 1560–1640* (Oxford, 1996), 313–24, 339–41.
67 Brinsley, *Ludus literarius*, 288–9, 290.
68 CLRO Journal 11, fo. 104v; Repertory 4, fo. 215; Journal 13, fo. 43.
69 *Statutes of the Realm*, iii. 329 (22 Henry VIII c. 12).
70 Beier, *Masterless Men*, 164–9; Ian W. Archer, *The Pursuit of Stability: Social Relations in Elizabethan London* (Cambridge, 1991), chap. 6, *passim*.
71 CLRO Repertory 11, fo. 153v.
72 CLRO Repertory 13 fos 52v–3, 292v–3. Cf. Repertory 13, fo. 401(402) (dual foliation); Repertory 14, fo. 472v; Nichols ed., *Diary of Henry Machyn*, 86.
73 CLRO Repertory 13, fo. 61v. Cf. Nichols ed., *Chronicle of the Grey Friars of London*, 78.
74 CLRO Repertory 13, fo. 61v.
75 CLRO Repertory 12, fo. 43; cf. fo. 418v.
76 CLRO Repertory 15, fos 278v, 498.
77 CLRO, Repertory 14, fos 169v; cf. fos 370v, 524v; Gairdner ed., *Three Fifteenth-Century Chronicles*, 125; CLRO Repertory 15, fo. 276. Cf. Nichols ed., *Diary of Henry Machyn*, 311.
78 Based on study of PRO CHES 21/1.
79 Beier, *Masterless Men*, 160.
80 Sir Anthony Fitzherbert, *The Newe Boke of Justices of the Peas ... Lately Translated* (1530), fo. 20; William Lambard, *Eirenarcha: or of the Office of the Justices of Peace* (1581), 222; Michael Dalton, *The Country Justice* (1618), 229.
81 Stone, *Family, Sex and Marriage*, 171.
82 John Foxe, *The Ecclesiasticall History Contaynyng the Actes and Monuments* (3 vols; 1570) iii. 2242, 2243. Cf. PRO STAC 8/107/1, m. 2.
83 Devon RO, Exeter City Quarter Sessions Minute Book, 1621–30, fo. 316, quoted in Mark Stoyle, *From Deliverance to Destruction: Rebellion and Civil War in an English City* (Exeter, 1996), 16.
84 C.L. Kingsford ed., 'Two London Chronicles, from the Collections of John Stow', in Camden Miscellany, Vol. XII (Camden Society, third series, 18, 1910), 8.
85 Robert Burton, *The Anatomy of Melancholy* (London, 1836 edn), 173, 174–5.

2
Dead Men Talking: Truth, Texts and the Scaffold in Early Modern England

Katherine Royer

In John Foxe's *Actes and Monuments* Martin Bucer's execution begins with a fire; burning in the middle of the marketplace, embers filling the air, smoke billowing up into the sky, the heat reflecting off the faces of the assembled crowd as the smell of burning flesh filled their nostrils. In many ways it was a typical Marian martyrdom: Bucer was tried and convicted of heresy, degraded by the bishops and turned over to the secular authorities, who paraded him through the marketplace, chained him to the stake, lit the faggots, and then threw his books into the fire as the flames reduced his body to ashes. What is intriguing about this execution was that when Martin Bucer was burned at the stake that day at Cambridge in 1557 he had been dead for six years.[1]

Why dig up a dead man and burn his decomposing body? Foxe writes that the Bishop of Chester, who presided over the exhumed Bucer's trial and condemnation, believed that the performance of this ritual was a divinely demanded necessity. The Bishop claimed that although God may be slow to wrath and vengeance, if the community permitted such 'execrable crimes' to escape unpunished, they 'should not lyue in quiete one houer'.[2] However, Foxe writes that this act struck many in the crowd as strange. Rather than being awed by the power made manifest in the public spectacle of Bucer's burning, the crowd was both repulsed and amused: 'Thus, every body that stoode by found faulte with the cruelnesse of the deed, either sharply or els lightly, as eury man's mynde gaue hym.'[3] Some wondered at the folly of men needing weapons to guard a corpse, others remarked that it hardly seemed necessary to tie the body to a stake, as if the authorities were afraid Bucer would run away. Of course, Foxe chose to tell the story of Bucer's posthumous execution for a particular purpose: to undermine the power of the Catholic state by illustrating that this execution was an exercise in futility and the object of popular derision. Foxe contrasts the sophisticated reading of this ritual by the 'countryefolke' with the superstition of the educated

Catholic clergy.[4] According to Foxe the burning of this exhumed body was necessary only to the Bishop of Chester, who believed that since Bucer had been buried with great pomp, he should be exhumed and executed with the same.[5] Bucer's was not the only body exhumed by papists in *Actes and Monuments*. James Treuisan was summoned from the grave in 1555 to appear before the Ordinary at St Pauls, and John Tooley, who was executed for robbery, was exhumed and burned for the heretical statements he made from the scaffold.[6] Foxe presents these posthumous executions as papist barbarism, while acknowledging that they were considered a sacred obligation by the Catholic clergy. Thus, in his text Foxe sets up a dichotomy between Catholic and Protestant readings of these rituals and in doing so he places the bodies of recently and long-deceased men at the centre of their struggle. However, Foxe is creating a false dichotomy. What he reveals is not so much a divide between Catholic and Protestant attitudes towards the body, but rather a shift in the role played by that body in the discourse of the scaffold. There is a subjectivity that emerges in Foxe's execution narratives and other sixteenth-century texts that renders the body of the dead less able to serve as the text of the execution. Thus, the real message of the narrative of Bucer's execution was that the time for his body to speak had long past.

Although Foxe attempts to frame the controversy surrounding these bodies as a matter of religious conflict, exhuming bodies in order to punish them was not an exclusively papist practice. Suicides, as well as Oliver Cromwell, were punished posthumously by good Protestants.[7] Since concern regarding the community's responsibility to see that no crime remain unpunished crossed the confessional divide, the Reformation had not altered the expectation that sometimes the arm of justice would need to reach into the grave. It was also not the Bishop of Chester's respect for the power of divine retribution that Foxe seeks to discredit in his narrative of Bucer's burning. As Alexandra Walsham comments, such providentialism was part of mainstream thought in early modern England: 'the ideological spectacles' through which individuals of all social levels and confessional positions viewed the universe.[8] Like other Protestant authors, Foxe employed divine retribution as a rhetorical strategy and devoted an entire chapter to 'God's punishment upon the persecutors and contemners of the Gospell'.[9] Despite his efforts to use Bucer's body to make a distinction between his Protestant world and the papist past, the body had long served as a sacred signifier and would continue to do so for Foxe and other Protestant authors. Like their Catholic counterparts, Protestants held a powerful belief that God's anger would be written in corporeal form. Judgment books, like those written by Thomas Beard and John Reynolds, illustrate that the body continued to serve as a text of sacred truth in Protestant England.[10] The hand of God frequently marked the bodies of murder victims in order to expose their wicked perpetrators.[11] In *Sundry strange and inhumaine murthers* the corpse of the murdered children bled afresh when their killer was nearby.[12]

Thus, the body served as a sacred symbol for Protestants, as well as Catholics. Foxe's Protestants even retrieved relics from the ashes of their freshly martyred saints. He writes that the people at John Hullier's execution sifted through the ashes for his bones and heart.[13] Using the body to commemorate the crime was also not an exclusively Catholic rhetorical strategy. Just as the Bishop of Chester burned Bucer's books along with his body to commemorate his heresy, Foxe describes how Bishop Cranmer thrust his 'unworthy right hand' into the flames because it was the hand he had used to recant.[14]

Despite the fact that Foxe relies on many of the rhetorical strategies of Catholic hagiographers, Bucer's story brings to light a critical distinction between Foxe and the papists. In *Actes and Monuments* only the bodies of the living serve as texts of truth. Unlike the Catholic hagiographers who point to the sweet-smelling bodies of dead saints as evidence of their salvation, Foxe reports that the unburied body of the good Protestant William Gouer smelled so foul that no man could stand to touch it.[15] This story stands in contrast to the thirteenth-century text *The Golden Legend* that describes how in death the body of St Elizabeth 'gave out a fragrant aroma' that was a sign of her cleanness and chastity.[16] Although Foxe does tell one story about a Christian Jew martyred by the Turks in Constantinople in 1528, whose body remained in the streets for nine days without evidence of decay, he refrains from using this rhetorical device when writing about Protestant saints.[17] Not a word is said in *Actes and Monuments* about the condition of Bucer's exhumed body, for in this text the word of God is written only upon the living.

The role of the body in Foxe's pages reflects both the medieval inheritance of this work and the sixteenth-century culture that gave it birth. It is also the product of the unique role that his text plays in English history. More than just a martyrology, it is also a political narrative that charts a history of English executions, and in doing so provides an opportunity to examine the discourse of the scaffold from late medieval to sixteenth-century England. Foxe's text is filled with narratives of executions from early Church history, the victims of the political conflicts of the medieval and early modern English state, and Protestant martyrs. Cast in the *longue durée* and reflecting the variety of sources that inform it, *Actes and Monuments* presents an opportunity to explore the ways in which the somatic discourse of the scaffold changed over time. Foxe's text reveals a transition from the late medieval execution narratives that were primarily catalogues of the dismemberment and disposition of body parts, to sixteenth-century accounts that focused attention on the behaviour of the condemned. What separates one from the other was the introduction of subjectivity into the discourse of the scaffold.

It is not my intention to argue that Foxe created a template which shaped the sixteenth-century scaffold discourses. In terms of its impact on early modern execution narratives, a genre that includes martyrologies, chronicles, pamphlets, and some private accounts, *Actes and Monuments* does not so much plow new ground, as follow a path that was being travelled simultaneously by other authors. Although John Knott argues that Foxe created a trope of heroic resistance to hostile authority through the determination to witness the truth regardless of the consequences, he admits that Foxe borrowed significantly from Eusebius and John Bale.[18] Knott claims that Foxe shaped an ideal of Protestant heroism that involved both confrontation and submission. However, such a combination was not a unique rhetorical strategy. The discourse of the scaffold which dominates in the second volume of *Actes and Monuments* was evident in other sixteenth-century texts, such as the *Chronicle of Queen Jane* and *The Chronicle of England during the reigns of the Tudors from AD 1485 to 1559*, both of which were written before the 1563 publication of the English version of Foxe's text.[19] According to these narratives, many of the men and women who fell afoul of Henry VIII practiced a subtle form of subversion on the scaffold that undermined the submissive tone of their last dying speeches. Neither terrorized by the sight of the axe nor threatened by the executioner, they undermined the coercive authority of the state by staking claim to their free will. According to the *Chronicle of Queen Jane*, although Thomas Palmer gave a speech submitting to the authority of the law, he declared that 'neither the sprinkling of the bludd, or the shedding thereof, not the bludy axe itself' would make him afraid.[20] Palmer even held the executioner at bay, telling him 'strike me not yet', until he was ready.

Any analysis of Foxe's contribution to sixteenth-century discourse must also keep in mind that he borrowed heavily from other authors. As Thomas Freeman has pointed out, Foxe lifted his account of the death of Leonard Keyser from Jean Crespin's *Actiones et Monumenta Martyrum*, and his description of Hugh Latimer's martyrdom closely resembled Augustine Bernher's dedicatory epistle to a collection of Latimer's sermons.[21] Thus, Foxe's narrative often reflected other influences, and like all historians, he was often the prisoner of his sources. This is reflected in Foxe's execution narratives and his descriptions of events on the scaffold ranged from brief to detailed. His account of the 1322 execution of Thomas of Lancaster, like the brief description in the *Vita Edwardi Secundi* from which it was drawn, mentions only that Lancaster was beheaded but not quartered because of the nobility of his blood.[22] In contrast, citing a much longer account from Eusebius as his source, Foxe's narrative of Polycarp's death is greater in both length and description.[23] The increased attention given by Foxe to certain figures may have been in part the product of his sources, which expanded to include first person accounts in the sixteenth century, but it also reflects the choices he made to advance his narrative. Thus, John Hus' execution was described in great detail, whereas the less notable Lollard Richard Hoveden rated only a single line.[24] As expected, Foxe concentrated his narrative focus on religious martyrs; yet, on occasion he would devote as much or more attention to the death of sixteenth-century political figures, such as Thomas Cromwell or the Duke of Somerset.[25] Thus, the attention paid in his text to any single execution was both a reflection of his narrative strategy in the name of English Protestantism, as well as the quality or quantity of his sources.

However, the execution narratives in the second volume of *Actes and Monuments* are much richer in detail than the accounts of the early Church martyrs and medieval political figures found in the first book. These narratives reflect another force at work in the sixteenth-century discourse of the scaffold that is manifest in the dynamic descriptions of Marian martyrs. These men and women were not the passive figures found in medieval martyrologies. There is a subjectivity that begins to surface in the second volume of *Actes and Monuments* that contrasts with earlier works. In the thirteenth-century text *The Golden Legend,* St Euphemia survived imprisonment, the wheel, starvation, pressing and beheading through divine intervention that paralyzed the headsmen, reduced the millstones to fine powder, and sent an angel to feed her.[26] Throughout this ordeal, this saint did nothing. Although she actively sought martyrdom by publicly announcing her faith, St Euphemia is described as being silent and passive as she faced these torments. According to *The Golden Legend,* when St Peter Martyr was attacked by his murderer, he 'does not turn away from his assailant but presents himself as a willing sacrifice, patiently submitting to the attacker's blows'.[27] This same passivity is also found in the martyrologies of *The Early English Legendary Lives of Saints*.[28] In contrast to these medieval martyrs, who let the will of God sweep over them as they patiently endure their fate, Foxe's sixteenth-century Marian martyrs actively participate in their executions. Bishop Latimer asked for a bag of gunpowder to help speed his burning; John Hullier grabbed one of the books thrown into the fire with him and read aloud as he burned; while Bishop Hooper helped adjust the chain about his waist.[29] According to Foxe, it was Bishop Cranmer, not the executioner, who placed his sinful hand in the fire.[30] Many a Marian martyr not only faced the fire with calm self-control, but kissed the stake. They used their bodies to do more than just endure their death, they embraced it. They helped wrap the chains about their waist, threw faggots on the fire, and embraced the stake as they shaped a somatic discourse that cast their fate as a matter of personal choice.[31]

Foxe's Protestant saints also actively employed their bodies as symbols of defiance. Thus, when George Marsh was denied the right to speak at his execution in 1555, as the fire consumed his body and many thought him already dead, he spread his arms like Christ on the cross and prayed as a signal to the crowd.[32] Like George Marsh, Foxe's other Marian martyrs did more than calmly submit to their persecutors; their's was a more dynamic form of martyrdom. William Coberley beat his breast with his blackened right hand as he was being burned at Salisbury in 1556, and Rawlins White found the will to stand 'bolt upright' in the face of death, although he was reportedly much stooped before.[33] Martin Bucer was one of the few saints in *Actes and Monuments* who was silent and still. Most of them, like

Christopher Wade, spoke, embraced the stake, and raised their hands to heaven.[34]

Such dynamism was more the product of the sixteenth century than it was a phenomenon exclusive to Foxe's Protestant martyrologies. This subjectivity was found in other sixteenth-century texts, such as the *Chronicle of Queen Jane* which describes a very busy Duke of Somerset, who gives a final speech on the scaffold, undresses himself, ties a kerchief over his eyes, and lays his head upon the block.[35] This dynamism is not so much the product of a particular genre, as it is part of the subjectivity that seeps into sixteenth-century discourse. That is why a text like *Actes and Monuments,* which relies on sources that range from early Church history to the sixteenth century, brings this change into focus. The dynamic nature of the deaths of the Marian martyrs and political figures stand in contrast, not just to the saints of *The Golden Legend,* but to the early Church martyrs and the victims of the political persecutions described in the first volume of Foxe's text, who face death with a passive resignation. According to Foxe, the early Church martyr Felicitas and her children 'sustayned also the cruelty' of whipping, scourging, pressing to death with weights, having their heads hammered, and their necks broken, all with passive resignation.[36] Although some of Foxe's pre-Reformation martyrs, such as Polycarp and John Hus, appear less passive in his text, it was primarily the men and women condemned to die in the sixteenth century who embraced the stake, helped their executioners wrap the chains around their waists, and raised their hands to heaven.[37] In contrast, when Foxe recounts the deaths on the scaffold of medieval political figures, the kind of passivity found in the execution narratives of *The Golden Legend* colours his descriptions. Thus, the execution of William Wallace is described in a single sentence, and Foxe succinctly states that Roger Mortimer 'as in cases of high treason suffered death accordingly in London'.[38] He says nothing about how either man behaved on the scaffold.[39] Drawn from medieval sources, the executions described in this first volume reflect the nature of the medieval execution narratives that inform his text. When Foxe writes that in 1322 Thomas, the Earl of Lancaster, 'for the nobility of his blood was beheaded', his description sounds very similar to Henry Knighton's fourteenth-century account of the execution of John Ball:[40]

> Sir John Ball, indeed, was taken at Coventry and brought to St. Albans, and there upon the king's orders he was drawn and hanged, and cut into four pieces, which were sent to different places to be displayed.[41]

Like other medieval authors, Knighton's narrative focused on the body of John Ball, while there was a silence about the rebel's behaviour on the scaffold. The condemned in most late medieval chronicles were passive: they neither act nor react. Medieval narrators like Knighton seem not so much concerned with the behaviour of the man beheaded by the axe, but why.

Thus, they focus their attention on the crime and not the criminal. *The Chronicle of Lanercost* reports that David of Wales was hanged as a thief, beheaded alive, his entrails burnt as an incendiary and homicide, his limbs severed as befitting a traitor, and his head mounted on a spear for the mockery of London.[42] In these texts each cut had a purpose, as the punishment commemorated the crime. Thus, according to Froissart, every mutilation of Hugh Despenser carried a specific meaning:

> First his private parts were cut off, because he was deemed a heretic and guilty of unnatural practices, even with the king, whose affections he had alienated from the queen by his wicked suggestions. His private parts were then cast into a large fire kindled close to him; afterwards his heart was thrown into the same fire because it had been false and traitorous.[43]

In the late medieval narratives, the body of criminals like Despenser served as a map of their crimes. Even after death these bodies continued to speak – the limbs from the gates of the city, the head from London bridge. Often described in the medieval texts as a document or banner, the severed body parts were a lasting reminder of the events on the scaffold, and were thus posted as the execution text.[44]

As the terrible nature of the crime was commemorated on the body of the criminal, the man said nothing in the medieval narratives. Although there were scattered reports of speeches by the condemned around 1350, most execution narratives written before 1500, and some after, make no mention of a last dying speech. Although these speeches have often been considered a Tudor innovation, there is evidence that this practice predated Henry VII.[45] *The Chronicle of Lanercost* from the fourteenth century does report a confession by John of Powderham on the gallows,[46] but this account stands out as exceptional as most of the executions described in this chronicle make no mention of such a speech. According to this text, William Wallace, David of Wales, Rismaraduc of Wales, Simon Fraser, the Earl of Athol, Thomas Bruce and Sir Henry Tynes all died in silence.[47] Occasionally descriptions of contrition and confessions are found in other late medieval chronicles. John Blake and Thomas Usk both spoke on the scaffold according to the *Westminster Chronicle*.[48] However, in the majority of the descriptions of executions in the chronicles of Henry Knighton, John Froissart and John Hardyng, the condemned do not speak from the scaffold. This is not necessarily to say that they did not give a confessional speech, only that the medieval narrators rarely reported one.[49] If men like Robert Tresilian, Hugh Despenser, Empson and Dudley spoke, these authors chose not to say so.[50] Foxe's martyrs, queens and politicians have plenty to say in the sixteenth century, but his descriptions of the deaths of earlier political figures such as Thomas, the Earl of Lancaster, William Wallace and Roger Mortimer make no mention of any words spoken from the scaffold.[51] Although the written record of the last dying speech certainly increased after 1500, even as late as the mid-century there were some authors such as Henry Machyn who make no mention of one. In his diary, Machyn describes the execution of the Duke of Somerset, but omits Somerset's frequently reported scaffold speech.[52] Thus, unlike Thomas Cromwell, who was reported to have spoken at length from the scaffold in *Actes and Monuments*, the condemned in the late-medieval narratives rarely spoke, confessed, suffered or complained.[53] Most of them, like Sir Hugh Despenser, were simply described as having been 'drawn at Bristol in his coat of arms and afterwards hanged and then beheaded'.[54]

Before 1500, there was little in execution narratives to imply that the condemned were offered any spiritual comfort on the scaffold or had any hope of salvation. They mostly faced their final moment without benefit of clergy until the fourteenth century when Pope Clement V moved to end the practice of denying confession to prisoners.[55] Despite the pope's efforts on behalf of the condemned, as late as 1549 Bishop Latimer felt compelled to implore the king to allow 'that such men as shall be put to death may have learned men to give them instruction and exhortation', for many 'die miserably for lack of good preaching'.[56] The spiritual needs and the potential salvation of the condemned man does not appear to have been a central concern of the late-medieval narrators. The *Chronicle of Lanercost*, however, does describe John of Powderham's gallows confession and the Earl of Carlisle's demeanour and contrition before his execution.[57] But such accounts were few and far between in late-medieval texts and were not the set pieces of sixteenth-century narratives in which confessions were presented as the centerpiece of the scaffold ritual. Before 1500, of the few men who were reported to have said anything on the scaffold, most refused to make any admission of guilt. When Thomas Usk was executed in the fourteenth century, he was reportedly very penitent, yet maintained that 'every word was true' of his defence.[58] In most execution accounts recorded in medieval chronicles, the condemned make no assessment of personal responsibility on the scaffold. Even in accounts sympathetic to them, their behaviour was not the narrative focus. The most common emotion described in late medieval execution narratives was that of the crowd. According to the *Westminster Chronicle*, the crowd at Nicholas Brembre's execution was moved to tears, and John Hayward wrote that those who watched Roger Clarindon's execution were filled 'with pittie and griefe by behouldling it'.[59] The crowd may have wept, but the condemned were portrayed as bereft of voice and will; without any hope or help. Most were presented as beyond the pale – past all hope and salvation. Dragged to their deaths on hurdles, fettered and dishonored, these men were passive, inanimate and silent in these texts – much like Bucer's corpse.

It was in the sixteenth century that authors like Foxe began to breathe life into the condemned. They give him a voice and a visibility little seen before;

the events on the scaffold proceed at a pace set by the condemned. He gave the final speech and the axe did not fall until he gave the signal.[60] In these texts the representatives of the state watched and waited as condemned men like Thomas Palmer bid the executioner not strike until they were ready.[61] Thus, these men and women are brought into focus in these narratives in a way that was denied their medieval predecessors. This was more than a matter of simply being given the opportunity to speak by the state. The subjectivity that suffuses these texts extended beyond the spoken word, as these authors employed the body as a means of expressing a message about the man instead of retelling the story of his crime. The sixteenth-century execution narratives are filled with speeches, farewells, prayers and the descriptions of the demeanour of the condemned, such as Foxe's account of Bishop Hooper, who with a 'cheareful and ruddish countenaunce', declared himself to be no traitor and stated that they need not have 'made such a business bringing me here'.[62] The practice of describing in detail the behaviour of men and women on the scaffold did not begin with Foxe. Writing contemporaneously of the executions in 1536 of Anne Boleyn and her brother, Lord Rochford, Charles Wriothesley described more than the distribution of their body parts.[63] He recorded their speeches, final prayers and Queen Anne's 'smiling countenance'.[64] Although the mechanical descriptions of the distribution of body parts found in the late-medieval narratives were echoed in some mid-sixteenth century texts such as Richard Grafton's chronicle and Henry Machyn's diary, this type of description became increasingly infrequent over the sixteenth century.[65] Interestingly, this shift is clearly discernible in texts whose narrative spans several centuries, such as *Actes and Monuments* and John Speed's *History of Great Britain*.[66] Speed wrote that 'Sir Humfrey Stafford was drawne and executed at Tyburne' by Henry VII, but described in detail the final speeches and behaviour of the Duke of Somerset and Thomas Wyatt, who were executed in the sixteenth century.[67] Like Foxe, Speed reported the execution of medieval traitors in much the same way as the late-medieval chronicles, but then writes in more detail about sixteenth-century executions. Because both Speed and Foxe's execution narratives were drawn from sources written in preceding centuries, their texts help bring into focus the transformation in this discourse that took place after 1600.

This shift in focus from the body to behaviour in the execution narrative transcended religious and political ideologies, as well as literary genres. Chronicles and pamphlets, as well as personal accounts written after 1550 all drew attention not to the distribution of body parts, but to the final moment of the man on the scaffold. The descriptions of the executions of the Duke of Somerset in *Actes and Monuments*, Lord Rochford in Wriothesley's chronicle, and Anne Boleyn in the 'Crapelet Lettres de Henry VIII' all focused on the speech and demeanour of the condemned.[68] Whether they were describing the execution of a common criminal such as Thomas

Appeltree or an unlucky queen, the story was the same.[69] This trope was also not exclusively Protestant, as the final moments of Catholics such as Raph Sherwine were described in much the same way by polemicists on the other side of the confessional divide.[70] Thus, the dichotomy in *Actes and Monuments* involved active and passive bodies. Like Thomas Palmer in the *Chronicle of Queen Jane* and Thomas Appeltree in *A briefe Discourse of the most traytorlike fact of Thomas Appeltree,* sixteenth-century executions are described in ways that shift the focus to the behaviour on the scaffold. Whether martyr or traitor, Catholic or Protestant, the narrative emphasis became the conduct of the condemned.

At the heart of this transformation was the *ars moriendi*. The literature on the art of dying well provided the framework for sixteenth-century execution narratives as the deathbed vigil moved to the scaffold.[71] What had once been described as a ceremony commemorating the crime, became in the sixteenth century the celebration of the sinner's good death. The condemned man given a voice on the scaffold so that he could teach others how to die well. The message of these narratives, therefore, was to take heed, but also to take heart, for all sinners can be saved – even on the scaffold. Whether Catholic or Protestant, the condemned was described by friend and foe alike as having died in voluntary submission to God's will, after confessing his sins and expressing true repentance.[72] The author of the *Chronicle of Queen Jane,* describes a dutifully repentant Duke of Suffolk who died a faithful and true Christian as the headman struck his blow and, according to Foxe, at his execution Thomas Cromwell reportedly told the crowd:

> I am by the law condemned to die, and thanke mye lord God, that hath appointed me this death for myne offence ... I have liued a sinner and offended my lord God for which I aske him heartilie forgiveness.[73]

Confession, repentance and submission to the will of God were the hallmarks of a good Christian death, on or off the scaffold. Once it became the sinner who was showcased on the scaffold, it was not his disembowelment that authors described, but his prayers. They focused on his demeanour, instead of his dismemberment, as the more physical components of the ritual gradually receded into silence in these texts. The disposition of the body was described briefly, but the focus of sixteenth-century narratives increasingly moved towards the scaffold speech. The account of the execution of Thomas Palmer in the *Chronicle of Queen Jane* includes his greeting to the men on the scaffold, his speech, his directions to the executioner, and finally a brief note that 'his corpse and head was buried in the chapel at the Tower'.[74] Even when authors like Foxe and the Catholic polemicists of the 1580 and 1590s sought to use their descriptions of the cruelty of the state to send a message, the centrepiece of their narratives remained the behaviour and final speech of the condemned. Thus, Foxe notes that when

George Eagles was cruelly mangled, he remained 'steadfast and constant in the very midst of his tormentes'.[75] Another pamphleteer illustrates that this interest in dying well trumped political and religious differences.[76] Even though the Scot in his dialogue condemned the Earl of Strafford's speech, he agreed with the Jesuit that the Earl had made a good end.[77] Transformed in the sixteenth-century narrative from object to agent, the final measure of the man was calculated from the manner in which he died. Like the Thane of Cawdor in *Macbeth*, death became the final self-defining moment:

> But I have spoke
> Wuth one that saw him die, who did report
> That very frankly he confess'd his treasons,
> Implor'd your highness' pardon and set forth
> A deep repentance: nothing in his life
> Became him like the leaving of it.[78]

What is striking about the sixteenth-century narratives is that so many men died well. Most executions in these texts served as exemplum – not only of the power of the state or its cruelty, but of the *ars moriendi*. There is a uniformity of behaviour on the scaffold that transcended the religious and political ideologies of the authors. Whether Catholic or Protestant, they described men and women who faced death bravely, calmly and with forgiveness in their hearts and prayers on their lips, whether they were like Catholic Thomas Awfeeld, 'a secret enemy' to their country, a glorious martyr like John Rogers, or simply a queen or courtier run afoul of the lethal politics of Tudor England.[79]

This is not to say that these narratives lacked conflict. From unlucky royal wives, unfortunate politicians, and the Marian martyrs to Roman Catholics, the scaffold was the sight of competing discourses.[80] Rawlins White disputed religious matters with the officers at his execution, and Henry Cuffe argued forcefully with Lord Grey and protested his innocence in 1601.[81] William Allen reports that the crowd at an execution of Catholic priests in 1582 was whipped into a fever by Protestant ministers crying 'away with them'.[82] Yet, at Edmund Campion's execution they were moved to 'such compassion and tears'.[83] Sixteenth-century polemicists wrestled with who was a true or false martyr, but they seemed reluctant to describe any man dying in despair or quaking with fear before the executioner. A Protestant author describes one Catholic priest as obstinate and another as penitent, but neither as afraid.[84] Although it was the cause and not the comportment that separated true and false martyrs for both Catholics and Protestants alike, either the reality of their stoic behaviour on the scaffold, or a deeply ingrained expectation of steadfastness in the face of death, led to few descriptions in which the condemned man expressed anything other than the calm assurance of his salvation.

Thus, sixteenth-century authors seemed reluctant to show condemned men in pain or in trepidation. A little pain here and there crept into these narratives, but not as often as one would expect. Although Foxe does not shy away from reporting the gruesome details of an execution, only rarely does he record any expressions of pain or suffering.[85] Thus, as the executioner did 'fouly mangle' the beheading of George Eagles, hitting his chin, neck and head with the axe, Eagles remained 'steadfast and constant'; and Cicely Ormes 'died as one feelyng no payne'.[86] For the most part, Protestants and Catholics preferred stoicism to expressions of suffering to make their case.[87] Of course, one man's stoicism could be another man's obstinacy. Thus, the Catholic account of the execution of Roger Dicconson in 1591 states that his calm demeanour on the scaffold was remarked upon by Protestants who noted that he died calmly, but 'desperately'. The Catholic narrators, on the other hand, wrote that when he was hanged, drawn and quartered, Dicconson 'endured so cheerfully and constantly and without any change of countenance'.[88] No matter how brutal the punishment, therefore, stoicism reigned supreme in sixteenth-century scaffold narratives.

For the most part, descriptions of the deaths of political figures resemble John Speed's account of the execution of Somerset, who 'meekely laide downe his head to the Axe and received at one stroke his rest by death'.[89] Thus, the desired swift and painless death dominated most accounts. Whether martyr or malefactor, most men died bravely and without any expression of pain – at least on paper. Although the condemned was given a voice in sixteenth-century narrative and an opportunity to self-fashion an identity on the scaffold, the construction of the 'self' was carefully constrained. There was only one role available to the man on the scaffold – that of a Christian dying well.

Although the last dying speech served as the centrepiece of these texts, authors did not immediately abandon the body. Words could not completely displace the body in these narratives because words were inherently problematic for Catholics and Protestants alike. Catholic writers such as Robert Persons had articulated a doctrine of equivocation that allowed the mental reservation of key details in answer to an incriminating question by an unjust magistrate.[90] The matter of words of betrayal uttered under torture required an explanation that led Catholic polemicists to further distance words spoken while suffering the intolerable torment of the rack from the 'truth'.[91] On the other side, Protestants were deeply suspicious of the veracity of anything uttered by a papist. However, the public and well-attended nature of these executions forced all authors to accurately report last dying speeches. Peter Lake and Michael Questier argue that execution narratives could not stray too far from the truth without damaging their credibility.[92] Brad Gregory addresses this issue when he compares Catholic and Protestant accounts of the execution of Edmund Campion to show that ideologically opposed authors told basically the same story about his behaviour on the scaffold.[93] Narratives written in the heated environment of the English Civil War also lend support to this claim. Both Laud and Strafford's executions generated pamphlets written from opposing political perspectives. Yet the demeanour and final speech of both men were reported in the same way by their supporters and opponents alike.[94] Thus, the thorny issue of true and false martyrs hovered over final speeches. Since one faith's martyr was another's heretic, behaviour was forced to yield to belief. In other words, heretics often died well and were tormented terribly, so all were forced to rely upon the Augustinian dictum that it was not the punishment but the cause that made the martyr.

However, this was more than a matter of one man's martyr being another man's traitor. Anxiety about the spoken word transcended religion, as evidenced by Hugh Latimer's concern over what he considered the transparent rhetorical strategy of many traitors: 'it hath been the cast of all traitors to pretend nothing against the king's person; they never pretend the matter to the king, but to others'.[95] Since words were suspect, John Bradford, the Protestant martyr burned at Smithfield, preached that it was better to pray from the heart than the lips, for 'God is the hearer of the heart and not of the voice'.[96] If, as Bradford believed, truth was locked in the interior, then it was a potential object of discovery and both Catholics and Protestants shared a similar inclination to imagine a corporeal location for it.[97] The authors of execution narratives, therefore, looked to the body as the window to the hidden interior of souls. Francis Bacon wrote of the many wise men who 'have secret hearts and transparent countenances'.[98] According to Thomas Bilson, inward affections make outward expressions on the body: anger, favour, fear – all appear on the face of man.[99] Thus, as the descriptions of dismemberment and degradation began to fade from view, a new role for the body emerges in these texts. Authors scrutinized the condemned's countenance for signs of fear; they described his body language; they analysed his voice for evidence of emotion; and they read his conscience from his corpus. The *Chronicle of Queen Jane* reported that Lady Jane Grey was not 'at all abashed', and the demeanour of Thomas Palmer at his execution 'never changed, but rather he seemed more cheerful in countenance then when he was at his libertye'.[100] According to Catholic William Allen, Edmund Campion addressed the crowd with a 'grave countenance and a sweet voice', and Raph Sherwine thanked God 'with stoute courage and strong voice'.[101] Foxe wrote that Somerset showed 'no maner of token of trouble or feare, neyther did his countenaunce change, but that before his eyes were couered there began to appear a red colour in the middle of his cheekes'.[102] Thus, with the emergence of a subjective discourse of the scaffold in the sixteenth century came a new role for the body – to reveal the inner man. If medieval truth had been written on the exterior for all to see, the Renaissance body possessed an interior space that contained its own mysteries. As a field of cultural inquiry in the sixteenth century, bodies were being explored not just in the execution narrative, but in the amphitheater of the anatomist, poetry and the torture chamber. Jonathan Sawday examines how the culture of dissection at that time was devoted to the acquisition and dissemination of knowledge of the 'mystery' of the body.[103] For authors of execution narratives, that 'mystery' was the truth contained within, which was reflected in the countenance of the condemned.

The sixteenth century therefore witnessed a growing ambiguity over whose truth the body told. Sawday argues that although the body was still considered, even by anatomists, as a sacred text, the artistic convention of the dissected human figure in self-demonstration was an example of the way in which the Renaissance body could be the product of both divine and human authors. The same can be said about the body on the scaffold.[104] Although sinners were assumed to have been denied God's grace, there was a sense that a dying man's demeanour was more than its product. After all, the whole project of the *ars moriendi* was predicated on the belief that what a dying man 'did mattered'. This literary genre was an instruction manual for self-fashioning in the face of death. Thus, the Renaissance body could be both the object of divine providence and the subject of a self-conscious construction of 'self'. The body served as the focus of twin discourses – one authored by God and the other by man.

As the boundaries between human activity and divine will began to blur, there was a growing instability surrounding somatic signification. Almost from the beginning concern was expressed that the body may not reliably reveal inner truths. Latimer had warned in 1549 that Anabaptists and other heretics had gone to their deaths joyfully, so who could know at the moment of death whether a man was truly saved.[105] This anxiety was more than a matter of separating true from false martyrs. If as Erasmus had taught, manners could make the man, could they not make him appear to be something he was not?[106] The self-conscious construction of identity found in Shakespeare's plays, the courtier's manuals, and the Elizabethan fiction of the 'stomach of a king' buried deep within the body of a female, reflected an erosion in what was inherently a medieval confidence in the ability of bodies to reveal truths.

In the sixteenth century this sentiment was more often reflected in literary genres other than execution narratives. When the Nobleman in Thomas Kyd's *The Spanish Tragedy* speaks of Alexandro's perfidy, he says: 'But now I see that words have several works, And there's no credit in the countenance'.[107] Although Erasmus wrote that men cannot see into other men's hearts, reflecting doubt about how demeanour might reveal secrets, it would not be until the seventeenth century that execution narratives would reflect these sentiments.[108] I am not suggesting that sixteenth-century authors always accepted a stoic performance on the scaffold as evidence of salvation, only that author's continued to describe the condemned man's countenance after 1600. In other literary genres authors expressed concern that a man's countenance may not have been as transparent as Bacon believed. But execution narratives were not yet ready to abandon the somatic discourses of the scaffold. *An Account of the Confession and Execution of Captain Vratz*, written in 1682, describes the repentance of Captain Vratz, John Sterne and George Baraski and their final speeches, but makes no mention of their demeanour on the scaffold, and the account of the execution of 19 rebels in 1685 simply states that they were conveyed to the place of execution and executed according to their sentence.[109] Execution narratives begin to abandon the body right at the same time – 1660 – that Alexandra Walsham claims that Newtonian scientists and Royal Society theologians began to link providentialism with the superstitions of the gullible multitude.[110] Jonathan Sawday also locates the dissected body's liberation from theology in the second half of the seventeenth century.[111] Thus, the power of somatic signification had eroded significantly by 1700 and it was reflected in the execution narrative.

In some sense, Foxe was the herald of this change. Just as Renaissance anatomists read bodies as texts written both by the hand of God and human agency – so did Foxe. Yet, he makes one critical distinction: only the bodies of the living serve as texts. This was at the heart of the tension surrounding Bucer's body. The body that so concerned the Bishop of Chester was the same one that had dominated late-medieval execution narratives; dead or alive, these were passive bodies that served as texts. For Foxe, however, Bucer's body had nothing to reveal, precisely because death had denied him agency. Thus, although the hand of God continued to make its mark on the bodies of the dead in other sixteenth-century texts, there were no messages written on the bodies of executed Protestants in *Actes and Monuments*. The dead did not speak in Foxe, or in other sixteenth-century execution narrative. In the discourse of the scaffold that emerges in the sixteenth century that was a role available only to the living.

Digging up the dead to burn them at the stake is only one part of the story of an age of spectacular justice that has often been portrayed as a primitive prologue to the modern practice of punishment. Late-medieval and early modern Europe has frequently been described as a world of socially accepted cruelty before Erasmus, emerging capitalism, rationality, and the absolutist state made men civilized – or in Foucault's formulation, the time for torture before the economy of punishment was redirected from the body to the mind.[112] The body, whether exhumed, dismembered or burned, has stood at the centre of this story as the symbol of the crime, the point of application of the vengeance of the sovereign, or the text of truth. However, the tendency in the historiography of capital punishment to lump together the fourteenth through the eighteenth centuries has led some to overlook changes that were taking place in the role of the body in the discourse of the scaffold. The shift in emphasis in the execution narrative from the body to behaviour reflected more than just the emergence of subjectivity in sixteenth-century discourse.

The ways in which the authors of the execution narratives chose to tell the story of the scaffold illuminates the changing ways punishment was presented to society over the course of several centuries. The body was read by late-medieval narrators as the text of a ceremony of retribution, which is why it was so important that they described how the punishment commemorated the crime. These texts shifted focus in the sixteenth century to the behaviour of the man on the scaffold, as telling the story of his repentance took precedence over the reenactment of the crime. As these narratives shifted focus from the crime to the criminal, they reflected a challenge to the retributivist concept of justice. The scaffold spectacle was born in the twelfth century into a world in which vengeance was the epistemiological framework within which men understood violence. Revenge was believed to be natural and necessary, a legitimate course of action for everyone from knights to kings to the Almighty. By the sixteenth century a culture thought too comfortable with vengeance was under attack on several fronts as the state sought to achieve a monopoly of violence.[113] Promoting the moralization of politics, the Tudor state encouraged the condemned to advertise their obedience to the will of God and the state in a final speech as part of the campaign to reign in the culture of revenge. In exchange for their submission, the condemned were given opportunity to redeem both their soul and reputation. This exchange moved dying well on the scaffold beyond the martyrologies and into the public discourse of punishment.

Thus, the shift from the body to behaviour in these texts was an early indication of a movement away from concern with retribution to an emphasis on describing how even the most heinous criminal was brought back into the fold through repentance on the scaffold. At its heart, this is the story of how the *ars moriendi* began to define the discourse of the scaffold, representing the beginning of a shift in attitude toward the purpose of punishment. The concept of reformative justice, so familiar to the modern world, began to challenge the retributivist discourse of the scaffold in the sixteenth century. Thus, the texts that describe these executions told a story much larger than what happened to the man standing on the scaffold.

Notes

1 John Foxe, *Actes and Monuments of Matters Most Special and Memorable, Happenyng in the Church, with an Uniuersall History of the Same, Wherein is Set Forth at Large the Whole Race and Course of the Church, From the Primitive Age to These Latter Tymes of Ours, With the Bloudy Times, Horrible troubles, and Great Persecutions Agaynst the True Martyrs of Christ, Sought and Wrought As Well by Heartless Emperours, and Nowe Lately Practiced by Romish Prelates Especially in This Realme of England and Scotland*, II, 4th edition (1583), 1961–63.

2 *Ibid.*, 1961.

3 *Ibid.*, 1963.
4 *Ibid.*, 1963.
5 *Ibid.*, 1961.
6 *Ibid.*, 1665, 1583–98.
7 See Michael MacDonald and Terence R. Murphy, *Sleepless Souls: Suicide in Early Modern England* (Oxford, 1990), 48, for a discussion of the treatment of the bodies of suicides in early modern England.
8 In *Providence in Early Modern England* (Oxford, 1999) 2, 73, Alexandra Walsham acknowledges the medieval inheritance of providentialism in early modern England, tracing it back from Thomas Beard through Foxe to the ecclesiastical histories of Eusebius, Rufinus and Bede. She contends that belief in divine providence was widespread and not just the product of a particular brand of zealous Protestantism.
9 Foxe, *Actes and Monuments*, II, 2099.
10 Thomas Beard, *The Theatre of God's Judgments* (1597); and John Reynolds, *The Triumph of God's Revenge Against the Crying and Execrable Sinne of Willful and Premeditated Murther* (1657).
11 In *Crime and Mentalities in Early Modern England* (Cambridge, 2000), 203–22, Malcolm Gaskill outlines the ways in which the body served as a divine instrument to both expose and punish the crime of murder.
12 *Sundry Strange and Inhumaine Murthers* (1591), folio A iiii.
13 Foxe, *Actes and Monuments*, II, 2004.
14 *Ibid.*, 1888.
15 *Ibid.*, 1715.
16 Jacobus de Voragine, *The Golden Legend*, II, trans. William Granger Ryan (Princeton, 1993), 313.
17 Foxe, *Actes and Monuments*, II, 972.
18 John Knott, *Discourse of Martyrdom in English Literature 1563–1694* (Cambridge, 1993), 2–8.
19 *Chronicle of Queen Jane*, ed., John Gough Nichols (1849) is believed to have been written in the 1550s, and Charles Wriothesley's, *The Chronicle of England During the Reigns of the Tudors From AD 1485 to 1559*, ed., William Douglas Hamilton (Westminster, 1874) was drawn from the chronicle of Richard Arnold for the first 11 years of the reign of Henry VIII. After 1520, Wriothesley's accounts were written contemporaneously.
20 *Chronicle of Queen Jane*, 22.
21 Thomas Freeman, 'Texts, Lies, and Microfilm: Reading and Misreading Foxe's "Book of Martyrs"', *The Sixteenth Century Journal*, 30 (1999), 23–46; Foxe, *Actes and Monuments*, II, 885, 1770.
22 Foxe, *Actes and Monuments*, II, 371, cites the *Vita Edwardi Secundi*, trans. N. Denholm Young (London, 1957), 126, as his source for the account of the execution of Lancaster.
23 Foxe, *Actes and Monuments*, I, 55–6, and Eusebius, *The Ecclesiastical History Vol. I*, trans. Kirsupp Lake and J.E.L. Oulton (Cambridge, MA, 1929), 347.
24 According to Foxe, Hoveden was a wool winder and a citizen of London who received 'the Crowne of Martyrdom' (*Actes and Monuments*, I, 665).
25 Foxe, *Actes and Monuments*, II, 1190, 1367–72.
26 de Voragine, *Golden Legend*, II, 181–3.
27 de Voragine, *Golden Legend*, I, 258.
28 *The Early English Legendary Lives of Saints I*, ed. Carl Horstman (1887).
29 Foxe, *Actes and Monuments*, II, 1770, 2004, 1510.

30 *Ibid.*, 1888.
31 According to *ibid.*, 1510–11, 1558, 1624, Bishop Hooper helped the authorities adjust the chains around his waist, Rawlins White helped arrange the straw around the stake, and John Bradford kissed the stake.
32 *Ibid.*, 1567.
33 *Ibid.*, 1895, 1559.
34 *Ibid.*, 1679.
35 *Chronicle of Queen Jane*, 21.
36 Foxe, *Actes and Monuments*, II, 44.
37 Foxe's account of the execution of Polycarp describes his request that he not be nailed to the stake in order to show that he had voluntarily embraced his martyrdom. He also claimed that John Hus reportedly sang with a loud voice as his body burned. See Foxe, *Actes and Monuments*, I, 56, 624–5.
38 Foxe wrote: 'Till at length the yeere following he [Wallace] was taken and sent up to London and there executed for the same' (*ibid.*, 342, 376).
39 *Ibid.*, 371, 376.
40 *Ibid.*, 371.
41 Henry Knighton, *Knighton's Chronicle 1337–1396*, ed. and trans. G.H. Martin (Oxford, 1995), 241.
42 *The Chronicle of Lanercost 1272–1346*, trans. Herbert Maxwell (Glasgow, 1913), 35.
43 Sir John Froissart, *Chronicles of England, France, Spain and the Adjoining Countries*, trans. Thomas Johnes, 3rd edition, I (1808), 32.
44 Henry VII considered posting the Cornish rebels' quarters as 'a document for other hereafter to beware', and 'instead of his banner' the severed limbs of William Wallace were 'his standards'. See Richard Grafton, *Chronicle of John Hardyng*, ed., Henry Ellis (1812), 576; and 'The Trailbastons and Execution of William Wallace', from *Peter Langtoft's Chronicle*, cited in Thomas Wright, *Political Songs of England from the Reign of John to that of Edward II* (Cambridge, 1996), 322.
45 J.A. Sharpe, Lacey Baldwin Smith and Mervyn James consider these speeches to have been a fixture of Tudor England. See J.A. Sharpe, '"Last Dying Speeches": religion, ideology, and public execution in seventeenth-century England', *P&P*, 107 (1985), 144–67; Lacy Baldwin Smith, 'English Treason Trials and Confessions in the Sixteenth Century', *Journal of the History of Ideas*, 15 (1954), 471–98; and Mervyn James, 'English politics and the concept of honour 1485–1640', in James, *Society, Politics and Culture: Studies in Early Modern England* (Cambridge, 1989).
46 *Chronicle of Lanercost*, 223.
47 *Ibid.*, 176, 35, 89, 178, 179, 237.
48 *Westminster Chronicle 1381–1394*, ed. and trans. L.C. Hector and Barbara Harvey (Oxford, 1982), 313–15.
49 *Westminster Chronicle*, 3, 13, and Knighton, *Knighton's Chronicle*, 499.
50 For example, Knighton, *Knighton's Chronicle*, 499, writes that Robert Tresilian 'was dragged from the Tower of London to the gallows at Tyburn, and hanged and had his throat cut', Hugh Despenser does not speak in Froissart's account; and according to the *Chronicle of John Hardyng*, 594, Empson and Dudley were brought to a scaffold on Tower Hill 'and there behedded'.
51 Foxe, *Actes and Monuments*, I, 371, 342, 376.
52 John Gough Nichols ed., *The Diary of Henry Machyn, Citizen and Merchant-Taylor of London, from A.D. 1550 to A.D. 1563* (Camden Society, 42, 1848), 14. This speech is reported in both the *Actes and Monuments*, Vol. II, 1372, and the *Chronicle of Queen Jane*, 21.

53 Foxe, *Actes and Monuments*, II, 1190.
54 *The Chronicle of Lanercost*, 252.
55 See Mitchell Merback, *The Thief, the Cross and the Wheel: Pain and the Spectacle of Punishment in Medieval and Renaissance Europe* (Chicago, 1999), 148, for a discussion of the movement in Europe toward spiritual consolation for the condemned man on the scaffold.
56 From the sermon delivered on March 29, 1549, cited in *Sermons by Hugh Latimer*, ed. George Elwes Corrie (Cambridge, 1844), 164.
57 *The Chronicle of Lanercost*, 223, 245.
58 See *Westminster Chronicle*, 315.
59 *Ibid.*, and John Hayward, *The First and Second Parts of John Hayward's The Life and Raigne of King Henrie IIII*, ed. John Manning (1991), 203.
60 *Chronicle of Queen Jane* and *A briefe Discourse of the Most Traytor like Fact of Thomas Appeltree* (1579); and Foxe, *Actes and Monuments*, II, 1558–9.
61 According to the *Chronicle of Queen Jane*, 212, 73, the executioner also held back until Lady Jane Grey and Thomas Wyatt gave him their signal.
62 Foxe, *Actes and Monuments*, II, 1509.
63 Wriothesley, *Chronicle*, 39–41.
64 *Ibid.*, 41.
65 Richard Grafton's continuation of the *Chronicle of John Hardyng* was begun around 1543. Henry Machyn's diary was written between 1550 and 1563.
66 John Speed, *The History of Great Britain Under the Conquests of the Romans, Saxons, Danes and Normans*, 2nd edition (1623).
67 Speed, *History of Great Britain*, 742, 837–8, and 847.
68 See Foxe, *Actes and Monuments*, II, 1367–72; Wriothesley, *Chronicle*, 39, and 'The Crapelet lettres de Henry VIII', 2 June 1536 in *The Calendar of State Papers Foreign and Domestic Henry VIII 1536*, 428.
69 *A Briefe Discourse of the Most Traytorlike Fact of Thomas Appeltree*.
70 Sherwine's behaviour and demeanour on the scaffold was described by the Catholic polemicist William Allen in *A Briefe Historie of the Glorious Martyrdom of XII Reverend Priests, Executed Within These…For Coinfession and Defense of the Catholike Faith*, diij, in much the same manner as Foxe's *Actes and Monuments*, II, 2023, account of the execution of the Protestant Cicely Ormes at Norwich in 1557.
71 As Brad Gregory points out in *Salvation at Stake: Christian Martyrdom in Early Modern Europe* (Cambridge, 1999), 30–62, the literature of the *ars moriendi* was extensively adapted and circulated throughout Europe in the fifteenth century and was part of the late medieval inheritance of the sixteenth century martyrs. According to Robert Wunderli and Gerald Broce in 'The Final Moment before Death in Early Modern England', *Sixteenth Century Journal* (1989), 259–75, the influence of this literature extended beyond martyrology to the last dying speeches of the political class in early modern England.
72 The essays in Bruce Gordon and Peter Marshall eds, *The Place of the Dead: Death and Remembrance in Late Medieval and Early Modern Europe* (Cambridge, 2000) discuss the changes and continuities in attitudes toward the dying and the dead in Christian Europe as it entered into and past the Reformation. It is not my intention to argue that all attitudes surrounding death crossed confessional lines, only that the desire to die well transcended religious differences. The *ars moriendi* survived the Reformation in England intact, although not unaltered. Thomas Becon's *The Sycke Man's Salve* (Edinburgh, 1600) and 'The Flower of Godly Prayers', in *The Writings of Thomas Becon* (London), which instructed good Protestants on how

to face the hour of their death, abandoned the saints, crucifix and holy water that assisted the dying man in his struggle with Satan in the *Ars Moriendi* from 1506. In 'The Flower of Godly Prayers', 113, Becon writes of a more personal and solitary struggle in which only a heartfelt repentance made in this life could save the dying man's soul. Both texts emphasized the role that confession of sins, true repentance, obedience to the will of god, and forgiveness of others played in a good Christian death. See Ralph Houlbrooke's essay, 'The Puritan Death-bed, *c.* 1560–1660', in Christopher Durston and Jaqueline Eales eds, *The Culture of English Puritanism, 1560–1700* (New York, 1996), 122–44, for an examination of puritan attitudes toward the correct conduct on the deathbed from the mid-sixteenth century to the Restoration.

73 *Chronicle of Queen Jane*, 63; and Foxe, *Actes and Monuments*, II, 1190.

74 *Chronicle of Queen Jane*, 22.

75 Foxe, *Actes and Monuments*, II, 2010.

76 *Great Satisfaction Concerning the Death of the Earl of Strafford in A Discourse Betweene A Scottishman and A Jesuite* (1641), presents a dialogue between a Scot and a Jesuit who disagree on the Earl's guilt, but both agree that he died well and made a 'good conclusion'.

77 *Ibid.*, 7.

78 William Shakespeare, *Macbeth* Act I, Scene IV.

79 *The Life and End of Thomas Awfeeld and Thomas Welby, traitors*, Aiiij; and Foxe, *Actes and Monuments*, VI, 609. See the description of death of Ann Boleyn in the 'Crapelet lettres de Henry VIII', 436, and the accounts of the executions of Lady Jane Grey, Thomas Wyatt and the Earl of Essex in John Speed's, *History of Great Britain*, 843, 847, 906.

80 Peter Lake and Michael Questier make this point in relation to the execution of Roman Catholic traitors in the 1580s and 1590s in 'Agency, Appropriation and Rhetoric Under the Gallows: Puritans, Romanists, and the State in Early Modern England', *P&P*, 153 (1996), 64–107, when they argue that the discourse of the scaffold was multivocal. The state, the criminal, and the crowd each attached their own meaning to the event. Lake and Questier chart a middle ground between what J.A. Sharpe described as events in which the state exercised ideological control and what Thomas Laquer sees as an unscripted carnival of inversion. See Sharpe, 'Last dying speeches', and Thomas Laqueur, 'Crowds, Carnival and the State in English Executions, 1604–1868', in A.L. Beier *et al.*, eds, *The First Modern Society: Essays in English History in Honour of Lawrence Stone* (Cambridge, 1989). Foxe's description of the reaction of the crowd to the burning of Martin Bucer and the account found in the *Westminster Chronicle*, 15–19, of the reaction to the executions in 1381 following the Peasants Rebellion are an indication that a multivocal discourse of the scaffold was not solely an Elizabethan phenomena.

81 Foxe, *Actes and Monuments*, II, 1558–9, and 'March 13, 1601', *Calendar of State Papers Domestic 1601–1603*, 14–16.

82 Allen, *Briefe Historie*, cij.

83 *Ibid.*, diij.

84 *A True Recitall Touching the Cause of the Death of Thomas Bales, a Seminarie Priest who was Hanged and Quartered in Fleet Street on Ash Wednesday Last Past* (1590), ij.

85 Foxe, *Actes and Monuments*, II, 1770, reports that Ridley leaped up and down because the fire burned too slowly and John Geninges wrote in *The Life and Death of Mr. Edmund Geninges Priest, Crowned with Martyrdom at London, the 10th day of Nouember, in the Yeare M.D XCI* (St Omers, 1614), 86, that his brother Edmund cried out during his dismemberment in 1591. According to Foxe, *Actes and*

Monuments, II, 2047, Thomas Benbridge recanted after the fire burned his beard and leather hose. He attributes Benbridge's momentary weakness to the fact that his tormentors did 'rather broyle hym, then burne him'. Benbridge later expressed his conscience and was burned at the stake a second and more successful time in 1558. Discomfort like that expressed by Thomas Benbridge was most often used by Foxe to either place a recantation in context or to make a point about the cruelty of the state.

86 Foxe, *Actes and Monuments*, II, 2010, 2023.

87 Some Catholic authors were more interested in the suffering endured in the torture chamber than on the scaffold and described it in greater detail. See William Allen, *Briefe Historie*, di–diij, for a description of the torture and execution of Father Campion, which emphasizes the former over the latter.

88 See John Hungerford Pollen, *Acts of English Martyrs* (1891), 94, for both accounts.

89 Speed, *History of Great Britain*, 838.

90 The Jesuit Robert Persons argued in *A Treatise Tending to Mitigation Towards Catholick Subjects* (St Omer, 1607) that under certain circumstances truth could be the product of both the internal and external voice. Elizabeth Hanson in *Discovering the Subject in Renaissance England* (Cambridge, 1998), 51, argues that the Catholic polemicists threaded this needle even closer when they tried to justify Campion's betrayal under torture of those who sheltered him. The Catholic construction was that Campion's words of betrayal were false; what he refused to reveal was the 'truth'.

91 Hanson, *Discovering the Subject*, 51.

92 Lake and Questier, 'Agency, appropriation, and rhetoric', 80.

93 Gregory, *Salvation at Stake*,18–36.

94 See *A True Copy of Certain Passages of the Lord Archbishop of Canterbury* (Oxford, 1644); *Canterburies Doom, Or, The First Part of a Compleat History of the Commitment, Charge, Tryall, Condemnation, Execution of William Laud, Late Archbishop of Canterbury* (1646); *Great Satisfaction Concerning the Death of the Earl of Strafford in a Discourse Betweene a Scottishman and a Jesuite*; and *An Impartial Account of the Arraignment, Trial and Condemnation of Thomas Late Earl of Strafford and Lord Lieutenant of Ireland* (1679).

95 Sermon delivered on 29 March 1549, *Sermons by Hugh Latimer*, 163.

96 John Bradford, *Two Notable Sermons Made by the Worthy Martyr of Christ, Master John Bradford* (1599), A4.

97 Elizabeth Hanson, *Discovering the Subject*, 24–55, examines the Renaissance obsession with the discovery of the truth hidden in each man's heart. She writes that in the discursive economy of English torture the body was used to both find and resist the discovery of the truth. In her essay, 'The Animated Pain of the Body' in *AHR*, 105 (2000), 36–68, Esther Cohen traces to the thirteenth century the belief that pain resided in the soul yet found expression on the body. Its expression (or nonexpression in certain circumstances) was a manifestation of more than a physical sensation; it reflected the state of the soul.

98 Francis Bacon, 'The Essays or Counsels Civil and Moral', in *Francis Bacon: A Critical Edition of the Major Works*, ed. Brian Vickers (Oxford, 1996), 384.

99 Thomas Bilson also wrote in *A Survey of Christ's Sufferings for Man's Redemption and of His Descent into Hades or Hell for Our Deliverance* (1604), 193, that 'a cheerful face is the token of the heart for good'.

100 *Chronicle of Queen Jane*, 55, 20.

101 Allen, *Briefe Historie*, d, diij.

102 Foxe, *Actes and Monuments*, II, 1372.

103 Jonathan Sawday, *The Body Emblazoned: Dissection and the Human Body* (1995).
104 *Ibid.*, 135, 101–5.
105 Latimer, *Sermons*, 160–1.
106 Or more specifically, not born to be. The self-fashioning that Stephen Greenblatt describes in *Renaissance Self-Fashioning From More to Shakespeare* (Chicago, 1984), 1–9, links manners and demeanour to the creation of an identity that was not rooted in inheritance, but was self-created. Norbert Elias in his study of the development of manners, credits *De civilitate puerlium* by Erasmus as a major influence in the development of an ideology of self-control which was an important component in this self-fashioning. See Norbert Elias, *The Civilizing Process: The History of Manners and State Formation*, trans. Edmund Jephcott (Oxford, 1994).
107 Thomas Kyd, *The Spanish Tragedy*, Act III, scene 4.
108 *The Second Volume of the Paraphrases of Erasmus Upon the Newe Testament Contenyng the Epistles of S. Paul and Other Apostles* (1549), A, iiii.
109 *An Account of the Confession and Execution of Captain Vratz* (1682); and *An Account of 19 Rebels That Were Executed at Taunton-Dean in the County of Somerset* (1685).
110 Walsham, *Providence in Early Modern England*, 333–4.
111 Sawday, *Body Emblazoned*, 38.
112 Pieter Spierenberg proposes in *The Spectacle of Suffering and the Evolution of Repression* (Cambridge, 1984), 12, 78, that the brutality of capital punishment in early modern Europe was the product of a violent society in which justice existed more in theory than in practice. Thus, an adolescent state was prone to make exaggerated statements on the scaffold in order to mask its inherent weakness. Drawing on the social theory of Norbert Elias, Spierenberg contends that the end of these spectacles was the result of a civilizing process which increased the sensitivity of the middle and upper classes to displays of violence. In *Rituals of Retribution: Capital Punishment in Germany 1600–1987* (Oxford, 1996), 208–9, 238–9, Richard Evans contends that this punitive aesthetic was rooted in folk culture and that the increasingly secularized German state set out to distance itself from the more vulgar elements of the popular culture. Richard van Dülmen in *Theatre of Horror: Crime and Punishment in Early Modern Germany* (Cambridge, 1990), 3, 137, similarly credits the Enlightenment for the change in attitude toward public executions that led to the move to the private and more humane forms of execution adopted in the nineteenth century. van Dülmen also cites the awareness of the state that excessive brutality was not deterring crime for the end of the spectacles of suffering. V.A.C. Gatrell and Thomas Laqueur are in agreement with this position. See V.A.C. Gatrell, *The Hanging Tree: Executions and the English People 1770–1868* (Cambridge, 1991). Michel Foucault in *Discipline and Punish: The Birth of the Prison* (New York, 1979) is less convinced that the state became any more humane, contending that it simply substituted one technology of power for another.
113 In 'English politics and the concept of honour', Mervyn James examines the role of revenge in late-medieval English society as well as explores how the culture of the sixteenth century supplanted it with other values.

3

Bodies and Souls in Norwich: Punishing Petty Crime, 1540–1700

*Paul Griffiths**

> This parallel between mind and body is precisely what one should expect if these are inward and outward manifestations of a single reality, as I believe they are. Whether we are made up of two substances or only one is a grizzled metaphysical debate, which I do not expect to settle here. In either case, we know that mind and body are intimately linked, that pain and well-being can leap over any gap there may be.
>
> (Scott Russell Sanders, *Hunting For Hope: A Father's Journey*, Boston, MA, 1998, 51)

I

A lack of balance affects our current knowledge of punishment in sixteenth- and seventeenth-century England. Up to now petty crime has nearly always played a poor second fiddle to felony and in the past, as now, commentators usually wrote about serious and shocking crime that could make stomachs turn. We historians are not that distant from the pamphleteers or balladeers of three or four centuries ago; we both mostly write about murder, witchcraft, or grand larceny when our thoughts turn to crime. This is certainly not wrong and it is perfectly understandable for good reasons. Matters of state often guided the prosecutor's arrow, and the depositions that narrated the facts of such crimes can be a wonderful journal of daily life. And once the verdict was announced and the sentence pronounced, the scene shifted quickly to the politically vital and buzzing gallows crowd.

* I would like to thank John Beattie, Randall McGowen and Moshe Sluhovsky for their very helpful comments, and audiences in Cincinnatti (Mid-West Conference on British Studies, 2000), Norwich (University of East Anglia, East Anglian Studies Centre Seminar), and Brisbane (at the Australian Historical Conference 2002, and at the Centre for Critical and Cultural Studies, University of Queensland), for listening to me and giving me such good advice.

To date, the 'fatal tree' and its consequences is not unfairly the linchpin of our histories of punishment since 1500. Impressions of change over time are mostly felony tales rooted in this tree, and it is from this same starting-point that the leaps, dips and pauses in crime-rates are often followed. We also commonly comb records of felony to map twists and turns in penal practices and ideas. Most controversially, the neat move from punishing criminal bodies to reforming minds (souls) in the eighteenth century, for instance is, in the hands of Michel Foucault and others after him, a fairly linear felony narrative in which privatising penalties and reforming offenders were the late outcomes of decades of penal debate, wrangling and testing in the enlightened sunshine of the eighteenth century and after. This account depends for its full force on a shift in scene from the dangling bodies at the noisy gallows to gloomy, lonely prison cells in which it was hoped that a tide of guilt-edged memories would wash away thoughts of wrong-doing. In this analysis, as fewer people dangled on the gallows, trained experts and their teams sought to 'alter' the criminal instincts and energies of lifelong offenders. As punishment softened, therefore, it reformed.[1]

For some time now, however, others working with felony cases have quizzed the neatness and suddenness of this shift. Better than ever before, we now know that ideas had already formed by 1700, that confinement along with backbreaking work was a suitable penalty for grand larceny, and that it was thought that imprisoned thieves could change their ways for the better. We also know that although fewer voices were raised to back penal reform before 1700, as after, a lobby had gathered steam that made much the same points that would lead to reforms later on. Nor should we treat punishing felony and petty crime apart from each other, but put them instead on a single continuum, as contemporaries did, where the death penalty was the last act after a string of lesser penalties had not been enough to put a stubborn felon on the right road.[2] Histories of penal change should be less tidy, and open to overlaps, inconsistencies and botched reforms, along with a few forward steps.[3]

Penal practices and cultures look different if we follow the historical development of penalty from a petty-crime angle. So far little work starts like this. We have good work on particular penalties and offences, but we still do not have a sound model of penal change from this perspective.[4] If we had one it would not challenge the long line of work on felony, but it would give us a fuller sense of past penal cultures by unsettling interpretations a little. Felony, after all, was only a tiny fraction of total caseloads of prosecuted crime; a little molehill next to the mountain of petty crime, even after we reckon with the petty crime that was dealt with in a flash by less well-recorded summary justice and has slipped our notice.[5] Petty crime was run-of-the-mill crime, and it was corrected day after day. Martin Ingram notes that 'lesser punishments' were 'commonplace'.[6] In this sense, the twice-annual gallows were less visible and more out of the ordinary.[7] It was such thoughts that persuaded

Beccaria, the eighteenth century's most influential legal writer, that short, sharp, shock penalties left a longer lasting mark on character:

> Since men are not induced on the spur of the moment to commit the gravest crimes, public punishment of a great misdeed will be regarded by the majority as something very remote and of improbable occurrence; but public punishment of lesser crimes, which are closer to mens hearts, will make an impression which, while deterring them from these, deters them even further from graver crimes.[8]

Early modern people believed that shocking crimes followed little slip-ups like tumbling cards in an irresistible motion. Crime had to be nipped in the bud to stop, in Beccaria's words, 'the graver crimes'. This was why the first penalty, however slight it might seem, was as urgent as the last noose. A whipping started the ball rolling, the end of the line was the gallows. Without petty crime there would be no felony, no final meeting with the hangman. In 1562 Norwich's mayor warned William Vincent, who had just escaped lightly with a whipping after a sex offence, that he had 'better hold upon God's grace and live in ye feare of God or ells he shuld come to ye rope'.[9] Time after time recidivists stepped into courts, adding local colour to this larger perception. Three such persistent pests in Norwich were Bridgett Nobbs, John Quantrell and Jane Sellars, who finally drained the magistrates' good will and patience. The bridewell was a second home for recidivists like these and the whipping post was like an extra limb; each of them was branded with hot irons, and after two decades of offending they all ended their lives on the gallows.[10]

The tumbling-cards idea was not the only one that was matched to the punishment of petty crime. In sixteenth- and seventeenth-century Norwich (the time and place of this essay), population soared by 75 per cent between 1560–1620 as migrant-flows reached new peaks.[11] Populousness was something to brag about when comparing cities when physical size was culturally a matter of pride,[12] but its unwelcome side-effects included a glut of workers, crime scares, environmental scars, and a resource-pinch that troubled both the peace and purse. All of this contributed to a *perception* that mounting crime was both the cause and the consequence of urban sprawl and squalor. The thinking about crime and its roots in preambles to urban by-laws, for example, brooded on the urban litany of decay, dirt, disease and disorder, an environmental sense of human predicaments to which penal cultures were always being adapted. The sudden and (often) spectacular growth of cities like Norwich challenged governments to come up with new ideas to cope with the flows of vagrants. Petty crime was punished both quantitatively *and* qualitatively differently in the sixteenth century and after, and much of the energy and ingenuity in penal planning was at the point of first or minor offences, like vagrancy or small-scale theft. One such spurt of creativity was the opening of bridewells (or houses of correction) up and down the land; a strategy that has been called 'revolutionary' and 'pioneering'.[13] From now on magistrates had a handy prison nearby, where the most flexible definitions of disorder were stretched to cover nearly all of the situations in which the poor broke the law.[14] We might also remember that transportation across the ocean was in its first colours a measure for rounding up vagrants, minor-league thieves, rowdy servants, and other petty offenders in the early seventeenth century.[15]

II

In what follows I will plot the course of punishing petty crime in Norwich between 1560 and 1700. The city had apparently just emerged with only a few scrapes and scratches from a trouble-free and 'quiet' Reformation by 1575,[16] although the catholics who were frog-marched to Quarter Sessions present a different case.[17] This fast-growing city was also apparently a stable place to live in, apart from the cut and thrust of civic politics when nonconformists rocked the boat.[18] Yet the idea of a stable city or 'quiet Reformation' seems like an objective rather than a reality. The civic leaders' unease as another plague took its toll or as a fresh surge of vagrants, inmates or country workers poured into the city was a more certain perception of its mixed fortunes. Norwich was not a stable city.[19] A landmark census of the poor was taken there in 1570 and, like welfare reform, the decision to count was usually spurred on by panic.[20] In Norwich, it was 'crewes' of 'contynuall beggars', 'brute people', troublemakers skulking in 'back corners', 'uncurable diseases' and workshy layabouts that prompted the authorities to check on the houses of the poor. Worse still, it was claimed in 1570 that this desperate situation had 'nowe of late' 'growen to the full'.[21]

This statistical snapshot of poverty and its problems had a lasting impact on penal cultures. Its grim count of suffering, sinning, sickness and split families was a launching-pad for the opening of a bridewell in Norwich and a brand of penal policy that was geared towards the luckless, feckless and rootless poor: beggars, sponging inmates, luckless jobhunters, the workshy, sinning singlewomen, masterless young people and breadwinning mothers.[22] The policies that followed the revelations of the census included a greater element of institutionalization (the bridewell, pauper service schemes, work-discipline, and the revamping of the hospitals and lazarhouses), more streamlined systems of information gathering, and police reforms. It was claimed that the 1571–72 policy-renovation was an overnight success, and the corporation reckoned that the city profitted to the tune of £3,118 1/4d in the year after the census.[23] Yet the scheme's weak points were exposed later on, though only a few of its pieces were scrapped.[24] A terrible plague struck the city in 1579, enough to rattle administrative systems, if only for a while. We are not even sure that the scheme survived intact until the end of its first decade. Problems would not conveniently disappear, and in matter of fact they cut deeper as time passed. 'Dayly experyence' still showed that begging at doorsteps was a survival strategy for paupers in 1587. 'Daylie complyent' of round-the-clock binge drinking and landlords who smuggled 'evill' sluggards into 'secret corners' in 1586 were rude reminders that families were still splitting up and that vice was deeply ingrained in the crust of the city.[25] The scheme had been designed before the population boom at the end of the sixteenth century, and no prior plan, not even one as stunning in its scope as this one, could cope with this high pressure. The cry in 1602 was that the 'number of the poore people' is 'greatly increased'. Two decades later, trade-laws seemed old-hat and lagging behind 'the change and alteracon of tymes', while the city's journeymen snapped that country workers 'filled' the city in 1634, taking precious jobs and working at sweatshop rates.[26] Not all the planks of the scheme were broken up, however, many of them continued to help the city to cope in the testing times ahead, including rate collections and hand-outs, medical services, work schemes, pauper services and the bridewell, though at a steep cost.[27] It was hard to keep pace with sudden bursts of growth or boom-and-bust cycles of plague or dearth, however, even though new additions to poverty policies were put in place almost as soon as the 1570s programme was up and running.[28]

The census was not the first time that Norvicians had been numbered like this; households had been added up as recently as 1563 by the ecclesiastical authorities.[29] Numbering was not new in sixteenth-century Norwich, but the city did participate in a more general increase of surveillance, registration and the alphabetical ordering of records across early modern Europe.[30] In England, this resulted in part from the growing reach of the State and its larger scope of activity, made explicit in bulging Poor Law files, orders to keep up-to-date parish registers, and the 'statute bookes' that lined the shelves of the Guildhall.[31] Surveillance was also stepped up, and discovering or counting people were part and parcel of day-to-day government.[32] The 1570 census was a starting point but in later decades a wealth of information was put within fingertip reach of magistrates. Data about people, places and problems was listed in books, censuses and certificates, sorted into rows and tables, and often listed by alphabetical order, date order or residence. The weekly, monthly or less frequent counts and searches by officers meant that these statistical snapshots were working archives for policy-makers. In such ways, data were collected about the poor and rate collections,[33] drunks, banned games, crooked landlords,[34] 'big wenches and boys' lounging at home who were fit for service and women 'that goe at theire owne handes',[35] births, marriages and deaths,[36] sabbath-day breaches,[37] 'strangers',[38] catholics[39] and large-scale counts of several problem groups at once.[40] Books and registers were crammed into the city archives; subsidy books, muster lists, books of strangers, apprentices and freemen sorted by occupation, and a 'booke of bastardy'.[41] The same sort of numerate mindset was evident in steps to keep track of crime and criminals. Starting in 1624, a multivolume A–Z listing of prisoners who were charged at the City Quarter Sessions was kept up-to-date with an index for easy cross-referencing. These long lists of names stretched to seven 'search-books' towards the close of the century.[42] Like a jigsaw puzzle, these statistical and biographical scraps were pieced together to form large pictures of the city, its people and its problems. The common denominator linking these profiles to penal practice and culture was a concern with character.

We know little so far about the rates at which petty crimes were corrected in public, apart from the fact that they slumped to zero in the nineteenth century.[43] Bridewells have loomed large in previous work, and cucking stools have also recently resurfaced, not least because they are seen to measure swings in gender tensions. We think that these stools and the spectator event of carting 'sleazy' people whose morals fell short of civic standards around busy markets were in the main urban penalties, and that the history of these public performances is tucked away in town archives, unwritten and urban.[44] It is also possible that their use accelerated in the sixteenth century.[45] Yet we still lack a full study of the range of public penalties in a single town or rural spot over the sixteenth and seventeenth centuries.

What Norwich reveals is possibly peculiar and a pattern of its own, and it is also incomplete, but for what it is worth this is what we see in the records.[46] The Mayor's Court put 433 offenders in the stocks from 1580–1645, 297 of them were men (68.6 per cent); whipped 2,093 men (65.8 per cent) and 1,086 women; ducked 25 women in the river; locked 32 pests in the cage (only one was a man); and dragged 41 people around the market in carts. These are not amazing rates, though an annual average of 49 floggings is no light matter, especially as it falls not long after 1600. Just 139 offenders were whipped between 1660–1700, and on a sliding scale as time passed (55 in 1660–69; 44 in 1670–79; 40 in 1680–89). Not one whipping was dished out by the Mayor's Court in the 1690s. The cage was last used in 1666 when two scolds were put in it for a short spell.[47] Just five men were put in the stocks after 1660, the last one in 1687.[48] Finally, Marie Clay was the last scold to sit in the stool under water in 1670 when she was 'dipped thrice over her heade'.[49] The city Quarter Sessions books, however, seemingly, show us something else. The justices dished out 627 whippings between 1570 and 1700 (records are lost from 1618–29): 454 men (72.41 per cent) and 173 women. Unlike the Mayor's Court, however, there is no eye-catching fall in whippings. Their number did drop after 1650, but they zoomed up again four decades later. Other public penalties were used sparingly by the Sessions justices. Just five men and one woman were put in the stocks by justices between 1570–1700, the same number and ratio that were locked in the pillory. The cucking stool stayed on dry land, it is not mentioned once in the Sessions records. The fall in floggings and shamings is also signalled in payments to workmen and whippers. These fees disappear from the city's account books in 1599 (hiring carts to drag people around the market), 1601 (whipping vagrants and others), and 1620 ('setting up and taking downe the pillorie').[50] Fees stayed the same until they vanished (twopence for each whipping and fourpence for shifting the pillory and for hiring carts), and the subsequent silence is probably no more than a mere bookkeeping matter. We cannot have a full record of punishment in early modern Norwich, however, as on a number of occasions that we will never know offenders were dealt with on the spot by officers, and other summary steps have left no trace. The select women who kept an eye on the poor after the 1570 census, for example, were asked 'to laye sharpe correccion' on disordered women who did not work hard enough.[51] Nor was there just one pair of stocks in Norwich. Along with the pair in the market, they were dotted through the wards, serving as handy holding devices and warning signs to stay on the right side of the law.[52]

We hold *recorded* pieces in our hands today, but sometimes bright trends cannot be dismissed out of hand, like the fall in public penalties in seventeenth-century Norwich. It is also risky to rely on the records of one court when measuring penalties in a single city. Someone working with Mayor's Court files may say that public penalty was running out of steam by 1700, though somebody flicking through the Sessions books would be less sure, any fall would not seem so sudden or smooth, but sluggish and prone to zigzaggery, as in the 1690s when whipping rates bounced back. We should ask what the various courts did, and where offences were channelled (even those like mayors' courts and city sessions, where the same aldermen could sit on both benches). Meeting weekly, the Mayor's Court was like the city's voice, responding to long-running issues or the latest scare to hit the city. It was a response court, crafted by the body of the city it served.[53] This was why it used the bridewell so much. Its staple load (the idle, lewd, workshy or jobless) was the bridewell's bread and butter too. Positioned right at the front line of tackling petty crime and at the core of penal policy, the bridewell was a valued resource.

III

Yet the penal order in sixteenth-century Norwich valued publicity. The type, timing and location of punishment was seldom random, as penalties and their scenes affected each other, setting limitations and possibilities. Public penalties were usually timetabled to meet a rush of people and traffic into markets in a neat fusion of weekly routine and the correction of anti-civic acts. In 1566 seven men who loosened gate hinges so that cattle stormed through corn fields were locked in the stocks for 'half an hower about the myddle of the daye in the chefe of the markett'. Alice Wilson, who screamed 'very slaunderous words' at an alderman sat in the stocks as shoppers streamed into the market in droves. Public whippings often happened in the busy Saturday 'open market',[54] and to make sure that the point hit home for shoppers, as they were whipped 'from one end of the market to the other' thieves like Robert Beecham, who was given 'three stripes under the signe of every house he passes that way', were made to stop at landmarks like pubs to drag out the shame a little longer.[55] Another good weapon, it seemed, was to punish offenders at the scene of the crime after the event, an emphatic expression of civic order at the exact spot where it had been smeared. This was doubtless a reassurance to the shearman John Swan, who watched as John Cuthbert, who snatched a 'piece' of his 'worstead stuff', was whipped on the same patch of ground where the stolen 'stuff' was hanging when Cuthbert grabbed it.[56]

Above all, these penalties were meant to set an 'example' to toe the line, and the papers that were pinned to offenders to sum up their offences in capital letters cautioned literate lookers-on and their listeners. When John Hallybred spread 'lewde talke' in 1553, he had to 'openly confesse his offence and declare his sorrowe' on a market day, 'to the end he may be an example to all misordered persons'.[57] The semaphore of these spectator events was signalled by other symbolic touches. James Ure, who slipped poison into his master's meal, was stripped and whipped by two 'ladds'. In 1568 Robert Archer was spotted 'goyng about lyke a vacabonde and deseyving the people with counterfett ringes', and he was put in the stocks 'with a paper and the rynges hangyng thereon that the people myght knowe of hym and souche as he ys'. Other visual cues included Emm Bucknellon, who pinched wool from a shop in 1543, and was carted 'about the market with the woll skyn aboute her hede and a writing in witness of the same to th'example of other yll doers', and the sight of a goose-thief sitting in the stocks with 'a goose aboute her necke'. Other thieves sat in the stocks with linen, flax, roots, hay, bread and bacon draped over their shoulders; Margaret Morley sat in them with a hen clucking 'abowte hir neck'.[58] This mix of civic–legal–moral values was also on show when whippings happened next to the market cross, cage or pillory.[59] Symbolic, too, were the overlaps between penal and civic maps of display, as when the routes of street punishments followed the same streets used by major civic parades. Spotted in a barn one day in 1561 in the middle of 'the abhomynable act of whoredome', widow Leman was punished like this: she was 'lede aboute the markett' in rush hour and by the mayor's house over Costamny brydge and to Seynt Georges and over Fybrigg with a bason tynckled before hyr', where she was ducked in the river and after, still wet, 'with a bason afore hyr', she was marched 'up by Tumland and Seynt Andrew' and at long last released from her shaming lap of the city's most public streets at St Stephens.[60]

This visual aspect to penalty made sound sense in a city where the visual validation of order was a general rule of thumb. In Norwich, a careful and 'contynuall eye' was kept on strangers creeping into the wards; the courts banished troublemakers who taunted the magistrates by sneaking back into the city in their 'sight' after they had been told to leave the city for good; and 'special watches' were warned 'to have an eye' for carriers of the plague.[61] A very watchful '*eye*' was kept on order in terms both of vigilance and in visual signs in all walks of public life. The themes of order were depicted in neat columns in the tables of laws hanging in the town hall near the branding iron (with its bold block capitals 'C' and 'N'), and stamped on people, places and objects. Beggars and the poor who were looked after in hospitals were badged as a stigma or 'conysaunce' of their lowly dependency.[62] Other visual civic tags included the beadles' and bellmans' staffs, staves and badges, and their 'blewe cloath' coats that were also worn by marshals and the master of the Bridewell, with 'the cities armes' printed on a sleeve 'as a cognizance', or the tailor-made blue gowns that were the standard issue clothes for the 'poore patients' in the Great Hospital and the Boys' Hospital. Visual order mattered in a city that, like all others, passed laws to stop people dressing above their station in 'monsterous fasshions'; and where steep fines were dished out to officers and officials who turned up for town meetings in shabby clothes, or for high points in the civic calendar like the mayor's feast in clothes of 'white or light color' rather than 'decent' 'black or sad color' ('as becometh citizens'). Payments were also logged in the city's account-books for 'colleringe' and 'paynting' the beadles' badges and staves.[63] Order was visualized in colours, clothes, sticks and signs, and also in the visualizing of the city in maps hanging on the walls of the 'counsell chamber', both to swell civic pride and to keep the boundaries of the city always in sight.[64] A growing number of civic portraits were painted at this time, and more care and money was spent on civic ceremonies, and it is quite possible that the optic order was growing in importance in Norwich and other cities towards 1600.[65]

Penalties were key parts of this optic order, and it was no accident that the market to where so many routes pointed was dotted with authority symbols. Here bellmen shouted by-laws; a 'hoggshead of wyne' was cracked open 'in shewe of joy and triumph' to toast the lucky escape from the Spanish match (1623); and 'libellous and scandalous ballets', 'popish pictures' and rotten meat were put to the flames.[66] This civic politics was made explicit in the layout of the market-square; the grandiose guildhall was on its edge with a cage by its porch for offenders; a whipping post was put next to the market cross in 1584 and the pillory was 'sett upon' it in 1685. While plans for a handy-sounding three-in-one unit had been made in 1550 – the pillory in the market-square was 'newe repaired in all things' and a cage was 'made' in its 'west parte' and 'a newe per of stoks' 'sette' on it,[67] these visual cues were arranged around the cross, the market's hub and symbolic focus. The possession of a pillory or stocks (and gallows) sent signals that this was a city with power and authority.[68] Fees are regularly recorded for 'oyling and colouring the cuck-stoole' and keeping it sound with fresh timber, locks and bolts; fixing new locks to the stocks; and for patching up the pillory.[69] Unlike the monarch-minded gallows propaganda, however, this penal politics was civic and its symbolic muscle did not always consist in the active use of penalties, but in their careful situating across the townscape like a text to caution and tutor the townspeople as they passed by and looked on.

This optic order was also guarded carefully as it was always open to the possibility of mockery, vandalism or opposition. A late-night drinker was punished for 'makeinge a signe upon his hand in contempt' of the law,[70] and peace and quiet were never inevitable in the market, its prime site. Markets were noisy and the reading of civic orders was sometimes drowned out;[71] like cities, markets were busy and messy. Townspeople traded punches and insults there and left litter and muck; it was a chore to keep them spick and span.[72] Norwich market was troubled now and then by pickpockets tracking easy pickings, ballad sellers or singers, shoddy goods, and by mutterings about high prices. John Cobb was put in the cage in 1551 after he was overhead 'by many persons' grumbling that 'the poore can bye no corne' in the market 'for the ryche chorles take it from them'. A labourer warned that 'yt woulde be a hott markett' if he could not buy food with the few pennies he picked up for a day's work.[73] Worse still were flashpoints when civic leaders were on the receiving end of abuse. 'Poore men will speke one daye', a cobler barked at an alderman when he was told to shave his beard. 'Oh Kette, God have mercye uppon thy sowle', a trader murmured, in a good example of the sort of cross-currents that unsettled markets.[74] The cross attracted actors, singers and musicians like a magnet,[75] when it was meant to be a civic platform free from grime for official news only. Its improper use was a blot on the landscape, painful to see.

Not only was the state of the market unpredictable, some people also turned the tables and used penal images/language to threaten those who crossed their paths. A blacksmith called alderman 'Quasshe vyllane and pillorye knave', and shoved him 'with the bak of his hand'. A locksmith who 'resisted' a warrant, said 'that he would not set in the stocks unles Mr Craske' who signed the warrant 'sett with him'. Nicholas Gyrdler was put in prison in 1584 for telling the sheriffs that 'he wold sett them in the stocks' if they ever set foot in his house to search it. And Joseph Hall shocked the aldermen in 1616 when he said that the mayor had pinched his cloak and 'thretened that he would whipp him unles he payed vis viiid'.[76] The gallows, as ever, added menace. Seething after a row about land-rents, Richard Smith was overheard in 1583 saying that Robert Johnson 'is a ranck traytor and therof he shalbe hangyd, drawne and quartered and his iiii quarters sett upp in sundry placys and his hed upon a jubytt'. A dutchman landed in court in 1610 for 'makeing the signe of a paire of gallowse at an Englishman'; while one of the English gang 'said openlie in the court that he had rather live to see 100 Duchmen hanged then all the prentices of the weavers in Norwich'. John Bradshaw, who was picked up late at night singing a 'revilinge' song, shouted 'hange [Justice] Craske, hange rogues, hange pedlars'. While in 1563 a skinner blabbed that Mr Mychells 'was never a pore mans frynd but allweys a mortall foe to all pore men'. 'I could fynde in my hart to be his hangman', he snapped.[77] Like vandalizing monuments,[78] these verbal appropriations damaged the optic order with their reverse intentions.

Such words should never have been let loose, and in order to keep a tight grip on penal order the authorities encouraged expedient eavesdropping and hunted loudmouths who spoke out of turn. But penalties also provided chances for showing off, resistance, malicious glee, or a lark and laugh. Strolling along the streets one Sunday morning, a woman watched three men toss the ducking stool in the river off Fybrigg bridge. One Emey's wife shouted 'unfytting wordes' from the cart when she was 'sente aboute the market' with basins ringing for 'suffring of whoredome and bawdrye' in 1558. While in 1584 Robert Croft and Cicely Rochester were whipped 'in the great chamber with rodds' for 'leawdly abusing their bodyes', but Croft grabbed a chance when nobody was looking and jumped out of the window.[79] Edward Muir writes that 'Both the gazed and the gazed upon participate in the creation of a ritual', yet we know that rulers could not count on the victims and onlookers at the gallows to toe the line; talk of ritual in early modern England is still largely one-sided, and the audiences are left waiting in the wings, mute and hidden.[80]

We know plenty about scripts, therefore, but not enough about their performance on the day. In fact most penalties passed off without hiccups, but, even so, enough cases exist of tampering to make them too risky for total ease of mind. A labourer standing in front of William White when his ears were nailed to the pillory and cut off for seditious words in 1550, muttered 'that if Whites eares shulde be cutte off by his hedde he thoughte he shulde dye', and he openly wondered if justice had been done. When Cicily Booty was whipped in 1567, John Lyttle 'swore and sayed he wold they wold whypp hym', and warned that he would 'be even' with the mayor one day. While Richard Toly's wife bumped into the mayor on the street in 1566, 'and emong other talke that she had for that her sonne was in the stocks for tollyng a bell in the tyme of the sermon', she 'unadvisedly tolde Mr Mayor yt he was foresworne'. The next day, it was the mother who was seeking 'forgevenes openly uppon her knees at the stockes'.[81] 'Yf ye laye a blocke on my hele', Thomas Ebbots, 'a great molester', warned the Mayor's Court, I will 'wronge' you 'everye waye'. I do 'as moche good in Norwich' as the magistrates, he growled, and I would like 'the cittie to be better governed'.[82] People did not like being shackled in the stocks or by clogs or blocks. Some people broke out of the stocks; a labourer freed '2 infamous wenches out of ye stocks'. After Bennet Goodwyn was spotted in a garden in 1562 in 'the abhomynable acte of whoardome', she was carted around the busy Saturday market with 'a paper on her hed and tycnkelyd with a bason', and then taken to the cokingstol' at lunchtime 'and duckyd in the water'. A tailor later said that as she sat in the stool waiting to be dipped, a servant standing at her side gave 'a twytche at the paper that was pynned on her hed and so losened thone corner of the paper'. The tailor 'pynned it to her hat ageyne', but a few minutes later the servant 'twytched the paper agyene of her hed and rollyd it in his hands and caste it into the ryver'.[83]

Lax officers also raised unease, as when a constable was ticked off in 1656 for putting people in the stocks without first checking that the locks were 'fast' shut, and they 'were soone after lett out'. The whipper was shoved in the stocks in 1585 after 'beyng comaunded specyally to whipp well Hugh Jones' but 'favouryng hym' instead. Other whippers were whipped for 'not whipping' offenders. One was sacked for fiddling fees, while another was taken to task 'for whippinge of Wagstaffe upon his cloathes' in 1652.[84] These were thorny issues and little else could be expected when entitlements to punish and their civic meanings were guarded so closely. This was also a cause of squabbles with the spiritual authorities. Two men 'dwelling in Christe Church' were summoned before the mayor in 1563 'and askyd by what aucthority' they put a miller's man in the stocks'. None, the pair answered, we did it of our 'owne rasshe heds'.[85] To stay politically sound, penalties needed to be always lawful and under the tight control of the authorities. Officers who took matters into their own hands were treated like loose cannons. Two beadles were put in the stocks for whipping a 'pore prentice without anye direction or warrant soe to doe'. While a pair of watchmen who locked a king's soldier in the stocks in 1687, 'knowing him to be a soldyer and having not misdemeaned himself other than by being late out of his quarters', were themselves 'set in the stocks for the space of an hower'.[86]

Much in keeping with the patriarchal politics that was present in all situations, masters and parents had green lights to punish their servants or children. When Titus Pyles was prosecuted for handling stolen goods, the court ruled that he could be flogged at home by his father. Two masters whose boys mixed with 'lewd company' were asked to whip them 'at ther owne howsys'.[87] In so doing, domestic heads were always warned to follow a lawful line: to be firm but fair. But this was a fuzzy code of practice that was often termed loosely through its opposites, like 'extraordinary' or 'excessive beating'. Titus Oates was told to whip his light-fingered servant 'with a rodd and to have eight stripes upon his buttockes', and given 'liberty to come at [him] with a rodd so as he give not above eight stripes at any one tyme'.[88] But this was a rare moment of clarity, however, and the line between fair and foul force was otherwise thin and rarely set out in numerical terms. But if it was crossed, heavy-handed household heads ran the risk of a drubbing in court, as happened to a mistress who hit her maid 'with a stycke in beting her bowte the showlders and armes tyll she was blacke and blewe', and ripped 'her skyne and fleshe with a woolcard casting salte upon her body to her great grefe'; and a joiner who cut his servant's face with 'an edge toole' and shouted 'he will geve hym a mark that he shall remember so long as he lyve'. Husbands who bashed their wives 'blacke and blew', or women who hurt infants trusted to their care, received little pity. Cicely Sharpley was put in the stocks 'for whipping knyttyng children with a whipp of lether of x or xi stringes and so many knotts'.[89]

It was hoped that court action like this would be a forceful expression of the sole right of civic leaders to confer entitlements to punish. Also relevant was the level of attention that meant that punishing petty crime was rarely random. Like penalizing felony, it was a selective and calculated decision-making process, in which the courts *could* think long and hard at each step. This was why wild lashes by hot-headed masters or officers were blemishes on penal politics. Heat-of-the-moment acts upset the sequence of decisions that resulted in a sentence. Flexibility was always fine, so long as it stayed safely within the regulatory reach of the courts. Far from being set in stone, however, the punishment of petty crime was capable of being adapted to the circumstances of each case. It is helpful for us to imagine a pecking order of penalties where physical pain and/or shame sharpened at each next step. So it was that offenders in the stocks were warned that they would be whipped in public if they ever offended again. Other cases imply that whipping at a post was a lighter penalty than whipping at a 'cart's arse'.[90] As well as this penalty-ladder, each case raised a range of responses from the courts on a pendulum stretching from pity to flat impatience. Once a verdict was reached, several details provided scope to choose a suitable penalty: its location, duration of exposure, the span of the sentence, the number of dippings or lashes, or even the type of rod to whip with, though the birch that was used to thread the brushes that swept the Guildhall was the most commonly used wood. Thomas Hubbered was 'betten with roddes of twoe byrcche' for running from his master. While another boy 'was whipped with ballyses for pyckyng and stealyng'.[91]

The amount of time spent sitting in the stocks is not often noted, though the little material that survives reveals patterns. It was men who sat in shame for the longest spells. Six hours is the longest recorded stretch; a sentence that was dished out to drunks lacking the money to pay their fines. The longest noted spell for a woman was two hours in a case of 'ill rule' with a man. Other men were humbled there for three or four hours for fist fights, 'cosinage,' sneering 'oathes' or for drinking too much. Still others swallowed their pride there for two or three hours for snapping at officers or for falling out with masters. Both men and women were locked in the stocks for one hour or less for their sharp tongues, light fingers, or cruel handling of children.[92] The longest time spent on the pillory was four hours (a female counterfeiter) and the shortest was one hour (three male 'cheats').[93] Elizabeth Smith sat longest in the cage; three hours for 'skoldinge and livinge unquietly amongest hir neybors' in 1661.[94] The highest number of lashes handed out to a woman was six 'stripes' (though Marie Langdon was threatened with 'xx yerkes' if Thomas Welsh was ever found in her house again).[95] Welsh was on the receiving end of the heaviest penalty given to a man: he was whipped at the post by two men 'with two whippes' in 1601 for not staying away from Langdon. Each man was told to 'give him xxtie yerkes', and Langdon's husband was probably one of them, as she was married to the city whipper, Barnaby Langdon.[96] Other offenders were given six, eight, 12, 25 and 30 lashes,[97] though more numerous are commands to strip both men and women to the waist and to whip them 'till the blood come'.[98] There were fewer options to be this selective when cucking stools made a splash; three 'ducskyngs' is the only number written down by the clerk, though 'for her abhomynable lyvyng and skolding', Agnes Richards was sentenced 'to be duckyd in the water iii tymes at the leaste'.[99]

Several clues suggest that the selection of penalty was often the outcome of negotiation and deliberation; it was not always a speedy or inevitable conclusion, and crossings-out and scribblings in courtbooks are the messy marks of a change of mind. A dice-playing servant had a stroke of luck in 1588: 'at the poast' is crossed out in the records, and a scribble in the margins lets us know that, much to his relief, he was whipped inside in the 'great chamber' instead. The entry continues: 'if he shall hereafter bee found disobedyent to his master he shalbe whipped at the poast and sent to Brydewell'. Less lucky was Marie Clay; she was locked in the cage and 'dipped' three times in the river, 'house of correction' is crossed out in the entry.[100] No doubt snap-judgments were made, but sentences were usually reached after consideration of the case, conversations in which offenders did not lack a voice. Bargains were made and penalties were sometimes softened or suspended if offenders agreed that their next offence could not pass unpunished. Anne Mallard, who was whipped in 1583 for 'running abut the contrye' with a married man 'very suspiciously', declared herself 'contented to bee whipped about the market' if the couple ever slipped away again. The scold Joanne Thunder had a lucky let-off when the court ruled that 'she ys content' that if she was ever again 'justly accused' by a neighbour, she would be 'whipped at the post' or dumped in the stocks with no right of reply.[101] The scene, however, caused most fuss and distress. If a choice was on the cards, offenders would have plumped for a fairly shameless indoor whipping. After he was caught red-handed having sex in a garden, William Vincent begged 'that his faulte might not be openly knowne for feare that yt shoulde be an occasyon yt he shold be put owte of servyce'. An alderman 'wishte yt for his masters and for his father sake', that Vincent might not suffer in public but receive 'close ponyshment'.[102] The view was limited inside with just a handful of onlookers, but outside, in the 'open', civic spotlights beamed brightly and magistrates' played on the stomach-churning chance of becoming lodged in public memories with a soiled reputation. If you 'shall be taken stealing of wood or thornes in any mans ground att any tyme hereafter', Joseph Acres was warned at Bridewell in 1644, you will be 'punished att the carts arse about the market'. He knew what would happen if he ever offended again.[103]

The grounds for selectivity in handling of cases are not always clear. One thing is beyond doubt, however, recidivists were treated more harshly. Richard Ancell made a return trip to the Mayor's Court in 1561 after being 'taken in bawdry': he 'hath had warnyng' before and been 'ponyshed in the stocks, and yet wyl not leve his yll and nowty behavyor', the magistrates moaned, and so he was whipped around the market, 'with papers on his hed for whoredome'. Thomas Smith was 'whipped at the post' in 1587 for 'myching beyng the second tyme'. A discriminatory note is also apparent once in a while when pesky recidivists were whipped 'seveerly' or on more than one market day. A persistent vagrant was 'grievously whipped' in 1580; a Cambridge scholar was whipped for 'evill rule' in the same year, and warned to leave the city 'or else to be greviously whipped'.[104] Repeat offenders limited the court's room for action, while flexibility was less evident in tense times like plague when the case for 'examples' was more pressing.[105] Others, however, were treated with more sympathy; the magistrates were not icy people without feelings. Agnes Barker punched a constable in the winter of 1600 and would not stop scolding, but after some thought her ducking was more kindly timetabled for the warmer summer weather and water. While even though she was a niggling nuisance to her neighbours, Ann Davy 'submitted herselfe and craved the favoure' of the court, who, 'moved to compassion', shelved her punishment so long as she kept her loose tongue in check. In other cases, pregnant women or sick offenders had their punishments dropped or softened.[106]

These sympathetic touches and contrite acts exemplified a culture of civic clemency, not least when city officials were the victims. In 1668, Jonathan Watts called Alderman Markham 'a beggarly tarr bottled knave' and told passers-by that 'his father had like to have died in a ditch'. Not long after Watts was grovelling in court: 'hartely' saying sorry and 'humbly' thanking the alderman for being 'pleased to accept' my 'acknowledgment'. I 'shalbe obliged to him soe longe as I live', he finished.[107] In much the same way as a monarch's mercy to felons sentenced to swing at the gallows is interpreted as a political move,[108] a mayor's sympathetic touches in court put his paternal face on show. Simple poverty, for example, was enough to pick up pity.[109] Things looked bleak for Robert Browne in 1680 when he was about to be locked in the stocks and kept in prison until the next Quarter Sessions for 'speaking base, scandalous and false words against Mr Maior'. But he fell to his knees before the court,'begging pardon of God, ye king and Mr Maior', and was set free 'by ye clemency of Mr Maior'.[110] A political advantage was also gained when 'gentyll submyssion' by rowdy apprentices reestablished the terms of their subordination, as when John Hawe ended up in court for taunting his master in 1551, but persuaded magistrates that his sorrow was sincere. 'He is sorry for his mysdemeanors', they noted, 'and doth graunt to amend his qualities and desireth his master to be good to him and will willingly serve' from now on. A public expression of his remorse was fixed for a later date. Other 'open' pleas for forgiveness were held in churches.[111] Political points were also scored in other cases when patriarchal politics were put back on an even keel after a domestic disorder, as when a husband's 'speciall request' or master's 'intreaty' won a reprieve for their trouble-causing wife or apprentice. Other offenders were let off after they agreed to marry soon or to settle down with a master as quickly as possible. Still others were set free following a 'good report' from neighbours, friends or kin. Quite typical was Thomas Parker, who was ordered to be 'whipped and burnte throwgh the grystell of the right eare' after he was spotted wandering aimlessly through the city in 1573, but was spared this grisly penalty when John Fayercliff, 'beyng moved with pyttie and charitie', agreed to take him as his servant. A patriarchal relation was patched up or established by each one of these decisions.[112]

The Kent justice William Lambarde wrote that punishment is 'for the amendment of the offendor' and 'for examples sake that others may thereby bee kept from offending'.[113] In Norwich reforming offenders was a top priority of penal politics and culture, both indoors and outdoors. It was music to the ears of courts when offenders buckled and dropped to their knees, asking forgiveness, seeming sorrowful or repentant, seeking a second chance, and vowing to become better. When offenders seemed 'sorrowful', 'repentaunte' or 'penytente', a note of it was usually made in the courtbooks. 'My words [about you] were false and untrue', John Wright said to Elizabeth Pickerel, 'syttyng upon his knees' and seeking her 'forgyvenes'. Bennett Goodwyn's lover, William Vincent, sobbed when the mayor lectured him to 'live more in feare of God': 'doest not ye knowe that thou art forbedeen by ye word of God to take ye membars of Jesu Cryste and to make them the membars of an harlott?' The mayor was moved: 'seyng tokens of repentance', he said, I 'cold not abstayne from weping myself'. Vincent's father also burst into tears. This puddle of tears reminds us of character and also of water washing away dirt, as when women were dipped or ducked in running water. And work on minds could begin before they touched water. Even as Goodwyn sat strapped in the cucking stool perched on the river's edge, an alderman's wife whispered in her ear, 'perswading' her to 'amende her evyll lyfe and confesse her faulte to the people'. [114]

The mind-designs of these short shocks have become lost in advice given to us by some scholars to split bodies (the physical) and souls (the emotional) in early modern penal ideas.[115] This tidy split would have seemed strange to early modern people: to the godly, for instance, who made minds their top concern; to advocates of spiritual medicine to soothe suffering; or in penal systems in which character could make or break cases, and mind-acts like penitence or amendment were perfect outcomes.[116] Physical and emotional matters were coupled, as in Erasmus's visual–verbal remark that the 'outward honesty of the body cometh of the soul well composed and ordered', or when Norwich's mayor grumbled that lazy beggars were riddled with disease and 'fylthynesse of body as they be browt into miserable state, to the great peril both of their bodies and souls'.[117] Emotions did not suddenly freeze in the stocks or when whip-sting burned; sensations of pain were always cultural, shaping sentiments. Hard work and punishment were mental corrections in this culture, not least because pain was understood to be a matter of the mind, turning thoughts with its spasms.[118] Time after time people were told to run through their consciences and to think about what they had done. This is even evident in the roll-call of failure: no amount of urging could put the Bate brothers on a better path, for instance, 'they will not bee by any frynds reclaymed', magistrates groaned; while John Baylie was turned out of the Boys' Hospital for running away day-after-day 'and other misdemeanours of which [it was said] he cannot be reclaimed [even] tho he hath bene corrected'.[119] Many wrongdoers walked free after a pledge to become better and to learn from their slip-ups, like the scold Martha Swanson who promised 'to live orderly' ever after; Thomas Hayward, who jeered at the mayor and was forgiven following his 'promys makyng never so to behave hymself ageyn'; and the tailor charged with 'ill rule' in 1559, who was let off after dropping to his knees and giving his word to 'becom a good and civill man' for the rest of his life. After Kett's Rebellion (1549), Doctor King visited the protestor William Mutton in his sickbed to 'exhort' him 'to be a newe man and to be sory for his offences'.[120]

These were all mind-actions or acts of will, involving changes of character and mind (or heart), amendment, submission and repentance. Not all vows to live cleanly were sincere, but most people crop up only once in records and disappear forever. Others, like Adam Mitchell, were more crafty. The amount of time he spent at Widow Nyckerson's house attracted attention in 1568, but he escaped with just a warning after pledging to lead 'a honest and vertuous lyfe'. Mitchell did not keep his promise, however, and he was later carted around the market for not being able to stay away from Nyckerson, 'contrary' to his vow 'and the godly admonicon' of the bench.[121] Character-change fitted well with the idea that first faults were the roots of awful felonies, and with the selectivity that was evident when people were put on trial. On top of this, reformation was *the* cultural issue of the day, and one of its symbols and strategies was to change people for the better. Piety and penalty were linked in 'godly admonicons' or 'exhortations' that were common in courts.[122] The Reformation offered symbols and strategies, and one of them was turning people into something else. Reforming manners was a long-running concern in the sixteenth and seventeenth centuries, and it would seem strange if it did not affect penal culture in Norwich where religious reform was warmly greeted early on.[123] The punishment of petty crime provided golden opportunities to push religious reform along, as when whippings were stopped after 'promise of reformation', when offenders were asked to look into themselves and to amend, and when the bowling alley addict Thomas Bunting was dumped in Bridewell and put to work to 'live in order'.[124]

IV

Work that links petty crime to reforming behaviour usually looks at opportunities for character change inside houses of correction or 'reformation', as the one in Acle (Norfolk) was aptly called.[125] The sharpest legal mind of the early seventeenth century said that few are sent 'to the house of correction or working house but they come out better'. While the leading justices handbook of the day urged courts to shove slack timewasters into one, so that 'by labour and punishment of their bodies their froward natures may be bridled, their evil minds bettered, and others by their example terrified'. We might also recall that the prisoners' mantra in the Sudbury house included these lines: 'the punishment wherewith we be now scourged is much less than our deserts', but our hope is 'that it may work with us a reformation of our former life'.[126] Even if the bridewell was first and foremost a discipline-structure, the hope that people would change there for the better was real enough. From its first days, Norwich Bridewell was a reforming place, and it did not lose this care for character. Mary Soamer was sent home from there in 1618 after her 'promise of reformacon'; Florence Beales was let out in 1672, following an allegation of 'leaud and scandalouse conversation' after her 'promise to reform her life'; while Margaret Rutter was released into her brother's care in 1683 after promising 'to reforme her evell and lewd life'.[127]

Like punishment, work was a mental correction, a moral tonic, and a social glue that helped society to stick together. So, the prisoners spent a large part of the day doing character-building work at Bridewell's own mills and looms, and maybe picked up a few extra pennies for cleaning the vault or some other dogsbody task.[128] They were paid to work, if only in kind (food and board), though it was hoped that the chief pay-off would be calculated in clean thoughts or saved souls. On top of work, a preacher picked from a parish floated pious thoughts through sermons and catechizing, as also happened in the city's other prisons and hospitals: the Great Hospital (opened in 1249), the Childrens'/Boys' Hospital (1621), or the Girls' Hospital (1650). Preachers picked up four pounds for reading prayers and testing catechumens in the early seventeenth century. A dreary 15-hour workday in summer at the Bridewell (it was shorter in winter) was lightened by meal-breaks (30 minutes) and a 15-minute pause for prayer. Like householders, it was hoped that Bridewell would turn troublemakers into sound citizens, using a stick when necessary (the mayor was called Bridewell's headmaster). Indeed, the Bridewell was called a 'house'. The household, the linchpin of the social order was a natural rhetorical resource, and this domestic spin to staff/inmate relations was meant to signify the Bridewell's model pedagogic purposes, ones in which identities and moralities would be constructed in better ways by solid work, sound religion and sharp correction.[129]

The explicit hierarchical ordering of the outside world was also expressed in descriptions of Bridewell's inmates as 'the poor', a designation that implied both subordination and responsibility, most revealingly in orders about bread rations and health care.[130] The anthropologist Mary Douglas writes that 'Institutions bestow sameness'.[131] This is what they try to do, though it does not always work out that way; but they do seek to confer similar identities on their inmates and to make them known around the city. The Bridewell gave institutional structure to attitudes towards the poor that were broadcast in local and central planning and policy: only the workshy and dangerous poor were locked up there. Its inmates were mostly poor, more or less evenly split between the sexes (though exact ratios seesawed over time), and likely to be family-misfits, unruly servants, rootless vagrants, or any other whose antisocial acts fell within pliable categories like idle, lewd or disorderly. The Bridewell was called on when other institutions like the family could not cool domestic disputes or patch up broken households. It was the last port of call in a domestic storm, as when Martha Thornton refused point-blank 'to live with her husband' and threatened 'to leave her child in the street', or when Grace Newton's son was stuck in Bridewell after abusing his mother 'and leavinge his masters worke'.[132]

We now tend to tone down the impact of bridewells, especially after 1600 when the pace of committals quickened and it is argued that with little time to spare for character reform, bridewells became mostly punitive places.[133] The extent of institutionalization was limited in Norwich, as it was in other towns and cities, and it is fair to question it.[134] No regular run of prisoner admission and discharge books survives today for Norwich Bridewell, and with only patchy evidence to work with (mostly committals or release-orders from the courts) we will never have a full picture of traffic in and out. For what it is worth, however, 1,085 people are recorded passing to the Bridewell from the Mayor's Court in the 75 years after Joan Gedding entered the history books by becoming the first person to make this trip in July 1571, after she got into trouble for 'mysrule'.[135] Movement was slow in the first three decades or so, but it soon speeded up: 64 committals were noted before 1600, though this number leaped more than tenfold up to 1640, and peaked from 1620–40 when 640 offenders were locked up (59 per cent of the total tally). Far fewer offenders were sent to the Bridewell from Quarter Sessions. Just a handful were shipped before 1600,[136] though this number rose after 1630 and stayed quite high over the rest of the century, almost entirely owing to the locking-up of thieves and acquitted or branded felons. The numbers sent from the Mayor's Court dropped after 1660, though not as quickly as the sudden plunge in whipping. The records reveal the names of just 57 men and 77 women who were carried to the Bridewell between 1660–1700, but as we shall shortly see, this number is unlikely to be the full picture.

In matter of fact, counting like this is only one way of measuring Norwich Bridewell's impact, and it is a limiting one at that. The Bridewell's importance cannot be understood in terms of the sum-total of its beds or cells, it had cultural and mental impacts too. Brand-new prisons (even ones in existing buildings) altered physical and mental landscapes for better or for worse. But there were a few flashpoints, however, as when Francis Barton stormed into Bridewell and 'cut the work' of his wife, leaving no doubt about what he thought of her being locked up. There were also some careless quips, like the one in 1613 when the bellman lost his job after he 'publiquely shouted' that 'yf any' are 'desirous to have their neckes broke yf they cam to Bridewell yt should be done', reminding us that bridewells were imagined as chilly places.[137] This was an idea that was used in calculated ways when the courts warned troublemakers that they would be slung in one unless they got back on the right track. 'Mere fear' of being put in Bridewell was a pressure that was commonely used, though it is impossible to quantify.[138] Civic rulers said that it was the 'feare and terror' of Bridewell that caused the number of 'whoremasters, whores, and vacabondes' to drop by nine-tenths not long after it first opened.[139] But the Bridewell was also a symbol of civic values and activism. It was a small comfort for the little ring of governors who ran the city, and also for anybody else who felt uneasy about the nasty side-effects of the city's quick growth. Civic-minded Norvicians liked to be associated with the civic glitter of Bridewell, and felt lucky to have it nearby working for their benefits, and so they reached into their pockets and gave money and materials quite freely.

Movement in and out of bridewells after 1600 is sometimes imagined along the lines of revolving doors, yet records show that offenders were not simply shunted in and out of Norwich Bridewell, one after another. It was not just a whipping place, it never had been. Significantly, its inmates were called 'prisoners' who were locked up in a 'prison'. Nor was this mere window-dressing; ideas of confinement as a tough corrective penalty existed at this time.[140] The metal gadgets listed in Bridewell's stock-rolls to limit freedoms and movement included 'cheans for prysoners', pothooks, 'blockes with shackles', manacles, handcuffs, and iron bars to block the windows.[141] Sentences varied greatly, doubtless depending on the character of the suspect or the offence. Henry Gigges was put in a cell from sunrise to sunset one day in 1614, while the perpetual recidivist Margaret Utting was packed off to the Bridewell in 1598 'to dwell and remaine for ever'. Some prisoners were only kept overnight, to shake them up a little. Others stayed longer than this, for a few weeks or months, or more. The tearaway servant Jeremy Beck was given a six-month dose of hard work in 1646 after his master could take no more of his bad behaviour. A number of women who gave birth to illegitimate children were shut up in Bridewell for a year, though nearly all of them were let free before the year was up.[142] In other cases it is simply said that prisoners had been locked up in Bridewell for a 'longe tyme', or that they would stay locked up there until a condition was met: Mary Bishop was not to be let free 'untill her husband shall desire to have hir out', and many others were asked to find a service to get their freedom back again.[143] The number of thieves sent in from the Quarter Sessions after being branded, acquitted or simply suspected of felony, or on lesser charges of petty theft, edged up after 1660, as it did in other places. Most of these thieves were sentenced to one month of grinding work, though longer stretches were not uncommon as when John Gidding and Edward Bunn were 'acquited of felony' in 1635 and put in Bridewell 'to remayne a yeare'.[144] These sentences might seem on the short side to us, and the 'faint' impact of bridewells on their inmates has indeed been measured by the amount of time spent there. But we should not make this calculation by today's standards when long sentences are common and pass almost unremarked, unless unfair. A few months of hard work may have been a scary prospect, enough to crush some people. Maybe the months seemed to stretch out into the dim and distant future. This, after all, was a culture that was not yet used to stiff or soft custodial sentences.

The opening of the Bridewell was a rare watershed in Norwich society and culture. From now on, the character-criticisms that lay behind reforming offenders were backed up by penalties which, after the Bridewell, included a much greater institutional slice. Indeed, Bridewell's domestic description as a 'house' nicely shows how punishing petty crime was becoming more and more of a private matter in the seventeenth century. Like a seesaw, the dip in whipping after 1660 was counter-balanced by a rush in the passage of prisoners to the Bridewell, and this balancing act was no accident; the Bridewell did change the nature of penalties in Norwich. The courts tested a larger range of penalties and matched them to crimes in fresh ways over the seventeenth century.[145] Most noticeably, significant shifts scattered the scenes of whipping. The locations of 1,902 whippings were jotted down by the Mayor's Court clerk (just over half the recorded total). In the quarter-century 1562–87, 231 offenders were whipped in the market, and 391 (63 per cent) were whipped behind walls in the 'great chamber', 'council chamber' or 'assembly chamber'. This situation then swings the other way in the period 1625–46, when just 94 offenders were whipped in front of the townspeople, and as few as 32 were flogged behind doors (though a portion of the committals to Bridewell are likely to have been for a whipping followed by a swift discharge). After 1660, however, it tips back, and the Bridewell and other indoor venues were the scenes for most whippings ordered by the Mayor's Court. By then, the sources even speak of a whipping as the 'usual corection' at the Bridewell.[146] The Sessions dished out most outdoor whippings after 1660 for this reason: petty larceny was commonly prosecuted there and it was almost always punished with the whip.[147] This was the main cause of the two views of whipping from the two courts. One thought that springs to mind after reading the Norwich materials is that the fall in the public punishment of petty crime was quickest (or earliest) in the corporation courts, while whipping had a longer shelf-life at the city Quarter Sessions where most petty thieves ended up.

We always take risks with accuracy when we use records of prosecution and punishment; we worry that some administrative switch or hitch might spoil what we find. This is certainly the case with correcting petty crime, and this state of affairs is muddled still further by the accelerating use of summary justice in the seventeenth century. When all is said and done, however, there were still fewer outdoor whippings as time passed, though there were a couple of slumps in whipping at the Mayor's Court that were so sudden that they cannot be easily explained by long-term adjustments. Twelve petty offenders were whipped by the court in 1683 according to the records, but just five floggings followed in the next seven years, and not one in the 1690s. Up to 1683 things had been ticking along slowly, though the overall pattern was still downwards. Government was not suddenly toppled or suspended after 1683, and the courts were still meeting. What did send shock waves through the city at this precise time, however, was its charter controversy. The charter was surrendered and redrafted in 1683, and the political debris from this hot-tempered partisan wrangle included a sweeping purge of Whig aldermen. It is quite likely that a period of administrative torpor followed this shake-up of civic government when splits occurred within as well as between the Tories and Whigs. The crown did have an interest in curbing the powers of boroughs, though no specific mention is made of entitlements to punish in the redrafted charter. Nonetheless, legal uncertainties may have lingered for a while. The spotlight also fell more heavily on dissenters. Quakers were piled up in prison in the 1680s, and this may well have rechanelled time, energy, money and strategies. At any rate, such troubles were shocks, adequate enough, one suspects, to rattle administrative systems for a while. And later maybe, when things began to settle down, some practices could have been altered for a good while.[148]

The charter storm occurred at a late point in the fall in recorded whipping and it could not have been its cause, though it certainly speeded it up. Towards the close of the seventeenth century, market-goers were more likely to buy medicine or ballads or to see puppet shows (the subjects of earlier bans) in the marketplace or on its edges than watch a whipping.[149] Rather than look on as a whip cracked open a back, the shoppers, strollers and drinkers watched dancing horses, dancing dogs, elephants, camels, tigers, porcupines, 'strange fish', a baboon that did strange feates', eight-foot high Joseph Farrell, 'a little dwarfe of 37 years of age with musicke', 'a fairy dwarfe', 'the girle without bones', 'a monstrous hayre chyld', 'a strange child with two heads', 'a child with six fingers on each hand and six toes on each foot', 'a woman without handes' who was given four days to show 'workes done with her feete', 'a monstrous man with two bodyes from the Indies', and 'a monstrous man' taken 'amongst the hills of Carinthia', who munched 'roots of trees'.[150]

Much existing work points to the eighteenth century as *the* century of pivotal change when explanations are most necessary for a number of telling changes in penal practice and culture. Some sloppy work may make us think that little happened in earlier centuries when it seems that whipping continued unrelenting. It was not like this in Norwich, however, as the penal limelight was dimming there before 1650, when the number of death sentences also fell from its Elizabethan summit.[151] The move of penalties inside has been seen for a long while as the result of the steady spread of civility and the taming of stormy instincts by a better-bred people who were calmer and cooler.[152] The apparent cruelty of these outdoor rebukes sometimes seals the case for historians who believe that early modern society was violent, whose people like taut strings were always on the point of snapping. The timing of some key turning points in Norwich muddles matters, however. In the first place, the course of whipping was never even over time, but confused by both dips and leaps in the seventeenth century. Nor is it certain that Norvicians were softer skinned or brimming with fellow-feeling after 1600. If they were, then we must fiddle around with the chronology of civility (if it ever happened in that way). But any explanation of the whipping slump must take on board the implications of the Bridewell for public penalty, and a better line of explanation may be a pragmatic one – that it was felt that the Bridewell was doing a good job in the scramble to keep order, and that punishments in crowded public spots were risky (that is why we spent some time looking at the scenes of optic order, like the market). We could also relax our critical categories a little and not always oppose private and public penalties in endless replacements or displacements (at least not yet before 1700). The Bridewell was not an absolute alternative to outdoor rebukes: its 1622 stock-take listed two whipping posts, a 'chaire for unruly persons', and a pair of stocks.[153] The courts did not keep all their eggs in one basket; they liked to work with all of their options in the best ways possible, especially after the Bridewell first opened its doors, and the punishment of petty crime went through one creative cycle after another.

* * *

Unless the records have tricked us, punishing petty crime in Norwich was moving out of public view after 1650. Not that the optic order was any less valued as time passed. Its propaganda value was just as evident in 1699 when paupers had to sew badges 'on the right shoulder of their outward garment' when they queued up for hand-outs; or when William Dodwell, lecturing at the Oxford Assizes half-a-century later, reminded the judges that 'the welfare of every worthy member of society is interested in bringing the wilful disturbers of it to publick shame and punishment'.[154] We know that public whipping rates bounced back in London over the eighteenth century after an earlier downswing,[155] but we do not yet know if this was so in Norwich, as the relevant work has not yet been done. But I suspect that they did go up in bursts and spurts in a century when some scholars tell us that empathy and sympathy at long last became expressed emotions after centuries of mean-spiritedness and numbness. Whipping's jagged chronology leaves this forward emotional march looking a little shaky to say the least. We are now back where we started, with the lack of balance in current coverage of punishment in the past. When it comes to punishment, shifting sentiments are more often than not reckoned in execution rates, themselves less helpful in this light than they might first appear. Things look different from a petty crime slant, they nearly always do. Just like five centuries ago, petty crime and felony should exist side-by-side in explanations of past penal practices and cultures. Only then will we get the full picture, as untidy as it is.

Notes

1 Michael Foucault, *Discipline and Punish: The Birth of the Prison* (Harmondsworth, 1991), 18. The better guides to Foucault for historians include David Garland, *Punishment and Modern Society: A Study in Social Theory* (Oxford, 1990), chaps 6–7; Randall McGowen, 'Power and humanity, or Foucault among the historians', in Colin Jones and Roy Porter eds, *Reassessing Foucault: Power, Medicine and the Body* (1994), 91–112; and Martin Dinges, 'Michael Foucault's impact on the German historiography of criminal justice, social discipline, and medicalization', in Norbert Finzsch and Robert Jutte eds, *Institutions of Confinement: Hospitals, Asylums, and Prisons in Western Europe and North America, 1500–1950* (Cambridge, 1996), 155–74. Good recent summaries of penal reform include Randall McGowen's chapter in this volume, and V.A.C. Gatrell, *The Hanging Tree: Execution and the English People, 1770–1868* (Oxford, 1994).

2 See, most recently, John Beattie, *Punishment and Policing in London 1660–1750: Urban Crime and the Limits of Terror* (Oxford, 2001); Peter King, *Crime, Justice, and Discretion in England, 1740–1820* (Oxford, 2000); and Randall McGowen's chapter in this volume.

3 J.A. Sharpe, *Judicial Punishment in England* (1990), chap. 2; and 'Civility, civilizing processes, and the end of public punishment in England', in Peter Burke, Brian Harrison, and Paul Slack eds, *Civil Histories: Essays Presented to Sir Keith Thomas* (2000), 215–30.

4 A pioneering study of petty crime is Robert B. Shoemaker, *Prosecution and Punishment: Petty Crime and the Law in London and Rural Middlesex, c. 1660–1725* (Cambridge, 1991). See also A.L. Beier, *Masterless Men: The Vagrancy Problem in England, 1560–1640* (1985); Joanna Innes, 'Prisons for the poor: English bridewells 1555–1800', in F. Snyder and D. Hay eds, *Labour, Law, and Crime: A Historical Perspective* (Oxford, 1987), 42–122; Martin Ingram, 'Juridical folklore in England illustrated by rough music', in Christopher Brooks and Michael Lobban eds, *Communities and Courts in Britain, 1150–1900* (1997), 61–82; Paul Griffiths, 'Meanings of nightwalking in early modern England', *The Seventeenth Century*, (1998), 212–38; and the chapters by myself and Martin Ingram in this book.

5 Bob Shoemaker writes that 'The impact of misdemeanour prosecutions was felt in all corners of society. Perhaps nine times as many defendants were involved in misdemeanour prosecutions as in felony cases, and they came from a wider range of social classes than other types of litigation' and 'included a far more diverse collections of offences than felonies' (*Prosecution and Punishment*, 6).

6 Martin Ingram, '"Scolding women cucked or washed": a crisis in gender relations in early modern England?', in Jenny Kermode and Garthine Walker eds, *Women, Crime and the Courts in Early Modern England* (1994), 48–80, quoting 60. There were, of course, eight hanging days each year in London.

7 However, Gatrell writes that 'until the collapse of the criminal code in the 1830s no ritual was so securely embedded in metropolitan or provincial urban life. Nor was any so frequent' as the gallows (*Hanging Tree*, 30).

8 Cesare de Beccaria, *On Crimes and punishments*, 1764, ed. Henry Paolucci (New York, 1963), 57.

9 Norwich and Norfolk Record Office (NRO) Norwich Mayor's Court (NMC) Interrogatories and Depositions Book 1C, fo. 26. All the following archival references are to manuscripts held at the NRO.

10 For Bridgett Nobbs see Norwich City Quarter Sessions (NCQS) minute books 1639–54, fos 81v, 101, 135, 166, 178; 1637–64, March Sessions 1646. For John Quantrell see NCQS minute books 1639–54, fos 9, 110, 130; 1637–64, fos 62, April Sessions 1659, September Sessions 1660, January Sessions 1661; 1654–70, September Sessions 1661, April Sessions 1663, December Sessions 1663; 1671/91, April Sessions 1674. And for Jane Sellars see my 'Masterless young people in Norwich, 1560–1645', in Paul Griffiths, Adam Fox and Steve Hindle eds, *The Experience of Authority in Early Modern England* (Basingstoke, 1996), 146–86, esp. 146–7.

11 Vagrancy figures are provided in my 'Masterless young people', 154–9. A brief guide to conditions in Norwich after 1600 is also offered there. Population data is presented in David Harris Sacks and Michael Lynch, 'Ports, 1540–1700', in Peter Clark ed., *The Cambridge Urban History of Britain, Volume II, 1540–1840* (Cambridge, 2000), 384.

12 See Paul Slack, 'Great and good towns', in Peter Clark ed., *Cambridge Urban History*, 347–76; and 'Perceptions of the metropolis in seventeenth-century England', in Burke *et al. Civil Histories*, 161–80.

13 Quoting Beier, *Masterless Men*, 164; and Innes, 'Prisons for the poor', 42, 53. See also Robert Jutte, *Poverty and Deviance in Early Modern Europe* (Cambridge, 1994), 169.

14 Innes, 'Prisons for the poor'; Shoemaker, *Prosecution and Punishment*, chap. 7; J.A. Sharpe, *Crime in Seventeenth-Century England: A County Study* (Cambridge, 1983), 151–2.

15 The early history of transportation is described in Joanna Innes, 'The role of transportation in seventeenth- and eighteenth-century English penal practice', in Carl Bridge ed., *New Perspectives in Australian History* (1990), 1–24; and in my forthcoming book, *Lost Londons: Crime, Control, and Change in the Capital City, 1545–1660.*

16 Muriel C. McClendon, *The Quiet Reformation: Magistrates and the Emergence of Protestantism in Tudor Norwich* (Stanford, 1999).

17 NCQS minute books 1581–91, fos 156, 185–5v, 191v, 198v, 204v, 214v, 219v, 229; 1591–1602, fos 13v–14; 1637–64, fo. 25.

18 John T. Evans, *Seventeenth-Century Norwich: Politics, Religion, and Government, 1620–1690* (Oxford, 1979), 42, 63–4; John Pound, *Tudor and Stuart Norwich* (Chichester, 1988), 85, 123–4, 161.

19 Paul Slack writes that 'In reality, godly cities were for the most part unquiet inhabitations' (*From Reformation to Improvement: Public Welfare in Early Modern England* (Oxford, 1999), 29). Epidemics in Norwich are described in Paul Slack, *The Impact of Plague in Tudor and Stuart England* (1985), 126–43. See also Norwich Corporation (NC) Assembly Books 5, fos 89v, 238, 244; Assembly Folio Books 5, fos 40v–1, 116v–17, 126, 349v; 8, fo. 48v; Clavors Book 1, fos 141, 142v; NCQS minute book 1630–38, fo. 103 (inmates); NCQS minute book 1630–38, fos 14, 30v, 42v, 46; NC Assembly Folio Book 5, fos 41, 175v, 195 (country journeymen).

20 Peter Burke, *A Social History of Knowledge From Gutenberg to Diderot* (Oxford, 2000), 117; Paul Slack, *Poverty and Policy in Tudor and Stuart England* (Harlow, 1988), 48–52, 53–5; id., *From Reformation to Improvement*, 154; Margaret Pelling, 'Healing the sick poor: social policy and disability in Norwich, 1550–1640', in Pelling, *The Common Lot: Sickness, Medical Occupations and the Urban Poor in Early Modern England* (Harlow, 1998), 79–102, esp. 101.

21 'The Mayors Booke for the Poore,1571–1580', fos 1, 2, mayoral proclamation (1571), fo. 11v, corporation letter to the Archbishop of Canterbury (1572), fos 16, 16v. Cf. Beier, *Masterless Men*, 110. John Pound plays down anxieties about beggars in the making of the census, most notably because the number of recorded prosecutions was so low in the years leading up to the census (Pound, *Census*, 7–8; and *Tudor and Stuart Norwich*, 110–11). He and others believe that the flashpoint leading to the census was the round-up of a pack of plotters in Norwich in the fall-out from the Northern Earls conspiracy (1569); a small scare, however, that was not even listed in the narrative of disorders in which the city wrote down its reasons for the census. See Dutch and Walloon Strangers Book 1564–1643, fo. 23; John F. Pound ed., *The Norwich Census of the Poor* (Norfolk Record Society, 40, 1971), 8–9; id., *Tudor and Stuart Norwich*, 141–2; McClendon, *Quiet Reformation*, 224–5, 229–30; Robert Tittler, *The Reformation and the Towns in England: Politics and Political Culture, c.1540–1640* (Oxford, 1998), 314.

22 This census (and surveillance more generally) will be more fully discussed in my forthcoming 'Numbering Norvicians: information, institutions, identities, 1570–1660', in C. Rawcliffe and R. Wilson eds, *History of Norwich*. I, of course, make use of John Pound's pioneering work on the census. Censuses of the poor in this and other towns and cities are discussed more fully in Slack, *Poverty and Policy*, 73–85. The findings of the census have been more fully scrutinized by Maggie Pelling in her 'Illness among the poor in early modern English towns', and 'Old age, poverty and disability in early modern Norwich: work, remarriage and other expedients', both of which can be found in her *Common Lot*, 63–78, 134–54.

23 'The Mayors Booke for the Poore, 1571–1580', fo. 5v. And see Pound, *Census*, 20–1; and *Tudor and Stuart Norwich*, 143.

24 The deacons and select women who were appointed in the wards were victims of uncertainty about the legality of the committal process to the Bridewell in 1588 (NC Assembly Book 5, fo. 39).

25 NC Assembly Books 5, fos 21–1v; Assembly Folio Book 4, fo. 38v. This is also noted by Pound, *Tudor and Stuart Norwich*, 146–7. Cf. Pelling, 'Healing the sick poor', 83.

26 Pelling, 'Old age, poverty and disability', 136; NC Assembly Book 5, fo. 273; Assembly Folio Book 5, fo. 169; NMC courtbook 16, fo. 470v.

27 Pelling, 'Healing the sick poor', 100–1; Pound, *Tudor and Stuart Norwich*, 147, 160.

28 NMC courtbooks 14, fo. 196; 16, fos 320v–1, 322–2v, 325–6v, 327–8, 3289–9v, 351v–2; NCQS minute book 1629–36, fos 27–7v, 30v–1; NC Assembly Folio Books 3, fo. 320; 6, fos 4v, 38, 70, 88v, 119v, 121; Assembly Book 5, fos 160v, 175v, 273–4, 427. See also Slack, *Impact of Plague*, 126–43; and my 'Masterless young people', 165–6; Pelling, 'Healing the sick poor', 100–1; Pound, *Tudor and Stuart Norwich*, 149.

29 NC Assembly Folio Book 3, fos 29v, 34v; Paul Slack, *From Reformation to Improvement*, 24. Carole Rawcliffe, *Medicine for the Soul: The Life, Death and Resurrection of an English Medieval Hospital* (Stroud, 1999), chaps 7–8; Pound, *Tudor and Stuart Norwich*.

30 The rise of the so-called 'surveillance' or 'paper state' in sixteenth- and seventeenth-century Europe, and the greater use of alphabetical order/indexing is described in Burke, *Social History of Knowledge*, 117–19, 184–7, and will be the subject of my forthcoming book *Paper States: Penal Cultures and Surveillance in Early Modern England*.

31 Two recent discussions of the growth of the state at this time are Michael J. Braddick, *State Formation in Early Modern England, c. 1550–1700* (Cambridge, 2000); and Steve Hindle, *The State and Social Change in Early Modern England, c. 1550–1640* (Basingstoke, 2000). Payments for buying and binding 'statute bookes' in Norwich include Chamberlains' Account Books 1603/25, fos 225, 417; 1625/48, fos 14, 104; Clavors Book 1, fos 54, 98v.

32 This point has already been made for Norwich by Rawcliffe, *Medicine for the Soul*, 190.

33 'The Mayors Booke for the Poore, 1571–1580', mayoral precepts 1573–74 (bound with 'The Mayors Booke for the Poore, 1571–1580'), fo. 164v; 'Mayor's Booke of the Poore, 1571–1579' charge to overseers, fo. 1; NMC courtbooks 25, fos 82, 198v, 225, 249v, 275v, 290v; 26, fo. 59v; NC Assembly Folio Book 3, fos 34v, 186v; Assembly Book 5, fos 278v, 283, 285, 286v; Clavors Book 1, fo. 123.

34 NMC courtbooks 15, fo. 138v; 25, fos 56, 236v, 260v; NCQS minute book 1602–18, fo. 187v; 'The Mayors Booke for the Poore, 1571–1580', deacons' orders, fo. 4v; 'Mayor's Booke of the Poore, 1571–1579', charge to overseers, fo. 2; NC Assembly Book 5, fo. 89v; 'Book for Innkeepers and Tipplers', *passim*.

35 'The Mayors Booke for the Poore, 1571–1580', deacons' orders, fo. 4v; orders for the poor (1576), fo. 206v (reissued fos 237v, 263v–4); NMC Courtbooks 25, fos 26v, 56, 81; 26, fo. 1; NCQS minute book 1654–70, August sessions 1668; Dutch and Walloon Strangers Book 1564–1643, fo. 61.

36 Clavors Book 1, fos 77v, 81v, 84v, 96v, 100, 103v; Chamberlain's Accounts 1625–48, fos 48, 106v, 127, 145, 168v, 186, 225v, 467v, 488v; NC Assembly Book 5, fo. 285v; NCQS minute book 1637–64, March sessions 1651.

37 NC Assembly Folio Book 6, fo. 21.

38 Dutch and Walloon Strangers Book 1564–1643, fos 22, 31v, 69v; Muster Lists case 10/H/number 11.

39 NMC courtbook 25, fo. 80v.

40 See NC Assembly Book 5, fos 244–5; MISC 21/a, order to constables.

41 NC Assembly Book 5, fos 83v, 86, 114, 374; Assembly Folio Books 3, fos 175, 180; 5, fos 143, 176; Dutch and Walloon Strangers Book 1564–1643, fo. 31v; Clavors Book 1, fo. 84; Chamberlain's Accounts 1603–25, fo. 107; 1625–48, fo. 143; NMC courtbook 15, fo. 179; 'Book for Innkeepers and Tipplers', *passim*; Muster Lists case 10/H/number 11; case 13a/1–39.

42 NCQS Searchbooks 1–7.

43 See Greg Smith, 'Civilized people don't want to see that kind of thing: the decline of public physical punishment in London, 1760–1840', in C. Strange ed., *Qualities of Mercy: Justice, Punishment, & Discretion* (1996), 21–51, esp. 37–41; *id.*, 'The state and the culture of violence in London, 1760–1840' (University of Toronto PhD thesis, 1999), 390, table 7.1; King, *Crime, Justice, and Discretion*, 272; and Bob Shoemaker's chapter in this volume.

44 David Underdown, 'The taming of the scold: the enforcement of patriarchal authority in early modern England', in A.J. Fletcher and J. Stevenson eds, *Order and Disorder in Early Modern England* (Cambridge, 1986), 116–36; Martin Ingram, 'Scolding women cucked or washed'; Sharpe, 'Civility, civilizing processes', 225.

Sharpe writes that carting 'seems to have been most often used in urban areas' (*Judicial Punishment*, 21). The European context is sketched by Pieter Spierenburg, 'The body and the state: early modern Europe', in Norval Morris and David J. Rothman eds, *The Oxford History of the Prison: The Practice of Punishment in Western Society* (Oxford, 1995), 49–77. Judith Bennett has recently described the medieval history of cucking stools in *Ale, Beer, and Brewsters in England: Women's Work in a Changing World, 1300–1600* (Oxford, New York, 1996), 104–5. See also John Webster Spargo, *Juridical Folklore in England Illustrated by the Cucking-Stool* (Durham, N.C., 1944).

45 Marjorie Keniston McIntosh, *Controlling Misbehaviour in England, 1370–1600* (Cambridge, 1998), 63–4, 106, 115.

46 All of my punishment figures are calculated from the minute books of the Mayor's Court – NMC courtbooks 11–20 – and the minute books of the extant City Quarter Sessions covering the period 1570–1700.

47 NMC courtbook 24, fo. 273. Two women were sentenced to 'be put into the cage [in 1668] for their abusive and rude language', but at their husbands 'engagement' that they would 'live orderly for ye future the punishment was remitted' (NMC courtbook 24–70v).

48 NMC courtbook 25, fo. 223.

49 NMC courtbook 24, fo. 144v.

50 For quotations and last mentions of fees see Clavors Book 1, fos 84, 106v, 135, 139; Chamberlain's Accounts 1580–89, fo. 110v; 1603–25, fo. 321v.

51 NCQS minute book 1639–54, fo. 129; 'Mayors Booke for the Poore, 1571–1580', fo. 4; NMC courtbook 9, fo. 72. See also Joan Kent, *The English Village Constable 1580–1642: A Social and Administrative Study* (Oxford, 1986), 26, 30–3, 200–5, 235, 265; McIntosh, *Controlling Misbehaviour*, 78, n. 78.

52 Clavors Books 1, fos 76, 77v, 80v. Cf. McClendon, *Quiet Reformation*, 231–2.

53 The provinces and powers of the Mayor's Court are well-described in Pound, *Tudor and Stuart Norwich*, chap. 9.

54 NMC courtbooks 8, fo. 411; 9, fo. 318; 8, fo. 506; NCQS minute books 1571–81, fos 68, 68v, 106v; 1581–91, fos 4, 11v, 48v, 115v, 147, 183, 198; 1637–64, fo. 62; 1639–54, fo. 70; 1691–1702, October sessions 1699, April sessions 1700. Whippings were also timetabled for the Wednesday market. See NCQS minute books 1571–81, fo. 176; 1691–1702, April sessions 1700.

55 NCQS minute books 1691–1702, April sessions 1699; May sessions 1698. See also NCQS minute books 1691–1702, May sessions 1698, October sessions 1698, July sessions 1700.

56 NCQS minute book 1671–91, January sessions 1687. See also NCQS minute books 1671–91, January sessions 1689; 1691–1702, May sessions 1698. Although these last two cases may refer to landmarks, in each case the house of a prominent citizen, rather than to a victim's house. Edward Girling made a 'publique confession' for 'speaking scandalous words' of an alderman, 'in the same place wher I did speake ye said words' (NMC courtbook 24, fo. 65v).

57 NMC courtbook 9, fo. 318. Cf. St George's Guild minute book 1452–1602, fos 79v, 80–0v.

58 NMC courtbooks 8, fos 430, 650; 5, fo. 149; 10, fo. 222; 8, fo. 461; 9, fo. 519; 12, fos 71, 179, 472; 13, fos 76, 173; 15, fo. 162.

59 NCQS minute books 1671–91, January sessions 1689; 1691–1702, October sessions 1692, April sessions 1699; NMC courtbooks 8, fo. 663; 11, fos 11, 150, 160, 190, 212, 231, 253, 270, 280, 294.

60 NMC courtbook 7, fo. 521. Cf. Laura Gowing, '"The freedom of the streets": women and social space, 1560–1640', in Paul Griffiths and M.S.R. Jenner eds, *Londinopolis: Essays in the Cultural and Social History of Early Modern London* (Manchester, 2000), 130–51, esp. 140–1. However, I am not so sure that this was 'a typically female progress of dishonour'. Some women were made to walk from the cage to the cucking stool (see, for example, NMC courtbook 24, fo. 144v).

61 St George's Guild minute book 1602–1729, fo. 59; 'Mayors Booke for the Poore, 1571–80', fo. 4v; Dutch and Walloon Strangers Book 1564–1643, fos 73–4. See also NC Assembly Folio Books 3, fo. 202; 4, fo. 38v; 'Mayors Booke for the Poore, 1571–80', fos 237–8, 263v–4.

62 Chamberlain's Accounts 1580–89, fos 2, 172; Clavors Book 1, fo. 63v; St George's Guild minute book 1452–1602, fo. 94; NC Assembly Folio Book 3, fo. 34v; Clavors Book 1, fo. 57; NMC courtbook 26, fo. 59v. See also Slack, *Poverty and Policy*, 118–19, 193–4. Badging in continental Europe is briefly surveyed by Jutte, *Poverty and Deviance*, 161–2.

63 St George's Guild minute books 1452–1602, fos 101v, 150v; 1602–1729, fos 34, 60, 61v, 66, 71v, 75v, 78, 83v, 127, 134, 134v, 137v, 152v, 158, 166v; Great Hospital General Account Rolls 1605–06, 1606–07, 1611–12; 'The Childrens Hospitall Booke', 1623–68, 1636–37, 1642–43, 1646–47, 1647–48; Chamberlain's Accounts 1589–1602, fos 243, 261, 278v, 297v; 1603–25, fos 76, 128, 244v, 263; 1625–48, fos 15, 46v, 105, 127, 468v; NC Assembly Folio Books 3, fo. 177; 5, fo. 37; Assembly Book 5, fo. 355v; NCQS minute books 1581–91, fo. 121; 1650–74, April Sessions 1667, January Sessions 1668. 'Red cappes' and blue coats were made for boys in the Childrens Hospital. See 'The Childrens Hospitall Booke, 1623–68', 1646–47, 1649–50, 1659–60; NMC courtbook 25, fo. 190.

64 Chamberlain's Accounts 1580–89, fo. 125; 1589–1602, fo. 235v; 1603–25, fo. 30; 1625–48, fo. 104. See also Burke, *Social History of Knowledge*, 132–5; Carl B. Estabrook, *Urbane and Rustic England: Cultural Ties and Social Spheres in the Provinces, 1660–1780* (Stanford, 1998), 56–61; David Buisseret ed., *Monarchs. Ministers, and Maps: The Emergence of Cartography as a Tool of Government in Early Modern Europe* (Chicago, 1992); M. Biggs, 'Putting the state on the map: cartography, territory, and European state formation', *Comparative Studies in Society and History*, 41 (1999), 374–405; and J.B. Harley, *The New Nature of Maps: Essays in the History of Cartography*, ed. Paul Laxton (Baltimore, 2001).

65 Robert Tittler, 'Civic portraiture and political culture in English provincial towns, *c.* 1560–1640', *Journal of British Studies*, 37 (1998), 306–29; R. Mackenny, *Traders and Tradesmen* (Beckenham, 1987), 155–65, 172; D.M. Bergeron, *Civic Pageantry, 1558–1642* (1971), esp. 105, 125, 134, 138.

66 NC Assembly Folio Book 8, fo. 68v; NMC courtbooks 24, fos 154v, 160, 186; 25, fos 43v, 57, 61, 124v, 170, 192, 330v; 26, fos 37, 56v, 69; 16, fo. 499; 25, fo. 186; Chamberlain's Accounts 1603–25, fo. 399v; 1625–48, fo. 124v; NMC courtbooks 20, fos 368, 415; 8, fo. 671; Clavors Book 1, fo. 92. See also Dagmar Freist, *Governed by Opinion: Politics, Religion and the Dynamics of Communication in Stuart London, 1637–1645* (London, New York, 1997), 41, 42, 46, 102, 103, 109; Adam Fox, *Oral and Literate Culture in England, 1500–1700* (Oxford, 2000), 387.

67 NMC Courtbook 11, fo. 135; Chamberlain's Accounts 1589–1602, fo. 102v. NMC courtbooks 12, fos 300, 312; 8, fos 505, 663; 9, fos 403, 601; 11, fos 451, 608, 680, 708; 5, fo. 149; 8, fos 582, 663; 9, fos 72, 132, 272; 10, fo. 30; 11, fos 135, 393; 6, fo. 83; 25, fo. 187v; 12, fo. 300. People were also publicly executed in the market

(NMC courtbook, 24, fo. 336v). See also Robert Tittler, *Architecture and Power: The Town Hall and the English Urban Community, c. 1500–1640* (Oxford, 1991), 28, 39; David Underdown, *Fire From Heaven: Life in an English Town in the Seventeenth Century* (1992), 97–8; McIntosh, *Controlling Misbehaviour*, 115. Cf. Tittler, *Reformation and the Towns*, 259; Michael Reed, 'The urban landscape, 1540–1700', in Clark, *Cambridge Urban History*, 289–313, esp. 301. Municipal prisons were also frequently located inside town halls. See Tittler, *Architecture and Power*, 125.

68 Kathy Stuart, *Defiled Trades and Social Outcasts: Honour and Ritual Pollution in Early Modern Germany* (Cambridge, 2000), 123, 124, 128; Pieter Spierenburg, *The Spectacle of Suffering: Executions and the Evolution of Repression: From a Pre-Industrial Metropolis to the European Experience* (Cambridge, 1984), 57; Ulinka Rublack, *The Crimes of Women in Early Modern Germany* (Oxford, 1999), 80.

69 Chamberlain's Accounts 1580–89, fos 28v, 317; 1589–1602, fo. 140v; 1603–25, fos 55v, 243; 1625–48, fos 71, 302v; Clavors Book 1, fos 74v, 76, 77v, 80v, 85v, 94v, 51v.

70 NCQS minute book 1630–38, fo. 45v.

71 Estabrook, *Urbane and Rustic England*, 51; Emily Jane Cockayne, 'A Cultural History of Sound in England, 1560–1760' (University of Cambridge PhD thesis, 2000), 131.

72 For example, NMC courtbooks 6, fo. 143; 7, fo. 130; 8, fos 502, 653; 9, fos 95, 622, 691; 11, fos 36, 654; 14, fos 290v, 291; NCQS minute books 1637–64, January sessions 1655; 1639–54, fo. 16; 1691–1702, April sessions 1696; Grand Jury Presentments, 1695. For orders to sweep the market and 'aboute the crosse', see NMC courtbook 25, fos 30v, 42v, 166; NC Assembly Folio Book 5, fo. 94; River and Street Accounts 1556–1618, *passim*; Clavors Books 2, fo. 149; 3, fo. 71; Chamberlain's Accounts 1589–1602, fo. 160v; 1603–25, fos 284v, 322; 1625–48, fo. 70.

73 NMC courtbook 6, fo. 98; NCQS minute book, 1630–38, fo. 44v. See also NMC courtbooks 9, fo. 410; 12, fos 133, 488, 595, 745, 820; 13, fos. 132, 133, 139, 387, 436; 14, fos 38v, 423v; 16, fo. 19; NCQS minute book 1630–38, fo. 27.

74 NMC courtbook 6, fos 373, 33. See also NMC courtbooks 6, fo. 136; 20, fo. 282.

75 NMC courtbooks 8, fo. 193; 20, fo. 484v; 25, fo. 134v; NC Assembly Book 5, fo. 253.

76 NMC Interrogatories and Depositions Book 1A, fo. 89v; NCQS minute books 1630–38, fo. 22v; 1581–91, fo. 93v; 1639–54, fo. 62; NMC 15, fo. 72v. See also NCQS minute book 1630–38, fo. 50; Rublack, *Crimes of Women*, 86; and Gowing, 'Freedom of the streets', esp. 143.

77 NCQS Interrogatories, Depositions, Examinations, 1580–85, Robert Worlyche interrog.; NMC courtbook 14, fos 290v, 291; NCQS minute book 1630–38, fos 70, 59v; See also NCQS sessions books 1630–38, fo. 71; 1639–54, fos 60v, 167; NMC Interrogatories and Depositions Book 1A, fos 5, 12, 37, 47; 1C, fo. 55; courtbook 23, fo. 120.

78 NMC courtbook 8, fo. 539.

79 NMC courtbooks 23, fo. 115; 7, fos 211, 212; 11, fo. 243. Croft was later 'whipped openly at ye cage'. See also NMC courtbooks 6, fo. 82; 8, fos 365, 542.

80 Edward Muir, *Ritual in Early Modern Europe* (Cambridge, 1997), 2. See also Gatrell, *Hanging Tree*, chaps 1–3; Thomas Laqueur, 'Crowds, carnival and the state in English executions, 1604–1868', in A.L. Beier *et al.*, eds, *The First Modern Society: Essays in English History in Honour of Lawrence Stone* (Cambridge, 1989), 305–55.

81 NMC courtbooks 6, fo. 82; 8, fos 365, 542. See also NMC Interrogatories and Depositions Book 1B, deposition of John Branthut (13 April 1557).

82 NMC courtbook 10, fo. 102. See also NMC courtbooks 6, fo. 55; 10. fo. 102.

83 NMC courtbook 25, fo. 183; NMC Interrogatories and Depositions Book 1C, fo. 39; NMC courtbook 8, fo. 24. Cf. *The Letter Book of John Parkhurst, Bishop of Norwich, Compiled During the Years 1571–5*, ed. R.A. Houlbrooke (Norfolk Record Society, 43, 1974–75), 60; NCQS minute book 1630–38, fo. 79.

84 NMC courtbooks 11, fos 414, 415, 253; 14, fo. 402; 23, fo. 32; NCQS minute book 1639–54, fo. 161v. See also NMC courtbook 11, fo. 318.

85 NMC courtbook 11, fo. 101. On occasion, the ecclesiastical authorities asked the permission of the civic authorities to punish an offender in the marketplace. See, for instance, NMC courtbook 13, fo. 211.

86 NMC courtbooks 14, fo. 271; 25, fo. 223. See also NMC courtbooks 10, fo. 534; 14, fos 57v, 263v. For some cases of citizens being punished for whipping without authority, see NMC courtbooks 8, fo. 379; 14, fos 57v, 271.

87 NMC courtbooks 12, fo. 491; 11, fo. 318v. See also NMC Courtbooks 9, fo. 165; 15, fos 169v, 230v.

88 NMC courtbook 15, fo. 125v.

89 NMC courtbooks 10, fo. 177; 9, fo. 23; 12, fo. 18; 7, fos 177, 241, 562; 8, fo. 379; 11, fos 301, 543, 567, 700; 12, fos 117, 147, 277; 13, fos 16, 92, 156, 276, 281, 338, 339, 356, 493, 514, 543, 712; 14, fos 84, 204v, 211, 261v, 445; 15, fos 8, 78, 107v, 123v, 180v; 25, fos 97v, 215; Interrogatories and Depositions Book 1D, Edmund Walpole examination (22/10/1567); NCQS minute books 1571–81, fo. 85; 1581–91, fos 33v, 87, 98v; 1602–18, fo. 187v; 1629–36, fo. 23; 1630–38, fo. 74v; 1637–64, fos 50, September sessions 1658; 1639–54, fo. 167; 1654–70, September sessions 1661; 1691–1702, October sessions 1692. Cf. Paul Griffiths, *Youth and Authority: Formative Experiences in England, 1560–1640* (Oxford, 1996), 313–18; Rawcliffe, *Medicine for the Soul*, 237.

90 NMC courtbooks 11, fos 89, 144; 13, fos 515, 723; 14, fos 75, 189v; 15, fo. 177. In the case of Mary Basham, a ducking in the river was counted more damaging than sitting in the stocks (NMC courtbook 14, fo. 166).

91 Clavors Book 1, fos 65v, 79, 89v, 95v, 97.

92 NMC courtbooks 7, fo. 290; 8, fo. 411; 11, fo. 217; 13, fos 321v, 634; 14, fos 259v, 394; 15, fos 21, 96, 142, 150, 197, 212v, 267, 281; 20, fos 305v, 359v, 388; NCQS minute books 1602–18, fo. 237; 1629–36, fo. 64.

93 NCQS minute books 1602–18, fo. 211; 1671–91, January sessions 1691; 1691–1702, October sessions 1699. The pillory is mentioned just a few times in the records. See also NMC courtbook 9, fo. 277; NCQS minute books 1571–81, fos 83–3v; 1671–91, January sessions 1691; 1691–1702, July sessions 1694.

94 NMC courtbook 23, fo. 152v.

95 NMC courtbooks 20, fo. 396v; 13, fos 568, 673. The six lashes were dished out for pinching hose.

96 NMC courtbook 13, fos 596, 673. Welsh, who had been in Bridewell for seven weeks was also warned that if he offended again with Langdon he would be 'whipt at a carts tayle iiii severall markett dayes one after another'.

97 NCQS minute books 1671–91, January sessions 1689; 1691–1702, April sessions 1699, October sessions 1699; NMC courtbooks 14, fos 399, 405; 15, fos 125v, 169v.

98 NCQS minute books 1639–54, fos 81v, 146v; 1571–81, fo. 143v; 1691–1702, October sessions 1698.

99 NMC courtbook 8, fo. 108. Three 'ducskyngs' is mentioned in three other cases. See NMC courtbooks 10, fo. 735; 15, fo. 8. The use of the cucking stool is only

mentioned on several other occasions and not once in the Quarter Sessions books that I have consulted. See NMC courtbooks 9, fos 263, 474; 20, fo. 454v; 24, fo. 144v.

100 NMC courtbook 12, fo. 165; 6, fo. 66; 7, fo. 428; 24, fo. 144v. See also NMC courtbooks 7, fo. 509; 10, fo. 749; 13, fo. 180.

101 NMC courtbooks 11, fo. 216; 14, fo. 189.

102 NMC Interrogatories and Depositions Book 1C, fos 24, 26–6v.

103 NMC courtbook 20, fo. 414. See also NMC courtbooks 8, fo. 658; 11, fos 145, 216, 251, 314, 615; 12, fo. 365; 13, fos 414, 515; 14, fo. 251; 15, fo. 102.

104 NMC courtbooks 7, fo. 444; 11, fo. 69v; 10, fos 493, 497. See also NMC courtbook 9, fo. 110; NCQS minute book 1691–1702, July sessions 1695, January sessions 1696, April sessions 1700.

105 See my 'Masterless young people', esp. 159–71.

106 NMC courtbooks 13, fo. 399; 9, fo. 692; 10, fos 476, 489; 12, fo. 205; 13, fo. 118; 14, fo. 154.

107 NCQS minute book 1665–87, January Sessions 1669. See also NCQS minute book 1571–81, fo. 162v.

108 See, especially, Douglas Hay, 'Property, authority, and the criminal law', in Hay *et al.*, eds, *Albion's Fatal Tree: Crime and Society in Eighteenth-Century England* (1975), 17–63.

109 For example, NMC courtbooks 8, fo. 692; 10, fo. 496; 15, fo. 123.

110 NMC courtbook 25, fo. 69.

111 NMC courtbook 6, fo. 135. See also NMC courtbooks 5, fos 28, 342; 6, fo. 66; 7, fo. 506; 8, fos 304, 498, 577, 677; 9, fos 132, 575, 692; 10, fos 427, 667; 11, fos 195, 457; 12, fo. 407; 13, fos 439, 533; 14, fo. 257; 15, fos 10, 265; 20, fos 349, 410v; 24, fo. 265v; 25, fos 293, 339v; 26, fo. 473v; NCQS minute books 1591–1602, fo. 82; 1654–70, December 1665; NC Assembly Folio Book 3, fo. 229v; St George's Guild minute books 1452–1602, fos 123, 172v; 1602–1729, fos 63, 139v.

112 NCQS minute book 1571–81, fo. 37. See also NMC courtbooks 8, fos 268, 365, 692; 9, fos 345, 631; 10, fos 16, 43, 496, 617; 11, fos 132, 181, 478, 638; 12, fos 24, 183; 13, fo. 589; 15, fo. 123. Cf. Pound, *Tudor and Stuart Norwich*, 115–16.

113 William Lambarde, *Eirenarcha or the Office of the Justices of Peace*, 1581 (The English Experience, 273, Amsterdam, New York, 1970), 67.

114 NMC courtbooks 5, fo. 28. See also NMC courtbooks 8, fo. 677; 9, fo. 132; NMC Interrogatories and Depositions Books 1C, fo. 39; 1A, fo. 30; 1C, fos 26–6v; courtbooks 5, fos 184, 526; 11, fo. 457; 15, fo. 146; NCQS minute books 1629–36, fo. 22v; 1654–70, August Sessions 1655.

115 Of course by Foucault, but also by many others including Pieter Spierenburg, 'Four centuries of prison history: punishment, suffering, the body, and power', in Finzsch and Jutte, *Institutions of Confinement*, 17–35, esp, 31–2, 35; and J.M. Beattie, *Crime and the Courts in England, 1660–1800* (Princeton, 1986), 617.

116 Andrew McRae, *God Speed the Plough: The Representation of Rural England, 1500–1660* (Cambridge, 1996), 67; Margaret Healy, *Fictions of Disease in Early Modern England: Bodies, Plagues and Politics* (Basingstoke, 2001), esp. 28–34; Rawcliffe, *Medicine for the Soul*, esp. 161, 170; Christina Vanja, 'Madhouses, children's wards and clinics: the development of insane asylums in Germany', in Finzsch and Jutte, *Institutions of Confinement*, 117–32, esp. 126; Rublack, *Crimes of Women*, 44–5. For a few contemporary indications see the Edwardian *Exhortation to Good Order*, quoted by McRae, *God Speed the Plough*, 120; *The Diary*

of Ralph Josselin, 1616–1683, ed. Alan Macfarlane (British Academy Records of Economic and Social History, New Series, III, 1976), 39, 58, 114, 438, 600; Edward Heron, *Physicke for Body and Soule* (1621); John Strype, *A Survey of the Cities of London and Westminster... by John Stow... Corrected, Improved, and Very Much Enlarged* (1720), 257; and *The Arraignement and Burning of Margaret Fern-seede, for the Murther of Her Late Husband Anthony Fern-Seede* (1609), sig. B2.

117 Erasmus is quoted in this particular context by Martin Ingram, 'Sexual manners: the other face of civility in early modern England', in Burke *et al., Civil Histories*, 87–109, at 93; The Mayors Booke for the Poore, 1571–1580', mayoral proclamation (1571), fo. 11. See also Ann Rosalind Jones and Peter Stallybrass, *Renaissance Clothing and the Materials of Memory* (Cambridge, 2000), esp. chap. 1; Patricia Allerston, 'Clothing and early modern Venetian society', *Continuity and Change*, 15 (2000), 367–90, esp. 367.

118 Esther Cohen, 'The animated pain of the body', *American Historical Review* (2000), 36–68, quoting 42. Cf. Peter Lake and Michael Questier, 'Agency, appropriation, and rhetoric under the gallows: puritans, romanists, and the state in early modern England', *Past and Present*, 153 (1996), 64–107, esp. 71. See also Elizabeth Hanson, *Discovering the Subject in Renaissance England* (Cambridge, 1998), 24–55.

119 NMC courtbooks 12, fo. 105; 25, fo. 307. Baylie was, in fact, readmitted into the Hospital as it was 'supposed' that his grandmother's death was 'the cause of his misbehavior'. But he was finally turned out three years later after a string of further offences (NMC courtbooks 25, fos 308, 333v; 26, fo. 18v.).

120 NMC courtbooks 20, fos 273, 368; 7, fo. 305; 8, fo. 11; 24, fo. 234v; 15, fo. 148; Interrogatories and Depositions Book 1A, fo. 30. See also NMC courtbooks 24, fos 206v, 237v, 385; 25, fo. 167.

121 NMC courtbook 8, fo. 568.

122 For some religious settings see Old Meeting Norwich, church book 1635–1839, fos 17, 18, 18v.

123 McClendon, *Quiet Reformation*, esp. chap. 6; Pound, *Tudor and Stuart Norwich*, 87; Evans, *Seventeenth-Century Norwich*, 84–6; Patrick Collinson, *The Religion of Protestants: The Church in English Society, 1559–1625* (Oxford, 1982), 141–5; Slack, *Poverty and Policy*, 119.

124 NMC 14, fo. 338v. See also NMC courtbooks 4, fo. 62v; 5, fos 149, 184, 200, 388, 499, 505; 6, fo. 107; 7, fo. 305; 8, fo. 104; 9, fos 252, 262; 12, fo. 105; 14, fos 183v, 251; 15, fos 108, 108v, 109, 195; 20, fo. 357.

125 Quoted in Innes, 'Prisons for the poor', 67.

126 Edward Coke, *The Second Part of the Institutes of the Lawes of England* (1644), 729; Michael Dalton, *The Country Justice* (1661 edition), 122; the Sudbury lines are quoted in Hindle, *State and Social Change*, 164. See also Sharpe, *Crime in Seventeenth-Century England*, 151–2, and his *Judicial Punishment*, 26–7; Innes, 'Prisons for the poor'. And for the European scene see Jutte, *Poverty and Deviance*, 169, who writes that 'a new reformative policy of punishment' inside institutions 'offered the authorities a kind of control over the offender without abusing his body'; and Stuart, *Defiled Trades and Social Outcasts*, 143–4.

127 NMC courtbooks 15, fo. 180; 24, fo. 206v; 25, fo. 137. See also NMC courtbooks 14, fo. 338v; 20, fos 321v, 334v; 24, fos 234v, 237v, 385.

128 Particular mention is made of weaving, hemp and the mills. See NMC courtbooks 14, fo. 417v; 15, fos 53v, 162; 25, fo. 302; Bridewell Treasurer's Accounts volume 1, fos 1585, 1592, 1593, 1594, 1595, 1600, 1611, 1614, 1616, 1618, 1620,

1622; vol. 2, fos 4v, 17–17v; Bridewell Treasurer's Accounts (bound with 'The Mayors Booke for the Poore, 1571–1580'), fo. 58; Clavors Book 3, fos 14v, 29v. Cf. Pelling, 'Illness among the poor', 65.

129 'The Mayors Booke for the Poore,1571–1580', fo. 2v; NMC courtbook 14, fo. 421v; Bridewell Treasurer's Accounts volume 1, fos 1616, 1617, 1629; Bridewell Treasurer's Accounts (bound with 'The Mayors Booke for the Poore, 1571–1580'), fos 58, 175v. This was the working day as it was described in 1571. For religious exercises and the purchase of service books and bibles in the prisons and hospitals, see NMC courtbook 25, fos 336; 26, fo. 2; Great Hospital General Account Rolls 1601–14, 1618–19, 1621–22, 1624–25, 1635–42, 1644–47; 'The Childrens Hospitall Booke', 1628–29, 1629–30, 1630–31, 1631–32, 1635–36, 1638–39, 1643–44; Chamberlain's Accounts 1603–25, fo. 30; 1625–48, fos 85v, 264. For the Childrens' Hospital see Margaret Pelling, 'Child health as a social value in early modern England', in her *Common Lot*, 105–33, esp. 111–12; and for the Great Hospital, see Rawcliffe, *Medicine for the Soul*, esp. chap. 8.

130 NMC 25, fo. 317v; Bridewell Treasurer's Accounts volume 1, fos 1585, 1604, 1605, 1606, 1609, 1612, 1629. Again, inmates in the hospitals were called 'the poor'. See NMC courtbooks 25, fos 311, 311v, 312, 318v, 331v, 333, 341v, 343; 26, fos 10, 11v, 13v; NC Assembly Folio Book 8, fo. 12v; Great Hospital General Account Rolls 1601–09 (payments to 'extraordinary poore people'). The Great Hospital was called 'the howse of the pore people' (NC Assembly Folio Book 3, fo. 121).

131 Mary Douglas, *How Institutions Think* (Syracuse, 1986), 63.

132 NMC Courtbooks 25, fo. 271; 24, fo. 99.

133 This idea emerges in both Beier, *Masterless Men* and Innes, 'Prisons for the poor'. Innes notes that 'A powerful case can be made for the insignificance of the bridewell as a regulatory institution' ('Prisons for the poor', 102).

134 As Maggie Pelling has done for medical services in Norwich. See her 'Healing the sick poor', 80; 'Illness among the poor', 63, 65; 'Child health as a social value', 131; and 'Old age, poverty and disability', 153.

135 NMC Courtbook 9, fo. 171.

136 NCQS minute book 1581–91, fo. 182v (three separate committals).

137 NMC Courtbooks 26, fo. 79v; 14, fo. 387v.

138 Quoting Innes, 'Prisons for the poor', 105. For some examples see NMC courtbooks 13, fo. 797; 14, fos 116, 165v, 167, 335, 345v, 387v; 15, fos 56v, 57, 182, 237, 256, 272v; 25, fo. 189v, 272v.

139 'Mayor's Booke for the Poore', 1571–80, fo. 5v.

140 NMC courtbooks 10, fo. 350; 15, fo. 149; The Mayors Booke for the Poore, 1571–1580', fo. 2; 1573–74 precepts (bound with 'The Mayors Booke for the Poore, 1571–1580'), fo. 165; Bridewell Treasurer's Accounts (bound with 'The Mayors Booke for the Poore, 1571–1580'), fo. 175v.

141 Bridewell Treasurers' Account Books 1, 1585 (inventory), 1600, 1610, 1622 (inventory); 2, fo. 17; Bridewell Treasurers' Accounts (bound with 'The Mayor's Booke for the Poore'), fo. 175v; NMC Courtbooks 7, fo. 550; 8, fos 236, 605; 9, fos 191; 10, fo. 677; 14, fo. 421v; 15, fos 189v, 275, 489v.

142 NMC courtbooks, 14, fo. 439; 13, fo. 183; 20, fo. 481; NCQS Minute Book 1654–70, May Sessions 1662; NMC courtbooks, 13, fo. 198; 14, fos 287v, 326v, 427, 436; 15, fos 1, 10v, 49v.

143 NMC courtbooks 14, fo. 439; 13, fo. 183; 20, fo. 481; NCQS minute book 1654–70, May sessions 1662; NMC courtbooks 13, fo. 198; 14, fo. 287v. Cases of women locked up for illegitimacy include NMC courtbooks 14, fos 326v, 427,

436; 15, fos 1, 10v, 49v. For examples of the range of sentences see NMC courtbooks 14, fo. 158; 13, fos 19, 596, 598, 712; 14, fos 102, 158, 397v, 402, 426v, 450, 459v; 15, fos 9v, 32v, 41v, 183. Utting was let out of Bridewell, however, as she reappears in the Norwich records a couple of years later.

144 NCQS Minute Book 1637–64, fo. 26v. However, it was ordered that both Bunn and Giddings would be set free 'if they be reteyned in service'. Cases of acquitted murderers being sent to Bridewell include NCQS minute book 1654–70, April sessions 1663, August sessions 1670. Other examples relevant here include NCQS minute books 1629–36, fo. 43v; 1630–38, fo. 103v; 1637–64, fo. 67v; 1639–54, fos 27v, 178; 1654–70, October sessions (1655), March sessions 1662; 1671–91, January sessions 1682 (after branding); NCQS minute books 1629–36, fos 22v, 43v, 61v, 65, 128v, 132v; 1630–8, fo. 78v; 1637–64, fos 44v, 47v, 51, 67v; 1639–54, fos 101, 110; 1654–70, May sessions 1662, January sessions 1669 (after felony acquittals); NCQS minute books 1629–36, fos 22v, 75, 114v; 1637–64, fos 8v, 39; 1639–54, fos 23, 101, 119, 148v, 178; 1654–70, March sessions 1665, 1671–91, January sessions 1674, April sessions 1682; 1691–1702, July sessions 1693, May sessions 1698 (after convictions for petty larceny). Cf. John Beattie's discussion of the uses to which London Bridewell was put by the London magistrates to punish small-time thieves (*Policing and Punishment in London*, esp. 24–33).

145 Spierenburg writes that 'the emergence of houses of correction, bridewells and similar institutions constitutes the foremost example of the retreat of the elements of publicity and infliction of physical suffering' ('Introduction', in Pieter Spierenburg ed., *The Emergence of Carceral Institutions: Prisons, Galleys, and Lunatic Asylums, 1550–1900* (Rotterdam, 1984), 2–8, quoting 5).

146 NMC courtbook 25, fos 181, 190. Whippings in the marketplace continued, but were by now infrequent. See NMC courtbooks 23, fo. 200v; 24, fos 5, 21, 21v, 67v, 257v, 383v; 25, fos 248v, 307.

147 Beattie, *Crime and the Courts*, 485–6; Sharpe, *Judicial Punishment*, 23–4, 42. Petty larceny was also the most common cause of referrals from City Sessions to the Bridewell, and this trend becomes particularly pronounced in the second half of the seventeenth century.

148 I must thank Paul Halliday, Martin Ingram and Mark Knights for their valuable advice on these matters. The events of the Norwich charter controversy can be followed in Evans, *Seventeenth-Century Norwich*, 277–305; and Paul D. Halliday, *Dismembering the Body Politic: Partisan Politics in England's Towns, 1650–1730* (Cambridge, 1998), esp. 222–4. The broader history and significances of such charter disputes across England is described with great skill in Halliday, *Dismembering the Body Politic*, chaps 5–6.

149 Earlier bans are discussed in Tittler, *Reformation and the Towns*, 328–9 (see NMC courtbook 14, fo. 423v). For puppet shows see 24, fos 161, 162; 26, fos 5v, 38, 38v, 68v, 73v. For stage shows see NMC 24, fos 160v; 25, fos 206, 210v, 227, 286, 290; 26, fo. 20v. For 'chirugicall cures' and 'manuall operations' after 1660 see 25 fos 42, 210, 227, 244, 272v, 300, 339v. By the late seventeenth century, however, ballad sellers and singers were given 'leave' to sell and sing in the marketplace (25, fos 68, 73v, 264v, 272).

150 The first such exhibit was noted in 1616, when Humphrey Bromley was given 'libertie to shewe' 'a strange child with two heads' (NMC courtbook 15, fo. 71v). Twenty-three years later, Lauzerus Colleretto was given 'leave to shewe a monster' (20, fo. 266v). Nearly all the other exhibits went on show after 1660, however. See NMC courtbooks 23, fos 216v; 24, fos 140, 161, 338v, 353v, 360v, 371,

380v; 25, fos 5v, 11, 35v, 139v, 189v, 193, 206v, 209v, 213, 225v, 227, 232, 257, 271v; 26, fos 52v, 54. See also NMC courtbooks 25, fos 164v, 229v, 237v, 260, 294v, 299v; 26, fos 39, 54v.

151 The justices issued 151 death sentences between 1570 and 1620 (127 men and 24 women) and 54 between 1630 and 1680 (40 men and 14 women). The number of sentences peaked in the 1590s when 44 felons (32 men and 12 women) were sentenced to hang, 21 per cent of the total number in these one hundred years. The number of felons branded also slumped: 76 felons were branded between 1660 and 1680; while 15 were branded between 1680 and 1700.

152 Most consistently by Spierenburg, *Spectacle of Suffering*; 'Four centuries of prison history'; and *The Broken Spell: A Cultural and Anthropological History of Pre-Industrial Europe* (1991), chaps 1 and 7. And, most recently in the English case, by Sharpe, 'Civility, civilizing processes, and the end of public punishment'.

153 Bridewell Treasurer's Accounts Volume 1, 1622 (inventory), 1587; vol. 2, fo. 17; Bridewell Treasurer's Accounts (bound with 'The Mayors Booke for the Poore, 1571–1580'), fos 58, 98.

154 NMC courtbook 26, fo. 59v; William Dodwell, *The Equall and Impartiall Discharge of Justice, With Respect Both to the Guilty and the Innocent. A Sermon Preached at St Mary's in Oxford at the Assizes…[on] July 16 1755* (1755), 22.

155 Whipping in the eighteenth century is discussed in Beattie, *Crime and the Courts*, 461–4 and 485–7; id., *Policing and Punishment in London*, 444–7; King, *Crime, Justice, and Discretion*, 262–6; and Smith, 'Civilized people don't want to see that kind of thing'.

4

Punishing Pardon: Some Thoughts on the Origins of Penal Transportation

*Cynthia Herrup**

In 1584, the explorer Richard Hakluyt argued that one advantage of creating settlements overseas would be their ability to provide work for England's 'excess' population – the wandering rogues and vagrants who were 'hurtful and burdensome to this realm'. Hakluyt believed that colonies would also mean opportunity for the great numbers of otherwise useful men who, through hard luck or bad advice or circumstance 'for trifles may otherwise be devoured by the gallows'.[1] Hakluyt was not the first English writer to suggest that the men and women whom elites considered to be idle and/or criminal might be valuable to the state as labour, but he may have been the first to incorporate that insight into arguments for English colonial enterprise and transportation. The Elizabethan government responded to his plea with little interest. The 1598 *Act for Punishment of Rogues, Vagabonds and Sturdy Beggars* allowed justices of the peace to banish 'beyond the seas' at county expense rogues whom they considered to be dangerous or beyond reform, but such men and women were not to be transported for any specific labour purpose. A proclamation five years later tried to further encourage justices of the peace to implement the law by specifically defining 'beyond the seas'; it meant not only 'the New Found Land' and the Indies, but also 'France, Germany, Spain and the Low Countries'.[2] Yet before the settlement of Virginia, justices seemed to have used these powers sparingly and seemed to

* I would like to thank the Huntington Early Modern British History seminar for their comments on an abbreviated version of this essay. I am grateful as well to Judith Bennett, Paul Griffiths, Margaret Hunt and Dana Rabin for criticism and encouragement on its revision; to Barbara Donagan for kindly allowing me to read her unpublished work; and to the Fletcher Jones Foundation and the Henry E. Huntington Library for the time and space to complete the initial draft. Unfortunately, I have not have time to incorporate into this essay in anything but a preliminary way the conclusions presented in J.M. Beattie's important new book, *Policing and Punishment in London 1660–1750: Urban Crime and the Limits of Terror* (Oxford, 2001).

have preferred to send men to war or to galley service rather than to the New World. While recognizing that labour itself could be redeeming, the central purpose of this early legislation was deterrence, the hope that 'a few of these examples will be more fearful to the thief and rogue than death itself'.[3]

In the seventeenth century, however, as private money built the colonies of which Hakluyt had only dreamed, something resembling his idea was slowly realized. In 1611, Sir Thomas Dale, the Governor of Virginia, wrote to the privy council in despair about the number and quality of his colonists. Instead of the 'disorderly' persons he had with him, he proposed building Virginia with convict labour. For the moment, he was ignored, but in 1615 (and repeatedly thereafter), the early Stuarts empowered commissions made up of privy councilors to reprieve for settlement overseas, condemned prisoners whom they believed 'might be rather corrected than destroyed'. In place of local rates (which had been expected and failed to fund both the 1598 scheme and prisoner galleys), the companies requesting prisoners were to underwrite the costs of resettlement. The privy councillors were merely to choose the convicts (usually on the basis of judicial advice) and hand them over to company agents.[4]

Like the 1598 legislation, these early provisions resulted only in erratic transportation of capital prisoners: probably fewer than 150 felons were resettled between 1615 and 1640. Most were sent to Virginia, but some went to Bermuda, St Christopher Island or Barbados. By the second half of the seventeenth century, however, there was a dramatic increase: between 1655 and 1699, nearly 4,500 prisoners left England for the same destinations or for Jamaica.[5] Between 1671 and 1673, from Newgate prison alone, the Restoration government transported nearly 250 felons.[6] By 1700, transportation had become the likely end of anyone convicted of serious felony. Government sponsored legislation in the early eighteenth century further expanded the range of crimes for which one might be transported, and formalized what was already effectively true, that despite growing resentment from the more established colonies, transportation had become the standard alternative to capital punishment.[7]

In the course of these changes, transportation shifted administratively from possibility to occasional option to routine practice. Legally, it morphed from a concession to planters into a mitigation promoted as a boon for convicts into a declared punishment for the public good. The story of transportation's rise must eventually incorporate changes in markets, capital flows, concepts of criminality and ideas about redemption. It must also explain the complementary rejection of older forms of discipline such as benefit of clergy. As John Beattie has wisely observed, changes in penal practice 'evolve within a larger social and cultural context that in imperceptible ways alters the limits of what is acceptable in society and what is not'.[8] The process was never simple and rarely straightforward. In this essay, however, I want to make a small start by adding a new complexity to the administrative tale of how prisoners came to be transported. In the mid-1650s, the government began to resettle prisoners under conditional pardons rather than reprieves. This is a change the importance of which Abbot Emerson Smith recognized more than 70 years ago, but without drawing out the implications of his insight.[9] The adoption of conditional pardons to accompany transportation coincided with other changes enacted in the 1640s and 1650s regarding the use of pardons. And it altered the use of pardons themselves, from a practice associated most closely with homicide to one associated most closely with theft. Exploring the shift from transportation by reprieve to transportation by pardon in greater detail shows not only how the use of pardons changed the practice of transportation, but also how the increased use of transportation changed both the meaning of pardoning and the relationship of pardoning to punishment. What follows is speculative, but it suggests that the shifting uses of pardons critically facilitated the large-scale adoption of transportation.

I

Most scholars have explained the adoption of transportation for felony primarily in material terms, pointing to the confluence of a growing need for labour overseas, a growing concern over property theft and vagrancy (especially in and around London), and a growing availability of entrepreneurs willing to pay prisoners' expenses. Philip Jenkins puts the position well by attributing the substitution of transportation for execution to the availability of 'the political and colonial accidents that gave England the need and the opportunity to exile their criminals to a distant land where cheap labour was in great demand'.[10]

Historians of transportation generally would agree, despite the fact that many of the material prerequisites for expropriating convict labour were present in the early seventeenth century when transportation for felons was seldom used. The economic viability of large-scale transportation depended on a complex labour benefit analysis, but merchant companies and private contractors appeared willing almost from the colonies' inception to underwrite sending labour West. Merchant companies sponsored extensive recruitment campaigns; royal commissions offered young poor men and women the opportunity to emigrate; statutes and proclamations encouraged the departure of known vagrants and orphans. When 100 poor children sponsored for emigration in 1620 by the London Common Council refused to appreciate their good fortune, the Privy Council 'in furtherance of so good a work' gave the London Council power 'as cause shall require' to persuade them. Children and vagrants were not the only conscripts available. Bridewells' governors sent away at least 1,000 petty thieves, nightwalkers and a variety of other minor miscreants in the early seventeenth century.[11] The demand for labour in the New World was great enough that it seems virtually to have created the modern crime of kidnapping, as men and women known as 'spirits' used false promises of New World plenty to clear the streets of London. As late as the 1670s, legislation was being proposed specifically to stop entrepreneurs who were happy to transport servants and children without waiting for the formality of an accusation or conviction. Joanna Innes has noted that renewed interest in convict transportation and in the 'productive' reeducation of the disorderly developed in tandem.[12] Yet before the 1660s, the annual total of felons transported numbered only in the dozens.

Without discounting the power of economic influences, scholars interested in legal history have further contextualized the growth of transportation by setting it among a succession of schemes tried in search of an effective and inexpensive alternative to execution. In the 1930s, Georg Rusche and Otto Kirchheimer argued that transportation and galley service should be understood together. More recently, John Langbein has pointed out that the language of the first transportation commissions echoed the galley orders adopted earlier in France and Spain. John Beattie has also drawn attention to how, in response to increasingly shrill concerns over property crime that current punishments seemed not to deter, the Restoration governments experimented with (among other things) new uses of fines, whipping, branding and imprisonment at hard labour.[13]

Doubts about the efficacy of execution as deterrence were not new in the Restoration nor, as the words of Hakluyt and others show, was the sense that there might be profit in the use of convict muscle. The English had spared condemned men for military service ever since the thirteenth century and continued to do so under the Tudors and the Stuarts. By the sixteenth century, benefit of clergy was an accepted sanction for the most commonly prosecuted felonies, and we have already seen how the early modern English state followed the French and Spanish in experimenting with pardons on condition of service in galleys. Krista Kesselring details a number of attempts under the Tudors to solve criminal problems by offering to exchange pardons for voluntary banishment.[14] These options proved too cumbersome or too expensive or seemed too lenient to succeed as an alternative to execution and, until the 1650s, reprieves and pardons rarely necessitated any promise of future service.[15]

Conflicting views of what it meant to go to the New World were one reason. Merchant companies enthusiastically advertised the colonies as sites of upward mobility; if that were true, transportation to such a place was not much of a punishment. Indeed, if the colonies merely needed labour, then transportation was an option that might encourage rather than discourage crimes. And if the colonies were to be profitable and orderly, then, as Sir Francis Bacon argued, mixing criminals and others would only 'spoil' the settlements. The confusion over what transportation was intended to accomplish mirrored contemporary ambivalence about the purposes of punishment: was it primarily deterrent, vengeful or rehabilitative.[16]

Legal obstacles were another problem: Magna Carta protected free English subjects from being compelled to leave the realm 'except by lawful judgement'. Judgement meant formal sentences such as banishment, not incidents such as transportation that were technically remissions of punishment rather than punishments themselves.[17] Some reprieves claimed that the petitioners had consented to or even requested transportation, but the sense of English rights was strong enough that at least some contractors thought it not worth the risk; they returned exiles to England if the exiles claimed coercion.[18] And administrative difficulties were a third dilemma. The government had asked judges who returned from circuit duty to submit lists of the condemned who might be spared the gallows, but keeping track of those who had been spared was much more difficult once they had been reprieved. In earlier decades, the solution was to keep reprieved prisoners in jail until they were either pardoned or hanged, but confinement was not practical for large numbers of prisoners whose reprieves lasted years and extended to other continents even if one extends the notion of prison to include ships and work sites. Both the 1598 vagrancy statute allowing transportation and the 1603 law intended to make that more feasible foundered partly on this problem.[19] Without some resolution of these issues, large-scale transportation was not efficient enough to be appealing.

II

To understand how changes in pardons affected changes in penology in the middle of the seventeenth century, it is necessary to begin with a brief introduction to the part that pardoning played in English governance. From the coronation of King Edgar in 993, every monarch in England promised at his or her coronation to offer mercy as well as justice. English monarchs were free to pardon anyone for a breach of the peace, whether or not that person had been convicted, tried, indicted or accused, and even if none of these had yet occurred. Legislation and judicial opinions advised against certain types of pardons, but until the Act of Settlement in 1701, no categorical bar existed to the pardon of any matter in which the monarch had an 'interest'.[20] Monarchs did not entirely supplant private claims to vengeance, but over time they succeeded in establishing the justice of their courts and the mercy of their pardons as superior to any other sort. By the 1530s, Henry VIII successfully claimed that a royal monopoly on pardoning in England and Wales was fundamental to his authority, contending that anything less would lead to a '... great diminution and detriment of the royal estate ... and to the hindrance and great delay of justice'.[21]

Such a monopoly was essential because the prerogative of mercy was not only a mechanism of legal sovereignty, but also one through which the monarch revealed a special affinity with God. Sir Francis Bacon considered royal pardons to be acts that 'imitated' the mercy of Christ; to

Sir Henry Finch, they were acts that proved kings had 'a shadow of the excellencies that are in God'.[22] Pardoning was a didactic as well as an authoritative act; in giving pardons, rulers allegedly taught the benefits of submission before authorities both secular and divine. Since mercy could never be commanded, only sought, a need to ask for pardon allegedly encouraged both hopefulness and humility. The language of salvation routinely used to describe pardoning referred not only to saving lives by remitting punishments, but also to saving souls by reminding observers of the Last Judgment.

The importance of pardoning had grown in tandem with the power of the medieval English state. As Naomi Hurnard has argued convincingly, in the twelfth century and beyond the royal right to pardon helped to reconcile subjects to legal changes that steadily enhanced royal power. The possibility of pardon softened the impact of the broader use of both public prosecutions and capital punishment; pardons allowed monarchs at once to expand the reach of their justice and to ameliorate its imperfections. '... The power to do, our justice to enforce and our mercy to pardon', declared Charles I, these are 'three such inherent prerogatives that as without them we are no King'. In his definitive *New Law Dictionary*, Giles Jacob defined pardons as 'inseparably incident to the crown'.[23]

The pardons that did this cultural work most obviously were called *special pardons*, so named because they were tailored for specific circumstances. These are the pardons that satisfy our image of pardoning – ones in which a grieving spouse moved a monarch to mercy, or a last-minute remission saved a life, or a powerful man or woman bought immunity from punishment. These were individual gifts of the king's grace, material as well as verbal favours, embodied in formal and sometimes elaborately decorated documents drawn in Chancery, authenticated with the great seal, and pleaded before the relevant court with considerable ceremony.[24] These pardons epitomized the essence of pardoning as an exchange: mercy for submission, forgiveness for guilt.

But, in fact, special pardons were numerically the exception among pardons and probably had been since the fourteenth century. Because petitioners for special pardons were reliant, first, on getting access to the monarch through ever growing layers of intermediaries and, then, on getting access to the great seal through ever growing layers of clerical bureaucracy, special pardons were beyond the financial reach of most petitioners. The price of access to the king was unpredictable; rumours told of thousands of pounds sterling changing hands.[25] Such instances were exceptional, but even the routine costs for a special pardon were prohibitive for most of the population. H. Maxwell-Lyte identified nine discrete administrative stages through which a seventeenth-century pardon passed on its way from petitioner to patent roll, many of them involving not only clerks, but also secretaries, doorkeepers and other officials who expected gratuities or fees. How much one paid depended on how many clerical hands were needed, how complicated the text of the pardon was, and how quickly it had to move from office to office. Having received the pardon, moreover, one still had to plead it: that took still more time and more money. For a pardon to cost more than most people's yearly income would not have been uncommon.[26] From the middle of the sixteenth century, special pardons incorporating numerous 'poor prisoners' into a single *circuit pardon*, considerably eased the financial burden. Often issued with the fees due to the government (although not those due to jailers) forgiven, these circuit pardons became the most common route to mercy for men and women of small means.[27]

While there was consistent recourse to forgiving crime through such grants by the late sixteenth century, the most unequivocal need for pardons had long been rooted elsewhere, with men and women trapped not by guilt but by the proper application of the law. The most common use of pardons in the middle ages originated with the fact that the common law had an absolute view of liability in homicide: a killer was equally culpable at law for acts that we would now call murder, manslaughter, misadventure or self-defence. Hence, whatever the circumstances, if a defendant had killed someone, the law said that a trial jury was compelled to convict that defendant of homicide. Hurnard estimates that more than 90 per cent of the pardons allowed in thirteenth-century England were responses to this problem. This mercy mitigated the punishment of individuals legally guilty, but morally exonerable because they had caused death in their own defence or by accident. As Bracton commented, these were convicts in need of pardons, but these were pardons that the king was virtually obliged to give.[28] By the early fourteenth century, such pardons were considered matters of course, *pardons de cursu*, rather than gifts of grace. They could be requested directly from the Lord Chancellor, and a fast-track process for obtaining them bypassed everything but the great seal (therefore reducing nine fees to two plus the costs of pleading). Although technically part of the same exchange as were special pardons, these *de cursu* pardons were asked for and received with minimal ritual, and at reduced cost.[29] Such pardons resolved the perceived injustice of the law, not injustices wrought by either investigative or trial process and not forgivable failings of character or will.

By the early modern era, the expanded use of benefit of clergy had dramatically reduced the need for pardons for homicide, but needs of a different sort for pardons to repair tensions created by the law had already developed.[30] The gap between practice and law in the control of property was already considerable in the early sixteenth century; Henrician legislation made it worse. Even before the dissolution of the monasteries vastly increased the number of tenants holding land directly from the king, Henry VIII's council understood the value of feudal dues as an untapped source of revenue. The passing of the Statute of Uses and the creation of the Court of Wards in conjunction with the dissolution set the government and the newly broadened classes of landholders at odds; the former hoping to increase its income from ancient obligations and the latter hoping to avoid them.[31] Here was another circumstance in which a class of offenders, albeit in this case not those in danger for their lives, considered themselves wronged not by a verdict but by the law itself. *De cursu* pardons for acts such as alienating land without a license essentially became *post-factum* licenses. Figures are unavailable for the Tudor grants, but pardons for alienating were the single most common sort of pardon granted by either of the early Stuart kings. Between 1625 and 1641, for example, the hanaper accounts record payments for 322 special pardons, 80 *de cursu* pardons for homicide, and 2,006 *de cursu* pardons of course for illegal alienation of property.[32]

Henry VIII's incorporation of the remaining secular liberties, Wales, and the ecclesiastical courts into his direct jurisdiction also inspired new courts and new legislation, so much so that by the late sixteenth century, justices of the peace complained bitterly about the difficulties of enforcing these 'stacks of statutes'. Because the new courts (Star Chamber in particular) and the new legislation focused on what we would call misdemeanours rather than on felonies, they impinged upon middling and elite individuals as defendants more regularly than had most of the older tribunals.[33] Perhaps to help offset this burden, Henry and his successors expanded another type of pardon with medieval precedents, this one called a *general pardon*. General pardons had originated as acts of grace to celebrate auspicious royal occasions, and anyone whose offences fell within their specifications could claim them for fees comparable to those for *de cursu* pardons. Each general pardon was different; most excluded heinous crimes, but forgave a comprehensive list of other thefts and statutory offences. Even before the sixteenth-century expansion of statutory crimes, general pardons were a popular means of avoiding financial penalties. Edward Powell estimated that Henry V's income from general pardons was about £4,500, while the lists of recipients of Henry VIII's coronation pardon were said to fill four Chancery rolls.[34]

The Tudors routinized general pardons by issuing them as special statutes at the conclusion of virtually every parliament. These pardons became acts of parliament, but unlike most acts, they arrived in Westminster already engrossed and inscribed with the sign manual and, in theory, they were not debatable. Henry VIII granted general pardons through parliament about every six years; Elizabeth I, about every four. The early Stuarts were less forthcoming, in part simply because fewer of their parliaments ended amicably, but James I issued an exceptionally generous pardon in 1624.[35] The accompanying rhetoric in such pardons explained them as 'gifts' in recognition of financial grants, but they were gifts of benefit to both parties. These *parliamentary pardons* were the least expensive sort of general pardon, since in most cases petitioners had only to claim the pardon's protection, not to obtain an actual document or to plead the pardon before a court. The sole cost was to record the claim (16d in the late sixteenth and seventeenth centuries). Because of this, parliamentary pardons are impossible to quantify from central records, but they seem to have been extremely popular. Attorney-General Robert Heath expected so many people to claim the pardon of 1621, for example, that he estimated the fines lost to be the equivalent of three subsidies.[36] Just as Hurnard had noted for the Middle Ages, an increase in the availability of pardons went hand in hand with an increase in the power of the king.

By the seventeenth century, pardons varied by form (special or general) and authority (grace or parliament or de cursu) as well as by content. They might or might not need to be pleaded (that is, formally presented to a court); they might or might not involve considerable fees. In any given year, for the handful of individuals pardoned by special pardons, hundreds were pardoned by *de cursu* pardons, and thousands might take advantage of a general or parliamentary pardon if one were available. Early modern punishments had simple rules (for example that the punishment for all felonies was execution) that disguised practical finesse; pardons had labyrinthine procedures that obscured simple results (for example that all pardons forgave penalties). The variations reflected the fee-driven nature of Chancery bureaucracy, but they arose as well from a changing understanding of what pardons needed to accomplish. In the early modern world, in courts and villages, towns and manor houses, pardons were if not ubiquitous, certainly not uncommon, a sign of the law's complexities rather than necessarily a sign of the incorrigible.

III

It is in this context that three developments in the 1640s and 1650s changed the meaning of pardons and their relationship to punishment. To begin with, parliament's use of the colonies for prisoners of war helped to emphasize the harshness rather than the possibilities of life in the New World. *De jure* and *de facto*, Commonwealth governments redefined pardons in ways that associated them more easily with deliberate offences worthy of punishment than with non-felonies, thereby enhancing the punitive implications of transportation. And lastly, a more efficient and more elegant means than the reprieve for authorizing prisoner transport was set in place. We know very little of how these changes originated or why they happened as they did. While the results fit many of the ends sought by contemporary law reformers (decentralization, rationalism, rehabilitation), nothing links these modifications directly to reformist pamphleteers or to the work of the Hale Commission. Yet deliberately or not, the effect of these changes was to revolutionize the possibilities of transportation, and in the process, to help change what it meant to receive a pardon.

Although some commentators continued into the eighteenth century to believe that transportation was more reward than punishment, by the 1650s four decades of colonial settlement had significantly qualified earlier idealizations of what it meant to be sent 'to the plantations'. More information meant more awareness of how severe and isolated such places could be, and the newer island colonies promised a life harsher still than settlement on the mainland. The conception of places such as Barbados and Jamaica as outdoor prisons became even clearer when parliaments began to send prisoners of war there after the siege of Colchester in 1648. Barbara Donagan sees the adoption of transportation for prisoners of war as itself evidence of the bitterness of the second civil war; after earlier battles, the norm was to exchange prisoners rather than to exile them.[37]

We do not yet know enough about the mechanics of this process, but having found the means to 'disburden the kingdom of their charge', Parliament appears to have turned to it repeatedly. Prisoners were ordered transported after the battles of Preston, Dunbar and Worcester, Penruddock's uprising and perhaps on other occasions too. Most were Scots or Irish; in the early 1650s, most were sent to Virginia; later the favoured destinations were Barbados and Jamaica. From 1653, the exportations also included large numbers of Irish poor, involving on at least one occasion 400 children.[38] According to Donagan, many of the prisoners died en route, escaped or ransomed their way free, but enough remained for the 1662 House of Commons to consider the possibilities of bringing them back home. And whatever the reality, royalists persistently vilified parliamentary skill at what the royalist poet Henry King called 'the Turkish art' of shipping away one's captured enemies.[39] By the mid-1650s, the association of exile with punishment was well-established.

At the same time that the government was making greater use of transportation to relieve Britain of those whom they considered dangerous, parliaments were also changing the public face of pardons. The Long Parliament abolished the ecclesiastical courts and Star Chamber and the Court of Wards; it ended feudal tenures and specifically the need for a pardon when alienating property.[40] The republican parliaments accepted pardoning as part of their sovereign responsibility: every special pardon was discussed and voted upon; the protectorate parliaments left most pardons to the discretion of the Lord Protector, but denied him control of pardons for murders and for treasons.[41] The unstable military and political situation (as well as the end of reliance on subsidies) disrupted the traditional rhythm of both general and parliamentary pardons; what replaced them were less frequent acts and commissions concerned primarily with indemnifying former soldiers.[42] Taken together, these actions ended the predominance of what had been the most common sorts of pardons. The biggest need for *de cursu* pardons disappeared; and general pardons to forgive statutory offences and small thefts were rare. And the sorts of special pardons most likely to touch the 'respectable', those for treason or murder, now (regardless of the final outcome) necessitated public and potentially fractious debates rather than just money and connections.[43]

In the 1640s and 1650s, much of the social middle ground of pardoning was cut away. With the abolition of feudal tenures, the end of prerogative courts and the decline of general pardons, the social profile of why one might need a pardon narrowed. For the first time, under the republic and protectorate, circuit pardons clearing the jails of felons freed more people than did any other sort of pardon.[44] The courts most likely to hear complaints about middling and upper-class involvement in non-felonious disorder were gone, as were the pardons that offered the most commercially involved individuals regular opportunities to immunize themselves against certain economic regulations.[45] Such changes as these identified pardons more closely with conventional notions of criminality and with the meaner sort who found themselves most frequently in need of them. Sending these men and women into what was effectively exile may have had renewed appeal for a government anxious about both local order and financial solvency.

Prisoners of war were, of course, a special case, covered by particular rights and regulations. Transporting non-combatants legally was more complicated since, as noted above, Magna Carta forbade unwilling expatriation. In Elizabethan and early Stuart England, the procedural prelude to sending prisoners overseas was the reprieve: typically, judges pronounced sentence, respited it, and ordered the convict returned to prison to await word of either pardon or execution. From the first of its transportation orders concerning non-combatants, in June 1654, the protectorate's convicts were ordered out of England under different terms: they were granted *conditional pardons*.[46] This may seem an administrative distinction without a difference, but in fact it had important repercussions; from the perspectives of both the government and the prisoner, conditional pardons had significant advantages over reprieves.

Reprieves saved convicts from hanging, but however long they might last they did not rescind the original sentence. The convict transported under a reprieve remained culpable. Even after years had passed, the sovereign could order an original judgment executed.[47] Conditional pardons, in contrast, seemed definitive. They exchanged a set amount of labour for freedom, putting clear limits on public supervision. Pardons erased rather than merely suspended prior sentences and some legal writers believed that pardons were able effectively to undo guilt as well.[48] Moreover, while governments had always claimed to honour Magna Carta's restrictions on enforced exile, conditional pardons embodied that claim in parchment. Because reprieves, were not 'of record', they had no official standing, and so left no detailed archive. Conditional pardons did. While this did nothing to eliminate the coercion behind such volunteerism, many conditional pardons specifically noted the cooperation of the prisoners.[49]

By adapting pardons as an instrument for transportation, the commonwealth found an administrative tool that was both practicable and valuable. As instruments of record, conditional pardons gave the government clearer control over convicts and the convicts clearer claims to freedom. Pardons with transportation combined public disapproval and tentative confidence in ways that reprieves and alternative punishments did not. While more punitive than whipping or benefit of clergy, they expressed faith in the redemptive powers of labour, particularly when combined with distance from 'bad company'. Having issued no large orders for convict transportation in its first years, Cromwell's governments issued pardons to clear the jails more than 25 times between 1656 and 1658, and ordered close to one-third of the released prisoners (about 90) to be transported.

IV

Within 15 months of his return, Charles II's government also began issuing conditional pardons to accompany orders of transportation. Transportation, the king declared, agrees with 'our royal clemency and [would] be likewise an advantage to the public'. In just three years, he had more than twice as many prisoners transported to the colonies from Newgate alone than his father and grandfather had done from all the country's prisons. The absolute increase in prisoners spared by circuit pardon was not dramatic, but now every circuit pardon spared some persons for transportation. Between 1671 and 1673 the colonies were the expected destination for more than two-thirds of prisoners freed. The House of Commons discussed and rejected bills making transportation into an optional sentence for forms of theft at several points throughout the 1660s before finally doing so on a small scale in 1670. Over the same decade, judges so favoured transportation that they routinely manipulated sentencing to make it the most common response to felonies within as well as outside the plea of benefit of clergy. By the 1690s, pardons on condition of transportation had become a fundamental aspect of what John Beattie has recently called the 'management of death at Tyburn'.[50]

The changes of the 1640s and 1650s altered not only punishment, but also pardoning. For those who could afford it, Charles II could still be copiously forgiving, but for poorer individuals, the price of a pardon had become not only the presence of mitigating circumstance but also their willingness to labour. Special pardons for humble felons perhaps now seemed excessive to the government; the chances of someone outside of the elite either needing or receiving such a pardon in the early 1670s seems to have been only half what it had been in the early 1630s. In the early 1670s, homicides and treasons – the sorts of crimes for which elites were most likely to be convicted – accounted for about 40 per cent of the special pardons granted; thefts (clergyable and not) – the sorts of crimes for which more modest folk were most likely to face death – for less than 10 per cent; in the early 1630s, the comparable percentages had been 17 and 30. In the early 1670s, about 7 per cent of special pardons went to men identified as labourers; 40 years before, the percentage was a bit over 20.[51]

By the Restoration era, pardons were more numerous than they had ever been, but more closely tied as well to punishment, to conviction for common theft, and to the 'meaner' sort. Under Charles I, only a small percentage of men and women condemned for felony were pardoned; under Charles II most of them would be. Pardons were still available to everyone, but for ordinary men and women a pardon was now a part of rather than an alternative to being punished. Scholars often stress the failures of reform in the 1640s and 1650s, but these decades show a creativity that belies the sense that productive reform had to await the eighteenth century. Not only an extended debate over the use of capital punishment, but also an extensive search for a reasonable alternative to it began in the Interregnum.[52]

My analysis points to many questions in need of further research both in terms of legal history and in terms of that history's role in social policy: was there a relationship between shifts in pardoning and a growing polarization between economic groups? How did the increased use of transportation for felons affect its position as a 'cure' for poverty? Does the large-scale adoption of transportation mark, on the one hand, a new stage in a perceptual move conflating the categories 'poor' and 'criminal'? Does it mark, on the other hand, a new stage in a perceptual move routinizing and so depersonalizing some uses of the royal prerogative? Abbot Emerson Smith wrote that without understanding pardons, 'no accurate idea of the criminal processes of the seventeenth century can be gained'.[53] There is much that we do not yet know, but it is already apparent that for criminal process and much more, he was surely right.

Notes

1 'Discourse on western planting', reprinted in the *Documentary History of the State of Maine*, ed. Charles Deane (Cambridge, 1977), II, 160–1. See also 36–44.
2 39 Elizabeth I, c.4; *Stuart Royal Proclamations*, ed. James F. Larkin and Paul L. Hughes (Oxford, 1973), i, 27 (1603).
3 BODL Tanner MS 76/160 (1602). See also HL Ellesmere MSS 6215–6 (1586).
4 *Calendar of State Papers, Colonial* (hereafter CSPC), ed. W. Noel Sainsbury (1860) I, 11–12; Abbot Emerson Smith, *Colonists in Bondage: White Servitude and Convict labour in America 1607–1776* (Chapel Hill, 1947), 92–9; an example of such a commission can be found at PRO C66/2599m.12.
5 Smith, *Colonists in Bondage.*
6 These and other statistics below are based on the recorded entries in the Crown Office docket book (PRO C231/7) for these years, cross-checked against the comparable records for the privy and great seals and the patent rolls. They are a part of broader in progress work on pardoning in the decades 1620–80.
7 22 Chas II, c.5 (1670) had made transportation an alternative for those convicted of certain thefts; 31 Chas II, c.2 (1679) confirmed its legality for convicts who requested it; 4 Geo I, c.11 and 7 Geo I, c.11 (1718 and 1720) expanded its scope to crimes within benefit of clergy and made it into an official sentence. On the colonies' diminishing enthusiasm, see Smith, *Colonists in Bondage,* 103–6;

J.M. Beattie, *Crime and the Courts in England, 1660–1800* (Princeton, 1986), 478–80. Cf Joanna Innes, ''The role of transportation in seventeenth- and eighteenth-century English penal practice', in Carl Bridge, ed. *New Perspectives in Australian History* (1990), 6, for the intriguing idea that those transported were a residual rather than a selected group of convicts.

8 Beattie, *Crime and the Courts*, 470.

9 Abbot Emerson Smith, 'The transportation of convicts to the American colonies in the seventeenth century', *AHR*, 39 (1933–34), 237–8, elaborated slightly in Smith, *Colonists in Bondage*, 95–7.

10 Philip Jenkins, 'From gallows to prison? The execution rate in early modern England', *CJH*, 7 (1986), x. See also, for example, Georg Rusche and Otto Kirchheimer, *Punishment and Social Structure* (New York, 1939, 1968), 58ff; Peter Linebaugh and Marcus Rediker, *The Many-Headed Hydra* (Boston, 2000), esp. chaps 2–3; A. Roger Ekirch, *Bound for America: The Transportation of British Convicts to the Colonies 1718–1775* (Oxford, 1987), chap. 5.

11 *Acts of the Privy Council of England, Colonial*, (hereafter *APC*) ed. W.L. Grant and James Munro (Hereford, 1908) i, 28–9; Smith, *Colonists in Bondage*, chap. 4; A.L. Beier, *Masterless Men: The Vagrancy Poblem in England 1560–1640* (1984), 162–4 estimates the number transported at several thousand for the entire century; Paul Griffiths, who generously shared with me Bridewell calculations from his forthcoming work on petty crime in London, notes slightly more than one thousand orders between 1619 and the 1650s. On kidnapping and 'spirits', see John Wareing, 'Preventive and punitive regulation in seventeenth-century social policy: Conflicts of interest and the failure to make "stealing and transporting children and other persons" a felony, 1645–73', *Social History*, 27(2002), 288–308.

12 On attempts to control 'spirits', see *CSPC*, i, 19; *Acts and Ordinances of the Interregnum*, ed. C.H. Firth and R, S, Rait (1911), i, 98; *Middlesex County Records*, ed. J.C. Jeaffreson (1888), iii, *passim* Leo Francis Stock, *Proceedings and Debates of the British Parliaments Respecting North America* (Washington, DC, 1924), I, 302–4, 357–61, 366, 375, 382, 397, 400; 21 Charles II, c.2; Innes, 'Role of transportation', 8–12.

13 Rusche and Kirchheimer, *Punishment and Social Structure*, 58ff; John Langbein, *Torture and the Law of Proof* (Chicago, 1977), 40–1; Beattie, *Crime and the Courts*, chap. 9.

14 Naomi Hurnard, *The King's Pardon for Homicide* (Oxford, 1969), 311–25; Thomas A. Green, *Verdict According to Conscience* (Chicago, 1985), 105–29; Krista Kesselring, *Mercy and Authority in the Tudor State* (Cambridge, 2003).

15 Cf. J.S. Cockburn, *Calendar of Assize Records: Introduction* (1985), 126–7.

16 Bacon, 'On plantations', in *The Essays or Counsels, Civil and Moral*, ed. Michael Kiernan (Cambridge, Mass, 1985), 106. Hope for rehabilitation was a standard rationale for reprieve, and some of the early Restoration pardons for transportation allowed the convict profits from the last years of his or her labour. See, for example, PRO C82/2305,2308 (1663). On the potential advantages of transportation's ambiguities for the government, see Simon Devereaux, 'In place of death: transportation, penal practices, and the English state 1770–1830', in Carolyn Strange, ed. *Qualities of Mercy: Justice, Punishment and Discretion* (Vancouver, 1996), 52–76; Beattie, *Crime and the Courts*, 476; Smith, *Colonists in Bondage*, 108–9, 136–52. In the seventeenth century, the practical distinctions between convict labour and free indentured labour are often very hard to see.

17 Clause xxxix; Sir William Holdsworth, *A History of English Law* (1938), xi, 569; William Craies, 'The compulsion of subjects to leave the realm', *Law Quarterly*

Review, 6 (1890), 392–402; Alan Atkinson, 'The free-born Englishman transported: convict rights as a measure of the eighteenth-century empire', *P&P*, 144 (1994), 88–115.

18 *CSPC*, i, 457–8. See also Jeaffreson, *Middlesex County Records*, iii, 100, 230. Cf *APC*, i, 28–9 where the Council overrode similar protests. Paul Griffiths tells me that among the Bridewell's records from about the 1630s, clerks often noted inmates' 'willingness' to be transported.

19 *Stuart Proclamations*, i, 27; 1 James I, c.7.

20 12 & 13 William III, c.2. The boundaries of royal 'interest' were ambiguous, but it was settled law that they did not include the right to pardon in suits of subject versus subject, in cases where fines belonged to informers, or in private suits for murder.

21 27 Henry VIII, c.24.

22 Bacon, letter to James I (1621) in Spedding, *Letters and Life*, vii, 240; Henry Finch, *Law or a discourse thereof* (1627), 81.

23 Hurnard, *King's Pardon*, 22–3; Charles I cited in Sean Kelsey, *Inventing the Republic: The Political Culture of the English Commonwealth 1649–53* (Manchester, 1997), 93; Giles Jacob, *New Law Dictionary* (1750), s.v. 'pardon'.

24 H. Maxwell-Lyte, *Historical Notes on the Use of the Great Seal of England* (1926), 267–70, 297–9, 332ff; Jacob, *New Law Dictionary*, s.v. 'pardon'; Krista Kesselring, 'To pardon and punish: Mercy and Authority in Tudor England', PhD thesis, Queen's University (Ontario), 2000, chap. 5; Thomas Forster, *The Layman's Lawyer* (1654), 187–9, describes pleading.

25 G.E. Aylmer, *The King's Servants: The Civil Servants of Charles I* (1961), 99–100, 197ff.

26 Maxwell-Lyte, *Historical Notes*, 94–6; For some other examples see *Calendar of the Committee for Compounding*, £13/8/6 in 1648; British Library (hereafter BL) Additional MS 46,500/92 close to £30 in 1655. Fees for pleading were much smaller. See, for examples, BL Egerton MS 2978/105–22.

27 Most of these pardons forgave between 10–20 persons each, but they could run as high as several hundred. See for example, Kesselring, 'To Pardon and to Punish', 110–12; PRO C231/45/72 (98 persons from Newgate, 1632).

28 Hurnard, *King's Pardon*, 246; Bracton, *On the Laws and Customs of England*, trans. Samuel E. Thorne (Cambridge, Mass, 1968), ii, 378.

29 PRO E215/397, E315/1645–94. The minimum cost seems to have been about 16s 8d for drawing such pardons and 12s for pleading.

30 Green, *Verdict According to Conscience*, chaps 2–4 is the best treatment of the development in homicide.

31 J.H. Baker, *An Introduction to English Legal History* (1990), 89–95.

32 PRO E351/1659–74; Maxwell-Lyte, *Historical Notes*, 217; BODL Bankes MS 2/3–3v; *A Perfect and Exact Direction to All Those That Desire to Know the True and Just Fees of These Courts…*, (1641), 57–9, 127–9 suggest that such pardons that by the early seventeenth century, clerical fees in Chancery were between £2–3. Alienations were not the only category for such pardons, but they were by far the most important.

33 William Lambarde, *Eirenarcha: Or of the Office of the Justices of Peace* (1581), 37–8; J.H. Bellamy, *Criminal Law and Society in Late Medieval and Tudor England* (1984), chaps 4–5.

34 Edward Powell, *Kingship, Law and Society : Criminal Justice in the Reign of Henry V* (Oxford, 1989), 91; Maxwell-Lyte, *Historical Notes*, 215. Examples of coronation pardons can be found in *Proclamations of the Tudor Queens*, ed. Frederic A. Youngs (Cambridge, 1976), 393–5; 452.

35 Kesselring, 'To Pardon and to Punish', 85–9, 92–102; David Dean, *Law-Making and Society in Late Elizabethan England* (Cambridge, 1996), 55–62; House of Lords Record Office Braye MS65/6–8 on procedure. The texts of the pardons are available in *Statutes of the Realm*, eds, A Luders *et al.* (11 vols.; 1810–28). On the problems such pardons caused for law enforcement, see Marjorie Blatcher, *The Court of King's Bench* (1978), 80–7.

36 Sir Edward Coke, *Institutes of the Laws of England* (1644), iii, c.55; and Ferdinando Pulton, *De Pace Regni et Regni* (1609), fo. 220; *Commons Debates 1621*, eds Wallace Notestein *et al.* (1935), iii, 526.

37 Donagan, 'War in England', unpublished manuscript.

38 *CSPC*, I, 360, 363, 373, 387, 401, 407, 409, 419, 421–8, 433, 435, 441; Stock, *Proceedings and Debates*, i, 204, 206, 241n, 444n; Smith, *Colonists in Bondage*, chaps. 5–6; Derek Hirst, 'The English republic and the meaning of Britain', *Journal of Modern History*, 66 (1994), 481–2.

39 Stock, *Proceedings and Debates*, i, 303; King quoted in Donegan, 'War in England'.

40 17 Chas I, c.10–11 (1641). See also the legislation that year abolishing 'feudal' occasions for pardon regarding the forest laws and knighthoods, in *Acts & Ordinances*, i, 833. Of these, only the ecclesiastical courts returned with the Restoration.

41 *Commons Journals*, vi–vii, *passim* for pardons; vii, 415 and 'Instrument of Government', clause iii for restrictions.

42 *Acts & Ordinances*, ii, 565–77 is a general pardon on the older order. Cf. 875–83, 1299–1304.

43 Blair Worden, *The Rump Parliament* (Cambridge, 1974), 89–90, 312; Austin Woolrych, *From Commonwealth to Protectorate* (Oxford, 1982), 290, 366–9.

44 The parliamentary and seals records indicate that under the Republic and the Protectorate together (to Oliver Cromwell's death), special pardons freed fewer than 120 individuals (most for treason), and circuit pardons around 650; the comparable figures for Charles I were 322 and 1068, but with more than 2,000 added *de cursu* pardons as well.

45 An increased need for pardons forgiving treason did not offset this trend, particularly since these were decades in which the line between what constituted treason and what constituted loyalty was itself in constant flux.

46 PRO C66/2912, contains the first set of conditional pardons; the earliest pardons I have found are for John Gale, theft, not to return for seven years and three prisoners from Surrey, theft, not to return for 10 years. The docket book from the Signet Office contains one earlier example, from June 1654, 47 Newgate prisoners 'provided that they shall be transported beyond the seas not to return in ten years' (PRO C231/6/291).

47 Sir Walter Raleigh (sentenced in 1604 and beheaded in 1618) was, despite his protests, recent evidence for this power.

48 Cf. Coke, iv, 235; Jacob, *New Law Dictionary*, s.v. 'pardon'. For a later opinion on some remaining problems, see Peter Brett, 'Conditional pardons and the commutation of death sentences', *Modern Law Review*, 20 (1957), 133–5.

49 See for example, PRO C82/2305, 2308, 2318, 2320, 2322, 2325. The formal phrase was 'upon agreement'. *CSPD* also often discusses prisoners' requests to be transported. Cf. Holdsworth, *History of English Law*, xi, 570–2. Transportation without consent, in fact without trial, was one of the inspirations for the *Habeus Corpus* Act of 1679; see Helen A Nutting, 'The most wholesome law: the Habeus Corpus Act of 1679', *AHR*, 65 (1960), 532–4.

50 J.M. Beattie, 'The Cabinet and the management of death at Tyburn after the revolution of 1688–1689', in Lois G. Schwoerer, ed., *The Revolution of 1688–1689: Changing Perspectives* (Cambridge, 1992), 218–33. Between 1671–1673, Charles II granted 23 circuit pardons, sparing 549 prisoners and delivering more than 360 for transportation. Beattie, *Crime and the Courts*, 474–84, now supplemented by Beattie, *Policing and Punishment*, 277–369, is the best summary of transportation under the later Stuarts.

51 1671–73: 85 men identified by status, 6 as labourers; 1631–33: 53 identified, 12 as labourers. See also BL Additional MS 32,518/117v for an undated memo from Lord Keeper Guildford directing 'no person to be inserted [in a circuit pardon] that is able to bear the charge of a particular pardon'.

52 In service to a different argument, Beattie, *Policing and Punishment*, 310–11, 318 offers some examples.

53 Smith, 'Transportation of convicts', 248.

5

Public Punishment and the Manx Ecclesiastical Courts during the Seventeenth and Eighteenth Centuries

*J.R. Dickinson and J.A. Sharpe**

On 8 November 1705 the consistory court of Thomas Wilson, bishop of Sodor and Man, issued an order of penance against William Kissack, a resident of the parish of Lezayre. Kissack had been presented and convicted for committing adultery and incest with his wife's sister's daughter, an offence against the island's morals which the consistory court clearly thought demanded exemplary punishment. He was sentenced to a month's incarceration in the Bishop's prison at St German's Cathedral, and before his release he was to give bonds to carry out a rigorous programme of penances. He was ordered to perform penance at each of the island's 17 parish churches on successive Sundays and at the market crosses of the island's four market towns on successive market days, these penances to be performed 'bare footed, bare legg'd, & bare headed, covered over with a white linen sheet, and a small white wand in his hand'. When performing penance at the churches Kissack had to stand at the church door 'at going in & coming out of the parishioners', while he was to spend two hours, from 9 to 11 a.m., at each market cross. He was not only to wear penitential habit, but was ordered to stand 'with a schedule on his breast intimating his crimes, which is to be read by the ministers of the respective parishes, and to be repeated by the above offender'. The text of this schedule was set out in detail. It began:

> I am thus justly censured for my abominable sin of incest & adultery with my wive's sister's daughter Anne Christian, whereby I am grievously fallen, & have given great offence to all good Christians here present, and to all other members of Christ['s] church who shall hear hereof. And, therefore I do must humbly and penitentially pray from the bottom of

* This essay was written during a period of research leave awarded to Professor Sharpe and funded by the Arts and Humanities Research Board.

> my heart, and upon my bended knees beseech God in his son Christ's name, who shed his blood for all sinners that they do truly repent and believe in him, to forgive me all my sins, but this especially. And I earnestly desire you & the whole Church of Christ to forgive this scandal given to the Christian religion; and that you offer up your fervent prayers to Almighty God our merciful father, that he wou'd raise me up again by true repentance.

The desired outcome of this process, so the schedule ran, was that Kissack should be 'rendered againe to a happy state of salvation, and by the indulgence of the church may be received again into the communion and fellowship of its members', so that he 'may both in body & soul be sanctified here on earth, and with you glorify'd in Heaven'. The schedule ended with the direction that Kissack should lead those present in the recital of the Lord's Prayer.[1]

The order of penance for William Kissack is a powerful statement of the great themes of the recognition of sin, of the value of true repentance, of the benefits of a public acknowledgement of fault, and of the desirability and possibility that the errant, indeed lost, sheep could be led back and reintegrated into the flock of believers. Underlying it was a strong belief in the possibilities and power of ecclesiastical discipline, and of the importance of using that discipline for the moral reformation of the individual sinner. And the key to the implementation of this discipline, and of the reformation and reintegration of the sinner, was clearly seen to be that public ritual of shame and redemption, penance. Both the fervour with which this disciplinary strategy was followed in William Kissack's case, and the power and complexity of the ritual involved were, as we shall see, typical of Manx ecclesiastical discipline in the early modern period.

I

The recent fashion for attempting an integrated history of the British Isles in the early modern period has largely ignored the Isle of Man, and the history of this small, yet institutionally interesting, component part of the Atlantic Archipelago is unfamiliar to the generality of early modern historians.[2] As far as secular government is concerned, the essential point is that, as Edward Coke put it, the Isle of Man was 'no part of the realm of England'.[3] The island had been under the Norwegian crown until 1266, and was subsequently disputed between the Scottish and English crowns until 1406, when possession of the island was granted by Henry IV to Sir John Stanley and his heirs to hold as a fief of the crown of England. The Stanleys, whose eldest sons from 1485 routinely succeeded to the earldom of Derby, enjoyed regal powers on the island, although the Tudor dynasty's ever more robust attitudes to what constituted treason meant that by 1600 overt reference to these powers had become very muted. Nevertheless, the Stanleys maintained complete control over the island's secular government between 1406 and the death of James, tenth earl of Derby, in 1736 (appeal from the Island's secular law courts to England, for example, although technically possible, was virtually unknown in practice), although their enmeshment in regional and indeed national English affairs meant that they were rarely resident on the island. For most practical purposes, the island's population was ruled by the earl of Derby's Governor and a surprisingly complex body of officers. Despite, by the late seventeenth century, the emergence of merchant communities in Castletown and Douglas, the island's population were for the most part Manx Gaelic speaking farmers who combined agriculture with fishing.[4]

Norwegian influence was also vital in the history of the Manx church in the Middle Ages,[5] the island having formed part of the Norwegian bishopric of Nidaros. The existence of the see now known as Sodor and Man was recognized in 1458, the papacy regarding it as part of the province of York, and litigants in the Manx church courts were indeed theoretically able to appeal to York throughout the early modern period.[6] The church history of the Isle of Man during the sixteenth and seventeenth centuries remains obscure. The findings of earlier writers imply that lack of sources makes writing the history of the Reformation in the Isle of Man impossible,[7] and it seems likely that the full impact of the Reformation did not hit the Island until 1610, in an important convocation presided over by an unusually active bishop, John Phillips (Phillips had been a very effective archdeacon on the island during the episcopates of the two previous, and largely absentee, bishops). Adequate materials survive for writing the history of the Manx church in the seventeenth century, but these have so far been little investigated. At present, the impression is of a backward and terribly under-resourced church, with ill-educated, poorly provided for, and sometimes delinquent clergy, and with a total absence of printed bibles and other printed works in the language spoken by the bulk of the population. Several of the bishops in the sixteenth and seventeenth centuries were rarely in residence on the island, although the episcopacies of John Phillips (1605–33), Isaac Barrow (1663 and 1670) and Henry Bridgeman (1671–82) constituted honourable exceptions to this sad record of neglectful leadership. The long episcopacy of perhaps the most famous bishop of Sodor and Man, Thomas Wilson (1698–1755) was, of course, characterized by a progressive reform of the Manx church and by attempts to impose a strict and efficient ecclesiastical discipline on the island's population.[8]

While Wilson's devotion and achievements should not be underestimated, it is nevertheless clear that he inherited a mature and complex system of ecclesiastical administration, which was marked by a distinctive structure of church courts.[9] There were summary courts, held twice yearly, whose main concern was with testamentary business, tithes and other church dues, and chapter courts, also held twice yearly, which dealt with disciplinary matters, granting of probate, and the admission of churchwardens and chapter quests. The running of these courts was split between the bishop (although they were most often presided over by his vicars general, of whom there were two) and the archdeacon of the island (sometimes represented by his official), each of them taking responsibility for running the courts. Full courts were held three times a year, meetings being organized over a circuit covering the six sheadings, or groupings, of the island's 17 parishes. To these circuit courts were added the consistory court, presided over by the bishop of the vicars general, which dealt with cases appealed from the lower courts, as well as matters (for example the disciplining of the clergy) which were felt to be too important to be left to the inferior courts.

John Keble, author of a hagiographic biography of bishop Wilson, commented that 'the episcopal archives, though abounding in curious details, have not been kept, even in Wilson's time, as to supply materials for a complete history of the insular discipline',[10] a sentiment which any modern student of the Manx church courts might be excused for sharing. Yet it would probably be more accurate to observe that the complexity of the Manx ecclesiastical courts system, and of the archives they generated, constitutes the real problem. A full account of the workings and business of the courts would be based on four archive series. Two of these, known as the Episcopal Wills and the Archidiaconal Wills, commencing in 1600 and 1628 respectively, record the meetings and business of the summary and chapter courts, these records being in effect a wonderful jumble of wills, records of testamentary disputes, presentments, and administrative orders. Thirdly, presentment books, surviving sporadically from 1644 and in an unbroken series from the late 1690s, as their name suggests, list presentments, but orders, depositions and notes of such matters as the performance of penance were also recorded in them. Lastly, there were the records of the consistory court, the Libri CAS arum, again running in a good series from the 1690s. These contain a few presentments and depositions, but are especially rich in orders and other documentation relating to church administration.[11] Constructing annual totals of presentments, given the current level of research into these records, is impossible. It seems that at the beginning of the seventeenth century the most consistently presented offence was fornication,[12] although from the mid-seventeenth century until well into the eighteenth perhaps the most commonly presented offence, surprisingly, was working on the sabbath. To these main staples of presentments were added cases of failure to attend church, defamation, and that great peculiarity of Manx cultural history, cursing.[13]

The system depended heavily on public participation. A sumner (this form was more used than summoner) general, roughly equivalent to an apparitor, was appointed for the whole island, but each parish also had its own sumner, an unpaid local official whose duties included whipping dogs away from the church door in service time, escorting prisoners to the episcopal prison in St German's Cathedral, helping to collect tithes in kind, and producing lists of those who had recently died intestate for the meetings of the ecclesiastical circuit courts. There were four churchwardens in each parish, whose duties were roughly equivalent to those of their English equivalents, and also four questmen. Although the presentments made by the churchwardens and the questmen look very similar, in theory the questmen had the distinctive task of acting as jury of presentment, and a few of the more zealous parishes seem to have, for at least limited periods, maintained the prescribed practice of holding meetings between the minister and questmen of each parish to make presentments on the last Sunday of each month. Given that the population of the island was probably not much over 10,000 in 1700, all this would seem to provide at least the framework for a very effective system of ecclesiastical discipline.

To those acquainted with the English church courts, perhaps the most remarkable aspect of the Manx system was the formidable range of sanctions which the Manx church had at its disposal. The bishop had his own prison, a dungeon in the crypt of St German's Cathedral, incorporated into Peel Castle. This probably dated, with other work on the cathedral, from 1229, measured 34 feet by 18 feet, and its only ventilation was provided by a barred opening which overlooked Peel harbour and which faced the north wind: incarceration there can hardly have been a pleasant experience.[14] Offenders might be made to give bonds, in effect recognizances, to guarantee either the performance of penance or future good behaviour. And the Manx ecclesiastical courts could fine. Even more remarkably, they regularly called on the assistance of the secular arm in the shape of soldiers from the island's various garrisons, who were constantly called upon to ensure that penances and other punishments took place. And the Manx system of ecclesiastical discipline could subject offenders to a wide range of physical punishments, most of which could assume an important symbolic tone.

One such physical punishment was the use of the stocks. A number of references occur to the Manx church courts punishment in the stocks, which was usually inflicted on offenders who were thought to be guilty of unusually heinous offences. One such was Katherine Cottier alias Kneall of Lezayre, who in 1659 cursed John Casement's posterity to the third or fourth generation and wished that his house might be 'ruenatted'. In a fine display of the spectrum of available punishments, she was sentenced to spend an hour in the stocks at Ramsey, to be whipped, to acknowledge her fault before the congregation in her parish church, to beg forgiveness publicly from Casement, and to pay a 12d fine.[15] The stocks were similarly used in conjunction with other forms of punishment in 1678, when Margaret Huiston of Braddan was found guilty of slandering Catherine Christian alias Finch as a whore, and of alleging that she 'gott peices of fustian from Scotchmen for lying w[i]th her'. The court ordered that Huiston:

> shall sit one hour in ye stocks at Duglasse in the height of the markett, and in ye same place to acknowledge her fault and to aske the s[ai]d

> Cath[erine] forgivenesse on her knees, and also to make two Sundayes penance in plena ecc[lesiastic]a where she is also to ask forgiveness on her knees and to confesse her fault.

This was to be followed by 40 days' imprisonment. The order noted the defamed person's good reputation, stating that 'it is well known to the whole country that the above Cath[erine] Christian al[ia]s Finch hath lived all her life time in a very good repute', and described Huiston as 'this most idle and wicked creature'. Here the stocks were clearly being used deliberately ('upon good consideration', as the order put it) as part of the sanctions against what was evidently regarded as an unusually annoying offender.[16]

As well as the stocks, the Manx church courts could make use of that instrument of punishment which has attracted so much attention from folklorists,[17] the scold's bridle. Here, as elsewhere, the exact chronology of the employment of various ecclesiastical sanctions on the Isle of Man will remain uncertain until the relevant records have been searched exhaustively, but there does seem to have been something of a short vogue in the use, or perhaps more accurately threat, of this punishment in the late 1630s. Although it should be noted that men were also subjected to it,[18] the bridle was apparently regarded in the Isle of Man as an appropriate punishment for women found guilty of defamation. One such was Elizabeth Cosnahan, wife of William Cosnahan, vicar of German. The vicar was suspended in 1638 for sexual immorality, drunkenness and irregularities in his conduct of marriages, and at the same time his wife was censured for defaming another woman for 'sorcerie or witchcraft'. The bishop was petitioned, probably by Elizabeth Cosnahan's relatives, that 'you will be pleased to forbeare the bridell because her shame & infamie will not profitt us', and in any case it seems that the defamed woman had also requested that the sentence be mitigated, and indicated that she would be content with an apology. But Cosnahan had defamed another woman as a witch, in this case it seems that the sentence that she should stand outside her parish church for half an hour 'when ye congregatio[n] come out of ye church from dyvine service & sermon ... with the bridle in her mouth' was carried out.[19] In 1640 Margaret Karren, her parish unknown, after defaming another woman, was similarly sentenced to stand at 'ye church yard stile in where she is parishioner after devine service' with a 'briddle' in her mouth.[20] And in 1637, when Mr Robert Quaile, Deemster, and Mary Corkill cleared themselves by compurgation of a fame of fornication, it was ordered that anybody subsequently repeating the slander should be fined £3, undergo imprisonment, and suffer the 'brydle' and 'other shamefull punishmente at ye Ordinarie's discrecon'.[21]

By far the most detailed order invoking the use of the bridle, however, came in September 1637 when Katherine Robinson, the wife of Edward Robinson of Castletown, was found guilty of defaming the bishop, at that point Richard Parr. When asked to drink the bishop's health in Arthur Caesar's house, she apparently said 'she would not pledge the bishop's health, or any black coat's, for yf he went in a black coate he could hardly be an honest man, and further said the devil goe w[i]th them all'. Unsurprisingly, the ecclesiastical courts decided that this was 'a greevous obloquy & matchlesse slander & aspersion uppon all the clergy', and that 'this most uncharitable, black & hellish imprecation & aspersion' deserved 'the most severe censure that the law alloweth'. It was therefore ordered that Robinson should

> submissively make her acknowledgement in penitentiall habitt, in all the parish churches of this isle, standing upon a forme im[me]diately after the reading of the second lesson untill the epistle & gospell be fully reade there & then shall aske every p[ar]ticular minister forgivenesse in their severall cures for her said high offence, & this acknowledgement to be maid in the churches one [i.e. on] the sabboath dayes w[i]thout intermission, according to the scheadule herewith anexed.

After this she was to be 'bridled at the crosse in the churchyard of KK Malew im[m]ediately after evening service & sermon there to stand w[i]th the bridle in her mouth in the face of the people for the space of half an houre'. The order stressed that this was 'accordiing to the law & practice of this church (though the offence be matchlesse)', but it seems that the sentence was never carried out. Robinson appealed against her sentence to secular authority in the form of James Stanley, then Lord Strange and the future seventh earl of Derby. The sentence was not imposed, and in August 1640, after standing excommunicate for three years, she finally made her peace with the bishop being at that point near to death, and fearful of the 'hassard of her soule' if she died excommunicate. Her sentence was remitted, although she still had to make an apology on her knees to the bishop.[22]

On the strength of Manx ecclesiastical court records so far consulted, the bridle appears to have been little used in the last decades of the seventeenth century, and it is therefore perhaps a little puzzling that its employment should have been noted by an early eighteenth-century observer. George Waldron, scion of an Essex gentry family and an Oxford graduate, served as a trade commissioner for the British government on the island, and in 1726 published the first edition of his *Description of the Isle of Man*. Waldron obviously regarded the island's way of life as somewhat lacking in gentility, and dismissed the Manx as ignorant, superstitious and priest-ridden. He commented on the use of the bridle as one aspect of the peculiar ways of the island:

> I know nothing in their statutes nor punishments particular, but this; which is, that if any person be convicted of uttering a scandalous report, and cannot make good the assertion, instead of being fined or imprisoned, they are sentenced to stand in the market-place in a sort of scaffold erected for that purpose with their tongue in a noose made of leather,

> which they call a bridle, and having thus exposed to the view of the people for some time, on the taking off this machine they are obliged to say three times, tongue thou hast lyed.

Waldron described this as 'a whimsical punishment', but reflected on its potential effectiveness, opining that after its use whatever the offender said 'would be certain to gain no credit'.[23]

Waldron seemed to think the bridle a regular feature of Manx life, and although this conclusion remains uncertain, there is evidence that the bridle's employment was revived in the early eighteenth century on the initiative of that great enthusiast for traditional Manx ecclesiastical discipline, bishop Thomas Wilson. Wilson noted in his personal memoranda book for June 1714 that 'I ordered a *bridle* to be made, as a terror to people of ill tongues: and it is now brought about the circuit by the General Sumner, and lodged in his hands for the time to come'. In October of that year the use of the bridle was once again threatened, in this instance against Mary Gibson, convicted of four separate slanders, 'by all which, and by the general complaint of the neighbourhood, it appears that she is a woman of a lewd and ungovernable tongue'. Gibson was sentenced to stand wearing the bridle on three separate market days at Castletown, but a little later appeared in court with Margaret Stevenson, the woman she had most defamed, and Stevenson's mother. Gibson, 'with the greatest submission and tokens of deep sorrow, begged that the severity of the law, in wearing the bridle, might be dispensed with'. The court, 'in Christian compassion', agreed to this, although it insisted that Gibson should ask public forgiveness in Castletown chapel the next Sunday.[24] Clearly, the bridle was regarded as a potent and shameful punishment, and something which offenders were anxious to avoid undergoing if at all possible, while it is once again equally obvious that the Manx ecclesiastical courts, as their equivalents elsewhere, were willing to accept considerable flexibility in their punishing policy.

But if Bishop Wilson reintroduced the bridle, his best remembered contribution to Manx ecclesiastical punishment was his revival of the ancient custom of dragging persons convicted of repeated sexual immorality behind a boat across one of the island's harbours. One such punishment, which apparently attracted little public enthusiasm (in particular, it proved difficult to find anybody willing to provide and man the necessary boat), occurred at Douglas in 1712,[25] although the most famous instance came in 1714, with the punishment of Katherine Kinred of 'Kirk Christ' (probably Lezayre). Kinred was described as 'a notorious strumpet, who has brought forth three illegitimate children, and still continues to stroll about the country, and to lead a most vicious and scandalous life on other accounts'. This could clearly not be permitted, and the Consistory Court thereforeordered that since all this tended to 'the great dishonour of the Christian name, and to her own utter destruction without a timely and thorough reformation':

> It is therefore ordered (as well for the further punishment of the said delinquent as for the example of others) that the said Kath. Kinred be dragged after a boat in the sea at Peeltown, on Wednesday the 17th instant (being the fair of St Patrick) at the height of the market. To which end, a boat and boat's crew are to be charged by the General Sumner, and the constable and soldiers of the garrison are, by the Governor's order, to be aiding and assisting in seeing this censure performed.

Given the difficulties encountered in finding people willing to assist with inflicting such a punishment two years earlier, the order also instructed that 'in case any owner, master, or crew of any boat are found refractory, by neglecting or refusing to perform this service for the restraining of vice', their names were to be noted by the General Sumner, and they were to be severely fined. Apparently, dragging offenders behind boats was the limit that public opinion on the Isle of Man put on acceptable ecclesiastical discipline.[26]

Yet, despite the stocks, the bridle and the water punishment, the standard punishment in the repertoire of the Manx church courts remained public penance. At the centre of Manx ecclesiastical discipline was the image of the penitent, standing in penitential habit, frequently with a schedule attached to their clothing giving details of their offence, making a full confession of their misdeeds, asking the congregation to pray for and with them, and seeking ritual and formal reintegration into the communities whose norms they infringed. Penance was a flexible form of punishment. As we have seen, the spectacular offender, like William Kissack, with whom we began this chapter, could be ordered to perform penance in all of the island's parish churches, and possibly in the market squares of its towns as well. More commonly, offenders might have to do one, two or three days penance in their own parish church. If they had offended against a specific individual (this was particularly true of defamation or cursing cases) penitents were usually enjoined to ask forgiveness of the person offended against, while there might be other touches. Throughout the seventeenth century it was customary to order (George Waldron's description of the use of the scold's bridle provides an added dimension to this) that the penitent should, as John Corkill of Andreas was after he defamed Jony Kneale in 1685, 'putt his finger on his mouth & say tongue thow hast lyed'. And in this case we find another element frequently present when penance was done for defamation. It was ordered that 'publication' was 'to be made in the parish church yt noe person revive ye s[ai]d slander un penalty of £3 to ye Lord's use 40 days imprissonm[en]t & further punishm[en]t at the court's discretion'.[27] The preservation of good relationships in the parish was an important objective of the church courts.

The objectives of all of these ecclesiastical punishments were essentially those of penance: the exposure of an offence, the warning which it was hoped the punished offender's fate might give to others, the reformation of the offender, and the consequent reinforcement of Christian values and of the Christian community and Christian commonwealth. The Manx Ecclesiastical Constitutions of 1704, which consciously built on the traditional Manx ecclesiastical law, were framed mainly to 'by all laudable means promote the conversion of sinners, and oblige men to submit to the discipline of the Gospel', and to 'provide for the instruction of the growing age in Christian learning and good manners'.[28] The discipline which the Manx church courts sought to impose was regarded as a vital part of that process, and the public and shaming punishments which were so frequently imposed upon offenders against that discipline were thought to be essential to its maintenance.

II

The Manx ecclesiastical courts operated in tandem with a system of secular justice, and this system too dealt in a currency of public punishments, and, on appropriate occasions, in the deployment of exemplary justice.[29] As in most of contemporary Europe, the Manx criminal justice system in the seventeenth and eighteenth centuries depended upon capital punishment for the correction of serious crime, and that capital punishment was carried out in public, and suffused with ceremonial and ritual. An account of the Isle of Man dating from c. 1665, which is especially strong on the island's legal structures and practices, gives a graphic description of the Manx public execution:

> Now the dayes of execucon are commonly frydayes, on which morninge the minister of the parish (which is Kirk Malew) comes unto the condemned persons which are brought before him in the Castle chappell and there reades prayers, gives them godly exhortacons, examines them of their beliefe, creed, to say the lords prayers, and to confesse their sins... and when they are brought to the place of execution, the minister goes alonge readinge psalmes, prayers or singinge psalmes, there being alsoe a guard of the soldiers with light matches, and, as the fashion is, many persons and young people comes there also for spectators... and before the fellon goes upp the ladder the coroner or lockman tyes a lynen cloathe about his forehead to cover his eyes, and soe ascends the ladder, with a roape about his necke, the ladder being commonly sett on the west side of the gallowes; and when the felon is on the topp, the people praying and frends bewailing him, if there bee no pardon, the coroner or lockman turnes the ladder, and soe hangs till he is conceived to bee deade; and then beinge taken downe, is by freinds layd in a windinge sheete and brought to the parish church on a beare or carr, and there buried.[30]

The public execution stands at the symbolic centre of the early modern Manx justice system, a more potent manifestation of authority than the church courts could provide. Yet it was also an infinitely rarer one. There could have been few, if any, Manx churchgoers who had not witnessed a number of public penances, for these were ordered at virtually every sitting of the ecclesiastical correction courts. Yet in the period 1680–1700, for example, only two executions are known to have taken place on the Isle of Man;[31] punishments inflicted by the ecclesiastical courts were much more common.

The Manx secular courts inflicted lesser public punishments, but even these, on the strength of surviving documentation, were far fewer than the penances and other censures inflicted by the church. The secular courts, for example, like the ecclesiastical courts, made use of the stocks, but surprisingly infrequently. A handful of petty thieves were stocked, one of them, an outsider, being put in the stocks 'for example to others' before being thrown off the island.[32] Others were put in the stocks for making false accusation, or for fishing for salmon against official order.[33] The only example of the use of the stocks from the secular court records which we have so far consulted that conveys anything like the intensity of the fuller ecclesiastical court orders concerning this form of punishment came in 1686, at the conclusion of a case which had commenced three years earlier. In that year, Thomas Clarke took out a traverse against a jury verdict in a case of assault between him and James Kissage. The traverse jury overturned the verdict of the original jury, declaring that the earlier jurors had ignored some of the evidence relevant to the case and hidden other parts of it. The jurors, four in number, were each fined 5 shillings and sentenced to sit for an hour in the stocks in Douglas marketplace in market time, each with a schedule on his breast announcing his fault.[34] Such sentences, it seems, were inflicted more commonly by the Manx ecclesiastical courts.

Something like the ecclesiastical punishments, indeed, occurred with the one example of the use of the pillory which we have encountered in the samples of Manx secular court records which we have studied. In 1680, Patrick Caly of Lezayre was accused of drawing blood on Thomas Stephen. Caly had cleared himself by swearing an oath that he was not guilty of the bloodshed, but subsequent evidence demonstrated that he had sworn falsely, and so he was accordingly punished for perjury. An order of 1684 sentenced Caly to go to the several churches and market crosses of the island 'with a paper upon his brest declaringe his offence', while the coroners (an office roughly equivalent to the English justice of the peace) of each of the island's sheadings were to oversee each act of punishment, and return certificates 'that the same was punctually done', while Caly was also ordered to stand in the pillory for an hour at the next meeting of the island's Court of General Gaol Delivery. Here we have a rare occasion on which the secular courts awarded a public punishment which was basically very similar to those regularly handed out by the ecclesiastical authorities.[35]

These secular punishments are familiar enough in most punishment systems of the period. The heavy reliance on shaming punishments in the Manx ecclesiastical courts does, however, suggest something rather different, although the identity of the particular qualities present in the Isle of Man which created this situation remains elusive. One possible line of approach to this problem lies in another phenomenon frequently referred to in the Manx church court records, *compurgation,* the practise by which persons accused of an offence before an ecclesiastical court might clear themselves by their own oaths and by the oaths of respectable neighbours willing to swear in their support. The practice was apparently fully established when records of the Manx church courts begin, with scattered references to it in the first decade of the seventeenth century.[36] More detailed accounts point to the seriousness with which it was taken. One such case came in 1637, when Mr Robert Quaile and Mary Corkill alias Vinch were defamed for fornication. Quaile (or Quayle) was a Deemster, that is one of the two judges who had considerable powers in the island, which included trying and sentencing in cases involving the death penalty. It is no surprise that he should be described as 'a man of soe eminente a place in the temporall state of the isle', while Mary Corkill, so the court insisted, was 'an honest matron of good & honest repute'. The bishop deputed the vicar of Braddan to call the couple before him, and they swore on the New Testament 'that they never had carnall dealings, knowledge, or copulacon one with the other'. The vicar noted that they had

> fully purged & absolutely cleered themselves from the s[ai]d uniust aspersion & undeserved defamation. And wee take in o[u]r consciences they have w[i]th a good conscience satisfyed the law in that behaulf & soe taken away the offence w[hi]ch anie charitable member of Christ his church might take uppon the former bruite & p[re]sentmente.

It probably helped matters that Quaile was a man of some standing. But the willingness to accept the accused couple's oath in this respect is remarkable. Manx society, like many other early modern societies, was one where reputation was vital. Yet it is striking how ecclesiastical compurgation, in this case without the assistance of additional compurgators, was so readilyaccepted, and apparently desired, as a method of reestablishing a good name.[37]

In 1637, compurgation, although a still regular aspect of church court procedures, was in decline in England.[38] But the practice was abolished there after the Restoration,[39] and by the early eighteenth century would only have been remembered by those running the English church courts as a long-obsolete practice. Yet, as with the active imposition of ecclesiastical discipline, what would have seemed an anachronism in England was still a live institution in the Isle of Man. In 1703, Mrs Lettice Salmon, at that point resident in Dublin, complained to the Manx ecclesiastical authorities that Henry Norris of Arbory was spreading rumours that he had enjoyed sexual relations with her. These rumours, Salmon claimed, were 'grounded only upon the bare report of the said Henry Norris, prompted for certain sums of money, which he had formerly borrowed from her'. Salmon,

> having voluntarily & earnestly desired that she might clear herself of the said scandalous imputation in due form of law ... accordingly came to KK Malew church on Sunday last, & then & there immediately after morning prayer before all the congregacon took her oath upon the Holy Evangelist, with two lawful compurgators, that she never at any time had any inconinent dealing with, or carnal knowledge of, the said Henry Norris.

Norris was, in fact, sentenced to penance, to 40 days incarceration in St German's prison, and a fine of £3. This case demonstrates not only the continuation of the old idea of compurgation (note that Salmon was aided by 'two lawful compurgators'), but shows again how this method of clearing one's name was seen as being appropriate and desirable in the early eighteenth century.[40] That the institution was an accepted one a generation earlier can be inferred from a case of c. 1677, which noted that Edward Pasley and Margaret Nelson of Rushen, suspected of fornication, 'came voluntarily on their owne accord & did purdge before the congregation'. The enthusiasm of the couple for this method of clearing their name is apparent, but on this occasion the minister presiding over the compurgation was admonished 'not to take ... purgation w[i]thout ord[e]r from ye court in form of law'.[41] The practice was obviously so popular and familiar that at least one Manx clergyman was willing to facilitate it without reference to higher authority.

Arguably, compurgation in the Isle of Man was the obverse of public punishment. Like public punishment, its efficacy depended upon the existence of face-to-face communities who possessed a shared morality, and who accepted that that morality should be upheld, either through the public shaming and punishing of offenders, or through that public vindication of individual morality and probity which compurgation represented. As yet, we have little insights into the mechanics by which Manx parish communities functioned, and we have little sense of how the 'politics of the parish' operated in the island;[42] assuredly, as yet we have no Manx Terling. Indeed, given the scattered nature of most Manx settlements (it is difficult to describe them as 'villages') the applicability of the concept of 'community' to the island's inhabitants remains problematic. But there is every reason to suspect that the inhabitants of these dispersed Manx settlements were evidently no less concerned with shared morality, with reputation, with the concepts of individual honour and symbolic capital than were their equivalents elsewhere in Europe. As ever, we must make due allowance for the rhetoric of court documents, but even when such allowance is made, some of the statements about the impact of disruptive individuals upon the smooth workings of neighbourly relations made in the Manx church court records is striking. We have already noted the case of Robert Quaile and Mary Corkill alias Vinch, who cleared themselves by purgation of rumours of fornication in 1637. The order exonerating the couple was anxious to prevent further gossip about them spreading, and took measures against 'caluminous rumo[u]rs, idle & lewd surmyzes falsly conceived & scandalously uttered by the virulent tongues of the ill disposed whose cheefe delight is to feed themselves or others infamie'.[43] Both the language, and the assumptions which underlay it, demonstrate a concept of individual honour which was essentially, potentially at least, public property, together with a concept of human relations which saw harmony and a shared sense of moral community as a desirable and attainable norm. Arguably, the public and shaming punishments inflicted by the Manx church courts made special sense in a culture where such concepts flourished.

But these concepts did not exist in an institutional vacuum: they were moulded, and avenues for their expression were provided, by the ideology of the Manx church and by the institutions which supported and promulgated that ideology. Let us return to our early eighteenth-century observer of Manx affairs, George Waldron. To the urbane Englishman, bishop Wilson's ecclesiastical regime was an unpleasant manifestation of priestcraft. He commented on the power of 'the ecclesiastick court, the clergy holding a kind of tyrannical jurisdiction over the Manks people',[44] and took a generally negative view of the clergy, claiming that they kept the Manx people in ignorance, the better to rule over them. Waldron declared that

> The discipline of the Church being perpetually dinn'd into the ears of the laity, and the indispensable obligation of submitting to it, the abject creatures are drove to prison like sheep to a fold, and from thence to public penance, as quietly as those beasts are to the slaughter; deterred, on the one hand, from murmuring, by the threatenings of severer punishments; and persuaded on the other, that patient submission to the inflictors is supremest merit in the eyes of heaven.[45]

At the very least, the public and shaming punishments inflicted by the Manx church courts, like there equivalents elsewhere, constitute a fascinating and important interface between official and popular culture, between the desire of communities to see what they conceived of as their disruptive members corrected, and the desire of officialdom to maintain control, to reform individuals, and to provide examples to the populace at large against future wrongdoing.

Such punishments also, arguably, have considerable implications for the general history of punishment in Europe. The public execution has attracted considerable attention from historians of punishment, but non-capital public punishments and shaming punishments more generally have so far been largely neglected by those constructing the broad accounts of penal history.[46] Rusche and Kirchheimer, for example, mention penance briefly, and also refer to the use of public exposure as an aspect of the punishment of offenders in late eighteenth-century France, but they do not explore either of these subjects in depth.[47] More recently, Michel Foucault, while awarding due emphasis to the importance of public spectacle and of the involvement of the populace in premodern punishment systems, restricts his detailed analysis to capital punishment. In so doing he misses a number of important points. In particular, his celebrated assertion that developments in penal practice around 1800 marked a shift from the punishments of the bodies of offenders to the bodies of their souls, 'a punishment that acts in depth on the heart, the thoughts, the will, the inclination', was clearly written in the absence of knowledge of the types of public penal ceremonies of shame and reintegration like those which we have found among the Manx records.[48] More recent general studies of the history of punishment rarely have anything very extensive to say about non-capital public punishments, and how shame and reintegration work as elements in society's repertoire of punishment.[49] This could well be part of a more general tendency to underplay what might be described as a cultural approach to punishment, to pay insufficient attention to problems of meaning.

It is intriguing therefore to speculate on how those punishments meted out by the Manx ecclesiastical courts, which we have described in this essay, stand in relation to some of the familiar theories on the punishment of criminals. Their functioning, in a general way, seems to fit in with that broadly Durkheimian model which would emphasise punishment's moral roots, and its assumed objective of assisting the production and maintenance of social solidarity. The chronology of the rise and fall of such punishments would seem a matter of concern both, as we have suggested, to the Foucauldian paradigm which interprets the punishment of offenders as a power-knowledge mechanism which operates within the broader repertoire of techniques of disciplining and dominating, and with a 'civilizing process' approach derived from Norbert Elias. Arguably, however, such punishments can be interpreted as being especially relevant to a certain stage of social development. The author of one of the few works to have examined how shame and reintegration might work as aspects of modern penal practices has argued cogently that

> a combination of shame at and repentance by the offender is a more powerful affirmation of the criminal law than one-sided moralizing. A shaming ceremony followed later by a forgiveness and repentance ceremony more potently builds commitment to the law than a shaming ceremony alone. Nothing has greater symbolic force in community-wide conscience building than repentance.

Yet for this symbolic force to operate at its strongest, the people on whom it is brought to bear must be 'individuals ... enmeshed in multiple relationships of interdependency', since 'societies shame more effectively when they are communitarian';[50] that is to say, of course, societies very much as we imagine early modern societies to have been. But, as we have suggested, the nature of Manx local communities, and how the early modern community was imagined by early modern Manx men and women, are still subjects which remain very much unexplored. What is obvious is that, however communitarian those undergoing or watching Manx ecclesiastical public punishments may have been, the impetus to inflict those punishments came not from the community, but rather from the Manx church, an organization which was evidently intent on using all the sanctions at its disposal to impose godly discipline on the population of an isolated and economically backward island on the periphery of Europe.

Notes

1 Manx National Heritage Library (hereafter MNHL), Liber Causarum 1703–09, 8 November 1705.

2 A.W. Moore, *A History of the Isle of Man* (2 vols, 1900), remains the best general introduction to the island's history, although it should be read with the more modern D. Craine, *Manannan's Isle* (Douglas, 1955), and R.H. Kinvig, *The Isle of Man: A Social, Cultural and Political History* (3rd edn, Liverpool, 1975).

3 Sir Edward Coke, *The Fourth Part of the Institutes of the Laws of England; Concerning the Jurisdiction of the Courts* (2nd edn, 1648), 284.

4 For the island's political and economic history in the seventeenth century, see J.R. Dickinson, *The Lordship of Man Under the Stanleys: Government and Economy in the Isle of Man, 1580–1704* (Chetham Society, 3rd series, 41, 1996).

5 A brief guide to Manx church history from the late middle ages to the seventeenth century is provided by Moore, *History of the Isle of Man*, I, chap. 5, 'The History of the Church and its first Struggle with the State', while Moore's findings on Manx church history are gathered in his *Sodor and Man* (SPCK, Diocesan Histories, Brighton and New York, 1993). Many important materials are gathered together in William Harrison, *An Account of the Diocese of Sodor and Man and St German's Cathedral: Also a Record of the Bishops of Sodor and Man and a Tabular Statement of the Rectors, Vicars and Chaplains in the Seventeen Parishes in the Said Diocese* (Manx Society, 29, 1879). John Gelling, *A History of the Manx Church 1698–1911* (Douglas, 1998) is a good introduction to later developments.

6 This right was apparently only very infrequently invoked. Dr Fay Bound, who has carried out extensive researches into the ecclesiastical court records of the Northern Province in the late seventeenth and early eighteenth centuries has found only two cases of appeals reaching York from the Isle of Man: BIHR references known to us. See also the papers collected in Borthwick Institute of Historical Research, 'Correspondence and Papers relating to the Diocese of Sodor and Man', Bp.C&P.XV/1–8. For a case dating from 1637 which was appealed to York, and provoked a minor constitutional crisis on the island, see Dickinson, *Lordship of Man Under the Stanleys*, 63–4.

7 See for example the comments of Moore, *History of the Isle of Man*, I, 347–52.

8 The classic biography of Wilson is John Keble, *The Life of the Right Reverend Father in God, Thomas Wilson D.D., Lord Bishop of Sodor and Man* (2 vols, Oxford, 1863), which includes numerous lengthy quotations from contemporary archival

sources. Although less well documented, Clement Crutwell, *The Life of Thomas Wilson D.D., Lord Bishop of Sodor and Man* (1782), does, in its 'Preface', print a number of contemporary encomiums on Wilson.

9 The standard introduction to the Manx ecclesiastical courts in our period is Anne Ashley, 'The spiritual courts of the Isle of Man, especially in the seventeenth and eighteenth Centuries', *EHR*, 57 (1957), 31–59, which should be read in conjunction with Neil Mathieson, 'Ecclesiastical Courts in the Isle of Man', *Proceedings of the Isle of Man Natural History and Antiquarian Society*, 5 (1952), 261–70. For some more recent comments, see J.R. Dickinson and J.A. Sharpe, 'The correction business of the Manx Church Courts, *c.* 1660–1720: a preliminary survey', in W.J. Sheils and Mark Jenner eds, *The Church Courts After 1660: a System in Decline* (Woodbridge, 2002).

10 Keble, *Life of Wilson*, I, 141.

11 Microfilms of the *Libri Testamentarum* relevant to our period are MNHL EW1–31 (Episcopal Wills, 1600–1723), and RB 512–26 (Archidiaconal Wills, 1628–1724. Microfilms of Presentment Books 1640–1800 exist as MNHL PRE 1–17. *Libri Causarum* are made available in the original, volumes for 1659–1704 and 1703–09 being consulted for this study. These sources are unpaginated, or at best paginated in an inconsistent fashion, and hence references have been cited by date. Generally, foliation of Manx documents for the early modern period is non-existent, misleading, or contradictory, and references to Manx secular court records given later in this essay follow the conventions laid down in P.J. Davey ed., *Notes for Contributors to Centre Publications* (University of Liverpool, Centre for Manx Studies, Douglas 1996).

12 MNHL EW1, *passim*.

13 Presentments for this later period are discussed in Dickinson and Sharpe, 'Correction Business of the Manx Church Courts'.

14 Gelling, *History of the Manx Church*, 7.

15 MNLI Presentment Book, 1659, no date.

16 MNLI RB 520, 19 June 1678.

17 See, for example, the comments of A.W. Moore, *The Folk-Lore of the Isle of Man* (Douglas and London, 1891), 176.

18 See for example John Corrin of Rushen, sentenced to wear the bridle for calling William Nelson's wife a bitch: Presentment Book 1668, 16 August 1668: cf. the Maughold man threatened with wearing the bridle in 1715 if he failed to perform penance for falsely claiming to be the father of an illegitimate child: Keble, *Life of Wilson*, I, 362.

19 MNHL RB514, 14 May 1638.

20 MNHL Presentment Book 1640, undated.

21 MNHL RB 514, September 1637.

22 MNHL RB514, September 1637, final order 5 August 1640.

23 George Waldron, *A Description of the Isle of Man*, ed. William Harrison (Manx Society, 11, 1865), 41. Yet, as Craine reminds us, the Manx bridle was made of leather, and thus 'not so formidable as the kind used in Britain' (*Mannanan's Isle*, 15–16).

24 Keble, *Life of Wilson*, I, 362.

25 *Ibid.*, 295–6.

26 *Ibid.*, 297–8. Craine, *Mannanan's Isle*, 136, similarly commented that this practice aroused 'great public resentment', and notes that the last order for drawing behind a boat, dating from 1634, was simply not carried out.

27 MNHL RB521, 25 July 1685.

28 Keble, *Life of Wilson*, I, 206.

29 The Manx secular court system formed the main focus of a project funded by the Leverhulme Trust, F224R, 'Crime, Litigation and the Courts in the Isle of Man, *c.* 1550–1704': for some initial findings from this project, see J.R. Dickinson and J.A. Sharpe, 'Courts, crime and litigation in the Isle of Man, 1580–1700', *Historical Research*, 72 (1999), 140–59.
30 Flintshire Record Office, Nantlys MS D/NA/905, 'An Account of the Isle of Man, *c.* 1665', fo. 59.
31 These involved Philip Cloage, executed for sheep-theft in 1682, and Isabel Kewley, executed for infanticide in 1683: MNHL Lib. Scacc. 1682, 24. 27; Lib. Plit. 1683, 96, respectively. For the background to the prosecution of serious crime on the island in this period see J.R. Dickinson, 'Criminal violence and judicial punishment in the Isle of Man 1580–1700', *Proceedings of the Isle of Man Natural History and Antiquarian Society*, 11 (2000), 127–42.
32 MNHL Lib. Plit., 1659, 45.
33 MNHL Lib. Plit., 1599, 57: Lib. Plit., 1688, 73.
34 MNHL Lib. Plit., 1683, 59.
35 MNHL Lib. Plit., 1680, 59, 60. On the Manx coroner, see Dickinson, *Lordship of Man Under the Stanleys*, 46–9. The samples of Manx secular litigation, civil and criminal, collected in the course of Leverhulme Trust Project F224R, included full details of cases coming to the Court of General Gaol Delivery, the Chancery Court and the Sheading Courts for two selected periods, 1580–1600 and 1680–1700, these being supplemented by cases coming to the Court of General Gaol Delivery (the island's equivalent of the assizes) for 1640–60. Together, these cases brought together in these samples number more than 15,000.
36 See for example EW1, 17 October 1601 (Lezayre); 3 February 1603 (Braddan); 4 February 1603 (Malew); 7 February 1603 (Patrick).
37 MNHL RB514, September 1637. On the office of Deemster, see Dickinson, *Lordship of Man Under the Stanleys*, 43–6. *Ibid.*, Appendix V, 360, shows that Quaile served as Deemster between 1636 and 1644, and held his main properties at Ballaquayle and Conchan.
38 For comments on compurgation in the English church courts, see Ronald A. Marchant, *The Church under the Law: Justice, Administration and Discipline in the Diocese of York 1560–1640* (Cambridge, 1969), 225, table 33, 231; Ralph Houlbrooke, *The Church Courts and the People During the English Reformation 1520–1570* (Oxford, 1979), 45–6, and appendix 3, 278–81; and Martin Ingram, *The Church Courts, Sex and Marriage in England, 1570–1640* (Cambridge, 1987), 51–2, 249, 280.
39 By 13 Charles II, cap. 12, sect. 4.
40 MNHL *Liber Causarum* 1659–1704, 6 April 1703; another order, *Liber Causarum* 1703–1709, 6 April 1703, records Henry Norris's punishment following Salmon's successful compurgation.
41 MNHL RB 519, date missing, c. July 1677.
42 The standard discussion of this concept is provided by Keith Wrightson, 'The politics of the parish in early modern England', in Paul Griffiths, Adam Fox and Steve Hindle eds, *The Experience of Authority in Early Modern England* (London, Macmillan, 1996), 10–46.
43 MNHL RB 514, September 1637.
44 Waldron, *Description of the Isle of Man*, 16.
45 *Ibid.*, 21.
46 But see Martin Ingram, 'Juridical folklore in England illustrated by rough music', in Christopher W. Brooks and Michael Lobbam eds, *Communities and Courts in England 1150–1900* (London and Rio Grande, 1997); and J.A. Sharpe, 'Civility,

civilizing processes, and the end of public punishment in England', in Peter Burke, Brian Harrison and Paul Slack eds, *Civil Histories: Essays Presented to Sir Keith Thomas* (Oxford, 2000). For some preliminary comments on the importance of shaming punishments, see J.A. Sharpe, *Judicial Punishment in England* (London, 1990), 19, 47–9.

47 Georg Rusche and Otto Kirchheimer, *Punishment and Social Structure* (New York, 1939), 9–10, 82.

48 Michel Foucault, *Discipline and Punish: the Birth of the Prison* (Harmondsworth, 1979), 16: at this point Foucault quotes Mably's formulation that 'Punishment, if I may so put it, should strike the soul rather than the body'.

49 This is even true of David Garland's excellent *Punishment and Modern Society: a Study in Social Theory* (Oxford, 1990).

50 John Braithwaite, *Crime, Shame and Reintegration* (Cambridge, 1989), 81, 14.

6

Sanctifying the Robe: Punitive Violence and the English Press, 1650–1700

Philippe Rosenberg

I

It has become almost commonplace to treat punishment as a self-contained sociological phenomenon to be interpreted in terms of sentences or patterns of prosecution. Unfortunately, this widespread approach tends to overlook how punitive power itself has been understood. Much like its ancient and medieval predecessors, modern punishment is supported by a set of rituals, rationales and explanations that serve to legitimize it. This symbolic apparatus not only underwrites punishment, but also marks it off as something distinct from 'mere' violence. Rationales are therefore every bit as crucial to the sociology of punishment as are the severity of sanctions, the frequency of punitive action, or the legal machinery that surround its application.

The work of several scholars, including a number of contributors to this volume, shows that the practice of punishment in early modern English history was a complex and highly varied matter. It combined harsh physical violence in some cases, and the discipline of fines, shame and indentured service in others, with the exercise of mercy and restraint. Mandates issued by the state, and ideas voiced by the theorists who struggled with the foundations of the right to punish, came head to head with local realities in the administration of justice. Contrary to appearance, however, a number of common threads linked these various elements. Punishment usually rested on a measure of popular consent: its deterrent message was addressed to popular audiences, and the authority to punish stemmed from juries and magistrates acting jointly in the name of the sovereign. With this in mind, we should seek to better grasp the views about punishment that were elaborated either by or for the national and local élites, and, better still, for the middling ranks of commoners who supplied accusations, entered evidence, served as jurymen or collaborated in the machinery of deterrence. What were the arguments that led these individuals to accept the courts' authority to inflict violence or other hardships as a matter of course? How did they decide that the violence carried out by the state, though sometimes quite brutal in its methods, was different from the violence carried out by the criminals? In what ways did they distinguish between proper and improper modes of administering retributive violence, long after any honour-derived rationales supporting direct retribution or 'composition' had ceased to persuade?

These questions all centre on the representation and ideology of punishment, a topic that has attracted some attention from historians. The two most entrenched arguments concerning the ideological dimensions of early modern punishment focus almost exclusively on the legitimization of state power and overlook questions about the legitimacy of violence itself. Followers of Michel Foucault claim that, before the rise of prisons and the internalization of discipline, punishment was an occasion for the state to advertise its power. Criminals were disturbers of the king's peace and the state's rituals of retribution provided a means for restoring lawful order as well as the integrity of royal power. The state effectively transformed the dismantled body of the criminal into a badge of its authority over its subjects.[1] A second prominent argument, congruent with the first, maintains that punishment was as much an occasion for social, political and spiritual contrition as it was a means of deterrence. Punishment was an occasion for asserting or reasserting the merits of obedience and submission to existing authority. In the view of J.A. Sharpe, the criminal's formulaic words of repentance supplied the necessary admission that the state was right to exact retribution. Faced with earthly punishment, the sinner turned to God for forgiveness in a process fundamentally akin to the experience of conversion. The pamphlets and broadsheets that summarized the criminal's life, confession and dying speeches showed where the sinner had strayed, but also offered reassurance that he or she had finally rejoined the fold of the political and religious community. The ordeal of punishment sent a warning to other potential criminals, but also served as a last-ditch instrument of salvation for the condemned.[2]

These arguments have opened up to discussion the ideology of punishment, but their limitations are beginning to show. The display of state power is an altogether obvious feature of the spectacle of corporal punishment, yet the argument which Foucault and his successors have put forward never truly gets beyond this issue of display. Unless one mistakenly assumes that subjects somehow lived in perpetual awe of their rulers, or that they mindlessly approved of the lessons of might, the argument fails almost entirely to account for the fact that the public supported the state's right to punish. More seriously still, it overlooks the considerable extent to which propagandists tried to *dissimulate* the state's power. In early modern England, as we shall see, pamphleteers routinely claimed that the violence witnessed in punishment was not the state's at all, but that of God.

Sharpe's contribution continues to hold a great deal more water than Foucault's, yet it overlooks a few important elements in the early modern ideology of punishment. Printing the criminal's acts of repentance certainly linked punishment with the wider narrative of human sin and divine judgment that held sway during this time. But if the whole point of these verbal performances was to commemorate submission and ultimate salvation, why, then, were dying speeches routinely accompanied by formulaic recitations of the criminal's cruelty or depravity? As we shall see, in seventeenth-century writings, the public vilification of the criminal remained as significant as the criminal's admission of guilt. It sustained what was, in effect, an attempt to expunge ambiguity: crime was crime, and therefore considered a form of violence; punishment was something else entirely.

While careful consideration of dying speeches and assize sermons, sheds light on retributive justice and its ideological moorings, these materials are more illuminating when considered in combination with other types of public commentary. The sketch that follows focuses mainly on print, especially the pamphlet press, leaving aside opinions conveyed through other channels of expression such as everyday speech and legal documents. It puts the emphasis on the *supply* of arguments, while dealing with their consumption and internalization in a more cursory manner. The quarry here, then, lies in the varied set of rationalizations which the shapers of opinion offered in order to justify punishment, including the effect of these rationalizations in fostering positive, as well as negative, evaluations of magisterial power. The focus is on the seventeenth century, with a special emphasis on its relatively neglected second half. This period, it bears noting, has received less attention than the late sixteenth and early seventeenth centuries, when the brutality of English law was at its peak, or than the eighteenth century, when an expanding 'Bloody Code' made a host of new property offences punishable by death, transportation, or imprisonment.[3]

Three concurrent trends affected the treatment of retribution during the late seventeenth century. The first involves a simple, quantitative proliferation of printed materials addressing punishment and similar categories of justified violence. The second and perhaps more surprising trend was one towards an increasing *sacralization* of punishment, the effect of which was to minimize its apparent violence. Sacralization, as we will see, represented a complex ideological pattern, keyed in part to a providentialist understanding of violence. The third trend was directly connected to the second; it involved an increasingly sharp dichotomy, opposing the benevolence of punitive authority to the cruelty of those who were subjected to it. Like so many dichotomies, this one was double-edged. It was used to justify the suppression of 'inhumane' elements in society, but could just as easily be turned against magistrates accused of judicial cruelty. As we shall see, the ideological fluidity that characterizes seventeenth-century discussions about retribution may well have stemmed from the fact that people were uncertain about whether the judges themselves were criminal or just, violent or benevolent.

II

The seventeenth century was a period of massive expansion in the volume and topical range of printed matter. The remarkable thing, however, is that the relative importance of punishment and retribution within this expanding field of print was more than keeping pace with the overall growth in output. Indeed, the proportion of these particular topics with respect to the whole did not decline until the eighteenth century, and then only gradually so. This finding is all the more surprising in that printers and booksellers had begun publishing on a vast array of new subjects that spanned everything from chemistry to the art of the flute.

Though imperfect, *The Short Title Catalogue* (*STC*) provides one of only a few usable sources for evaluating the production of print. Its chief and most obvious limitation lies in the fact that it only lists the titles of surviving materials, leaving out many works that are no longer extant. It also fails to provide any record of the numbers of copies produced or sold. It is problematic, furthermore, in that cataloguers entered different editions, reprints and sometimes copies of the same works, as separate records. A certain number of titles, therefore, appear more than once in the list. With these limitations in mind, by dividing the production of print into discrete 25-year periods, we find that between 1550 and 1749, words such as 'justice', 'revenge' and 'punishment' made up a steady 0.8 to 2.7 per cent of total production[4] (Table 6.1). These were significant figures that compared favourably with those obtaining for other important topics of the day. In 1650–74, the word 'government' accounted for 2.2 per cent of titles; in 1675–99, it was 2.1 per cent. In the same range of years, 'Jesus' accounted for between 1.5 and 2.8 per cent of titles. The words 'popish', 'popery' and 'papist' which evoked the great bugbear of the late seventeenth century, the Catholic threat, appeared in some 1.0 to 2.5 per cent of the period's titles. Counting the appearance of certain keywords is, of

Table 6.1 Titles containing specified keywords per each 25-year period

Years	*Range of occurrence (%, no.) of:*					*Total*
	'execut (ion/ed)'	*'justice'*	*'punishment'*	*'revenge'/ 'vengeance'*	*'hang (ed/ing)'*	
1550–74	0.13% (5)	0.15% (6)	0.28% (11)	0.15% (6)	0.13% (5)	0.84% (33)
1574–99	1.10 (74)	0.10 (7)	0.60 (40)	0.10 (7)	0.06 (4)	1.96 (132)
1600–24	0.80 (93)	0.07 (8)	0.32 (37)	0.17 (20)	0.13 (15)	1.49 (173)
1625–49	0.51 (145)	0.65 (184)	0.58 (164)	0.15 (42)	0.25 (71)	2.14 (606)
1650–74	0.75 (235)	1.04 (325)	0.34 (105)	0.17 (52)	0.26 (80)	2.56 (797)
1675–99	1.36 (624)	0.67 (307)	0.26 (120)	0.14 (66)	0.29 (134)	2.72 (1251)
1700–24	0.76 (433)	0.47 (264)	0.24 (136)	0.08 (43)	0.12 (67)	1.67 (943)
1725–49	0.58 (317)	0.37 (200)	0.26 (140)	0.07 (39)	0.06 (32)	1.34 (728)

Source: RLG's Eureka, ESTC (*English Short Title Catalogue*): http://eureka.rlg.org; June 2002.

course, an imprecise yardstick. A given word will recur, or several different keywords coincide, within a single title. The choice of words itself is always somewhat arbitrary. Rubrics like 'execution', 'justice', 'punishment', 'revenge' and 'hanging' (including related adjectives and verbs) only stand out because they recurred frequently. Meanwhile, words such as 'condemned' and 'condemnation' occur too often in discussions having nothing to do with punishment to be of any use; in early modern titles, to take a banal example, one 'executes' orders less often than one 'condemns' opinions.

Although these figures constitute only a rough guide to the diffusion of materials on punishment, they tell a revealing story. The preponderance of references to execution within the overall distribution of titles is this survey's most obvious result. Over the course of the period examined, 'execution' was a more prevalent term than 'punishment'. Many of the titles that discussed 'executions' conformed to the pattern described by J.A. Sharpe; they publicized the capture, trial, conviction and dying behaviour of various felons, most of them traitors and murderers. But while considerable, the amount of attention bestowed on executions varied over time. In the 75 years from 1600 to 1674, the proportion of titles that referred to executions declined slightly relative to what it had been in the closing decades of the sixteenth century, the volume of titles that referred to 'justice' expanded to fill the gap. The proportion of titles that directly invoked 'punishment', 'hangings' and notions of vengeance, fluctuated only moderately throughout the entire seventeenth century. We should note, too, that the appearance of terms connected with vengeance underwent a very progressive decline as of 1675. Allusions to punishment had begun to fall a little earlier, after reaching a high point of just over half a per cent of surviving titles in 1625–49.

On the whole, punishment held its own – this, in spite of the fact that it might easily have been overshadowed by a flood of new interests and new printed materials. But given the rapidly expanding pace of publication, even the most stable percentages would have translated into a dramatic expansion in the *exposure* of English-speaking subjects to materials on justice, executions and punishment. A brief review of the totals expressed in absolute numbers bears this out more clearly. The 25-year totals increase from 33 titles in 1550–74 to 173 titles in 1600–24, and then to a staggering 1251 titles by the closing decades of the seventeenth century. The public's familiarity with the sorts of materials surveyed here would have depended, ultimately, on such factors as the number of copies printed and sold, the network of geographical distribution, and the more intangible exposure of illiterate or partially literate audiences to these texts through reading aloud. Although diaries hold some clues that these materials were read and publicly discussed, we have little further evidence of the diffusion and reception of these texts.[5] What we can say is that they were produced and published on such a scale as to suggest that the supply must have corresponded to a substantial demand. We also should keep in mind that the numbers given here are, if anything, much too low. Many titles, especially those of short, cheaply-produced leaflets, simply did not survive to be entered into the *STC*. Not only this, but countless more books and pamphlets discussed punishment, retribution and their rationales even though their titles never directly alluded to this fact. Works on topics as diverse as military campaigns, the upbringing of children and apprentices, or the materiality of hellfire, often included theories or discussion about the appropriateness of punishment. Printed newsbooks, though not primarily concerned with reporting on punishment, also commented on executions, punitive measures, martial law and other instances of retaliatory violence. The exact numbers, however, would still say next to nothing about the rationales that authors offered to justify punishment, and this makes it preferable to move to actual contents.

III

Criminal biography, which accounts for a good proportion of the printed materials surveyed above, has been noted for its combination of sensationalism and fatalism. It typically presents punishment as a natural consequence of crime, just as crime itself was considered an outgrowth of sin. Alexandra Walsham and Malcom Gaskill have commented that crime narratives often portrayed criminals undone by the miraculous discovery of their deeds, as when corpses suddenly began to bleed in the presence of the murderer, or when mute children regained their voices just in time to identify their parents' killers. The agent in these stylized tales of retribution was an all-seeing God who invariably found some way of exposing criminals. Gaskill maintains that providential narratives were reassuring in a period in which the machinery of policing and the methods of prosecution remained rudimentary and therefore unreliable. He also claims that, by the latter half of the seventeenth century, these kinds of stories were on their way out, partly because the reliability of investigations improved and therefore lessened people's psychological reliance on the expectation of divine justice as a corrective.[6]

In fact, many authors in the late 1600s persisted in seeking providential underpinnings to explain the criminal's violent fate. Older tales recounting providential downfalls, like John Reynolds' collection in *The Triumphs of God's Revenge* (first published in 1635) continued to be reprinted and sold as before. Meanwhile, contemporary authors simply adopted more subtle forms of providential thinking, in which the intervention of a miracle gives way to a more diffuse sense of divine agency in bringing about the criminal's downfall. This shift may have been due to tamer stylistic norms, and not to any alteration in the authors' or the public's expectations concerning the efficacy of the judicial system. Be that as it may, these various forms of expression converged in purpose and effect: they worked to deflect attention away from the violence of executions. In so doing, they contributed to the greater legitimacy of capital convictions.

One of the claims common in accounts of crime and punishment in the latter half of the seventeenth century was that felons were self-victimizers. A ballad published in 1675 offers an excellent example of this link between self-victimization and punishment. It tells the story of Henry Symball and William Jones, sentenced to die in Fleet Street, London, for the murder of Sir Richard Sandford.[7] In describing their demise, the balladeer reminded readers that the punishment of hanging would deter other potentially violent individuals from committing murder, but he also framed his discussion of exemplary justice in terms that emphasized the murderers' self-defeating fury. In this balladeers' view, Symball and Jones were sentenced to die as a 'reward for impiety'. Death by strangulation was *'their due'*. Following this reasoning, the murderers could never have hoped to escape detection and eventual punishment. Thus, their thoughtless actions ended up causing not one, but rather three pointless deaths. The law, in this case, was only a means of redress.[8] In evoking 'dues' and 'rewards', the author drew attention to the deadly wages of sin; to the fact that the criminals' deaths were foreordained as part of an economy of retribution independent of the actual workings of the law. The two men had earned the fate that awaited them.

Some authors were more sparing in their descriptions of punishments. The anonymous author of *The Cruel Murtherer, Or the Treacherous Neighbour* (1673) provides an example of a certain curtness in the description of punishment. Although he lavished great attention on every detail of the murder of Alice Stephens and her young daughter in the parish of Stocksay, Shropshire, when it came time to describe the murderer's fate, the author switched to a more muted style of rhetoric:

> On Tuesday last, the 11th of March, [Thomas Reignolds] received his trial; he pleaded guilty and on the Thursday following the sentence was passed upon him; he was adjudged to be hanged in chains on Aldon's Mind, near the place where he did the murder. Accordingly, on Thursday March the 20th he was executed.[9]

The violence that the criminal had committed required a lengthy explanation, but the violent destruction of the criminal did not. There is no sign of providentialism here. This author's assumption, to the extent we can that detect it through his silences, seems to be that violent punishment was simply normal. The gruesome addition of leaving the corpse to rot on the gibbet somehow befitted the crime. On the title page, however, the reader was confronted with another interpretation of punishment, in the form of biblical citation: 'The wicked', he or she learned, 'is snared in the work of his own hands'. Whether this was the author's inclusion, or merely the publisher's matter-of-fact pronouncement on punishment, it reinforced the idea that the criminal had victimized himself.

This kind of emphasis was found in many pamphlets and songs, as well as in tales belonging to more elaborate literary genres. The literature of wonders stands out in this respect. John Reynolds' previously mentioned *Triumphs of God's Revenge* offers one of the finest examples of the wonder genre. His best-selling set of stories was initially produced in installments between 1621 and 1625, but in 1635 they were bound in a single volume and the compilation was subsequently reprinted in various editions well into the eighteenth century.[10]

Reynold's tales presented the reader with a stereotypical portrait of the murderer swept away by his or her own violence. One of these tales, for example, begins with the return from service in the Adriatic of de Salez, who finds his father pressing him to marry a colleagues' crippled daughter. Salez, we learn however, is already in love with a notoriously loose woman by the name of Mademoiselle de la Hay. His descent into violence begins when a rival challenges him to a duel and loses. Meanwhile, la Hay eliminates her own rival (the cripple), with the help of a poisoner. With the rivals out of the picture, Salez rides off to Paris to ask for his father's blessing to marry, but when the latter refuses, Salez stifles him in the middle of the night. After a brief mourning period Salez braves public scandal and marries la Hay, but after only three months, she offers her favours to another man. At last, Salez repents the murder of his father, but as he begins to talk of divorce, la Hay's fear of destitution leads her to slit his throat. Everything unravels from here. As de Salez lies dying, his servants hear him accuse his wife. The *lieutenant criminel* arrives on the scene, and de Salez confesses his own parricide before he finally expires. Shortly thereafter, la Hay is seized in a church and racked until she admits to having murdered her husband. Finally, the judges condemn Salez' dead body to public desecration, and sentence la Hay to public burning after prior strangulation. But, as she confesses, la Hay unwittingly reveals her guilt in the death of Mademoiselle de la Frange, and the judges proceed to stiffen the penalties against her, ordering that she be burnt alive rather than dead. Even the poisoner ends up being caught and broken on the wheel.[11]

Although this story was likely meant to titillate, the author felt a need to rationalize these criminals' violent ends, something he accomplished by inserting punishment into a tragic progression of violent acts. In the story, Salez and la Hay, unable to restrain their passions, set in motion a train of events to which they inevitably succumb; from victimizers, they become self-made victims. Reynolds' running commentary on the events in this sorry tale confirms the case for unavoidable consequences. At one point, for instance, he inveighs against la Hay, as if to warn her: 'if thou proceed and finish this infernal and bloody stratagem of thine, although thou chance to go unpunished of men, yet the Lord (in his due time) will find thee out and both severely scourge and sharply revenge and chastize thee.' Similar words of warning threaten both the poisoner ('beware for the sword and arrow of

God's just revenge and revenging justice threatens ye with no less than utter confusion and destruction') and de Salez ('we shall shortly see this mask of his devilish hypocrisy pulled off and this inhumane parricide both shamefully and sharply revenged by the just judgement and finger of God').[12] When the judges perform their function by condemning all three murderers to death and degradation, Reynolds intervenes once again and denies them agency, turning to divine Providence to provide his ultimate justification. But while it was 'God's revenge' that triumphed over murder, God was not interested in taking lives. The criminals themselves triggered the process. Punishment qualified as the 'bitter fruit' of their own actions.[13]

Although these various allusions might be viewed as simple devices meant to drive the action of a sensational tale of deceit and murder, they coincide nicely with the didactic purposes of Reynolds'stories. For Reynolds, stories offered fresh and vivid reminders of Biblical lessons – reminders that left 'a better imprint on the mind' than the Bible itself. One of the lessons he self-consciously sought to impart was that divine justice implied perfect redress: the redirection of violence towards its point of origin. As he explained in his preface, the human tragedies which murder provoked proved the truth of David's words: 'whosoever maketh a pit for others shall fall into it himself; for his mischief will return upon his own head and his cruelty fall upon his own pate.'[14] God's customary recourse was to let the effects of violence run their course, so that the instigators found themselves caught at their own game.

For Reynolds, the idea that violence would boomerang against the perpetrators of violence was intricately tied to the notion of divine justice. The same idea, however, circulated without necessarily being tied to providential explanations. An abridged, pirated version of Reynolds' very own stories, published by a certain T.M. in 1661, illustrates this well. The dominant themes in T.M.'s version of Reynolds' tales include disobedience, honour and the proper uses of punishment – themes which correspond to the author's own preoccupations with the Regicide and the 'judicial murder' of Royalists following the Civil Wars.[15] For T.M., punishment stemmed from murder, and murder stemmed from disobedience without further ado. Providence played only a cursory role in this trajectory.

Yet the author still made a careful point of talking about the many 'miseries' that caught up with the criminal as part of the cycle of violence. The title of his compilation itself bears the stamp of a residual concern with divine retribution in that it links murder and vengeance (*'Murthers Revenged'*) to a biblical injunction customarily associated with *lex talionis* (*'Blood for Blood'*). There is, in other words, ambivalence here. In T.M's hands, the story of de Salez and la Hay is turned into a straight narrative with only the shallowest of didactic pretensions; the purpose of the story is to provide 'a lesson for all people not only to detest these foul sins in themselves but [to] abhor and hate them in all others'. On the other hand, the calamities that befall the three villains are still very obviously the logical culmination of their own violence.[16]

The points raised by Reynolds and T.M. apply to murder pamphlets and ballads in general, as well as to writings dealing with treason and rebellion. Similar points also obtain in materials treating less serious offenses, such as robbery, breaking and entering, and other property crimes.[17] What differentiated all of these various works was not their subject matter – murder as against treason or theft – but rather, the greater or lesser extent to which the authors relied on providential arguments in order to justify the punishments meted out to the guilty. The providential treatment of retributive justice worked, in effect, to write the violence out of punishment. Punishment, according to the providentialist perspective, pertained to God not to human beings. The violence of punishment was nothing more than the justly redirected violence of the criminal. God, the source of all judgement, stood as the author of this redirection, but was not usually described as violent in his own right. Judges and jurymen, for their part, were almost invariably treated as the mere instruments or conduits in the supernatural accomplishment of 'justice'. Against this transcendent view of justice, less providentially-minded authors presented a complementary idea, that of immanent justice. In this view, violence bred violence and 'the wicked' were 'snared in the work of their own hands'. These authors did not seek to substitute God's agency for that of men and women, but they usually paved over the actual violence of punishment by making a point of describing it as a direct 'reward', 'wage' or 'product' of the criminal's misbehaviour, rather than as a new and separate instance of aggression.

Putting aside differences in emphasis, both of these interpretations shared a good many traits in common. Following both views, punitive violence was the outcome of an unstoppable sequence of events that began and ended with the criminal. Justice, whether it was imagined to be transcendent or immanent, was portrayed as a process independent, in important respects, from the agency of the courts or the state. The propensity of commentators to describe punishment in these terms forces us to call into question the standard Foucauldian case: early modern executions, it seems, were *not* supposed to be interpreted as conscious and deliberate displays of state authority. Far from drawing attention to the state's triumph over the criminal, authors and pamphleteers insisted that violence originated from the criminal's own actions; in their accounts the state is a participant, but an inessential one – the simple instrument of a natural ordering of things.

A common pattern of sacralization appears, in effect, to inform these two somewhat divergent approaches to the abstraction of punitive violence. This is the juncture at which Foucault's history of punishment fails as an analytical guide and René Girard's model of the relation between violence and 'the sacred' emerges as a more appropriate one. Girard's claims have centred on the role sacrifice plays in archaic cultures. In his view, the ritualized killing of preselected scapegoats in ancient societies served to restore peace to communities threatened by cycles of revenge killing. The scapegoat, according to Girard, was typically an innocent, selected either at random or according to ritualized prescriptions. In slaying this innocent sacrificial victim, the community confronted the spectacle of its own violence. It simultaneously distanced itself from and, to some extent, rid itself of this violence. Following archaic modes of religious explanation, the sacrificial victim was 'taken' by a god whose power was identified with the community's own violence (roughly to the point of being conflated with it), but who was nevertheless considered separate and more powerful than the community. The spheres of sacrificial violence and of the sacred were therefore essentially one and the same; angry divinities transcribed the violent dealings of human beings.[18]

In formulating this admittedly schematic account of the sacrificial process, Girard notes that modern societies, governed by law, have short-circuited the logic of sacrifice. In modern societies, legal institutions mediate between individuals and the threat of cyclical violence. These institutions either intervene, or are called upon to intervene, whenever a dangerously conflictual situation arises. Their role is to identify a guilty party, condemn or sanction that party, and thereby help people avoid taking recourse in private vengeance. But while Girard would not readily accept that this type of modern legal machinery ever produces or involves 'sacredness', there remains reason to suspect that, in the course of their historical development, legal institutions did, in fact, invoke 'the sacred' in order to foster legitimacy. Although we should reject a crudely evolutionary account of the transition from 'archaic' modalities of sacredness to modern, secularized modalities of law, early modern accounts of punishment still smacked of the 'in-between.' Several pieces that we have been examining, in particular those that were most overtly providentialist in their outlook, impute the violence of punishment to God. Virtually all the rest of these materials pave over the actual role of the law's agents or institutions in their descriptions of punitive violence. And the majority of them portray the liquidation of a given individual (or individuals) as the final act bringing cycles of strife, homicide and possible revenge to an end. In these various respects, early-modern arguments duplicate the process of sacralization described by Girard, including: (1) the tendency to read violence as something transcendent; (2) the denial of active violence on the part of the community; and (3) the closure which this 'final act of violence' is meant to provide to a community previously destabilized by violence.

The one principal disagreement between Girard and the early modern commentators has to do with the identity of the 'sacrificial victim.' In the legally-minded framework of seventeenth-century polemics, 'scapegoating' was irrelevant and deterrence far more to the point. The seventeenth-century 'victim' was a criminal, not an innocent made to bear the community's guilt. He or she had to be *truly*, not only metaphorically guilty and, in many cases, not only guilty but also unrepentant.[19] The legal machinery, when it functioned properly, was there to ensure that this stipulation (the determination of guilt) was met before punishment was carried out. The criminal's guilt, in the eyes of both God and man, was the absolute precondition of a logic that made 'punishment' synonymous with 'justice'. The insistence on guilt in early-modern English culture thus clashes with the arbitrary selection of victims so vital to Girard's case. Girard's sacrificial victims were only retrospectively made to appear 'guilty' in the eyes of the sacrificial community. The victims of English justice, by contrast, were supposed to be guilty *tout court*.

John Seller's picture book on *The Punishments of the Common Laws of England* (c. 1678) supports this case for sacralization quite nicely.[20] Seller's bookplates described the various forms of punishment in ascending order of severity. The illustrator ignored the fairly common punishment of fining, beginning instead with the drunkard's punishment of the stocks. From this point forward, we move through a list of increasingly serious sentences; from the 'cage' for the unruly, to the house of correction, whipping at the carts' tail, hangings, burnings and the punishments reserved for traitors. In all of these plates, save one (the house of correction), a crowd of onlookers beholds the violence taking place. Most of these spectators are quiet, but a certain number of figures gesture towards the criminal, perhaps as a way of marking the exemplarity of punishment. Whether the gaze is public or institutional, however, it virtually always signals the public's acquiescence in the punishment. The community is an explicit participant in the process of punishment. By contrast, the justices and juries responsible for handing out sentences are nowhere to be seen in these plates. The constable who oversees 'the punishment of the whipping post for vagrants and sturdy beggars', the beadle who carries out the whipping, and the mounted guards who keep order are the only reminders of the role of public authority in the infliction of sentences. The tendency towards sacralization, in Girard's sense of the term, is fairly clear here. The sacrificial crowd is present to stare down the guilty, but at the same time it distances itself from the violence taking place under its very nose.

On its own, a few tales on punishment and a single picture book cannot be treated as conclusive evidence that early modern authors sought to sacralize, rather than celebrate, the violence of judicial authority. But much of what is already known about the religious component of punishment, from existing historiography, dovetails with the framework of analysis suggested here. Sharpe's main point, namely that the convict's dying words provided an opportunity for the affirmation of authority and for the sinner's reconciliation with God, makes all the more sense if one considers that the people who recorded, edited and published these speeches also had a keen interest in sacralizing retributive justice. Any confessions or admissions on the part of the criminal that contributed to the commentators' efforts to transform a scene of violent punishment into a scene of contrition in the face of divine judgment would indeed have been ideal fare for appropriation.

In general, the sacralization of punishment fits in nicely with basic tenets in early modern religion. There was a strong overlap between the justifications for human punishment on the one hand and prevailing views of divine justice on the other. Homilists liked to remind their readers of the continuum between the spectacle of the gallows and the threat of hellfire. Until a changing theology in the eighteenth century began to cast doubt on the earlier image of hell as a place of endless torment, and until assumptions about the purposes of punishment began to change in its latter half, the organizing framework for interpreting punishment centred chiefly on the figure of a just, vindictive God at the head of a just and orderly state.[21] The image of human punishment and that of divine punishment were, in fact, mutually reinforcing. Sacrificing the guilty helped to preserve the community by discouraging further violence. Since it was thought that deterrence created peace, punishment could easily be regarded as an enactment of God's desire for order on earth. Thus the assumptions made about divine judgment itself were connected to the logic of contemporary punitive practice.[22]

Yet religion, as always, was not all-encompassing. The ideological impetus to sacralize punishment, to sanitize it as well as turn it into abstraction, was consistent with more mundane realities reflected in such things as the geographical positioning of the gallows. In certain cases, convicted felons might be executed in some central space associated with their crime, but the gallows were deliberately erected in the liminal spaces outside cities and towns.[23] Although this exercise no doubt owed something to a concern with public hygiene and crowd control, it also suggested an attempt to symbolically rid the city of its moral 'pollution'. The criminal was not only removed from the human community through execution, but also physically exiled to the outer margins of public space, just as the violence inherent in capital punishment was removed to a no-man's land.[24]

But if liminality was meant to convey sacrality, the well-known unruliness of crowds gathering for a public hanging would certainly have detracted from the purported solemnness of the event.[25] Ordinary spectators were bringing their own expectations to executions and these expectations were not fully consistent with the tendency towards sacralization one finds in the printed pamphlets. Spectators made their own comments about the criminal's fate and their emotional responses varied from one execution to the next (they could be sad, somber, silent, angry or enthralled, depending on the case). One popular concern does, however, suggest that spectators subscribed in some part to the broad logic underlying sacralization: they expected complete proficiency from the hangman. The delivery of punishments had to be both appropriate and swift enough to spare the convict any unprescribed suffering. In cases where the gravity of the convict's crime mandated contrition, many spectators apparently expected it as a matter of course, as part of the requirements for 'making a good end'.[26]

The responses of spectators at executions take us beyond the pale of the literate world discussed above into a sphere of unwritten ideology that holds its own important implications for the normalization of punishment. As Susan Amussen has recently explained, in early modern communities 'discipline was the justification for punishment, and punishment was central to many other forms of violence'.[27] Outbursts of violence were keyed to the administration of discipline in the home and the local community.[28] To those involved in brawls or domestic disputes, what we would take to be violence did not necessarily register as 'violent' at all; almost any form of violence could be legitimated insofar as it was used to redress a wrong or discipline the unruly. These categories were unstable of course, and some people might well expose what some considered to be 'discipline' (wife-beating, for instance) for the violence that it really was, giving rise to a game of mutual accusations. Yet many men and women were clear on their categories and probably tended to view the machinery of legal prosecution as an extension of their own aspirations to discipline those who gave offence.

IV

Following the logic of sacralization described above, the exoneration of judicial authority from the infliction of violence required, as a counterpart, that spectators be absolutely convinced of the criminal's guilt. We should therefore expect to find that, aside from obscuring the violence of the criminal's end, authors would also use rhetorical mechanisms for underscoring and intensifying the criminal's guilt. Appealing to Gods' all-knowing gaze was one such device. God never erred: those who stood guilty before Him must therefore be at fault. References to witnesses, depositions and the court's judicious scrutiny of evidence constituted another register to much the same end: proving that the condemned must be guilty because reasonable people had found that it was so. Another mechanism, however, and one that played a preponderant role in the vast majority of tales and reports was simple vilification. Recent scholarship has tended to place strong emphasis on the theme of redemption. Historians and critics have shown, again and again, that early modern authors were bent on the criminal's atonement and salvation, something which depended, in part, upon being able to show that the criminal's condition was similar to that of other sinners.[29] By shining their light on the redemptive element in criminal biography, these critics and historians have unwittingly left an equally important component of these tales out of the account: the part of the story in which the criminal is shown to be unlike most sinners and unlike most human beings. The condemnation of criminals in the press mobilized a convention-laden, highly stylized practice of name-calling. Much like older traditions of blame, this rhetorical practice relied on set formulas, the point of which was to sharpen perceptions of the criminal's guilt. Authors claimed repeatedly that criminals were inhumane, bloodthirsty, barbaric and cruel in the case of murderers – or sinful and hardened in the case of thieves. This was another way of saying that criminals, as a type of people, were *depraved* and not merely guilty in a legal sense.

The deep tension between the redemptive and accusatory strains in criminal biographies is especially clear in the story of Mary Cook, who killed her infant daughter in 1670 and instantly became the subject of two separate pamphlets.[30] Cook exemplified the case of a woman beleaguered by her relatives and her own severe bouts of depression; 'melancholy' was how contemporaries described her condition. The authors who wrote about her were visibly divided between sympathy and an urge to demonize her as the embodiment of the stereotypically 'unnatural' mother. Their aspersions therefore have something of a hollow ring; they read like a recitation of pieties one finds hard to believe but cannot refrain from mouthing anyway. Yet the pieties in this case worked to a specific effect. They simultaneously assigned guilt and vilified the guilty. According to one author, Mary Cook was a 'cruel mother'. Her heart was 'obdurate and impenetrable', or else simply 'wicked'. She was the author of an 'unnatural, inhumane, notorious, material bowelless cut-throat murder'.[31] Partridge and Sharp, the authors of a second pamphlet, referred pointedly to Cook's 'horrid murder', the 'ghastly' way in which she cut her child's throat ('laying aside all motherly bowels'), as well as the 'barbarous' tenor of her actions.[32]

One might assume that the outrage expressed through these labels was entirely related to the fact that the murderer was a mother and the victim her own child. The allusion to 'motherly bowels' certainly owed something to ideas about gender, which assumed that women – and especially mothers – were supposed to exhibit a 'natural' sense of pity toward the young. In virtually every other respect, however, the authors' formulas drew upon a rhetoric that carried well-beyond the representation of 'unnatural motherhood' *per se*. The kind of language that was here directed against infanticidal mothers was also invoked with uncanny frequency throughout the seventeenth century to describe all manner of enemies and outcasts, be they papists, regicides, persecutors, cannibals, tyrants, pirates or plain murderers. The language in question also served to identify and castigate abuses of power and virtually every category of illegitimate violence.[33] The specific ways in which different authors deployed the formulas that made up the language of illegitimate violence and criminal responsibility varied. Authorial inclinations, the criminal's identity, and the context of crimes and atrocities all had some bearing on the themes and labels that were selected. In the case of Mary Cook, the organizing principle lay in the theme of 'bloodshed'. The readers of both pamphlets were exposed to a barrage of allusions to the shedding of blood: Mary Cook's hands were 'colored by blood;' her knife was 'bloody;' her crime was likewise 'bloody'.[34]

This choice of imagery can be imputed to sensationalism as well as to the urge to make a strong impression, since blood is a potent reminder of victimization. The graphically physical image of spilling the body's vital fluid (blood) concretizes an otherwise abstract offence (murder). The broader importance of the image of blood, however, was based on a biblical formula which the authors invoked repeatedly. As Partridge and Sharp observed: 'No sin committed against the commandments of the second Table, cryeth louder to God for vengeance, and unto Man for Justice than the shedding of innocent blood'. Society, in their view, could not ignore this insistent cry, and there was no way for it to 'purify the land from the guilt of innocent blood, but by executing Justice upon the blood-shedder.'[35] The author of the other tract steered clear of direct biblical references, but he was nonetheless convinced of Cook's guilt and was eager to associate her guilt with the stain of blood. In his view, the miscarriage which Cook suffered in Newgate prison was not enough to kill her because, as he put it: 'Providence had otherwise decreed, she must live to satisfy the justice of the Law, and be a terror to deter all others from being guilty of the like crime nay, if they have any Grace, from having any thoughts of *so horrid a blood-guiltiness*.'[36] The stress on deterrence, so apparent in this statement, correlates with a conviction that Cook's guilt was not only undeniable, but also particularly odious and worthy of punishment because she had shed the blood of an innocent.

Seventeenth-century historians are already familiar with the theme of blood-guilt because it constituted one of the principle charges brought against Charles I at his trial in 1648. Charles was condemned as a 'man of blood'. Ironically, the regicides would themselves be accused of the same crime when the tide turned against them in 1660–61. Blood-guilt was a fairly common theme, which appeared in seventeenth-century biblical commentary as well as discussions of power relations and violence. Religious enemies – in particular, the papists – were routinely accused of wallowing in innocent blood. The principle of blood-guilt hinged upon a distinction between 'innocent' and 'guilty' blood. Innocent blood represented a source of pollution, which, following biblical logic, could only be purged by restitution. The murderer's blood, in other words, was the only substance capable of atoning for the blood of the innocent. Since the 'cry' of unavenged innocent blood offended God, there was strong incentive to slay the guilty as the only means of making the necessary restitution.[37]

The imagery of blood was therefore a perfectly convenient shorthand for further sacralizing crime and punishment. Characters like the beleaguered Mary Cook might have provoked sympathy. But if the dichotomy between innocence and guilt were to hold, it was necessary to describe Cook's actions in such a way as to undercut this sympathy. The imagery of blood did exactly that. It drew attention to the innocence of the victim, exacerbated the guilt of the murderer, and concealed the workings of justice by conflating it with 'divine anger' and a presumed duty to rid the land of the filth of blood pollution. Other labels describing the illegitimacy of murder further reinforced the contrast between violence and justice. Cook's actions were 'barbarous', meaning here that they were unrestrained and undiscriminating. Her punishment, by contrast, was limited and proportional. Cook was 'inhumane', while her judge apparently qualified as clement because he at the very least invoked God's mercy for her soul.

Most of the terms which authors employed to couch their recriminations against Mary Cook and other criminals had long precedents, which included classical *topoi* and biblical rhetoric. This terminology had been part of the battery of execrations commonly found in medieval oral and literate culture, including clerical culture.[38] By the sixteenth century, the countless authors whom we now group together under the unspecific heading of 'the press' had already transformed the language of blood-guilt, cruelty and inhumanity into mainstays of international and domestic propaganda. English-speaking pamphleteers, journalists and orators throughout the British Isles had become keen observers of how power was exercised in Europe and elsewhere. They frequently responded to international events through the use of diatribe of this type. But the process that made terms like 'cruel', 'bloody' and 'barbarous' commonplace was self-perpetuating, inasmuch as the reiteration of a common set of themes and expressions in ever-widening contexts of discussion gave them rapidly increasing currency. By the seventeenth century, many of these expressions had crystallized into stereotypes for describing illegitimate violence: the 'cruel tyrant', the 'inhumane savage', and the 'treacherous papist' bent on massacre.

In themselves, these formulas did not automatically have any bearing on the legitimization of judicial punishment. But several of them were likely to become relevant whenever retribution was at stake in the description of events. An excellent illustration of this is Sir Gerrard Lowther's inquisition in Ireland in the winter of 1652–53. As head of the High Court of Justice set up to try Sir Phelim O'Neill for the atrocities committed against Protestant settlers, Lowther presented himself as the human instrument in an 'inquisition for blood'.[39] Lowther did not limit his purview to the description of Irish atrocities, as was the case with most books and pamphlets. For obvious reasons, he was also concerned with the judicial context, the trial and punishment of an Irish 'rebel'. His words at the trial thus invite comparison with the demonization of Mary Cook 17 years later. In both cases, the use of formulas meant to vilify the criminal fit into an explicitly judicial context.

Lowther was convinced that an 'impartial inquisition for innocent blood' was essential in order 'to put away innocent blood from the land'.[40] In order to sustain the notion of a divine mandate, Lowther contrasted the 'wickedness' of the Irish rebels with the image of 'the innocent blood of Christians' which the Irish had 'wickedly and cruelly shed' against 'the Laws of God and man, of Nature and of nations, the Laws of the Land, and the rights and rules of war, and the bonds of Humanity and humane society'.[41] As in the case of Mary Cook, the themes of blood and blood-guilt were modulated by a series of other references alluding to a loss of self-restraint and to a descent into cruelty. Several witnesses had allegedly seen the rebels devise a 'variety of tortures and cruel deaths of the living' including exposure, starvation, burnings and similar acts. The 'savage cruelty', 'execrable malice' and 'hellish rage' of the Irish rebels had turned into outright 'devastation'. The rebels had targeted virtually everything connected with the protestant religion, the English nation and 'civility' itself; they had even murdered children and ripped unborn babies from their mothers' wombs. It seemed 'as though Infidels, or rather the wild beasts of the wilderness, wolves, and bears, and tigers, nay fiends and furies, had been brought into the Land'.[42]

For Lowther, the stereotype of the cruel Irishman, popularized by countless pamphlets, supported a caricatural distinction between brutal violence and the just rule of law, which he represented. The distinction was, in fact, a tricky one to sustain. Lowther had to explain why, under an infamous double-standard dating back to a statute of Henry VII (10 Hen. VII, c. 21), Irish murderers had to be punished as though they were traitors, 'both with torture and with death'. Lowther could reason that Gaelic law had taught the native Irish that murder was a relatively minor offence, easily settled by the payment of blood fines. But the cruelty and barbarism of the Rebellion stood as better confirmation that, in Ireland, English customs were insufficient. Force, even though brutal, constituted a providential means of self-preservation. Thus, by invoking the ruthlessness of the Irish Lowther conveniently side-stepped any residual moral problems.[43] Dramatizing the guilt of criminals was a good way of drawing the reader's attention away from the inherent violence of executions and corporal punishment, effectively robbing the condemned of his or her status as a potential victim.

The references to bloodshed and atrocity that filled the pages of murder pamphlets may have supplied convenient arguments for the killing of murderers, but what then of the men and women executed for lesser offences, including theft? To some extent, executions for theft were becoming less of an issue. In the late seventeenth century, sentences of transportation came to supplement the pardons, benefit of clergy, and the habit of convicting felons on lesser charges (punishable by whipping and branding) as an alternative to the death penalty.[44] Many of the felons who ended their days on the gallows were either recidivists or guilty of aggravated crimes, such as highway robbery or house-breaking. But the guilt of these convicts still needed to be demonstrated, and protests about their cruelty and acts of bloodshed were both inappropriate and hard to justify given the context. Authors, therefore, found ways to compensate. Some chose to emphasize the sinful course of life that led to a progressive state of brutalization, and some pointed to the violence implicit in the work of the more notorious thieves. A cursory look at the literature reveals that these references to the audacity, 'notoriety' or callous indifference of particular convicts performed much the same function as allusions to blood and cruelty did in murder pamphlets. It has become fashionable to think that portraits of hardened criminals and their punishment enabled readers to infer moral lessons from the demise of these, their fellow-sinners. Many pamphleteers, however, seemed only marginally interested in stirring up deep feelings of empathy for these fallen brothers and sisters. Their sharp, caricatural distinctions between untainted innocence and exacerbated guilt prevented any easy identification between readers and even the most repentant convicts.

The accumulation of all of these accounts suggests that many of these writers were driven by a need to appease an underlying uncertainty about the legitimacy of punitive violence. The frequency of physical 'discipline' as a feature of early-modern English culture suggests that people were probably not particularly squeamish about the infliction of pain itself. One should not therefore assume that they were markedly troubled by the *violence* involved in punishment, in its own right. On the other hand they may have entertained reservations as to whether or not the guilty party really was *guilty*, or at least guilty enough to warrant the full severity of the law. How could they be sure that verdicts were reliable, or that punitive violence was *legitimately* punitive?

V

Punishment is a bit of a catch-all category. The punishment of self-confessed killers was one thing; that of mere thieves or, for that matter, of dissidents and marginals (a standard practice in Restoration Britain) was another. The formulas which authors and pamphleteers mobilized to castigate criminals – and thereby whitewash the violence of punishment – were not, in fact, the exclusive property of any one ideological grouping. They were available for appropriation by propagandists speaking on the behalf of any one of a variety of groups that had reason to regard themselves as persecuted. One of the lines of thinking which these spokespeople often pursued involved maintaining the received categories and rhetorical formulas, but deploying them in such a way as to redirect blame. Under usual circumstances only the target of punishment would be identifiable as 'cruel' or otherwise depraved. But when the agents of punitive violence were found to be cruel – and the 'punished' innocent – the logic of punishment failed.[45]

By the second half of the seventeenth century, no group was more assiduous in turning the conventional language of justice and punishment against their persecutors than the Quakers.[46] Friends actively compared the actions of the informers, local officials, clergymen and judges who persecuted them to those of European Catholics who martyred Protestants. From as early as 1660, motivated by a conviction that suffering constituted a powerful form of religious testimony, Friends had begun to collect reports from all over the British Isles and, indeed, from all over the world. By 1676, the sheer volume of their record-keeping necessitated the creation of a 'Meeting for Sufferings' which would compile and publicize reports of persecution.[47] The resulting pamphlets and petitions were steeped in the rhetoric of cruelty and blood, and the fact that this rhetoric was often absent in the original reports demonstrates that it was being added for the purpose of dramatizing persecution. The overcrowding of men and women in tiny gaol cells translated into the worst form of tyranny, and even comparatively mild forms of pressure – the levying of fines, the distraint of poor people's goods, and the 'haling' of Friends gathered at religious meetings – were now framed in terms of 'barbarous cruelty'.[48]

Friends were not alone in portraying themselves as innocent martyrs pursued by depraved persecutors. From the inception of the Reformation, Protestants in the British Isles had refused to regard the prosecutions against their co-religionists at home, or in Catholic Europe, as legitimate 'punishments'. By the second half of the seventeenth century, the rhetoric of Protestant martyrology was being freely appropriated by almost all Nonconformists within the British Isles.[49] Even Irish Catholics and uncompromising Scottish Conventiclers drew upon this cache of stereotypes and rationales to reprove their accusers.[50] All of these groups sought, in effect, to de-sacralize the violence that other propagandists were trying very hard to sacralize.[51]

The best-known example of this kind of reverse smear campaign stems from the Whig martyrology created between 1688 and 1690, which chronicled the violence committed under James II. The figure dominating this martyrology was not James himself but rather his Lord Chief Justice and eventual Lord Chancellor, George Jeffreys. Jeffreys, as is well-known, had presided over the treason trials of 1685 following an uprising in south-western England in support of Charles II's illegitimate but Protestant son, the Duke of Monmouth. In 1685, following a now familiar pattern, Jeffreys had saddled his victims, the rebels, with the responsibility for severe reprisals that he himself was meting out. By 1689, however, Whig propagandists had redefined his proceedings as a mockery of justice and as an act of overt cruelty involving the brutalization of innocents. Their success was such that, to this day, the Jeffreys' trials are still remembered as 'the Bloody Assizes'.[52]

High politics, religious controversy and the propaganda it generated were obvious settings in which one might expect the validity of punishment to be questioned. But the tendency of even the unlikeliest of pressure groups to exploit the dichotomy between punitive justice and cruelty suggests that this dichotomy held sway in more banal contexts as well. The misgivings of the spectators who witnessed bungled executions may owe something to this habit of distinguishing between punishment and excessive violence.[53] Clearer expressions of the popular desire to keep punishment distinct from cruelty routinely emanated from the press. The 'children's petition' against school whippings in the fall of 1669 is a case in point. The authors of this satirical pamphlet were not overly worried about the validity of corporal punishment itself, but they deplored the 'accustomed severities of school-discipline' on the grounds that England's schoolmasters so routinely brutalized their pupils that punishment had become as meaningless as it was pervasive. The schoolmaster's apparent sadism threatened to turn the rationale for punishment on its head, transforming the laudable goal of discipline into a cruel abuse of power.[54]

If this rhetoric meant anything, it would seem to be this: that England and the rest of the British Isles abounded in subjects bent as much on *resisting* as on applauding the rise of a potentially repressive legal system. Under Elizabeth, at a time when the English legal apparatus reached the height of its severity, commentators had turned to the press to debate the differences between punishment and violence, or punishment and cruelty. By the second half of the seventeenth century, at a time when new practices and new inclinations served to temper the severity of the law, justifications and condemnations of 'punishment' had both become regular topics of debate.

Both sides of this polemic, the justifications as well as the condemnations, must be regarded as twin facets of a common process. While many commentators sought to sacralize punishment, a number of their immediate contemporaries were doing the exact opposite: they questioned the legitimacy of punishment by pointing to its many abuses and drew as much attention as they could to the violence inflicted in the name of justice. In effect, the sacralization of punishment was a negotiated process that presupposed ideological conflict. People's willingness to buy, read or listen to stories about 'just' punishments was symptomatic of a context in which the arbitrary quality of punitive violence was under serious discussion. Far from accepting that violent punishments were normal or desirable, they needed to be reassured that punishment was not, in fact, violence – that it only targeted a minority of truly depraved individuals and, in so doing, helped to sustain a benevolent ordering of society.

By the seventeenth century, would-be defenders of public authority could exploit the increasingly mainstream machinery of the press to make their reassuring pieties heard. They were joined by a variety of hacks whose motivations were more mercantile. Money could be made by satisfying the demand for moral pieties, and publishers were on the lookout for materials that fit the bill. The pious competed with the chorus of dissenting voices who accepted the theoretical possibility of just punishment, but who bitterly resented the realities of seventeenth-century punitive practice. In this essay, I have put the purveyors of salacious stories and the odd balladeer on the same footing as a judge bent on condemning an Irish rebel, an engraver who thought it might be profitable to produce sensational plates depicting common forms of punishment, and a variety of sectarian pamphleteers. But this was a diverse cast of characters who occupied widely varying positions within the network of print culture.

Given the inherent diversity of these individuals' motivations, the fact that this propaganda should have been fairly consistent in its effects seems all the more revealing. Wherever we happen to look, we find the abstraction of punitive violence, the drawing of stereotypical dichotomies which opposed innocence to guilt and justice to cruelty, and the reinforcement of these categories through a stock of common formulas and examples. Reiteration was key, and the press itself was one of the most important driving forces in this respect. For all the attention historians have paid to juries and crowds, we should remember that only a minority of Englishmen and Englishwomen had any real contact with the criminal courts and their dealings. The majority simply glimpsed the punishment of offenders now and again. If they were to make sense of what punishment meant, they would have had to combine what they themselves knew about the subject with what the purveyors of opinion were telling them.

Between the consumers of opinion and the variety of producers and distributors, then, stood the press. It was the press, ultimately, and not religion or changes in the extent or effectiveness of prosecution, that lay at the heart of the cultural moment from which modern views of punishment emerged. The words of Chief Justice Gerard Lowther would not have mattered a minute after they had been uttered in the Winter of 1653, had it not been for the fact that they were printed up as part of Borlase's *History of the Execrable Irish Rebellion* in 1680. Without the press, the protests of the Quakers would likewise have passed into silence after victims complained and petitions were sent up to the relevant authorities. An expanding press was what drew these many voices into a public field of rhetoric, imbuing these arguments with some form of persistence. The press likewise fostered the rehashing of arguments by feeding people's uncertainty over the legitimacy of punitive violence and by fostering a need for frequent reassurance on this matter. Finally, the press was also the mechanism that transformed pre-existing rationales and formulas into what would become widely-used clichés.

When one reads about criminals on their way to Tyburn, greeted by acquaintances and strangers and plied with drink, one begins to wonder how far the opinions and rhetoric I have been exploring in this essay really extended. Britain would long be home to a set of cultures in which the ideological priorities of the literate classes proved a matter of popular indifference. The sacralization of punishment would therefore remain an unfinished process, extending only to a number of social strata.[55] Yet it seems fairly clear that by the time the 'Bloody Code' was expanded, an entire class of 'respectable', literate individuals – the *gens bien-pensants* of the British Isles – had been saturated with the message that punishment belonged to an order of violence so completely distinct from commonplace aggression that it simply did not count as any kind of victimization. Individual members of this broad group had had opportunity to develop a set of ideological proclivities encouraging them to overlook the potential similarities between criminal and executioner. As early as 1650, anyone who wished to be so persuaded could have found ample assurances that the punished brought their 'just desserts' upon themselves. By the close of the seventeenth century such assurances had only become more plentiful. In such a context, the death penalty would not have seemed particularly violent, and the substitute punishments that did away with the immediate display of violence, such as transportation or imprisonment, could be hailed as the very epitome of 'civility'.[56]

Notes

1 M. Foucault *Discipline and Punish: The Birth of the Prison, trans.* A. Sheridan (New York, 1979), chap. 2; R. McGowen, 'The body and punishment in eighteenth-century England', *Journal of Modern History*, 59 (1978), 661–6; D. Hay, 'Property, authority and the criminal law', in D. Hay *et al.*, eds, *Albion's Fatal Tree: Crime and Society in Eighteenth-Century England* (1975), 26–9. F. McLynn (*Crime and Punishment in Eighteenth-Century England* (London and New York, 1989), 258.

2 J.A. Sharpe, '"Last dying speeches": religion, ideology and public execution in seventeenth-century England', *P&P*, 107 (1985), 144–167. See also P. Lake, 'Popular form, Puritan content? Two Puritan appropriations of the murder pamphlet from mid-seventeenth century London', in A. Fletcher and P. Roberts eds, *Religion, Culture and Society in Early Modern Britain* (Cambridge, 1994); and P. Lake, 'Deeds against nature: cheap print, protestantism and murder in early seventeenth-century England', in K. Sharpe and P. Lake eds, *Culture and Politics in Early Stuart England* (Stanford, CA, 1993), 274–5; L. B. Faller, *Turned to Account: The Forms and Functions of Criminal Biography in Late Seventeenth- and Early Eighteenth Century England* (Cambridge 1987), chap. 5.

3 The expansion began immediately following the Glorious Revolution in 1688 and involved some 170 new capital offenses created between 1688 and 1818. For a brief overview, see H. Potter, *Hanging in Judgement: Religion and the Death Penalty in England from the Bloody Code to Abolition* (1993), 3–6.

4 My methodology involved calculating the sum of the titles containing particular keywords published *within* the specified range of years. STC codes were as follows: 'fi tiw execution and pyr 1550–1574'; 'fi tiw executed and pyr 1575–1599 not tiw execution'; and so on. I then controlled the resulting samples of titles so as to discard any titles that made use of any of the relevant words but did so in the wrong context (e.g. the 'execution' of orders). The resulting number of records is subsequently expressed as a percentage of the total number of titles published in that specific range of years.

5 Diarists sometimes recorded the circulation of the types of stories one associates with the penny-press. This was certainly the case with Thomas Rugge who left a number of entries on sensationalistic tales of crime and punishment. *The Diurnal of Thomas Rugge*, BL Add. MSS 10117, fos 94(v)–97; 100(v), 102–3, 150, 159(v). In describing executions, Narcissus Luttrell occasionally referred his reader to printed confessions. See *A Brief Historical Relation of State Affairs from September 1678 to April 1714* (Oxford, 1857), I, 170 (10 March, 1681/2).

6 M. Gaskill, *Crime and Mentalities in Early Modern England* (Cambridge, 2000), 206–26; A. Walsham, *Providence in Early Modern England* (Oxford, New York, 1999), chap. 2.

7 W.P., 'A Sad and True Relation of the Apprehension, Tryal, Confession, Condemnation, and Execution of the Two Barbarous and Bloody Murtherers ...',

in H.E. Rollins ed., *The Pepys Ballads* (Cambridge, MA, 1930), 24–5. The same story was the subject of two separate pamphlets: *The Bloody Murthers Executed; or, News From Fleet-Street* (1675); and *Bloud Justly Reveng'd* (1675).

8 W.P., 'A Sad and True Relation', 24–5.

9 Anon., *The Cruel Murtherer, Or the Treacherous Neighbour* (1673), 7. On the same murder see anon., *Bloody Nevvs from Shrewsbury* (1673).

10 T. Reynolds, *The Triumphs of Gods Revenge Against the Crying and Execrable Sinne of (Wilful and Premeditated) Murther* (3rd edn, 1657). Other editions were printed in 1635, 1639, 1640, 1656, 1663, 1669, 1679, 1704, 1708, 1726, 1740, 1753, 1770 and 1778. On Reynolds' models see Walsham, *Providence*, 66–7.

11 Reynolds, *Triumphs of Gods Revenge*, 141–59.

12 *Ibid.*, 153–7.

13 *Ibid.*, 159.

14 *Ibid.*, preface, fourth page. The reference is to Psalm 7.

15 T.M., *Blood for Blood: Or Murthers Revenged* (Oxford, 1661).

16 *Ibid.*, dedication and 123.

17 For instance, E.S., *The Witty Rogue Arraigned, Condemned, and Executed* (1656). See also S. Smith, *A True Account of the Behaviour, Confession, And Last Dying Speeches Of the Seven Criminals* (1690).

18 R. Girard, *Violence and the Sacred*, trans. Patrick Gregory (Baltimore, 1977), chap. 1.

19 On the importance of contrition as a condition of mitigation, see C.B. Herrup, 'Law and morality in seventeenth-century England', *P&P*, (1985), 118–9.

20 J. Seller, *A Booke of the Punishments of the Common Laws of England* (*c.* 1678).

21 R. McGowen, 'The changing face of God's justice: the debates over divine and human punishment in eighteenth-century England', *CJH*, 9 (1998), 63–98. For a close study of eighteenth-century assize sermons see also R. McGowen, '"He beareth not the sword in vain": religion and the criminal law in eighteenth-century England', *Eighteenth Century Studies*, 21 (1987–88), 192–211.

22 McGowen, 'He beareth not the sword in vain', 200–3.

23 See A. Babington, *The English Bastille: A History of Newgate Gaol and Prison Conditions in Britain 1188–1902* (1971), 33–4. A. Marks, *Tyburn Tree: Its History and Annals* (1908), 63 and 213.

24 I am expanding here on S. Mullaney, *The Place of the Stage: License, Play, and Power in Renaissance England* (Chicago, 1988), 38–40. The fact that hangings were consigned to a geographical periphery did not detract from the public nature of these events. As Peter Linebaugh has noted, executions were well-advertised. P. Linebaugh, 'The Tyburn riot against the surgeons', in D. Hay *et al.*, *Albion's Fatal Tree*.

25 See T. Laqueur, 'Crowds, carnival and the state in English executions, 1604–1868', in A.L. Beier *et al.*, eds, *The First Modern Society: Essays in English History in Honour of Lawrence Stone* (Cambridge, 1989), 305–55. See also McLynn, *Crime and Punishment*, 274–5.

26 On the expectations weighing upon the hangman, see McLynn, *Crime and Punishment*, 269–70. On the variability of crowd responses, see J.A. Sharpe, 'Civility, civilizing processes, and the end of public punishment in England', in P. Burke *et al.*, eds, *Civil Histories: Essays Presented to Sir Keith Thomas* (Oxford, New York, 2000), 220–2.

27 S. Amussen, 'Punishment, discipline, and power: the social meanings of violence in early modern England', *JBS*, 34 (1995), 5.

28 *Ibid.*, 23.

29 This is especially true of J.A. Sharpe, Peter Lake and Lincoln Faller.

30 Anon., *The Cruel Mother* (1670); and N. Partridge and B. Sharp, *Blood for Blood Or Justice Executed for Inhumane Blood-Shed* (1670). For discussion of the case itself, see M. Francus, 'Monstrous mothers, monstrous Societies: infanticide and the rule of law in Restoration and eighteenth-century England', *Eighteenth-Century Life*, 21(1997), 138–41.

31 *The Cruel Mother*, title and 6.

32 Partridge and Sharp, *Blood for Blood*, 1 and 15–16.

33 On the conventions and uses of this language in England and the British Isles see P. Rosenberg, 'The Moral Order of Violence: The Meanings of Cruelty in Early Modern England, 1648–1685' (PhD thesis Duke University, 1999). For an earlier parallel see C.A. Patrides, '"The bloody and cruell Turke": the background of a Renaissance commonplace', *Studies in the Renaissance*, 10 (1963), 126–35.

34 *The Cruel Mother*, title, 3; Partridge and Sharp, *Blood for Blood*, title, 'To the Reader', 16–17 and 19.

35 Partridge and Sharp, *Blood for Blood*, 1–2. This symbolism carried over into a discussion of the blood of Jesus and its powers of atonement. If Cook was genuinely repentant, Christ's blood would wash away her own blood guilt. See 'To the Reader' and 41–2.

36 *The Cruel Mother*, 6 (emphasis added).

37 P. Crawford, 'Charles Stuart, that man of blood', *JBS*, 16 (1977), 41–61; S. Baskerville, 'Blood guilt in the English Revolution', *The Seventeenth Century*, 8 (1993), 181–202; E. Tuttle, *Religion et Idéologie dans la Révolution Anglaise, 1647–1649: Salut du Peuple et Pouvoir des Saint* (Paris, 1989), chap. 9.

38 See B. Rosenwein, T. Head and S. Farmer, 'Monks and their enemies: a comparative approach', *Speculum*, 66 (1991), 771; H. Wieruszowski, 'Roger II of Sicily, rex-tyrannus in twelth-century political thought', *Speculum*, 38 (1963), 65–6.

39 The transcript of Lowther's speech appears under the title 'The Lord Lowther's speech, at the opening of High Court of Justice, at the trial of Phelim O Neal', in Edmund Borlase, *The History of the Execrable Irish* (1680), 305–14.

40 Lowther, in Borlase, *History*, 306.

41 *Ibid.*, 306.

42 *Ibid.*, 311.

43 *Ibid.*, 311.

44 J.M. Beattie, *Policing and Punishment in London, 1660–1750: Urban Crime and the Limits of Terror* (Oxford, 2001), chap. 6.

45 Once again, this bears comparison with the arguments for abolishing the death penalty voiced during the Interregnum. See Zaller, 'The debate on capital punishment', 131–5.

46 This is a habit that Restoration Nonconformists shared with Elizabethan and Jacobean Catholics – the earlier specialists in this brand of rhetoric. For the catholic discourse on capital punishment see M. Questier and P. Lake, 'Agency, appropriation and rhetoric under the gallows: puritans, romanists and the state in early modern England', *P&P*, 153 (1996), 64–107.

47 On the Meeting for Sufferings and its work see W. C. Brathwaite, *The Second Period of Quakerism*, 2nd edn, (Cambridge, 1961; reprinted, York, 1979), 282–5; and C. Horle, *The Quakers and the English Legal System, 1660–1688* (1988), 161–5.

48 See, for instance, Anon., *A Relation of the Inhumane and Barbarous Sufferings of the People Call'd Quakers* (1665); [R. Allen], *The Cry of Innocent Blood, Sounding to the Ear of Each Member in Parliament* (London?, 1670); W. Penn, *The Continued Cry of the Oppressed for Justice* (1675); Anon., *The Sad and Lamentable Cry of Oppression and Cruelty* (1682).

49 See N.H. Keeble, *The Literary Culture of Nonconformity in Later Seventeenth-Century England* (Athens, GA, 1987), chap. 2; and more crucially, J.R. Knott, *Discourses of Martyrdom in English Literature, 1563–1694* (Cambridge, 1993), chaps 6–7.

50 Irish examples include R. S., *A Collection Of Some of the Murthers and Massacres Committed on the Irish in Ireland* (1662); P. Walsh, *A Letter Desiring a Just and Mercifull Regard of the Roman Catholicks of Ireland* (Dublin?, 1662); N. French, *The Bleeding Iphigenia* (1675). For the Scottish Conventiclers see J. Stewart, *Naphtali, or the Wrestlings of the Church of Scotland* (1667); (A. Shields?), *A Hind Let Loose* (Edinburgh?, 1687); A. Shields, *A Short Memorial of the Suffering and Grievances… of the Presbyterians in Scotland* (Edinburgh, 1690).

51 Orthodox Protestants, it is worth noting, felt a distinct need to defend their honor against Nonconformist allegations of persecution. A particularly vivid example is N. Brisbie, *Prosecution No Persecution* (1682).

52 See the introductory remarks by J.G. Muddiman ed., *The Bloody Assizes* (Edinburgh and London, 1929), 6–8; and M. Zook, '"The Bloody Asizes": Whig martyrdom and memory after the Glorious Revolution', *Albion*, 27 (1995), 372–96. Variants include J. Tutchin, *The Protestant Martyrs: or, The Bloody Assizes* (1688?); J. Bent (J. Dunton), *The Bloody Assizes* (1689); [J. Tutchin], *The Dying Speeches, Letters, and Prayers, &c. of Those Eminent Protestants* (1689); *id.*, *A New Martyrology, or, The Bloody Assizes* (3rd edn, 1689).

53 See, for instance, Luttrell's comments on the executioner's failure to properly decapitate the traitor, Lord Russell, in July 1683 (*A Brief Relation*, 271). The incident itself was thought to warrant a printed explanation: J. Ketch, *The Apologie of John Ketch, Esq., the Executioner of London* (1683). For a German perspective see R. van Dülmen, *Theatre of Horror: Crime and Punishment in Early Modern Germany*, trans. E. Neu (Oxford, 1990), 113–18.

54 Anon., *The Childrens Petition* (1669), esp. 18–22, and 46–7.

55 For discussion of this point see, amongst others, Peter Linebaugh, *The London Hanged: Crime and Civil Society in the eighteenth Century* (Cambridge,1992), chaps 1 and 2.

56 On 'civilization' and the shifts in sentencing which began in the 'long' eighteenth century, see Sharpe's 'Civility, civilizing processes', and *Judicial Punishment*, 36–49. For trends in the nineteenth century see R. McGowen, 'Civilizing punishment: the end of the public execution in England', *JBS*, 33(1994), 257–82.

7

The Grotian Moment: Natural Penal Rights and Republicanism

Mark Rigstad

I

From the Civil War to the South Sea Bubble, English republican writers endeavoured to legitimate various modes of political violence as instances of just punishment despite apparent deficits in regular legal authority and applicable civil law. These political acts – some completed, others merely compassed or threatened – included regicide, assassination, conquest and impeachment. Each posed an obvious problem of ideological coherence in light of avowed republican commitments to the rule of law.[1] From the ancient Roman republic on, the precept that 'there can be no punishment without law' (*nulla poena sine lege*) remained one of the enduring basic principles associated with the rule of law. According to this principle, which is sometimes called the principle of legality, in the absence of applicable law or regular legal authority, political violence remains political violence and cannot be deemed to be just punishment. English republicans were therefore obliged to explain how their ostensibly extra-legal acts of political violence could be construed as just punishment and made consistent with the rule of law.

One fairly well-known aspect of this ideological project was the republican reinterpretation of the rule of law that Montesquieu later championed. As Montesquieu discerned, English republicans often subordinated the traditional Aristotelian preoccupation with the strict governance of universal reason in public action to a more politically loaded conception of the rule of law as that concrete set of institutions whereby citizens manage to restrain their governors and vindicate an extensive sphere of private prerogative.[2] Still, republican allegiance to this politicized notion of the rule of law rarely initiated an outright repudiation of the principle of legality. Instead, republicans attempted to avoid the implication that they were subverting public reason and legality by arguing that their acts of seemingly extra-legal violence were in fact rooted in the ethical foundations that make legal order possible. In each case, responding to such political crimes as 'tyranny' and 'corruption', leading republican punishers (or would-be punishers) justified their efforts on the basis of the radical doctrine that the ethical principles of 'natural' or 'transcendent' justice that *ground* the rule of criminal law also ought to *complete* it by supplying warrant for punitive action when the regular offices and written records of the law are found wanting. Thus, republicans not only politicized the notion of the rule of law, they also invoked recent innovations in natural law theory to extend the justificatory reach of that notion beyond the warrant of established jurisdictions and traditional legal documents.

One of the chief philosophical resources for this latter aspect of republican argument was Hugo Grotius's innovative and influential theory of the natural obligation and right to punish. As English republicans were quick to point out, although the Grotian natural obligation and right to wield the secular sword of justice might be fully alienable to a public magistrate, it is not always fully alienated. When fortune favours the people at the founding moment of their polity, or at the conclusion of a civil war or constitutional crisis, they may reserve to themselves and their parliament a part of their original natural penal rights. Since Machiavellian republicans believed that fortune favours those who exhibit political virtue – those who 'prefer the good of the public to any private interest'[3] – they naturally preferred Grotius's moral theory to the more selfish individualism of Thomas Hobbes.

II

Grotius's primary aim in *The Laws of War and Peace* (1625) was to provide a theory of just warfare capable of imparting a certain degree of moral order to the conduct of nations, which in recent years had exhibited, to his mind, an unusually ferocious tendency towards 'lawlessness in warfare' (Prologue, 28).[4] Once Philip II's dream of a pan-European empire had been defeated, it seemed less plausible than ever to suppose, as Francisco de Vitoria had in the previous century, that 'the world as a whole' was 'a single state' with the authority to create positive international laws that would be 'just and fitting for everyone'.[5] In the absence of international magistracy, Grotius believed that relations between states could only be intelligently ordered in accordance with universal principles of human morality, or 'natural' laws. He therefore construed the right of every nation to defend itself against foreign aggression on analogy with the natural right of every individual, in the absence of civil authority, to preserve and defend herself against harm. And beyond this, he supposed that every nation should also be understood to have an international right of punitive warfare, which derives from an analogous pre-civil right and obligation of every individual to punish anyone who offends against universally valid moral standards of justice.[6]

Grotius's doctrine of the individual's natural right to punish was a conspicuous innovation.[7] He wrote *The Laws of War and Peace* at a time when philosophical dialectics, being rooted in debates over whether Conciliar or Papal power was supreme, varied between the view that the right to punish belongs originally and chiefly to the community as a unified whole, so that it may govern the conduct of its parts or members, and the view that the right to punish belongs in the first instance to that part of the community which is set above, and ordained to rule over, the whole. Within an international society which was neither unified nor ruled by any single nation or alliance, both of these competing traditional views failed to invest the several independent nations of the world with the right to punish those guilty of unjust aggression. To Grotius's mind, such a conclusion was morally intolerable. In his view, nation-states, like private persons, are moral agents that should be judged and punished according to natural standards of moral conduct. Accordingly, morally responsible and 'brave' nations will not limit their independent use of arms to the requirements of self-defence. Rather, they will also endeavour to enforce natural standards of justice as if violations of those standards were breaches of their own territorial boundary lines (Prol., 19, 24). In Grotius's view, not only this right of punitive warfare, but also the state's right of domestic criminal jurisdiction, ultimately derives from each citizen's original right to 'the sword of justice'. He plainly states that 'the liberty of inflicting punishment for the peace and welfare of society, which belonged to individuals in the early ages of the world, was converted into the judicial authority of sovereign states and princes' (II. xx. 40).[8]

Grotius systematically draws conclusions about the right conduct of nations from reflections on our natural moral capacities as individuals. Foremost among these capacities, he emphasizes our ability to distinguish between just and unjust violence without appealing to the declared will of any positively instituted civil authority, as well as our ability to resist natural injustices for the sake of our common interest in peaceful and intelligently ordered social life. Thus, it is in large measure as a motive to natural law enforcement that Grotius posits, as 'the source of all law which is properly so called', a uniquely human, paradigmatically rational, and morally 'mature' form of social appetite (Prol., 7, 8). We are by nature socially inclined but pugnacious beings. We have a natural desire to live together in a peaceful society ordered primarily through the exercise of our intellectual capacities for speech and rule-following. But since we tend naturally to follow our own judgments and to be somewhat partial to our own interests, we are prone to controversy and conflict, or (broadly speaking) 'war' (I. i. 2).

There are, however, rationally demonstrable and empirically discoverable rules for limiting interpersonal conflict in ways consistent with the 'peculiar' bent of the human social appetite; these rules are what Grotius calls 'the laws of nature' (I. i. 2). According to Grotius, if we are attentive to the claims of human sociability, then we will recognize as unjust forms of action and inaction that are directly inimical to peaceful and intelligently ordered social life. Far from aiming to maximize some highest human good, the Grotian laws of natural justice merely describe the minimal moral conditions that make pre-civil sociability possible. These fundamental injustices include breaking a promise, taking what belongs to another, failing to restore what has been wrongfully taken, and failing to compensate another for a loss negligently caused. At the end of this short list of universal natural injustices, Grotius also includes the claim 'that it is right to punish men who deserve it' (Prol., 8).

When Grotius speaks not only of the 'right' but also of the 'obligation to punish', he has in mind a moral necessity that arises through coordinate application of the natural laws of justice and beneficence (III. xiii. 2). A violation of natural justice creates in the offender an obligation to suffer punishment (II. xx. 2; III. xxii. 4). The principles of natural justice also permit that 'anyone of competent judgment, who is not implicated in similar or equal offences' may impose this punishment (II. xx. 7, 9). Thus, upon murdering his brother, Cain gave expression to his 'sense of natural justice' when he acknowledged that 'whosoever finds me shall kill me' (I. ii. 5). In response to serious injustices, the innocent may indeed throw the first stone. The relative innocence that conditions attributions of natural penal rights is not always a product of self-interested fear, however. Indeed, the fear that arises from the instinct for self-preservation – which Hobbes would later make the cornerstone of his theory of political subjection – often figures in Grotius's treatment of the state of natural society as motive of cowardice and a poor excuse for unjust anticipatory attacks on neighbours or neighbouring states (II. i. 5, 17, 18; II. ii. 13; II. iv. 6; III. iv. 13). We discover other, altruistic motives to justice in those who exhibit such moral qualities as 'temperance, fortitude and discretion', and we are 'bound' by the natural law of beneficence to exhibit these virtues in many situations (II. i. 9).

Hence, the natural law of beneficence dictates that, quite apart from egoistic concerns, 'the very injustice of all offences ought to be a general motive with men, to restrain them from the commission of them' (II. xx. 30). The virtuous individual's concern for 'the public welfare', 'the common good' or 'general utility' arises not only for the sake of her own selfish investment in public peace and safety, but also 'for the sake of others'. Further, 'all men of sober judgment and enlarged information deem the public interest of higher moment than their own' (II. i. 9). Individuals who exhibit such public virtue are natural punishers, 'designed by nature for the office of perpetual magistracy' (II. xx. 9). In sum, whereas the natural law of justice grants every relatively innocent person the right to punish an offender, the natural law of beneficence sometimes makes the exercise of that right a moral necessity for 'good men'. In this respect, the execution of punitive violence, under certain circumstances, is an obligation-fulfilling natural right.[9] It is for this reason that Grotius thinks that (other things being equal) 'neglect' of appropriate punitive action 'amounts to a sanction of the offence' and constitutes 'a sin against human nature' (III. xx. 23, 30). And, in his view, it follows that 'the state or nation, which has neglected to punish the aggressions of its own subjects ... is a proper object of hostility and attack' (I. i. 2).

By locating the source of natural law morality in a uniquely human form of social appetite, Grotius was clearly signalling his departure from the classical Roman conception of natural law as that law which nature 'has taught all animals'.[10] The laws of natural justice are not grounded in an instinct common to all brute creation, such as the instinct of self-preservation.[11] Accordingly, Grotius is very careful to distinguish between the egoistic goals of self-defence and the altruistic goals of punitive justice, and this difference is further reflected in his treatment of the corresponding natural rights. The right of self-defence 'derives its origin primarily from the instinct of self-preservation, which nature has given to every creature, *and not from the injustice or misconduct of the aggressor*' (II. i. 3, my emphasis). By contrast, in his treatment of natural penal rights, he claims that 'he who punishes, if he is to punish correctly, must have a right to do it, *a right growing out of the crime of the offender*' (II. xx. 2, my emphasis).[12]

Moreover, unlike Hobbes, Grotius does not see self-preservation as a moral absolute under conditions of natural or civil society. The Grotian state of natural society is a 'community of goods' in which everyone is entitled, within the bounds of justice, and from a prudent concern for their own preservation and well-being, to take what is ready to hand and unclaimed by any other. After the formation of civil society, under circumstances of 'extreme necessity', exceptions may be made to positive laws of property, and the 'primitive right to the use of things' may be 'revived' (II. ii. 6). Such exceptions to positive law arise not because the right to self-preservation is absolute, as it is for Hobbes, but because it is weightier than the right to property as a means to exalted well-being. Although Grotius famously acknowledges that the instinct to preserve and care for our bodies is our 'first duty' (I. ii. 1), he means here only that it is first in what was sometimes termed the order of creation as distinct from the order of reasons. The duty of self-preservation is less weighty than our moral duty to live sociably with others in conformity with natural justice. Accordingly, instances in which we can take what belongs to others for the sake of self-preservation are limited and 'cannot be granted where the owner is in an equal state of need himself' (II. ii. 7). Under circumstances of equal need 'the owner's claim is superior'. On this point, Grotius quotes Cicero with evident approval:

> Suppose a wise man were starving to death, might he not take the bread of some perfectly useless member of society? Not at all; for my life is not more precious to me than that temper of soul which would keep me from doing wrong to anybody for my own advantage. (II. ii. 7)[13]

Nothing could be further in spirit from the absolute liberty and purely self-interested calculations of Hobbesian moral agents than this Ciceronian sentiment.

III

Writing at the outbreak of the Civil Wars, Philip Hunton presented the first substantially Grotian understanding of the conflict between King and Parliament. Although he was not in the habit of citing the sources of his intellectual inspiration, Hunton's *Treatise of Monarchy* (1643) adhered closely to Grotius's nuanced account of natural right and state-formation. Accordingly, he hung his argument for Parliament's cause upon, first, a moral affirmation of every individual's effective sense of justice and, second, an historical point of constitutional interpretation.

For Hunton, as for Grotius, natural law is neutral as between different forms of government (I. i. 1, p. 3).[14] For every distinct nation, it is the original historical will of the community, or 'the original contract and fundamental constitution', that determines the legitimate form of political subjection (I. i. 1, p. 6; I. ii. 6, p. 16). It happens that the ancient constitution of England established a 'mixed and limited monarchy' (II. iii. 1). Like every other form of government, limited monarchy has its peculiar form of 'inconvenience'. Whereas democracy, aristocracy and absolute monarchy involve the risks, respectively, of chronic confusion, destructive faction and irremediable tyranny, limited monarchy opens the door to constitutional crisis and civil war. This inconvenience of limited monarchy arises from the precarious balance of its constitutional origin and design. On the one hand, 'the law of the land' limits the legitimate power of the king and declares that tyranny will have its remedy. On the other hand, for the task of enforcing the king's compliance with the law of the land, 'there can be no judge legal and constituted within [a monarchical] frame of government' (I. ii. 7, p. 17). Parliament could raise a constitutional 'tribunal' to depose Charles I only if it were itself absolutely sovereign. But England was not a constitutional democracy, according to Hunton. Therefore, the constitution that limits the king's power can only have an 'extraordinary' mode of enforcement:

> The Fundamental Laws of that Monarchy must judge and pronounce the sentence in every man's conscience; and every man (as far concerns him) must follow the evidence of truth in his own soul, to oppose, or not oppose, according as he can in conscience acquit or condemn the act of carriage of the governour. For I conceive, in a case which transcends the frame and provision of the government they are bound to. (I. ii. 7, p. 18)

The constitution of limited monarchy affords no regular 'legal' remedy for tyranny, but it implies, instead, the legitimacy of a 'transcendent' and 'moral' remedy. In other words, paradoxically, the 'law of the land' in England is legitimately enforceable only by means of extra-legal violence, which men dutifully enact as subjects of natural morality, not as subjects of civil law. The people do not fully alienate their natural penal rights when, at the founding moment of their polity, they agree only to a conditional contract of subjection to monarchy. In accordance with natural law, every armed individual may therefore judge the monarch's rule and, if conscience finds cause, reclaim the original right to the sword of justice. The citizen who thus raises arms against an unjust monarchical regime does not exercise the authority of a superior civil office. He exercises, rather, that pre-civil 'moral' right that Grotius and Hunton credit to every relatively innocent person:

> This power of judging argues not a superiority in those who judge, over him who is judged; for it is not authoritative and civil, but moral, residing in reasonable creatures, and lawful for them to execute, because never devested and put off by any act in the constitution of a legal government, but rather the reservation of it intended: For when they define the superiour to a law, and constitute no power to judge of his excesses from that law, it is evident they reserve to themselves, not a formal authoritative power, but a moral power, such as they had originally before the constitution of the government; which must needs remain, being not conveyed away in the constitution. (I. ii. 7, p. 18)

Thus, in Hunton's account, the English Civil Wars could be understood as a conflict between parliamentary and monarchical forces that met as natural equals, and the execution of Charles I could be understood as a morally legitimate act of extra-legal justice.

Repudiating Hunton's relatively moderate view of the ancient constitution, Henry Parker was the first English republican thinker to offer an explicitly Grotian argument for parliamentary sovereignty and penal rights.[15] Moreover, to this end, he was also the first to adopt Grotius's scriptural argument for natural penal rights in opposition to the view (of which Filmer was to become the most famous proponent) that civil magistracy is a patriarchal right, immediately instituted by God.[16] In his *Jus Populi* (1644), Parker argues that if Adam had possessed the right of magistracy over his sons, then he 'ought to have arraigned Cain at his bar, and to have required blood for blood'. Instead, as Grotius emphasized, we find that 'the whole stock of mankinde then living, were the judges that Cain feared' (*ibid.*, 33).[17] Before the institution of kings or judges among the Israelites, 'the people by common consent did rise up to vindicate common trespasses'. Thus, like Grotius, Parker emphasized the importance of common consent in the origination and punitive maintenance of private property. In this form of democratic punitive action, the people do not exercise an unbridled self- interested liberty. Rather they exercise a generous, obligation-fulfilling right, for 'God so required it at their hands'. For Parker, who (like Grotius) repudiated voluntarism, the moral requirement of impartiality in punishment provides the reason for God's universal distribution of the obligation and right to wield the secular sword of justice:

> If judgement should be left to parents only, much injustice might be expected from them, which is not so much to be feared from the people not yet associated: For the offence of the son is either against the father, or some other: If against the father, then is he judge in his own case; and that is dangerous; the father may be partiall to himselfe: If against another, then the father is a stranger to the plaintiffe, not to the defendant: and that is more dangerous. (*Ibid.*, 33)

Exclusive patriarchal power offers no inherent assurance of impartiality. By contrast, if the obligation and right to punish originally fall to all those who live together as equals, then those who are generous enough to risk taking punitive action will be sure to secure the consent of others in order to avoid being punished themselves for unjust unilateral violence.

Hence, the universal distribution of penal power ensures that its exercise will be based upon broad consent, which in turn ensures that it will be exercised impartially. In the institution of a just civil government, the people's *manner* of pursuing punishment 'flows' to the chief magistrate without loss of its original impartiality and generosity, or, in Parker's preferred vocabulary, without loss of its original 'honour and splendour' or 'honour and glory' (*ibid.*, 16). In order to ensure that the natural moral quality of punitive action will not be 'wasted' when the people invest their power in the office of the 'supreme commander', it is necessary that this power should never entirely 'passe from the people', but should always ultimately remain their legal possession (*ibid.*, 17). This moral imperative is enshrined in the ancient constitutional rights of the people's parliament. Therefore, contrary to Hunton's contention, there is no reason to suppose that parliament lacks the legal power, during an 'inter-regnum', to erect a 'Tribunall' for the purpose of prosecuting 'all the common disturbers of mankind' (*ibid.*, 10). If parliament had conducted the regicide, it could have been viewed, in light of Parker's theory, as a positive legal enactment of the people's natural rights.

The trial and execution of Charles I were carried out, however, not by parliament, but by Cromwell's New Model Army. In *The Tenure of Kings and Magistrates* (1649), John Milton would explicitly invoke Grotius's authority on behalf of the Army's proceedings, but he would depart significantly from the orthodox Grotian view of natural penal rights. In particular, Milton did not embrace Grotius's contention that the obligation and right to punish malefactors for the sake of the public interest is already fully constituted in advance of the formation of civil society. Unlike Grotius, he strongly suggests that the 'bond of nature' does not reach beyond self-interest. Milton's state of nature is as Hobbes would have it: individuals in that condition have unlimited natural rights of self-preservation and defence. But they apparently have nothing like the Grotian moral faculty for discovering, and responding with duly measured force, to actions that are intrinsically unconformable to the normative conditions of natural society.

Miltonian duties for the vicarious use of coercive and violent force depend, instead, upon the creation by mutual covenants of a civil society which is no longer purely natural, even when it is not yet (or no longer) ruled by duly-appointed governors. With this intermediate stage of social organization, everyone's natural right of self-defence is transformed into a civil obligation and right of mutual defence against common enemies. The legitimate public use of coercive and violent force hinges upon a political criterion of alliance and not upon any moral principles of natural justice other than the duty of promise-keeping. Consequently, Milton's account of the right to punish accommodates a remarkably sparing range of moral distinctions. Apart from registering degrees of danger or harmfulness, Miltonian punishers will also distinguish between enemies simpliciter who were never bound by the covenants of the society they attack (foreign invaders), enemies who have defected from the social contract (domestic criminals), and enemies who have breached the contractual terms of political governance and subjection (domestic tyrants). Of these three, the latter deserve the harshest treatment.

It was, of course, ideologically expedient for Milton to conceive of civil society as a defensive military alliance. Earlier protestant resistance theorists typically maintained that the right to take up arms against a domestic tyrant resides exclusively with parliamentary magistrates. Justification of the military proceedings against Charles I would therefore require a quite different and novel account of the right to punish. Milton set out to provide such an account in his treatise, though he attempted to mask the novelty of it on the title page of the first edition, which asserted:

> That it is lawfull, *and hath been held so through the ages*, for any, who have the power, to call to account a tyrant, or wicked King, and after due conviction, to depose, and put him to death; if the ordinary magistrate have neglected, or deny'd to doe it.[18]

Milton's theory of state-formation is more philosophically radical than Grotius's, because he did not wish to hang his case against Charles I on the uncertainties of interpreting the ancient constitution of England. Since he did not wish to allow for the possibility that the people of England may have completely and permanently alienated their liberty to punish, he chose a more decisive mode of argument than any appeal to the 'primitive will' of the people could provide. In his view, the common public right to punish is a creature of the original pact of civil society that the people can never fully alienate to a sovereign ruler. Accordingly, the legality of tyrannicide is established, not by direct appeal to pre-civil standards of natural justice, nor by appeal to the historically contingent constitutional settlement of England, but by the implicit promise that is universally inscribed in the very nature of civil society.

Writing after the conclusion of the Civil Wars, in his *Case of the Commonwealth of England Stated* (1650), Marchamont Nedham invoked Grotius's authority both in order to justify the punitive execution of Charles I for violating parliament's rights (with the purging of Presbyterians from the Commons characterized as the punishment of 'accessories') and also in order to justify submission to Cromwell's rule. Unlike Milton, however, Nedham would find in Grotius's theory of 'formal' warfare a jus gentium argument that would elude the difficulty of resting the people's claim to the sword of justice upon an uncertain interpretation of the ancient constitution.

As a central tenet of this particular treatise, the mercurial Nedham maintains that England is a mixed monarchy. Speaking of the balance of rights characteristic of such a regime, he quotes from *The Laws of War and Peace* what would become the favourite passage of English republicans:

> If the Authority be divided betwixt a King and his People in Parliament, so that the King hath one part, the People another; the King offering to incroach upon that part which is none of his, may lawfully be opposed by force of Arms, because he exceeds the bounds of his Authority. And not only so, but he may lose his own part likewise, by the Law of Arms. (I. iv)

Nedham leaves no doubt that, in a mixed monarchy, the people retain their natural penal rights and that the people of England exercised such rights in the execution of Charles I. To Nedham's morally sceptical mind, however, others might reasonably disagree about the legitimacy of the regicide. Insofar as the legitimacy of parliament's initial cause in the civil wars ultimately hinges upon an 'immemorial' point of historical fact, there is room for reasonable doubts about every effort of Parliament at armed resistance against the King's forces. Nevertheless, in Nedham's view, the moral contestability of the war efforts of Parliament and Cromwell should have no bearing upon the issue of engagement. The Civil Wars represented a time of 'miserable Confusions' in which the determination of constitutional and natural right was uncertain business. Whether or not the initial cause of the Civil Wars was truly just, it was advanced in good faith under conditions of moral uncertainty. Viewed in this light, Cromwell's eventual victory gave him a legitimate right, under the putative *jus gentium* convention of formal warfare, to impose his preferred conditions of political subjection. Here Nedham cleverly seizes upon a singularly Hobbesian subdivision of Grotius's multifaceted treatment of the laws of war. As Grotius allows, 'when for instance, a kingdom is so equally divided between two parties, that it is a matter of doubt which of them constitutes the nation ... the kingdom may be considered as forming two nations at the same time' (II. xviii. 2). In the settlement of such Civil Wars, Nedham avers, 'necessity sometimes gives birth to new rights in violation of former rules'.[19] This implies that the new regime may 'use such means as nature instructs them in, and erect such a form [of government] as they themselves conceive most convenient for their own preservation'. At the conclusion of a formal civil war, the conquered party's duty of obedience is sufficiently grounded in the fact that the conquering party possesses irresistible power and provides the service of protection.[20]

IV

Nedham is best-known for the leading role he played in bringing Machiavelli's republican thought to bear upon English political affairs. In frequently citing the authority of both Machiavelli and Grotius, however, he also appears to have been the first to suggest a philosophical synthesis that would occupy the minds of many later republican thinkers, from Edward Sexby to Algernon Sidney. Notwithstanding the great extent of Grotius's influence, late seventeenth-century English political thought has also been aptly described as the heyday of Machiavellian republicanism. Many English republicans endeavoured to bring these two strains of political theory together, despite the apparent tension between them.

According to orthodox Grotian republicans, this was a tension between the view that might makes right and the view that the legitimacy and stability of political power depends upon its conformity with antecedent standards of natural justice. We find this tension in Grotius's own criticisms of Machiavelli, which were published in England in 1654 as *Politick Maxims and Observations*. In this work, Grotius is concerned at nearly every point to insist upon a fundamental moral difference between Machiavellian 'reason of state' and just government on the basis of 'equity' (*ibid.*, 32).[21] Similarly, we find that some staunchly Grotian republicans repudiated Machiavellian political thought as divisive, atheistic, and subversive of natural and constitutional law. Parker and Gilbert Burnet, for instance, thought that their Grotian convictions placed them opposite Machiavelli on the heavenly side of the divide between 'piety' and 'policy'.[22] In their view, the trouble with Machiavellian republicans is that they do not properly subordinate the assertion of their civil liberties to obligations of natural law and Christian religion.

Note, however, that when it comes to punishing tyrants for their absolutist pretentions there may be (depending upon the nature of the relevant historical constitution) no fundamental conflict between a pious observation of Grotian obligations and a shrewd Machiavellian defence of republican liberty. In the face of tyranny, there may be little conflict between having a clean conscience and having dirty hands. Such was clearly the view of Edward Sexby, who systematically educed the most radical implications of the Grotian notion that every man is naturally equipped to execute justice. In his *Killing Noe Murder* (1657), Sexby drew upon Grotius's individualistic theory of natural penal rights in order to support his own independent assault upon the protectorate. Sexby was an ally of Cromwell's during the Civil War, but he soon came to believe that Oliver had betrayed the republican cause and that his rule was as tyrannical as Charles I's. Accordingly, he plotted to assassinate Cromwell. In justifying his attempt (which failed and ended in his own death), Sexby did not feel compelled to defer to any constitutionally enshrined penal powers or any common convention among nations. Instead, he argued that Cromwell ruled by force and fraud rather than by law, that he lacked any legitimate claim to magistracy, and that he had therefore placed himself in the state of nature, outside the protective cover of the English constitution, and within the moral jurisdiction of Sexby's or anyone else's natural right to punish.[23]

While invoking his Grotian natural obligation and right to punish Cromwell, Sexby also argued that even 'his Highness' own Evangelist, Machiavelli' would condemn him (*ibid.*, 367). From a Machiavellian standpoint, he suggests, Cromwell's rule relied too heavily on the excessive timidity and pious self-restraint of the people. One can only realistically expect, in his view, that the people will endeavour to vindicate their civil liberties, once contested, by fierce and violent means. Sexby was not simply grafting a Grotian obligation and right onto what was already a commonly accepted Machiavellian expectation of actual political behaviour. Writing 20 years before the reception of Grotius in England, Barnabe Barnes complained that, when it comes to defending their civil liberties, modern English citizens are not Machiavellian enough:

> The reason why so fewe free people and States are in comparison of former times, and such a defect of true lovers and of valiant champions of liberties in comparison of former ages … is, that people in hope of beatitude, and towards the fruition of a second comfortable life, devise in these dayes how to tollerate and not to revenge injuries.[24]

One might reasonably suppose, however, that if this same Christian people were to become convinced that toleration of serious public injuries is, as Grotius put it, 'a sin against human nature', then their actual pattern of political behaviour might change. Accordingly, in the case of Cromwell, Sexby could embrace a Machiavellian prediction of rebellion, not because he was a deeply Machiavellian thinker (he suggests that he was not), but because he recognized, and he was optimistic that the English people would also recognize, a Grotian obligation and right to punish tyrants.

Nearly a generation later, we find Henry Neville repeating Sexby's Machiavellian warning of the consequences of tyranny in his *Plato Redivivus: or, A Dialogue Concerning Government* (1681).[25] Unlike Sexby, however, Neville was a devoted follower of Machiavelli. In order to answer the complaints of such critics as Burnet (a pious 'Court Whig'), he endeavoured to convert Machiavellian political thought from atheism to reformed theology. His 'divine Machiavelli' was merely the enemy of popish clergy, and was therefore a friend not only of republicanism, but also of the reformation.[26]

Thus, by invoking the account of civil conflicts set forth by Grotius, who was especially popular among the English clergy, Neville could maintain that his brand of republicanism was compatible with a reformed conception of the duties that citizens owe to God as human beings and as Christians. Like Hunton, Neville holds that no judge could ever have authority to adjudicate civil conflicts between the 'coordinate' powers of a mixed government. Therefore, when one civil power has committed an injustice against another, the conflict is best settled by the exercise of natural penal rights. Unfortunately, as Nedham had argued, the English civil wars began not over a clear 'point of right', but over an immemorial and uncertain 'matter of fact'. In this case, according to Neville, 'both parties pretended and believed they were in the right; and that they did fight for, and defend the government' (*ibid.*, 150). The Civil Wars began with a good-faith disagreement. Thus, citing both Machiavelli and Grotius, Neville endorses an ideological consensus according to which, under the extraordinary circumstances of the civil wars, a legitimate settlement could be achieved only by means of superior arms.

Of all republican thinkers, Algernon Sidney presented the most thorough amalgamation of Grotian natural law and Machiavellian policy. Sidney composed his *Discourses Concerning Government* (1698) at the time of the Exclusion Crisis (1681–82), and like other leading exclusionists, such as James Tyrrell and John Locke, he rehearsed Grotius's interpretation of the natural law implications of Cain's guilty apprehensions (ch. 2, s2; ch. 3, s1).[27] Following Parker, he held that when the people come together to form a 'mixed' or 'popular' government, they invest part of their original natural rights in parliamentary penal powers which they institute in order to impose legal limits on the powers of their chosen king and his ministers:

> These are the kingdoms of which Grotius speaks, *where the king has his part, and the senate or people their part of the supreme authority*; and where the law prescribes such limits, *that if the king attempt to seize that part which is not his, he may justly be opposed*. Which is as much as to say, that the law upholds the power it gives, and turns against those who abuse it. (*Ibid.*, ch. 2, s30; my emphases)

Further, there is a certain natural coordination between the people's right to the punitive enforcement of constitutional limitations of kingly power and their inalienable right to defend themselves. In Sidney's view, the people may justifiably take up arms against their rulers for the very reasons of self-defence that Grotius put forth: 'On account of [the rulers'] great savagery' and 'when the king hastens to the ruin of his people' (*ibid.*, ch. 2, s27).[28] Since the people are disinclined by nature to cause extreme harm to themselves, these 'mischiefs and cruelties', and their ensuing defensive rebellions, are much less likely to occur when the people are ultimately in control of their own government. In short, when the people federate their natural penal rights in a parliament and actively prosecute violations of constitutional divisions and limits of power, it is unlikely that they will need to rely upon their monarch's benevolence or to defend themselves against his malevolence.

Moreover, according to Sidney, in adhering more closely than absolutist regimes to Grotian principles of natural right and justice, mixed governments draw upon and foster civic virtue and liberty. When the people retain the right to limit and punish their king and their king's ministers, they are not only much less likely to suffer from the vices of those rulers, they are also much less likely to fall into vice themselves (*ibid.*, ch. 2, s19). Of course, any form of civil society can fall into a state of 'corruption' in which virtue no longer flourishes. But, according to Sidney, absolute monarchy is 'rooted' in the corruption of virtue as a matter of 'principle', because the exercise of absolute power can only reach its full extent (as is the tendency of all power) when citizens become passive in the face of injustice. In his efforts to bring about such passivity in his subjects, the absolute monarch invariably becomes an enemy of virtue: 'The absolute monarch always prefers the worst of those who are addicted to him, and cannot subsist unless the prevailing part of the people be base and vicious' (*ibid.*, ch. 2, s19). Passivity in the face of injustice would therefore appear to be the first and greatest vice to be found in any people. While it makes them fit for subjection to an absolute monarch, it also makes that very form of government unstable because vulnerable to external aggression. Citizens who lack the moral vigour to resist a domestic tyrant are also likely to make poor soldiers when it comes to resisting the similar injustice of foreign domination (*ibid.*, ch. 2, ss11, 15, 21). In sum, both the virtue of the citizenry, and the liberty of the commonwealth (which in the Machiavellian sense is its freedom from external domination), are best maintained when the people invest part of their natural penal rights in an independent parliament.

Sidney was not the only Whig exclusionist to embrace the idea that Grotian principles of natural justice and right describe the basic conditions under which Machiavellian civic virtue and liberty tend to flourish. His thoroughgoing synthesis exemplified and clarified a widespread pattern in English republican thought. By this time, most Machiavellian republicans had acquired a quick sense of Grotian natural justice. Milton's more philosophically radical mode of justifying extraordinary or ostensibly extra-legal violence failed to have a lasting influence on republican thought, in part, for the same reason that Hobbes's political theory was unpopular among Royalists. The unlimited natural right of self-preservation, guided only by the bare criterion of political alliance, is a double-edged sword. In conflicts that exceed the authority of any positive civil jurisdiction, prudential considerations of allied self-preservation weigh equally on opposing sides. Barring rational mediation by other right-conferring moral criteria (such as the fundamental injustices of Grotian natural law), only superior power can tip the balance in favour of one side or the other. Further, the bare principle of self-preservation was a meager medium for those who wished to appeal directly to natural law morality in order to advertise the legal character of political violence. A reasonably cogent resolution of the problem of legality would require a greater degree of ethical continuity between natural and civil law than the principle of self-preservation could supply. Unlike the law of self-preservation, the natural right to punish implied the existence and relevance of some standard of justice and legal (or quasi-legal) order. According to Grotius and his followers, since the penal powers of civil society accrue from natural penal rights, the legitimacy of any exercise of those powers depends in part upon its conformity with the principles of natural law morality which would give everyone the right to punish under pre-civil conditions. Civil magistrates have a duty to enforce positive (common or statutory) laws, but only insofar as those laws are consistent with natural law. Therefore, according to Grotian thinkers, principles of natural law provide the interpretive framework within which the meanings of positive laws should be determined. This idea would hardly have seemed unusual to magistrates and members of parliament schooled in the thought of Edward Coke, who held that the immemorial customs of the English common law were ultimately grounded in 'the immutable law and light of nature, agreeable to the law of God'.[29] Not surprisingly therefore, Grotius's influence was particularly pronounced where we find the tendency in republican thought to combine natural law and historical-constitutional arguments in favour of parliament's right to the sword of justice. And this mode of argumentation was especially popular among Machiavellian republicans who paid the most lip service to the idea of the rule of law.

Shaftesbury's own *Letter from a Person of Quality to his Friend in the Country* (1675) presented the definitive Machiavellian-Grotian conception of the ancient constitution. The *Letter* defers to Grotius's understanding of the admonitions contained in natural and ordained law against swearing 'oaths promising something in an uncertain future' (*ibid.*, 15).[30] The relevant precept of Grotius's theory of natural law states that 'it is best and most useful and most in harmony with a rational nature to refrain from oath-swearing, and to habituate oneself to speaking the truth that one's word may be accepted in place of an oath'.[31] Immediately after stating this precept, Grotius proceeds to argue that, as a consequence, 'obviously, if a people has set up a king without absolute authority, but restricted by laws, any acts of his contrary to those laws can be rendered void by them, either as a whole or in part, because the people has reserved for itself authority to that extent' (*Law*, II. xiv. 2). On the face of it, this connection between the virtue of truth-telling, the problem of oath-swearing, and the power of the people to 'void' kingly acts might seem obscure. But the connection seemed clear to the Shaftesburean Whigs. For the First Earl, the apparent implication of Grotius's account of public oaths was that members of English parliament could not possibly swear oaths of allegiance and, at the same time, speak the truth about their duties and rights under both natural law and the ancient constitution of their limited monarchy. According to the *Letter,* members of parliament cannot legitimately swear oaths never to take up arms against their king because such oaths would cast doubt on the ancient constitution itself. The ancient constitution is a 'golden chain' which binds together the interest of the king with the interest of his people by placing 'his safety ... in them, as theirs was in him' (*ibid.,* 16–17). It is a sacred bond of 'trust' which conforms to the laws of nature. But it is also a trust that is enforced and made legally binding by mutual 'fear'.[32] Accordingly, no oath can supplant honest dealing as a guarantee of peace between a people and their government, and the constitutional condition of mutual fear, which provides inducements to honest dealing, can be maintained only if parliamentary representatives retain some part of the original penal rights of the people. In this way, the First Earl's conception of the constitution implies that 'they overthrow the government that suppose to place any part of it above the fear of man' (*ibid.,* 16). Therefore, the notion that members of parliament should, by oaths of allegiance, foreswear their obligation and right to take up arms against a tyrannical king 'necessarily brings in the debate in every man's mind, how there can be a distinction left between absolute, and bounded monarchys, if monarchs have only the fear of God, and no fear of human resistance to restrain them'.[33] Here we see how, at a moment of constitutional crisis, Grotian obligations and natural penal rights could be embraced as complementary to a Machiavellian understanding of the political dynamics involved in a putatively republican constitution.

V

During the last quarter of the seventeenth century, with the emergence of the Machiavellian–Grotian synthesis, the notion that the penal powers of civil society accrue from the aggregation of natural penal rights reached its zenith as an instrument of English oppositional politics. It was in this context that John Locke abandoned the convictions of his earlier systematic reflections on natural law (his *Essays on the Law of Nature*) and, following James Tyrrell, jumped on the Grotian bandwagon in asserting what he considered to be the 'strange doctrine' of natural penal rights.

In the early 1660s, when he composed his eight *Essays,* Locke was already familiar with Grotius's theory of natural penal rights.[34] But he did not embrace it. Although he acknowledges in *Essay VI* that 'the laws of the civil magistrate derive their whole force from *the constraining power of natural law*', he never suggests that any part of this constraining power involves a punitive mode of response between individuals situated in a natural condition of equality (*Essays,* 189, my emphasis). On the contrary, he allows only that the laws of nature may be enforced immediately through divine sanctions, or mediately through sanctions imposed by human superiors who have acquired rights of 'dominion' either by donation or by contract (*ibid.*, 185).[35] Locke's early natural law is not enforceable within a pre-civil community of equals. The obligatoriness of certain actions and forbearances stems not from their intrinsic moral qualities, as in Grotius, nor simply from fearsome threats of sanctions for doing otherwise, as in Hobbes, but from the 'authority and rightful power' of superiors to issue commands and prohibitions (*ibid.*, 187, 189). Whereas natural obligations arise directly from the 'intrinsic force' of divine authority, familial and civil obligations arise indirectly from the 'delegated power' of parents and kings (*ibid.*, 187). Locke maintains that our moral conscience will tell us 'that we deserve punishment' whenever we rationally apprehend that we have transgressed against the declared will and authority of a rightful superior (*ibid.*, 185). So remorse of conscience may combine with the penal powers of superiors in giving force to natural and civil laws. Locke credits no such effect, however, to resentment of injuries arising from the judgements we are inclined to pass on the actions of our less conscientious equals. Parents may judge their children, kings may judge their subjects, and everyone may judge herself according to the judgements of her superiors. But no one is morally competent to judge her equals, and no one can assert rights of dominion over others simply in virtue of her greater innocence in the eyes of nature.

Locke first argued for the Grotian doctrine of natural penal rights in the second of his *Two Treatises of Government* (1690), which (if David Wooton's conjecture is correct) he composed immediately after the appearance of James Tyrrell's like-minded *Patriarcha Non Monarcha* (1681).[36] Like Tyrrell, he adopted the Grotian view as part of what he considered to be the most compelling philosophical alternative to Robert Filmer's patriarchal theory of the origin and rightful succession of sovereign power. From 1679 to 1681 Filmer's theory quickly became the orthodox view of royalists opposed to Exclusion. Although Locke did not publish his *Two Treatises* until after the Glorious Revolution – perhaps in order to justify revolutionary actions already taken, and perhaps also in order to present his arguments at a moment some distance from the heat of political conflict, when they might plausibly claim to enlighten the reader from a standpoint of cool philosophical detachment – nevertheless, it appears to have been the Exclusion Crisis which provided the occasion for his conversion to the Grotian view that, on the basis of their natural penal rights, the people may determine who shall wield the public sword of justice, how such officials should wield it, and when they may be said to have relinquished it and to have merited punishment themselves.

Locke, however, departed from the emerging republican orthodoxy by repudiating the Grotian method of arguing from a consensus of natural and customary law. He thought it was a mistake to give greater or equal weight to legal history in determining what rights parliament may claim to have against the king. In his view, the actions of 'the executive' should be held accountable to the standards of natural law 'not by old custom, but by true reason' (*Second Treatise*, chap. 13).[37] And in virtue of his insistence upon this dichotomy between the real authority of reason and the pseudo-authority of custom – redolent of Hobbes's insistence that 'experience concludeth nothing universally'[38] – Locke was perhaps the least Grotian of all the exclusionist writers.

At the time of the Glorious Revolution, shortly before Locke published his *Two Treatises*, the influence of Grotius on Whig thought was even more pronounced than it had been during the Exclusion Crisis. Indeed, Grotius's authority on natural law and natural penal rights so dominated the scene that Charles Blount, author of a pamphlet entitled *Proceedings of the Present Parliament Justified, by the Opinion of the Most Judicious and Learned Hugo Grotius* (1689), believed that sufficient justification for the revolution, and for submission to William's regime, could be given simply by stringing together numerous and long quotations from *The Law of War and Peace* pertaining to the conditions under which a people may justifiably punish an unruly king and reform their government.

Gilbert Burnet's *An Enquiry into the Measures of Submission to the Supream Authority* (1688) is also an especially important indicator of Grotius's influence in this context because it came closer than any other relevant work to presenting an 'official' justification of the Glorious Revolution.[39] Burnet regularly preached to William of Orange before the revolution, while exiled in Holland, and after the revolution as the Bishop of Salisbury. And during William's invasion, both Burnet and large numbers of his largely Grotian *Enquiry* accompanied the Prince's landing party. The slender pamphlet they distributed upon arrival all but proclaimed William to be King of England in the name of Grotius.[40] Speaking on behalf of William, Burnet follows Grotius in denying that monarchs ever rule on the basis of 'immediate warrants from heaven' (Burnet, 1688, sect. 4). Instead, civil governments are formed when individuals entrust their natural rights to exact 'revenges or reparations' to a single person or body of executives (*ibid.*, sect. 3). Like Milton, and unlike Grotius, however, Burnet supposes that the natural right to punish the enemies of society is grounded in the 'duty of self-preservation' (*ibid.*, sect. 2). This departure from Grotius's own doctrine was not uncommon among Whigs who professed their allegiance to the Dutch philosopher-jurist. They rarely accepted or, more likely, rarely discovered his distinction between the instinctual basis for the right of self-defence and the moral basis for the natural right to punish.[41] Also in the typical fashion of the Grotian Whigs, Burnet combines arguments from natural law and immemorial custom in his 'Enquiry'. His Grotian natural law does not specify which form of government a natural society should institute (*ibid.*, sect. 4). He therefore follows Grotius, and not Milton, in maintaining that the limits of monarchical power, and the corresponding obligations of citizens, 'must be taken from the express laws of any state ... or from immemorial prescription' (*ibid.*, sect. 7). When those who have been 'trusted' with the execution of justice fail to abide by the constitutional laws that specify the terms of their trust there is, however, a real 'dissolution of government' (*ibid.*, sect. 4). Similarly, the government is dissolved when members of parliament 'corrupt' themselves by swearing and abiding by oaths of non-resistance to the king; for parliament thereby abjures its duty and right to punish an unruly executive (*ibid.*, sect. 14).[42]

In light of the widespread influence of Grotius in this period, it is extremely unlikely that, by calling the Grotian doctrine of natural penal rights 'strange', Locke meant to signal that he was innovating (as Leo Strauss insists and as Peter Laslett and James Tully seem to allow).[43] When Locke composed his *Two Treatises*, and especially when he published them, it is difficult to imagine that his readers would have thought the doctrine unusual. It could hardly have been more familiar. It therefore seems more likely that, by calling the doctrine 'strange', Locke was giving direct expression to the awkwardness of his newly adopted position, because it did not sit well with his own earlier reflections on the subject of natural law.

VI

Grotius and his English followers made their case for the natural right to punish in opposition to the traditional view – which, it is worth noting, prevailed as a cultural mentality long before it achieved the status of a formal theory in the seventeenth century – that worldly rulers were appointed directly by God for the execution of His divine wrath. Grotian thinkers who wished to displace this traditional view maintained that God only acts as a remote but providential cause in the natural constitution of the state's power to punish. The immediate cause of legitimate penal power, in their view, is a wholly natural and human form of moral agency. In this context, it would be surprising if we could not find Grotian theorists willing to resort to the obvious alternative notion that the immediate source of this power must be some form of human wrath. Grotius himself denied that anger was ever a just motive to punishment, and he was otherwise uninterested in conducting a naturalistic examination of moral motivation. But certain of his followers maintained that there must be some connection between affect and action, and consequently between justifiable anger and justifiable punishment. Hence, we find that, in the first quarter of the eighteenth century, Grotian proponents of natural penal rights often drew upon a sentimentalist language of 'just resentments', and even 'noble and generous resentments'.[44] Natural-law arguments containing references to popular resentments were especially pertinent to Parliament's use of bills of attainder calling for the impeachment of those who had perpetrated egregious 'public crimes' for which there was no regular statutory remedy. So that these popular resentments might escape the charge of being partial to factional interests, leading republican thinkers argued that reflective impartiality could be achieved through a procedural division of powers.

In his *Discourse Concerning Treasons and Bills of Attainder* (1716), Richard West attempted to demonstrate the 'natural justice' of bills of attainder on the basis of a thoroughly Grotian theory of natural penal rights. He indicates that 'all authors' allow that every individual in the state of nature has a right of self-defence, and that some have endeavoured to derive the magistrate's right to punish 'from this principle *solely*' (West, 1716, 97, his emphasis). Following Grotius, however, he argues that the principle of self-defence is not a 'sufficient foundation, for the whole extent of political power'. Instead, 'the power of the sword' is 'fully deriv'd' from a combination of principles: one of self-defence, and the other of mutual consideration and aid:

> Let it be, therefore, farther considered, that the state of nature is not without a law. Reason is that law. And that teaches, that all men being naturally equal; no man ought to prejudice another, either in his person or property; but on the contrary, *they ought to assist one another by all means justifiable*. For as the law of nature willeth the peace and preservation of all mankind, every man is equally concerned in the observation of it: and therefore, that all men might be restrain'd from acting contrary to it; the execution of the law of nature is in that state vested in every man; *and in consequence of that law, every man may punish* (that is, inflict pain upon) *every transgressor of it*, to such a degree, as may hinder its violation for the future. (*Ibid.*, 97, my emphases)

West then employs this Grotian theory of natural penal rights in order to answer the objection that bills of attainder are unjust because they are used to punish people for actions which are not expressly prohibited by the published laws of civil society. The objection assumes that the legitimate rule of law is limited to the rule of positive laws, and that citizens are justified in feeling secure in doing whatever those laws do not expressly prohibit. According to West, this objection 'destroys the very notion of right and wrong, and makes the whole of morality to be purely accidental and political' (*ibid.*, 99). To suppose that there are no moral standards over and above what is established by positive law is not only to suppose that laws can never be unjust; it is also to suppose that the most 'monstrous crimes', those crimes which are the most difficult for human legislators to foresee, should pass with impunity (*ibid.*, 101). In West's view, the positivist's objection is sufficiently met by drawing a distinction between actions that are wrong because prohibited by positive law (*mala quia prohibita*) and actions that are intrinsically wrong (*mala in se*) because contrary to natural law. The only reason why 'notice' is necessary for the former sort of wrong is that 'no man can know whether such a particular action be criminal, until he be informed of its being prohibited' (*ibid.*, 102). But since 'all mankind' will agree that natural injustices are wrong, no positive enactment is required in order to justify parliament's power to punish those who commit such wrongs. If this power (or the natural penal rights upon which this power is based) is denied, civil society is 'dissolved' because the normative conditions that make such a society possible cannot be upheld.

West's treatise was repeatedly cited with approval in Thomas Gordon's *The Justice of Parliaments on Corrupt Ministers, in Impeachments and Bills of Attainder, Consider'd* (1725). And Gordon – who is best-known as co-author (with John Trenchard) of *The Independent Whig* (1719) and *Cato's Letters* (1721) – conjoined West's Grotian theory of punishment with a political analysis of the proper place and limits of popular resentments. Gordon concurs with a common assumption of the Old Whigs in holding that it is most prudent to assume that rulers will not be benevolent and to adopt legal measures to restrain them accordingly, for 'men that are above all fear, soon grow above all shame'.[45] He also similarly maintains that 'places' should be distributed according to an impartial standard of public merit alone, and that contrary practices ought to be severely punished (*ibid.*, 8).[46] But when 'delinquents' engage in the treasonous practices that corrupt parliament they often grow 'too big and potent for the common process of justice', and they must therefore be punished according to higher laws – the laws of nature and 'the laws of nations' (*ibid.*, 29, 31).

Gordon's reference to the *jus gentium* is especially striking given that, as Michael Zuckert points out, 'in nearly one thousand pages of essays, Cato never once betrays the kind of interest in the laws of nations that forms the very core of Grotius's concerns'.[47] The absence of explicitly Grotian ideas in the otherwise synchretistic essays of Cato (which bring the likes of Hobbes, Locke and Machiavelli into a semi-cohesive political vision) must have been owing to Trenchard's cast of mind. For Gordon not only follows West in grounding parliament's impeachment powers in Grotian laws of nature and of nations (in *The Justice of Parliaments*), but he also cites Grotius on the question of natural penal rights at the end of his *Three Letters to a Noble Lord* (1721).

The occasion that animated all of Gordon's forementioned political writings was the scandal of the South Sea Bubble. Certain members of parliament, those with particularly close ties to the court, had enjoyed the 'privilege' of receiving shares in the South Sea trading company without having to pay any advance consideration (other than their promise of support for legislation favourable to the company). They then received the difference between the 'purchase' price and the value of the rising stock, but they did not share in the burden of the losses when the bubble finally burst.[48] There being no regular legal sanction against these scandalous dealings, opposing members of parliament turned for satisfaction to the 'transcendant justice' of natural penal rights.[49] Those who committed this crime against the commonwealth were said to be 'guilty by the highest conviction upon the earth, the general consent of mankind'. And, in typical Grotian fashion, these Whig opposition writers joined their natural law arguments with historical arguments showing 'with what impartiality and rigour our ancestors… punished those crimes which had the publick for their object'. The claim that Parliament retained the original natural penal rights of the people they supported with numerous historical instances of 'the interposition of the legislative power in criminal cases of an extraordinary nature'. Consequently, they maintained that it was not unjust for Parliament 'to punish facts which are in their own nature criminal, though not within the verge of the law'. In their view, only 'inferior courts' are 'govern'd by the letter of the law'. The ancient constitution was itself 'above the laws', because it obliged parliament under a higher law of nature 'to preserve the commonwealth'.[50]

Accordingly, bills of attainder designed to give force to 'the just resentments of the people' were not only the most effective available instrument for punishing elite criminals who were far too powerful for the lower courts to confront effectively, but they were also said to be 'the highest proceeding known in the constitution'.[51] Robert Molesworth was one of the most outspoken advocates for the impeachment of the South Sea directors and their parliamentary accomplices. Indeed he may very well have been among the anonymous authors quoted in this paragraph. And the fact that he believed the constitutional practice of retaining and exercising a basic part of the people's natural penal rights in Parliament to be of Roman origin (as he averred in his *Account of Denmark*), would explain why he felt Parliament should declare the leaders of the South Sea scandal guilty of parricide and then impose upon them the peculiar ancient Roman punishment for this crime – being enclosed and drowned in a large sack along with a monkey and a snake.[52]

Joining this opposition cause, Gordon argued that even if the civil laws of England should allow the directors of the South Sea scandal 'to escape', nevertheless 'the law of nature would demand satisfaction'. In support of this claim, he cites the usual authority: 'Every man, says Grotius, might right himself; and execute the sentence his own uncorrupt judgement should dictate to him.' And he agrees with the other opposition writers that, as a product of 'arbitrary power', the excesses of the South Sea scandal should inspire 'a free people' to give effect, through the powers of Parliament, to their 'noble and generous resentments for the publick good'.[53]

Four years later, when he presented a more comprehensive account of parliament's impeachment powers in *The Justice of Parliaments* (1725), Gordon embraced a more nuanced view of the legitimate force of popular resentments. He continued to maintain that, when the government is in 'imminent danger', when the offenders are 'too big for regular justice', and when the crime in question is 'sheltered from the law', parliament ought to execute 'that justice which every injur'd people had a right to exact' (*ibid.*, 32–3). And he continued to base his argument on the Grotian theory of natural penal rights, this time as elaborated in West's oft-cited *Discourse*. He was also concerned, however, to answer the objection that in parliamentary impeachment proceedings the accused tends to be judged by those who 'out of resentment, and a desire to retaliate the injury, may let their prejudice get the better of their judgement' (*ibid.*, 27). At the time, such allegations of partiality typically went hand in hand with the more pointed complaint that because impeachments are animated by popular resentments they amount to no more than collective acts of disobedience, defiance and unruly violence against the crown.

Gordon's response to this standard line of objection hinged upon a clear division of the power of impeachment between the two houses of parliament. To his mind, a procedural division between Commons and Lords, as between prosecutors and judges, is sufficient to ensure that the execution of natural justice will embody the kind of impartiality and public-mindedness that virtuous persons are able to achieve by means of moral reflection. In Gordon's view, only the House of Commons is directly beholden to the task of prosecuting popular resentments, whereas the House of Lords is uniquely charged with the duty of rendering a final, impartial judgement concerning the justice of those resentments. Thus, he concedes that 'sentiments of grov'ling malice' are incompatible with the nobility and the ties of honour that bind the members of the House of Lords together, but he maintains that this 'assumption of integrity' among 'persons of their quality' is precisely what makes the Lords the appropriate final judges in all treason trials (*ibid.*, 28). When such trials are conducted within the lower courts, by judges who occupy their offices at the pleasure of the Crown, actions punished as treasonous tend to be those which adversely affect the king 'as distinct from the public' (*ibid.*, 30–1). There is even less justice in this manner of proceeding than there is in those cases where the king's ministers are unreflectively sacrificed to 'the resentment of the Commons', because popular resentments tend more than the King's personal malice to promote the good of the commonwealth as a whole (*ibid.*, 23, 38).

Popular resentments also tend to support a just distribution of punishments, because they tend to rise to their highest pitch against criminals who occupy privileged and powerful social positions, which is precisely where punishments ought to be the most severe (*ibid.*, 1–3). It is therefore appropriate that members of the House of Commons should act as 'the general inquisitors of the realm', and they should even 'prosecute with earnestness', and with 'heat and resentment', the crimes of Lords (*ibid.*, 15, 23–4). But in the end, they must submit their cases to the more reflective and impartial members of the House of Lords for a final approval and execution of their 'just resentments'. Popular resentments tend to express narrowly self-interested desires for revenge, and therefore cannot alone provide sufficient warrant for the exercise of Grotian natural penal rights. Being essentially a right to punish vicariously, on behalf of the social body as a whole, the natural right to punish must therefore ultimately reside with persons who possess an uncommon 'dignity and unbyass'd integrity'. And, according to Gordon, this exceptional quality of character is more presumable among persons of 'high rank and nobility' (*ibid.*, 27). This expectation that the English nobility will display an extraordinarily high level of civic virtue is, therefore, at once the reason for subjecting them to a higher and 'more dreadful' form of justice, and for placing the final execution of that justice in their hands.

Notes

1 James Harrington, for example, articulated his quarrel with Hobbes by drawing a contrast, in the 'First Preliminaries' to *Oceana* (1656), between 'the empire of laws' and 'the empire of men'. John Wildman, in *The Leveller: or the Principles and Maxims concerning Government and Religion* (1659), insisted that government should be decided by 'laws and not by men' (5). And Henry Vane, in *A Needful Corrective or Balance in Popular Government* (1660) maintained that a government formed by voluntary association between individuals who are originally in equal possession of natural sovereignty is 'that of laws, and not of men' (4).

2 Judith Shklar, *Political Thought and Political Thinkers*, ed. Stanley Hoffmann (Chicago, 1998), chap. 2.

3 Niccolo Machiavelli, *The Art of War*, Bk I, trans. Ellis Farneworth (Cambridge, MA, 1990), 12.

4 The quote in the heading is at II. xx. 9.

5 *Relectio* on *The Laws of War*, trans. John Pawley Bate (Washington, DC, 1917), 419.

6 Separate from both the right of self-defence and the right to punish, there is a third right to reparations, which will not concern us here.

7 I present detailed arguments for this claim in 'Two Essays on Philosophy and Penal Power' (PhD thesis, Johns Hopkins, 2001). In my view, Quentin Skinner is mistaken in attributing the same doctrine to Jacques Almain and George Buchanan (*The Foundations of Modern Political Thought*, Cambridge, 1978, II). These thinkers held that the right to punish belongs originally and chiefly to the whole community as a unified political body. They did not conceive of punishment, in the later Grotian fashion, as a right that one individual moral agent may exercise over another in a natural state of equality.

8 Compare James Tully's analysis of this point in *An Approach to Political Philosophy: Locke in Contexts* (Cambridge, 1993).

9 This is only one of the many ways in which Grotius's natural law theory belies Knud Haakonssen's characterization of the 'subjective rights tradition' in *Natural Law and Moral Philosophy* (Cambridge, 1996), 5–6.

10 *The Institutes of Justinian*, I. ii, trans. and ed. J. B. Moyle (Oxford, 1913), 4.

11 Compare the views presented in Richard Tuck, *Philosophy and Government, 1572–1651* (Cambridge, 1993), 199–200.

12 Unfortunately, the great care that Grotius takes here to distinguish the moral basis for the right of self-defence from the moral basis for the right to punish has gone unnoticed in some of the most influential recent secondary literature. Richard Tuck, for example, conflates the two (*Philosophy and Government*, 199–200).

13 Here Grotius quotes Marcus Tullius Cicero, *De Officiis,* trans. Walter Miller, Loeb Edition (Cambridge, MA, 1913), II, vi, 29.
14 All page references are to the 1689 edition.
15 According to M.A. Judson, Parker was the first English writer to offer any sort of argument for Parliamentary sovereignty. See her 'Henry Parker and the Theory of Parliamentary Sovereignty', in Carl Frederick Wittke ed., *Essays in History and Political Theory in Honor of Charles Howard McIlwain* (Cambridge, MA, 936). For a qualified reaffirmation of this thesis, see J. W. Gough, *Fundamental Law in English Constitution History* (Oxford, 1955).
16 Grotius's argument for natural penal rights from Genesis 4.14 was repeated by many prominent republican thinkers, such as: Edmund Ludlow, in *A Voyce from the Watch Tower,* ed. A.B. Worden (Camden Society Publications, 4th series, XXI, Cambridge: 1978); James Tyrrell, *Patriarcha Non Monarcha* (1681), I, 11; John Locke, *Two Treatises of Government* (1690) II, ii. 8; and Algernon Sidney, *Discourses Concerning Government* (1698), I. ii; III. i.
17 Note that this argument represented a significant departure from the traditional way of distinguishing between patriarchal power and that form of penal power proper to public systems of criminal justice. In drawing this distinction, Marsilius of Padua, and those conciliarists who implicitly followed him, also acknowledged that Cain's impunity would have been inconsistent with the requirements of public justice, if any had been in force at that time. In contradistinction to the new Grotian argument, however, they maintained that Adam had complete discretion and every right to 'pardon' Cain precisely because the only legitimate pre-civil punishments are those which belong to the absolute domestic jurisdictions of patriarchs.
18 Demonstrating the truth of this claim remains the stated aim of the second edition of 1650; but it is no longer given unequivocal support in the text, which now includes the testimonies of protestant divines to the effect that 'to doe justice on a lawless king, is to a privat man unlawful, to an inferior Magistrate lawfull' (47).
19 *Case of the Commonwealth,* 19. Here, a truly Grotian statement of the aims of state-formation would add 'and for the maintenance of impartial justice'.
20 *Case of the Commonwealth,* 17–18.
21 Moreover, apropos of my argument (in section III above) that Grotian natural penal rights are obligation-fulfilling rights, Grotius argues that punishment for injustices is 'to be commanded' because the 'evill of punishment' differs in moral quality from the 'evill of offence' in that it alone benefits the public (*Maxims,* 38).
22 Gilbert Burnet, *Sermon before His Highness the Prince of Orange* (1689). Parker similarly impugns Machiavelli's authority in *Jus Populi* (1644), 30. Felix Raab traces the reception of Machiavelli in early modern England against the background of this discursive dichotomy in *The English Face of Machiavelli* (1964).
23 Reprinted in David Wooton ed., *Divine Right and Democracy: An Anthology of Political Writings in Stuart England* (Harmondsworth, 1986), 360–88, to which edition page references are made.
24 *Foure Books of Offices* (1606), 173; quoted in Raab, *English Face,* 85.
25 Reprinted in Caroline Robbins, *Two English Republican Tracts* (Cambridge, 1969), to which version all page references are made.
26 See also his *Nicholas Machiavelli Secretary of Florence His Testimony Against the Pope and his Clergy* (1698).
27 Here Sidney cites *The Law of War and Peace,* I. iv. 13.
28 Here Sidney quotes *The Law of War and Peace,* I. iv. 11.

29 Quoted in the anonymous *Vox Populi: or the People's Claim to Their Parliaments Sitting, to Redress Grievances* (1681), 3.
30 This reference is to *The Law of War and Peace,* II, xiii. 21, where Grotius cites Philo's commentary on the Decalogue (as natural law) and Matthew 5: 34, 37 (as ordained or positive divine law).
31 Here Grotius quotes Philo, *On the Decalogue,* XVII.
32 Note that George Buchanan would have been a problematic authority for the proponents of this conception of the English constitution, because he argued that it is inconsistent with 'the true representation of a king' that he should be conceived as 'ever fearing others, or making others afraid' (*The Right of the Kingdom in Scotland,* trans. Philolethes [1689], 30).
33 *A Letter from a Person of Quality to His Friend in the Country* (1675), lii.
34 Locke quoted and borrowed citations from the prologue and the first book of *The Law of War and Peace,* and there is strong evidence in the essay he devoted to refuting Culverwell's neo-Grotian *a posteriori* method (of demonstrating the existence of natural laws from consensus) that he had at the very least read well into the second book. A complete examination of this evidence is beyond the present scope. But see Wolfgang von Leyden's astute references and comments in the footnotes to Locke's *Essays* (Oxford, 1958), 37, 111, 161, 202–4, 282. All page references are to this edition.
35 As in his previous two tracts on the civil magistrate, he remains agnostic on the question of whether the crown is granted directly by God or indirectly by those who would become its subjects.
36 The period of composition for Locke's second treatise is controversial. In addition to David Wooton's introduction to *John Locke's Political Writings* (New York, 1993), see Peter Laslett, *Two Treatises of Government: Student Edition* (Cambridge, 1988), and Richard Ashcraft, *Locke's Two Treatises of Government* (1989).
37 *Second Treatise,* chap. 13.
38 Thomas Hobbes, *Elements of Law* (1640), I. iv. 10.
39 See Lois J. Schwoerer, *The Declaration of Rights, 1689* (Baltimore, 1981), 117–18; and Michael Zuckert, *Natural Rights and the New Republicanism* (Princeton, NJ, 1994,) 106.
40 Towards the end of 1687, Burnet had expressed his hope that a 'commonwealth' could be established in England as the result of 'a rebellion of which [William] should not retain the command' (Christopher Hill, *The World Turned Upside Down: Radical Ideas during the English Revolution,* Harmondsworth, 1991, 359). But he soon changed his tune and regularly praised God for William's rule.
41 This error of interpretation was later revealed by Jean Barbeyac in his footnotes to Samuel von Pufendorf's *Of the Law of Nature and Nations,* ed., Basil Kennet (1717), including large notes from Barbeyrac's 1712 Amsterdam edition. Citing Locke, Barbeyrac defends Grotius's doctrine of the natural right to punish against Pufendorf's contrary view (which happens to resemble the authoritarian account of the right to punish set forth in Locke's *Essays*).
42 According to Burnet, such oaths can only apply to ministers of the king's own executive powers.
43 See Leo Strauss, *Natural Right and History* (Chicago, 1953), 222; and Laslett's introduction to Locke's *Two Treatises,* 97.
44 *Salus Populi Suprema Lex; Shew'd in the Behaviour of Brittish Parliaments Towards Parricides, etc* (1721), 2; *Three Political Letters to a Noble Lord Concerning Liberty and the Constitution* (1721), 3 of Letter I.

45 *Cato*, 17 June 1721.
46 See also the *Independent Whig*, 24.
47 *Natural Rights and the New Republicanism* (Princeton, 1994), 299.
48 John Carswell and Nicholas Goodison, *The South Sea Bubble* (1997).
49 *A Modest Apology Occasion'd by the Late Unhappy Turn of Affairs with relation to Public Credit* (1721), 9.
50 *Salus Populi*, 5, 35, 35–7.
51 *Modest Apology*, 9.
52 Frank McLynn, *Crime and Punishment in Eighteenth-Century England* (1989), 152. I suspect Molesworth of being the author of the *Salus Populi*, which refers to the offenders as 'parricides' (5).
53 *Three Political Letters*, 9, 1.

8
The Problem of Punishment in Eighteenth-Century England

*Randall McGowen**

Although judges, as well as the ministers who delivered the assize sermons, regularly intoned about the glories of English justice, other observers took alarm at at what they saw as evidence of a disturbing situation. 'There are more Men and Women hang'd here (I mean in London) in a Year, than in Amsterdam' and all seven United Provinces, complained a pamphleteer in 1695.[1] 'More are condemn'd at one Newgate-Sessions', announced Lawrence Braddon in 1717, 'than are execut'd in some Countries within three years'.[2] Such expressions, far from rare in the opening decades of the century, increased in frequency by mid-century. 'There are more Persons hanged in England', the *London Magazine* commented in 1735, 'than almost in all Europe besides'.[3] 'I have heard it affirmed', wrote Charles Jones in 1752, 'that there are more Persons executed in the British Dominions, than in all Europe besides'.[4] These somber reflections on the number of executions in England were scarcely offered in a spirit of national congratulation. The nation, they worried, had achieved an unenviable distinction. Whether the figures are accurate or not, the complaints testify to a concern experienced in some circles about the condition of English justice. This lament was offered by people who took the unsatisfactory state of English penal arrangements as evidence of a profound problem in the body-politic.

The attack upon the gallows was only the most striking expression of the discomfort some Englishmen felt with the character of punishment in their day. A few writers expressed unhappiness with such public inflictions upon the body as whipping and branding; others challenged the management of the pillory; and prisons and transportation also inspired concern and dissatisfaction. The unhealthiness of places of confinement excited special anxiety, and the plight of debtors elicited repeated attention. There were

* This essay was written during a term in residence at the Humanities Research Centre at the Australian National University. I would like to thank Donna Andrew, John Beattie, Simon Devereaux, Jo Innes, Peter King, Iain McCalman and Nicholas Rogers for their comments and encouragement.

various proposals to reform prison administration, and a few authors questioned the absence of what they described as a rationale for the penal regime, but these voices were seldom united in support of any particular proposal. The sentiments were more often expressed in a few paragraphs in a magazine than in entire books devoted to the subject. Still, the regularity of such comments, widely scattered though they were, suggests that they reflect not isolated outbursts but deeper currents of unease about penal arrangements.

The repetition of such opinions ill-accords with the usual portrait of eighteenth-century justice. For many years the discussion of the period's penal thought and practice began and ended with a description of the 'bloody code', the numerous capital statutes passed with increasing regularity over the course of the century. The passage of these measures, their number and often trivial nature, suggested to historians the operation of a blind reflex. The recourse to the gallows, they argued, implied that legislators held human life in low regard, and that they saw no other recourse than terror as a way of holding the populace in check. This conclusion was all the easier to sustain because silence seemed to surround the question of punishment in this period. Capital legislation seldom provoked debate in Parliament. The occasional comment of a Mandeville or Fielding could be dismissed as the musing of an exceptional individual. The apparent lack of discussion became a singular fact that reinforced the impression created by the size of the capital code itself. It lent weight to the argument that the early modern penal order was static and homogeneous. Thus, these accounts announced, the history of punishment waited in suspense the explosion of reform oriented works that appeared in the 1760s. After the English publication of Beccaria's *On Crime and Punishment* in 1764 the complaints against a regime that relied upon the gallows multiplied as penal reformers attacked its inhumanity and irrationality. The demand for a transformation of incarceration followed, and new ideas and programme multiplied. The epoch of the unthinking response at last gave way to a period of sophisticated discussion and debate.

Much of the recent scholarship on the operation of eighteenth-century justice has made this deceptively simple story of judicial thinking and practice harder to sustain. 'We need to resist the notion', John Beattie has convincingly argued, 'that significant changes only occurred after 1770 and that before that there had been a jumble of inflexible, archaic, and unchanging institutions and practices'. He supports this argument by demonstrating that the century's most important development, the rise of transportation, took place in 1718. Transportation involved a decisive shift in the character of English punishment. It inaugurated an intermediary punishment that fell between branding and the gallows, and the authorities quickly embraced it and the state moved to facilitate its operation. They acted, Beattie contends, because they hoped that here was a measure that would satisfy the mounting demand for an infliction that employed labour to reform offenders.[5] In his subsequent work, Beattie has elaborated on this argument, demonstrating that the period between 1690 and 1720 saw a remarkable number of proposals for dealing with crime, at least some of which were actually instituted. 'The sheer number of ideas developed and options explored, their overlapping character and their wider significance, made the generation after the Revolution a period of significant transformation in the criminal justice system.' Practical innovations in street lighting and policing occurred throughout the first half of the century. These developments were usually the product of local initiative, and were seldom linked to a wider or more abstract programme. Their cumulative effect, however, was profound. After Beattie we can no longer talk in terms of an unchanging penal regime.[6]

The recent work of Peter King reinforces and extends Beattie's conclusions. King has shown how complex and nuanced judicial deliberations could be, not only on the part of judges and the Crown, but at every level of decision-making. A significant number of people – victims of crime, magistrates, jurors, the community at large – influenced the outcome of a case. 'The whole criminal justice system', he concludes, 'was shot through with discretion.' For our purposes, King's most important discovery is that these decisions were regularly based upon considerations such as those of the age or sex of the accused, and the circumstances of the crime. In choosing how to proceed in particular cases, people were more likely to be guided by shared principles than influenced by personal connections. The implication of this research is to support the idea that people at all levels of society had to think about crime, and that they brought to the problem a rough and ready set of calculations about the meaning and goals of punishment. There may be few traces of what went on in these deliberations, but King has left us in no doubt that they took place.[7]

While Beattie has shown us that the authorities were experimenting with different strategies for punishing offenders, and King has demonstrated that as people were drawn into the operation of justice they had to make decisions that depended upon consideration of the goals of punishment, what continues to be missing is the context for these deliberations. What we lack are the words that might help us to explain what was going on in the minds of the people who promoted transportation or decided not to prosecute a young offender. The outcome of their actions strongly implies a deliberative process but to date we have not had their own words to tell us what ideas influenced them.[8] In this essay I want to address this challenge, the question of what kinds of ideas about punishment were circulating in the early to mid-eighteenth century. Were there people who saw a 'problem' with existing punishments? Were they content or unhappy with the current system? These questions cannot be answered directly; there is no substantial body of material that suddenly opens up the 'eighteenth-century mind' to us. What does exist, however, are scattered comments in magazines, newspapers and obscure pamphlets that suggest the presence of considerable uneasiness with prevailing penal options and the existence of conflicting views of punishment. Such commentary varied in intensity as well as content. There were more opinions offered in the 1690s and 1750s than at other periods. Some years saw a flurry of contributions, such as the succession of letters to the *Gentleman's Magazine* in 1738 over the justice of the death penalty.[9] But no decade was without some commentary on the issue. No doubt these sources are selective; they perhaps reflect views current in London, and probably exaggerate the influence of complaint and reform. Still, the magazines and pamphlets were influential, circulating widely among the well-to-do in the country, spreading metropolitan values. The important point, however, is the mere fact of the existence of these reflections on punishment.

Penal change in the early eighteenth century was something more than a simple reflex to the experience of rising crime rates or a sudden outbreak of a particularly disturbing crime. The issue was very much alive, even if we only catch occasional glimpses of the kind of ideas then in circulation. The most familiar note struck in these writings was one of distress. Some of the remedies proposed sound much like those offered at the end of the century; others appear to fit less well into the usual frame for discussing the evolution of penal ideas. Far from being static, the situation appears fluid and dynamic. The expressions seldom assumed the shape of anything so definite or settled as a debate, but they point to the existence of a concern with punishment and suggest a richer stock of notions about what should or should not compose it, than we imagined operating in this period. They represent a murmur rather than an insistent appeal. But they do help us to make sense of the conduct of the authorities that Beattie has charted, and the behaviour of prosecutors and juries that King explores. It is no doubt significant that these comments were more dispersed than they would be at a later date. With the publication of Beccaria, Blackstone, and Eden, we enter a different period, but it may be one marked more by the volume of commentary, and the extent of its dissemination, rather than by the novelty of the ideas. With a fuller understanding of the kinds of sentiments circulating in earlier decades, we are in a better position to comprehend what was new about the end of the century controversies.

Of course the history of changing attitudes towards punishment does not begin with 1700 or even 1650. The later Tudor period saw a dramatic rise in the numbers executed, followed by an equally spectacular decline in the early seventeenth century, although the reasons for the later development remain unclear. We encounter sustained criticism of the death penalty in radical circles during the Revolution, at least as it was applied to minor thefts. Some complained about the disproportion between an article of property and the life of an individual, and many claimed that the severe penalty in such cases lacked scriptural sanction. 'One mans life', a barrister argued in 1651, 'is of greater value and esteem, than all the treasure upon the earth'. Samuel Chidley offered a ringing appeal for a reform of the criminal law, and for a time these arguments even caught the ear of Cromwell. In the end little came of these proposals, but they expressed a disquiet with existing practice that would reemerge powerfully at the end of the century.[10]

The two decades after 1689 saw significant efforts to increase the effectiveness of police and penal measures, and the changes introduced during these years went a considerable distance towards installing the regime that would dominate the eighteenth century.[11] While much of the focus of historical work has been on the changes that increased the severity of the criminal law, it now seems clear that a wider range of penal experiments took place. There was a revival in interest in the house of correction and the creation of a number of new establishments,[12] and this period of experimentation also culminated in the transformation of transportation in 1718. The rise of an effective intermediary punishment as an alternative to death, however, did not mean a retreat from the latter. A number of new capital statutes were passed during these decades, and the early 1720s saw an unusually high percentage of executions in relation to those condemned.[13]

Despite the continuing alarm at high levels of crime, particularly of the sort that made travel on the roads around London dangerous, not everyone endorsed the resort to severe measures. There was an undercurrent of concern that the remedy might be worse than the problem, and evidence of this unease can be found in an unlikely source. In the face of a panic about rising crime, the anonymous author of *Hanging Not Punishment Enough*, published in 1701, demanded dramatic action be taken to heighten the severity of penal inflictions. He justified new penalties by pointing out that punishments were intended to terrorize the wicked; when criminals became beasts, he argued, society had a right to punish them as such. Since bad men had grown worse, good men must 'grow less merciful'. Here was a familiar argument for explaining the necessity of capital punishment, one frequently heard at the assizes.[14] Yet this author assumed a more modest stance, one that acknowledged that there was something extraordinary about his recommendation. 'I doubt not', he wrote,

> but any Community may secure it self, as it best can, without the imputation of Cruelty; since one would judge so well of Human Nature, as to believe, that such harsh methods would not be made use of, before they are absolutely necessary, anymore than a Physician would Cup or Sacrifice his Patient, unless to prevent his Dissolution, a greater evil.[15]

Throughout his work this author adopted an apologetic tone for the argument he made, as if recognizing that he was urging upon his fellow citizens a course he suspected they would be reluctant to pursue. It is his characterization of this resistance that is of particular interest. He conceded that his proposals ran counter to what he called the spirit of English law and conflicted with what he described as the natural sentiments of humanity. 'I know', he offered, 'that Torments so unusual and unknown to us may at first surprize us, and appear unreasonable'. 'I am sensible', he added, 'that the English Clemency and Mildness appear eminently in our Laws and Constitution'. His call for increased severity, he confessed, might even be said to conflict with history, since when Rome turned Christian, it turned away from capital inflictions. Finally, he even endorsed the idea that as a general rule, if 'ill men' could be made good, the state was obliged to follow such a course.[16]

The author of this pamphlet also recognized that he would encounter more than philosophical and moral objections to his programme. He presented a portrait of his countrymen as reluctant in practice to take human life, and this impulse, he accepted, was a worthy sentiment. He was, he wrote, 'sensible, that tho' I argue for severity, in general we ought to be tender of shedding humane Blood'. There were those, he implied, who would object to his measure: 'It's frequently alledg'd', he conceded, that it was taking away a better thing in depriving someone of life for stealing a worse thing, 'money and goods'. In principle the law should respect the idea that 'crimes are certainly very unequal, by the Laws of God and the consent of nations'. There was a difference between stealing five shillings and murder (it was 'a rule of reason'); murder, doubtless, should be punished more severely. Still, he thought, there were moments when public safety demanded harsher measures. His design, he protested, was not to shed blood needlessly, but to prevent the additional loss of life. A few particularly shocking examples of justice, he hoped, would soon diminish the need for such inflictions.[17]

The comments of other defenders of English justice offer further evidence of a sensitivity around questions of the gallows. Oftentimes complacent in their acceptance of existing arrangements, at other moments they felt it necessary to answer critics of those institutions. Such voices acknowledged the existence of doubts about the death penalty and the uneasiness of a public weary of large numbers perishing on the scaffold. One minister, in an assize sermon in 1739, alluded to those who argued 'that there is such a Cruelty in all capital Punishments, as is altogether inconsistent with the meek and gentle Spirit of the Gospel'. He responded that this charge misrepresented Scripture and sought to disarm government of one of its most important sanctions. Ministers often took the occasion of the sermon to warn listeners about the dangers of a too easy charity and a misplaced leniency.[18] John Shebbeare, in a political fantasy published in 1760, argued that too many criminals were lightly punished. 'He was convinced, that a short perserverance of unrelenting punishment would ultimately prove the greatest act of mercy'. 'This vigorous act of justice', he added, 'to superficial understandings appeared the most sanguinary and remorseless', but he was convinced it would prove 'to be the most humane and commiserating'.[19] Thus, in this roundabout fashion, even those who defended the gallows appealed to sentiments that they shared with their opponents, although harnessing them to a different conclusion. In 1731, George Ollyffe wrote expressing his dismay at the great numbers who had no dread of the 'infamy and misery attending executions'. They took no warning and dared to defy the message. The only answer, he feared, was to make punishment even more terrifying. Perhaps, he speculated, a slower and more painful death, one full of 'the most exquisite Agonies', might gain their attention; then only a twentieth part of the current number who died would perish. He admitted that some would oppose his recommendation: 'The tender and innocent part of mankind' might not be able to bear such a spectacle. 'If such methods be censured as too severe', he replied, 'it may be considered whether they may not have the greatest use; when if they sufficiently terrify, the happy end is answered, by their being none or very few capital crimes committed.'[20] This was not the language of one who cherished the death penalty; rather it expressed the view of one convinced of its necessity.

If necessity formed one justification for severe measures, doubts about the viability of alternatives to the gallows formed another. Daniel Dolans, in a charge to a Middlesex Grand Jury in 1726, acknowledged the accusation that death did not deter because potential offenders rarely reflected on their possible fates. But how, he asked, could replacement punishments 'have any efficacy upon them, without thought and consideration, any more than the former'? 'The miserable habit and temper of such wretches minds, is only to think on the gratification of their own vicious and wicked inclinations and passions, without any, or but little regard, to the means, ends and consequences of such unlawful satisfactions.' Death, Dolans announced, was more likely to work upon such people; it was a terrible spectacle, one capable of awakening a sense of one's situation.[21] 'If, nowithstanding the terror of an infamous death to be inflicted', another essayist remarked in 1738, 'roguery is yet unrestained; and even the gallows cannot terrify numbers from the commission of crimes made legally capital, what might we expect from the fear of the work-house only, or from the hazard of making restitution, tho' it were four-fold'.[22] These remarks by authors defending existing arrangements offer compelling evidence not only of the existence of alternative proposals for punishment, but of what they detected as a widespread if diffuse reluctance to employ more terrifying penalties.

These pamphlets and sermons were scarcely ringing endorsements of severity. The author of *Hanging Not Punishment Enough* made large concessions to what he portrayed as a wider public opinion reluctant to extend the sway of the gallows. One example of the kind of sentiment he faced can be found in another pamphlet, published in 1695, by an author who called himself *Solon Secundus*. Much about the tone of his work suggests his association with the movement for the reformation of manners. He denied any disrespect for English laws, but felt strongly that they stood in need of improvement. 'I find no Fault with our Establishments', he confided, 'they are Good in the main; however, they could be better, if mended a little'. His pamphlet breathed the spirit of the age of projectors. 'While we are in this World', he wrote, 'we shall see Reason for the redressing some Things which will be always amiss, and out of order. There must be some Reformation, (I don't mean in Religion, for that's well enough, if we can be quiet).' 'Some soft and weak Heads' might point to the 'Dangers and Difficulties that attend such a Change', but he was convinced of the opportunity for improvement. He began by expressing sorrow at the number of young men and women who rode up 'Holborn-Hill alive in carts', and returned corpses. 'I have pitied them from my very Heart, and wish'd it in my power to mitigate their Doom.' It was folly, he argued, for a nation to sacrifice so many valuable subjects. 'Is it not a thousand Pities that so many handsome, jolly, lusty, brisk young fellows, in their very Bloom, should be tied up to that cursed Tree?' Sadder still, many of those in danger had never heard of the statutes under which they were condemned. The authorities were culpable for their deaths because they had done nothing to encourage them to quit their idle habits. 'Tis Natural and Humane', he concluded, 'to preserve rather than destroy; and therefore I shall end with this, That if my kind Tender of my Services to my Country were reduc'd into practice, not One in Ten would be hang'd that are'.[23]

This note was struck time and again over the following decades. It expressed the sense that death was a sad waste of something precious; it was a miserable and lazy expedient. A medical analogy sprang to mind. 'Ketch is a cruel hard-hearted Doctor', *Solon Secunus* wrote. Hanging was 'the last stroke, and which is, by much, the worst of them all'.[24] 'Death is not necessary, nor such a power just', an essayist explained in 1738. Quacks, he added, were too ready to cut off limbs, while the skilful physician 'tries all remedies'.[25] Custom could not justify such expedients. 'Almost all the laws that can boast an antiquity in their behalf', protested one author in 1754, 'seem very reluctant and unwilling to pronounce the cruel decree of death'.[26] Even those who wrote in defence of English justice found it necessary to make room for these sentiments. 'The good nature of our ancestors', announced Robert Burrow in an assize sermon in 1729, 'under the divine goodness has taken care for us that our laws are "not wrote in blood", which was a character of some ancient laws remarkable for their vigour and severity'.[27]

The most frequent complaint against the criminal law was that it violated a sense of due proportion between offences and punishments. Sollom Emlyn, writing in 1730, believed that the greatest evil lay in the failure to discriminate between crimes. While it was true, he conceded, that England did not inflict a 'cruel death', still 'it must be also observed that our laws are very liberal of the lives of offenders, making no distinction between the most atrocious and heinous felonies and those of less degree'. 'So little regard', he suggested, repeating a familiar formulation, 'is had in proportioning the punishment to the offence, that the letter of the law makes no difference between picking a man's pocket and cutting his throat'.[28] For some this lack of proportion violated the principles laid down in Scripture. For others, it conflicted with reason. One author in 1735 complained that the existing law was inconsistent with 'right reason and natural equity'. 'All punishments', this essayist concluded, 'ought to be exactly apportioned to the Nature and Effects of the Crime; for if the Punishment exceeded the Crime, then that Excess can only be imputed to the Cruelty and Injustice of the law'.[29] Some contrasted the English practice with that of other nations. 'Almost all Nations but Ours', lamented Charles Jones in 1752, 'adopt their punishments to the Nature of the Offence. We make no difference in the Sentence of our Laws, between a poor Sheepstealer that takes wherewith to feed his wretched Family, and the most inhuman and blood-mangling Highwayman or Murderer'.[30] 'This inequality in the Punishment', one pamphleteer suggested in 1733, 'is the principal Reason of the Frequency of the Crime'. He called for 'a juster Proportion' between the punishment and the offence.[31] Another author, in 1754, argued that 'if there be a medium in the crimes, there ought to be a medium in the sentence'.[32]

Although some version of this grievance appeared most often when authors criticized the capital code, at other times essayists voiced different concerns or linked the issue to an indictment of a particular party. These views were sometimes expressed in opposition papers such as *The Craftsman* or *Fog's Weekly Journal*. When *The Craftsman* came to condemn the criminal laws in the 1730s, it used criminal justice as a means to ridicule the legislators responsible for passing the acts and the magistrates charged with their enforcement. 'The *moral Laws* of most Nations have been nearly the same, in all Ages', one author explained in 1739. 'The differences is not so great in the *Laws* themselves, as in the *Magistrates*; the Vigilance and Steadiness of the *latter* would be much more conducive to the Well-ordering of a Nation, than *severe* and *sanguinary Punishments*.' 'The *bare Increase of a Crime*', he wrote, was 'not always a Reason for making *Punishments more severe*'. Ill-considered laws had done more harm than good to the country. 'If *Vengeance* is more concern'd in the forming of *Laws* than *Justice*, and *severe Penalties* are encreas'd, upon the Suggestion of a *few*; or, perhaps, on account of a *private Pique*, and to severe *particular Ends*; they are Shots at Random amongst a Crowd, by which many will be hurt, but no Body knows upon whome the bullet might light.' Harsh laws were a symptom of abuse of power. These failures on the part of rulers were of much greater consideration than the misdeeds of subjects. Such criticism had the Walpolean regime in its sights. 'When *Ministers* and *Magistrates* are earnest to multiply *penal Laws*', this author charged, 'and not as vigorous in the *Execution of them*, it may be more strongly concluded, that they act from a *Thirst of Power*, not a *Principle of Justice*, and that their least Aim is the making People *honest*'. The ill-consequences of such conduct flowed through society. Where magistrates were immoral or were 'partial in their administration of the *Laws*', justice became odious in the eyes of the public. The situation in England had become highly precarious. The good magistrate, he cautioned, would decline to enforce excessive laws, for 'the severer the *Penalties* are, the greater will be the Opposition and Disobedience of the People.' 'Surely' 'the author continued, '*Laws* not fit to be *executed* are not fit to be *made*.'[33] Walpole's opponents used the state of the criminal law, as they did the operation of excise administration, in an attack on what they portrayed as an abuse of power and mismanagement of the nation. The important point is that they thought the situation with respect to capital punishment would be widely recognized as an instance that supported their contention.

The discontent with existing punishments focused most insistently on the gallows; it was the penalty most symbolically charged, and the infliction most clearly associated with criminality. But other institutions, such as the prison, came in for criticism as well. As early as 1681 Thomas Firmin complained that it was 'very unreasonable that Prisons should be places of pleasure, delight, and choice; yet some such there are'. He thought felons should be forced to labour, even if they could provide for themselves. 'This would be a good means to prevent much of that Wickedness which is practiced in those places.'[34] One contributor to a magazine in 1746 expressed dismay that 'the Prisoners are indulg'd in so great a Liberty in Rioting and Debauchery, which the Keepers, who have the Advantage arising from Sale of the Liquors, find their Account in promoting'. 'The young Novices are permitted to contract so intimate an Acquaintance and Familiarity with the old Offenders, that our Gaols are rather the Schools and Nurseries of all Manner of Roguery and Wickedness, than proper Places for Correction and Amendment.'[35] Here was a charge repeated frequently throughout the first half of the century. Far from curtailing crime, prisons bred it; the young mingled with the old and soon lost all virtue. In all of these accounts the fate of the young offender in the prison was a subject of special anxiety. The author of *Hanging Not Punishment Enough* worried that when the experienced thief mixed with the youth, the latter were inevitably 'corrupted by 'em'. It would be better, he thought, to isolate the notorious so 'that they might not improve each other in wickedness'.[36] 'Our common Gaols and Bridewells (as now managed)', Braddon charged in 1717, 'rather harden than reform their Prisoner's'.[37]

By so early a date, then, the fear that would produce mounting alarm by the end of the century was already a common concern. Even the terms used, especially the notion of the 'hardened' offender, had become conventional. 'All punishments below capital', Emlyn wrote, 'are intended to reform the criminal, and deter him from offending again: but as our gaols are commonly managed, it is to be feared, they breed up and harden more rogues, than the law either reclaims or removes'. Emlyn lamented the many oppressions inflicted by gaolers, crediting them with producing swarms of criminals.[38]

These writers were in no doubt about how this pernicious influence operated. 'As evil Communications corrupt good Manners', Jones wrote in 1752, so the morals of the innocent were 'tainted' by the prison experience, 'insomuch as never to be reclaimed'.[39] The only change over time lay in the length of the indictment and the drama of the charge. 'The misery of gaols is not half their evil', one author wrote in 1759:

> They are filled with every corruption which poverty and wickedness can generate between them; with all the shameless and profligate enormities that can be produced by the impudence of ignominy, the rage of want, and the malignity of despair. In a prison the awe of the publick is lost, and the power of the law is spent; there are no blushes. The lewd inflame the lewd, the audacious harden the audacious. Every one fortifies himself as he can against his own sensibility.[40]

Despite these often scathing comments on prisons, they continued to be the focus of hope for those who wanted to reform punishment. Almost without exception, those who condemned the frequent reliance upon the gallows had an alternative punishment in mind, that of confinement with labour. Such schemes had been regularly discussed since at least the 1670s, drawing upon an extensive literature concerned with issues of vagrancy and management of the poor. Workhouses and labour regimes had been offered as a cure for many of the problems associated with poverty since the sixteenth century. What was new was the effort to apply such proposals more particularly to facilities for dealing with criminals. In the 1690s, several unsuccessful measures proposed establishing work as an alternative to the gallows. In 1706 a Hard Labour Bill was actually passed into law, providing for judges 'to sentence clergied felons to a period of six months to two years at hard labour in a house of correction or workhouse'. While this act was soon superceded by transportation, it provides evidence of the degree to which a labour regime remained the ideal against which the short-comings of other punishments were increasingly measured.[41]

Certainly the critics of the gallows in the early eighteenth century were unanimous on this score. Should 'capital punishment', the author of one pamphlet asked in 1727, 'whereby the crimes have in no measure abated of their force, be esteemed an undue treatment of the person'? 'Must a whole nation be bound up', he demanded, 'by a fond superstition, to a growing mischief, and instead of redressing the grievance, tamely permit it to obtain under those conditions'? He was in no doubt as to the answer. Far better, he concluded, would it be to bring in a new dispensation, one which involved 'the saving of life, the reformation of offenders, the exercise of strict discipline, correcting the contumacious, the discountenancing the trade of begging, vagrancy, and idleness'.[42] Emlyn wrote that while the law of retaliation justified hanging for murder, 'as to other less offenders, it would be more equitable and effectual punishment to confine them to hard labour at home'.[43] 'Would not a *Magistrate* deserve much better of his Country', another correspondent wrote, 'who preserv'd the Lives of Men, by forcing them into *Industry* and *Labour,* than in procuring them to be hang'd for *Offences,* which *Idleness* and *Want* had tempted them to commit'.[44] One essayist, in 1731, called for legislators 'to invent such punishments for criminals as may reclaim the offender, if the crime be not capital'.[45] Bishop Berkeley shared this conviction; would it not be better, he asked in *The Querist,* in 1735, to find some way 'for making criminals useful in public works, instead of sending them either to America, or to the other world'?[46] Despite the failure to establish a successful work regime in the houses of correction, it remained the goal towards which many authors thought punishment should move. By 1751 Joshua Fitzsimmonds was merely repeating a familiar refrain when he announced that 'such punishments as branding, whipping, and even transportation might be very properly changed to hard labour and correction, suitable to the nature of the crime'.[47]

Few who argued for labour as an alternative to the death penalty offered details of what they thought this regime would look like. *Solon Secundus* went further than most; he was confident that it was better to 'retrieve life' than destroy it. 'Confinement and Labour', he thought, would produce a far more satisfactory outcome. 'Working will do more than Whipping', and he proposed a graduated scale of punishments. When a person stole a tankard, for instance, he 'would have him sent to a Work-house, and there to remain till he should, by his Labour, pay the Prosecutor the full sum', in addition to whatever it cost to maintain him in prison. A highway robber 'should be sentenced to Imprisonment, and painful bodily Labour, till Money, should arise by his Sweat'. 'This long Confinement, and hard Service, would baulk his Stomach, and spoil his Appetite to the old way of Padding, and very Gang and Knot would be broke and dispers'd.' This author made clear that his scheme was not motivated solely by a concern with humanity. He was convinced that it would bear hard on those who experienced it. Confinement, he concluded, was an especial threat to his countrymen. 'This to an *English Man,* so fond of Liberty, would be more formidable than that ignominious Death.' An execution was no more than a moment of pain, soon over. 'But loss of Liberty will make a deep Impression, will make a hole in their Hearts, and give them a great deal of Melancholy.'[48]

For most other authors the idea of prisoners forced to labour was self-explanatory. Even as work was universally admitted to be a superior solution to either hanging or transportation, commentators had few specifics to provide. Some thought that the Dutch Rasp-house was worthy of imitation. 'I do not doubt', Braddon wrote in 1717, 'but TWO or THREE Doses of such DUTCH PHYSICK as have cured Thousands of that Disease in Holland, will have as good effect upon our British Constitution'.[49] No-one found other merit in the idea of confinement. There was just a hint that time-limited punishment might be quantifiable in a way that better calibrated offence to penalty, but noticeably absent were the discussions of solitude and the soul that would become the focus of concern by the 1770s. There was little mention of prison architecture, almost no discussion of kinds of labour except that it should be 'hard'. There was the usual mixture of beliefs that work would both reform and punish, that it was a more humane penalty and a more fearful one. The valuable labour of members of society might be saved; the cost of punishment could be reduced. The nation would convert loss into gain. The psychological assumption behind this punishment amounted to little more than that individuals forced to take on industrious habits would continue them once released. 'By this means', one author explained, 'these lesser kind of Thieves and Felons, who now generally return to the same Course of Life again, will be enabled to get an honest Livelihood after their Time of Servitude is expired, which they will do with the greater Cheerfulness and Spirit, as they will be so much the more inured to it'.[50] Perhaps the brevity of such discussions merely reflects the fact that this analysis was deeply entrenched, having been a staple of arguments about the poor for several centuries.[51] Still, there was no description offered of a place within England where this regime already operated, and beyond these hints the authors made little effort to elaborate on a notion that was universally shared.

Here then were the common themes that appeared with some regularity among the authors who wrote about punishment – the dismay at the gallows, the belief that some form of confinement organized around labour would be more effective, and the conviction that prisons as then managed produced great evil. But it would be a mistake to focus only on those proposals that foreshadowed developments that would become more common later in the century. Occasionally, at some moment of crisis or following on an expression of frustration with current means employed to deal with crime, authors suggested extreme and unusal measures. These proposals remind us of the fluidity of thinking about punishment in this period, and that certain inhibitions that would circumscribe later debates were still in process of formation. The recommendations sometimes appealed to foreign examples, and often mingled concerns with severity, labour and bodily inflictions in ways that would appear outlandish at a later date. For instance, in the midst of an exchange of letters in the *Gentleman's Magazine* in 1738, one author wrote that if the gallows did not seem to inspire fear, then he favoured burning at the stake. Still, he confided, he placed more faith in the discovery of some means for putting prisoners to work.[52] These proposals often emerged at a moment of panic, and they spoke of a hope that Parliament would address the issue. After a series of alarming crimes, the *Derby Mercury*, in 1736, repeated a call for action. 'Those shocking Barbarities', it wrote, 'undoubtedly deserve a severer Death than bare Hanging, and methinks that Burning Alive, or Breaking upon the Wheel, wou'd not be at this Juncture unseasonable, to check a growing Proneness to Cruelty.'[53] The paper had issued a similar call three years earlier, at which time it noted obstacles in the way of such a change. 'Some say 'tis inhuman to punish one of our own Species in so tormenting a Way, but surely they do not attend to what they say, for Murtherers are People that have divested themselves of all Humanity, and therefore can be intitled to no share of it.'[54]

Other writers sought for alternatives to the gallows, since daily experience seemed to show that 'Hanging only signifies nothing'.[55] One pamphlet writer proposed making criminals slaves for longer or shorter periods, putting them to work on the roads or in the ports, building canals or dockyards. Mandeville thought that offenders might be used to redeem slaves captured by the 'several Powers of Barbary'.[56] Another contributor to a magazine thought that setting those sentenced for capital crimes to 'perpetual hard Labour' would strike more terror than death, especially if they worked at cleaning the streets while chained, and were kept on a bread and water diet.[57] These proposals are significant because they testify to the frustration felt for a regime believed to be too dependent on the gallows. 'Stop', one author announced, 'the torrent of blood, its effusion answers not the end proposed'. Transportation, he claimed, worked no better; it 'hides too many of the offenders from those who ought to learn to beware from their example'. 'Hang a few, and keep the rest to labour'; that was his solution.[58]

The middle decades of the century saw an unusual number and variety of such suggestions. One writer in 1751 offered the idea that male prisoners be employed in galleys. These boats, he reasoned, might be of great service to the nation, helping to curtail smuggling or to repair harbours, and they would constitute a valuable reserve in case of war. One powerful argument in favour of such a scheme was 'the saving of the lives of so many condemned' which 'on a moderate computation, must be upwards of 500'. 'If the soul of one of them could be thus saved, it would be well worth the experiment.'[59] Another correspondent wrote to express dismay at the wave of murders and robberies sweeping the nation in 1744. The author wondered whether, if murder were punished more severely, or theft less so, the result might not be better. 'All other nations', he explained, 'adapt Punishment to Crimes.' By way of illustration, he described in exquisite detail the tortures employed by the French for specific offences and different degrees of seriousness. Perhaps if particularly heinous offenders were fed to the lions and tigers kept in the Tower, he suggested, such a tremendous penalty might produce the desired effect. At the same time he praised the Rasp-house as a suitable model for dealing with the average prisoner.[60] Here was a grab-bag of remedies, a series of measures thrown off that would be hard to categorize as mild or harsh. In many respects this hodge-podge captures an important aspect of the thinking about crime in the period; certain themes recurred time and again, yet the lines of argument had not become fixed around a few solutions.

Another significant change during these years was the growing prominence of the press, not simply London-based, but provincial as well, in providing publicity for law-and-order issues. Perhaps the development of the latter was especially important. For instance, by the late 1720s the *Derby Mercury* gave considerable space to reports of crimes, the outcomes of trials, and to executions. Much of this news, however, concerned London rather than the immediate vicinity. These provincial papers had few facilities for collecting local news; it was much easier for them to copy stories from the London papers. What was more, London had more exciting crimes to report, and thus few issues passed without a report of several highway robberies or spectacular assaults from the metropolis. Sometimes the crime earned only a brief mention; at other times a fuller account followed. The paper dutifully repeated the results of trials at the Old Bailey, paying particular attention to those capitally convicted, and to the king's deliberations over the fate of the condemned. It would continue the coverage with details of the execution days. Justice and mercy drew the most attention, as well as the most comment. The paper repeated rumours of Parliamentary action, and it provided summary numbers of those transported. The effect of this coverage was to create a national experience of problems of crime and punishment, one that gave especial prominence to London crime and Parliamentary solutions. In 1735 the Derby paper offered a particularly full account of gangs especially active near London. Despite frequent executions the challenge did not appear to abate. 'And since the Gallows will not deter them', the paper reported, 'tis talked the Legislature will take Cognizance of these Proceedings, in order, by some Punishment more terrifying to put a Stop to them'.[61] In this way the press added a crucial new dimension to the experience of crime, magnifying its significance and circulating proposals for dealing with the threat.

By 1750, however, there is some evidence that the disparate thoughts about punishment were beginning to form into a settled debate. In that year, William Webster, vicar of Ware and the author of a number of books on a variety of topics, offered a dialogue between a gentleman and a clergyman on an important moral subject, that of the proper relationship between anger and forgiveness. There was nothing particularly remarkable about this study of manners and morals; it was simply one among a number of semi-popular religious works on this theme. Inevitably Webster found himself discussing punishment, and his discussion captures something of the flavour of the argument of his day. The two figures in his dialogue quickly came to an agreement that in principle 'the Degree of our Anger ought to bear a Proportion to the Nature of the Crime, and other Circumstances, and, in this Respect, the Laws of England are greatly defective'. 'There is', both conceded, 'frequently no difference in the Degree of the Punishment, where there is a wide Difference in the Degree of Guilt'. Still, the gentleman, who was identified by Webster as serving in the legislature, defended existing practice. God, he pointed out, could apportion blame precisely; human government could not. 'Therefore all that we can do is to enact such Laws as we judge necessary to the Peace and Happiness of the Community, and to annex such Sanctions as shall seem, to our most deliberate Judgment, necessary to secure

Obedience to those laws.' Whatever penalties were necessary to achieve the end of security were 'justifiable, let them be ever so severe'.[62]

Significantly, in Webster's imaginary debate it was the clergyman who set forth a more moderate position, as he cast his eye over the penal situation in England. 'I am against such frequent Executions as are in Use in our Country', he remarked. 'I think', he added, 'the Law should be exceeding tender of human blood, and never shed it but when no other Punishment will do.' Besides, he quickly pointed out, severity was ineffective. 'What signifies, I was going to say, the Fear of Death, to a Parcel of illiterate, ignorant, hardened Creatures, who have no Notion at all of it, unless it be this, that it puts an End to Existence, which, while they are in their Courses of Wickedness, they do not think worth keeping?' Far better, the clergyman thought, would be a punishment involving work. 'Hard Labour is the most dreadful Thing in the World to Persons habituated to Idleness; and, therefore, were they daily to see Examples of Offenders confined to a disgraceful and labourious Life, it might make a great many think to get an honest Maintenance.'[63] Webster was scarcely novel in any of these observations; rather he drew together a collection of sentiments that were often rehearsed in literate circles over the previous half century. Another author, summarizing the situation in 1751, noted that 'some have, with reason, proposed softening the laws, and making them more mild, and adequate to the different degrees of injustice; others are for increasing the pains and penalties, and endeavouring to extirpate such iniquities by severer punishments'. He was convinced, like Webster, that it was 'a vain attempt to put a stop to such crimes by the halter; the nation may thereby be depopulated, but never amended'.[64] What was changing by mid-century was less the ideas themselves than the frequency with which they appeared in print. The criticism had become more pointed, more passionate, and more self confident.[65]

In 1754 the *Monthly Review* discussed a new book dealing with crime. The author, the reviewer noted, sought to show 'the inexpediency and unfitness of our present laws, for the punishment of capital offences. He would have no criminal put to death, but for murder and treason; and also thinks it absurd to continue transporting our felons to the colonies, when we might dispose of them to more advantage at home'. The reviewer implied support for these suggestions, but found little novelty in the proposals. 'In all his arguments, he offers little but what hath been frequently urged before'.[66] Indeed, when Beccaria's *Dei Delitti e delle Pene* was published in 1764, a reviewer of the Italian edition argued that an English reader would not 'find many things that are new to him, however novel and strange they may appear to the Italians'.[67] It has been the argument of this essay that these reviewers were right, at least in some measure, that a variety of complaints had been offered of English penal measures throughout the early eighteenth century. These views, perhaps, never became a majority opinion, but their presence suggests a more serious consideration of punishment, with a greater variety of positions, than has been previously acknowledged.

Two questions remain. First, given this level of discontent, why did not more change? The nation continued to rely on transportation, and prisons regularly excited criticism, but little in the way of reform. The legislature continued to pass capital legislation, while Tyburn went on receiving a steady stream of victims. Webster was in no doubt as to why so little had altered. 'The Gallows and Transportation', he explained, 'are the Shortest, and cheapest, Methods of getting rid of them [offenders] without further Trouble'.[68] If inertia is part of the answer, other factors may have been just as important. As Peter King has demonstrated, many people in eighteenth-century England had confidence in their ability to influence the course of justice; perhaps so long as they believed that this individual and collective mercy worked, they accepted the situation. The scattered nature of much of this commentary on punishment also points to an obstacle to reform. Occasional comments and vague sentiments did not amount to a programme for change; indeed, it was also far from clear to contemporaries what should be done and who should do it. The diffuse opinions described here could not yet overcome the settled conviction that authority required spectacular punishments in order to instruct in habits of obedience.

The second question concerns the issue of continuity. Given how many of the familiar themes that would surface later in the century were already present much earlier, does this mean that nothing had changed over its long course? Was the reviewer of Beccaria right that his work presented nothing new? Certainly the enthusiasm generated by those who read Beccaria suggests that they found something fresh in his work, some challenge put with especial urgency, that demanded a more energetic response than had been true earlier. He managed to transform a preexisting disquiet with capital punishment into a clear vision not only of what needed to be altered, but how to do so. Still, the excitement provoked by his work would not have been so great if the ground had not been prepared in the preceding decade. Penal questions agitated the public more in the 1750s than earlier; for a variety of reasons the issue had become more pressing, but it also assumed a subtly different form. Samuel Johnson, in his essay of 1751 in *The Rambler*, not only articulated what we now see were familiar themes, but more sharply posed a new issue. 'Rigorous laws', he argued, 'produce total impunity'. The practice of mercy, which had for long been taken as evidence of English humanity, was now presented as a symptom of disorder and a cause for concern. Severe penalties, Johnson argued in a closely reasoned presentation, reduced the law to a nullity.[69] Another author took a slightly different tack when he wrote in 1754 that people should not be 'shocked at the useless effusion of blood'. 'I have brought forward', he explained:

> these prudent laws and customs of other countries, and those of our own likewise, to show that tho' we have more malefactors executed now in

> one month, than we formerly had in a whole century, that it is not owing to the supposed corruption and depravity of mankind, but that it is owing to the unaccountable, not to call it unhuman, alteration in our laws, which like rivers that have been wrested out of their easy natural channels, have ruined and laid waste those very countries they were intended to secure and support.[70]

Here were two ways of casting the argument that suggest a shift from earlier formulations of what was wrong with the criminal law. The target of the criticism became sharper; the sense of the evil more pronounced. Earlier complaints had been more matter of fact, pointing to the waste of human life. By mid-century the critics drew upon enlightenment principles and the language of sensibility to fashion a more sweeping indictment.

The number and length of commentaries on the criminal law expanded rapidly by the end of the century, and the analysis offered became more elaborate. What had been general and lacked specificity now became more carefully worked out. Book-length treatments replaced the isolated comments that occasionally bubbled to the surface, and new constituencies took up the cause. No doubt the agitation of Wilkite reformers had something to do with this phenomenon, and the activities of rational Dissenters and reforming lawyers is also conspicuous. The demand for criminal law reform assumed an entirely different dimension in the 1770s than it had earlier in the century.[71] Howard and Hanway, operating under the spell of Evangelical ideas and emotions, shifted attention from labour to the condition of the souls of prisoners. They came to advocate solitary confinement, and more attention was devoted to the design and construction of prisons. In response to this agitation, William Paley offered a novel defence of English practice, one that sought to coopt the utilitarian argument that Beccaria launched against older forms and conceptions of punishment. By the time Romilly took up the cause of criminal law reform in the early nineteenth century, the discretion exercised by the judges had become a pivotal issue. All of this bustle, all of these various changes in the character of debate, can cause us to miss an obvious point; the reformers did not discover the inhumanity of the gallows, nor did they invent the prison; rather, something more complicated went on as they transformed the notion of humanity and proposed a different relationship between society and punishment.

Notes

1 *Solon Secundus, or Some Defects in the English Law with their Proper Remedies* (1695), dedication.
2 Lawrence Braddon, *The Miseries of the Poor are a National Sin, Shame, and Charge* (1717), xxxiv.
3 *London Magazine* (1735), 598–9.
4 Charles Jones, *Some Methods Proposed Towards Putting a Stop to the Flagrant Crimes of Murder, Robbery, and Perjury* (1752), 11.

5 J. M. Beattie, *Crime and the Courts in England 1660–1800* (Princeton, 1986), 13, 470–83, 500–13; Roger Ekirch, *Bound for America: The Transportation of British Convicts to the Colonies 1718–1775* (Oxford, 1987).

6 J. M. Beattie, 'London crime and the making of the "Bloody Code", 1689–1718', in Lee Davison *et al.*, eds, *Stilling the Grumbling Hive: The Response to Social and Economic Problems in England, 1689–1750* (New York, 1992), 70, and more generally, 49–76. J. M. Beattie, *Policing and Punishment in London, 1660–1740* (Oxford, 2001). Of course other scholars have challenged the significance usually accorded to the 'Bloody Code'. See, for instance, John Langbein, 'Albion's fatal flaws', *P&P*, 98 (1983), 96–120; Joanna Innes and John Styles, 'The Crime wave: recent writing on crime and criminal justice in eighteenth-century England', in Adrian Wilson ed., *Rethinking Social History* (Manchester, 1993), 200–65; Randall McGowen, 'Making the "Bloody Code"?: forgery legislation in eighteenth-century England', in Norma Landau ed., *Law, Crime and English Society 1660–1840* (Cambridge, 2002), 117–38.

7 Peter King, *Crime, Justice, and Discretion in England 1740–1820* (Oxford, 2000), 1, and esp. chap. 2.

8 'The changes that one can see taking place in several aspects of the law and criminal administration of the period', Beattie reports, 'were accompanied by very little public discussion' (*Policing and Punishment*, 5).

9 A column in the July, 1737 issue of the *Gentleman's Magazine*, produced responses in January, April, and June of 1738. John Beattie has mined London grand jury presentments for their discussions of the nature of the criminal threat. Particularly interesting are the repeated calls for an attack on the 'roots' of crime, suggesting the presence of a widely accepted version of what the causes of crime were, and what needed to be done about them (*Policing and Punishment*, 51–6). A charge to the grand jury at the Guilford Quarter Sessions in 1740 summarized the conventional wisdom. 'As no man is completely wicked at once but become so insensibly by a gradation of wickedness, wch would continually gain Strength by Impunity, till the Offender loosing all Sense of fear & remorse, grows harden'd to the Commission of Crimes of the deepest Dye.' Reprinted in *Charges to the Grand Jury, 1689–1803*, ed. Georges Lamoine, (1992), 293.

10 Robert Zaller, 'The debate on capital punishment during the English Revolution', *The American Journal of Legal History*, xxxi (1987), 133, and more generally 126–44. The earlier shift in the frequency of capital punishment has been explored by Philip Jenkins, 'From gallows to prison? The execution rate in early modern England', *Criminal Justice History*, vii (1986), 51–71. See also Beattie, *Policing and Punishment*, 278–82; Nancy Matthews, *William Sheppard, Cromwell's Law Reformer* (Cambridge, 1984), esp. 168–72.

11 Beattie, 'London crime', 49–76; and esp. Beattie, *Policing and Punishment*.

12 Joanna Innes, 'Prisons for the poor: English Bridewells, 1555–1800', in Francis Snyder and Douglas Hay eds, *Labour, Law and Crime: An Historical Perspective*, (1987), esp. 79–81, 89–90; Beattie, *Crime and the Courts*, 492–500. Robert Shoemaker, *Prosecution and Punishment: Petty Crime and the Law in London and Rural Middlesex, c.1660–1725* (Cambridge, 1991), 166–97.

13 Beattie, *Crime and the Courts*, 513–18.

14 It is worth remembering that there was a well-articulated defense of capital punishment, one that employed Christian symbolism and theology to explain the necessity for such measures as arising in humanity's fallen nature. The dread day was meant to make spectators consider the still more awful day of divine

judgment that awaited all. For more on this subject, see my articles, '"He beareth not the sword in vain": religion and the criminal law in eighteenth-century England', *Eighteenth-Century Studies*, xxi (1987–88), 192–211; 'The body and punishment in eighteenth-century England', *The Journal of Modern History*, lix (1987), 651–79; and 'The changing face of God's justice: the debates over divine and human punishment in eighteenth-century England', *CJH*, ix (1988), 63–98.

15 *Hanging Not Punishment Enough* (1701), 2, 15.

16 *Ibid.*, 2, 3–5. This pamphlet has long been offered as an example of the brutality of the age. Beattie, however, recognizes the more subtle character of the argument offered by the author (*Crime and the Courts*, 488–89). Many authors claimed that English punishments were milder than those on the continent. 'As for Breaking on the Wheel', Edward Chamberlayne wrote, 'and other like torturing Deaths, common in other Christian Countries, the English look upon them as too cruel to be used by the Professors of Christianity' (*The Present State of Great Britain* (37th edition, 1735), 95).

17 *Hanging Not Punishment Enough*, 3–5, 8–9. This discussion in the pamphlet foreshadows the distinction drawn by Henry Fielding in 1751 between the 'good mind' and the 'bad mind'. See King, *Crime, Justice, and Discretion*, 327–9.

18 Fifield Allen, *The Reasonableness and Necessity of Human Laws and Penalties* (1739), 15.

19 John Shebbeare, *The History of the Excellence and Decline of the Constitution of the Sumatrans* (2 vols, 1760), I, 165–6.

20 George Ollyffe, *An Essay to Prevent Capital Crimes* (1731), 4–10, 12.

21 Daniel Dolans, *Charge to the Grand Jury of Middlesex* (1726), 8.

22 *Gentleman's Magazine* (1738), 179.

23 *Solon Secundus*, dedication, 2–5, 8–9, 25.

24 *Ibid.*, dedication, 8, 12–14.

25 *Gentleman's Magazine* (1738), 14–15.

26 *Proposal to the Legislature for Preventing the Frequent Executions and Exportations of Convicts in a Letter to Henry Pelham* (1754), 12.

27 Robert Burrow, *Mercy and Truth are Met Together* (1729), 23.

28 Sollom Emlyn, *A Complete Collection of State Trials and Proceedings for High Treason* (1730), ix.

29 *London Magazine* (1735), 598–9. *The Gentleman's Magazine* (1735), 654, used almost the same words to express this idea: 'For if the Punishment exceed the Crime, then the Excess of Punishment can only be imputed to the Cruelty, and Rigour of the Law.' Sir George Mackenzie, in his volume on Scottish law in 1699, appealed to such principles in his discussion of punishment. 'I will not dispute', he wrote, 'the Power of Princes and States, yet I incline to think, that for simple Theft, a Thief should not die'. Such a severe penalty found sanction in neither moral nor divine law. 'As Crimes grow more frequent', he contended, 'the punishment may be augmented, but I deny that they should be so augmented, that suitable Proportion should not be keeped' (*The Laws and Customs in Matters Criminal* (Edinburgh, 1699), 99, 101).

30 Jones, *Methods*, 7–8.

31 Eboranus (T. Robe), *A Collection of Political Tracts* (1735), 43.

32 *Proposal to the Legislature*, 20–7.

33 *London Magazine* (1739), 31–5. A decade later the number of executions once again sparked critical comment. 'Seventeen malefactors condemned for capital offences, and the gaols already crowded with more? Does this reflect more dishonour on the people or the G—T'? (*Gentleman's Magazine*, 1750, 532).

34 Thomas Firmin, *Some Proposals for the Imployment of the Poor* (1681), 41. Doubtless it is no accident that authors like Firmin, Braddon, and Hay, men who took a leading interest in proposing new arrangements for the poor, also disliked what they saw as the waste of the gallows.
35 *London Magazine* (1746), 433–4.
36 *Hanging Not Punishment Enough,* preface, 15–20.
37 Braddon, *Miseries,* xxxiv.
38 Emlyn, *Complete,* xii. Of course many features of this complaint against prisons appeared in Defoe's *Moll Flanders* in 1722 (London, 1989), 135: 'We all know here, that there are more Thieves and Rogues made by that one Prison of Newgate, than by all the Clubs and Societies of Villains in the Nation.'
39 Jones, *Methods,* 11.
40 *London Magazine* (1759), 30–1. These comments were drawn from Samuel Johnson's *The Idler,* 38.
41 Beattie, *Policing and Punishment,* 310–11, 323–35. For a suggestive treatment of the longer history of institutions and arrangements for the poor, see Paul Slack, *From Reformation to Improvement: Public Welfare in Early Modern England* (Oxford, 1999).
42 *An Essay Concerning the Original of Society, Government, Religion and Laws, especially those of the Penal Kind* (1727), 63–7. The author added that he was in expectation of a work on 'reforming the penal scheme' which was in press and would propose replacing 'capital animadversion' for theft. See also William Hay, *Remarks on the Laws Relating to the Poor* (1735), 17–18.
43 Emlyn, *Complete,* ix.
44 *London Magazine* (1744), 433–4. The author drew heavily on Emlyn for his conclusions.
45 *Gentleman's Magazine* (1731), 60.
46 *The Works of George Berkeley, Bishop of Cloyne,* eds A. A. Luce and T. E. Jessop (London, 1953), VI, 109.
47 Joshua Fitzsimmonds, *Free and Candid Disquisition on the Nature and Execution of the Laws of England* (1751), 45.
48 *Solon Secundus,* dedication, 8, 12–14, 16. This author also doubted the value of transportation. It 'won't do the business', he explained, 'though that's a great deal better than hanging'. 'I am utterly and absolutely against Transportation of Fellons (tho' it was thought Mercy by our Law)'. The difficulty lay in the fact that offenders returned too soon, usually to take up their old trade. They were seldom made better by the experience (9–10). George Ollyffe also thought it might be better to put offenders to work to cover the expense associated with their confinement (*Essay,* 4–10). One author proposed that 'the Time of their Servitude should be according to the Kind and Degree of their Crimes' (Eboranus, *Tracts,* 45).
49 Braddon, *Miseries,* 54; Eboranus, *Tracts,* 45. 'It is known from experience', wrote Sir George Mackenzie, 'that many men fear hanging, less than being constantly keeped in Correction-houses, or in the places where they may be kept working, as they do in Holland, for the good of the Commonwealth' (*Laws,* 99, 101).
50 Eboranus, *Tracts,* 46.
51 Innes, 'Prisons for the poor', 81–2.
52 *Gentleman's Magazine* (1738), 287–8.
53 *Derby Mercury,* 4 November 1736.
54 *Derby Mercury,* 3 May 1733.
55 *Ibid.*

56 *Proposals to the Legislature*, 20–7; Bernard Mandeville, *An Enquiry into the Causes of the Frequent Executions at Tyburn* (orig. 1725, Los Angeles, 1964), 48–9.
57 *London Magazine* (1737), 386.
58 *Gentleman's Magazine* (1751), 368.
59 *London Magazine* (1751), 82–3.
60 *London Magazine* (1744), 506–9.
61 *Derby Mercury*, 17 April 1735. On 2 January 1734, the paper reported that some 6,000 offenders had been transported from Newgate over the previous 15 years, and some 500–600 from county jails. On the press and reporting of crime, see Peter King, 'Newspaper reporting, prosecution practice and perceptions of urban crime: the Colchester crime wave of 1765', *C&C*, 2 (1987), 423–54; Hannah Barker, *Newspapers, Politics and English Society 1695–1855* (Harlow, 2000), 29–45.
62 William Webster, *A Casuistical Essay on Anger and Forgiveness* (1750), 53–5.
63 Webster, *Casuistical*, 58–60, 64. He had no kinder words for transportation: 'And what an insignificant Scarecrow is Transportation to those who will naturally persuade themselves that they can more safely, and as easily, get a Livelihood abroad?' Ollyffe thought the punishment failed because transportees retained the hope of returning home (*Essay*, 4–10, 12).
64 *London Magazine* (1751), 307.
65 For a discussion of these years, see Nicholas Rogers, 'Confronting the crime wave: the debate over social reform and regulation, 1749–1753', in L. Davison *et al.*, eds, *Stilling the Grumbling Hive: The Responses to Social and Economic Problems in England, 1689–1750* (New York, 1992), 77–98.
66 *Monthly Review* (1754), 155.
67 *Monthly Review* (1764), 533–4.
68 Webster, *Casuistical*, 53–5.
69 Samuel Johnson, *The Rambler*, 114 (1751), in Samuel Johnson, *Works* (New Haven, 1969), iv, 241–7. Johnson's reflections were widely reprinted; see *Bath Journal*, 29 April 1751.
70 *Proposal to the Legislature*, 16. The publication of Montesquieu's *The Spirit of the Laws*, in 1748, was of particular significance for the development of certain arguments against the reliance upon the penalty of death.
71 John Brewer, 'The Wilkites and the law, 1763–74', in John Brewer and John Styles eds, *An Ungovernable People: The English and Their Law in the Seventeenth and Eighteenth Centuries* (New Brunswick, NJ, 1980), 128–71; McGowen, 'The body and punishment', 651–79; Simon Devereaux, 'The making of the penitentiary Act, 1775–1779', *HJ*, 42 (1999), 405–33.

9
Streets of Shame? The Crowd and Public Punishments in London, 1700–1820

*Robert Shoemaker**

Early modern punishments frequently involved an element of popular participation. Penance (for defamation and sexual immorality), whipping (primarily for petty larceny) and the pillory (largely for 'unnatural' sexual offences, seditious words, extortion, fraud and perjury) were performed in public, and an important dimension of the punishment was the damage to the offender's reputation which resulted from public humiliation. This is even true of public executions, since the spectacle of the scaffold served both firmly to identify the culprit for posterity as a convicted felon, and, if he or she behaved appropriately, to rehabilitate him or her as a repentant sinner. But arguably the main purpose of carrying out capital punishment in public was in order to deter others from committing crime. In the case of public corporal punishments like whipping and the pillory, deterrence was also important, but the significance of the publicity of these punishments was to a much greater extent that they shaped reputations. The public labelling of the recipient as deviant was intended to identify him or her as someone who could not be trusted, to damage his or her reputation as a respectable member of the community. This infamy lasted long after the punishment was completed and any bruises healed. In petitioning the Middlesex Justices in 1725 to keep Mary O'Bryan bound over by recognizance for suspected theft, for example, Margaret Fox described O'Bryan as 'an old offender and was pilloried at Charing Cross in the late Queen's reign for forgery' – the punishment was still remembered, despite the fact it had occurred at least 10 years earlier.[1] Penance was also intended to shape reputations (in defamation

* I would like to thank John Beattie, Penelope Corfield, Simon Devereaux, James Epstein, Louise Falcini, Karen Harvey, Peter King, Tim Hitchcock, Greg Smith, and the participants in the 'Long Eighteenth Century' seminar at the Institute of Historical Research, London, for helpful advice and archival references, and Donna Andrew for permitting me to read a forthcoming publication.

cases, this included restoring the victim's reputation as well as humiliating the offender), but there was an additional aim of restoring the sinner to the community through an act of repentance.

Over the course of the 'long' eighteenth century these punishments were abandoned, restricted or moved indoors in London, *before* they were formally repealed or restricted by statute. This chapter will examine some of the reasons why public punishments declined in the metropolis. It will take into account the explanations advanced by previous historians, notably changing elite attitudes, including a growing intolerance of violence and concerns about the growth of public disorder. But it will focus on a neglected aspect of this problem: the changing attitudes of the audience, the 'public', who were expected to play a crucial role in carrying out these punishments. Over the course of this long period the ways Londoners used and conceived of their streets were fundamentally transformed, making it much more difficult for shame and public humiliation to work as forms of punishment.

I

Pre-industrial penal strategies were characterized to a considerable extent by judicial discretion, and judges and justices selected only a small fraction of convicts for public punishments, except in the church courts, where penance was routinely imposed. For those selected, the judicial authorities attempted to ensure that such punishments achieved maximum publicity by paying considerable attention to where and when they were staged. Penance was supposed to take place in the culprit's (or victim's, in the case of defamation) parish church, where the community gathered for Sunday worship. The pillory was usually set up in places, such as Cheapside or Charing Cross, with markets and considerable traffic; and timed at midday when the streets were busiest.[2] In other cases it was set up near the scene of the crime. Jasper Arnold, who tore two pages out of the parish register of St Andrew Holborn in order to destroy the evidence of his bigamy, was sentenced to stand in the pillory in front of the church.[3] When Thomas Lyell and Lawrence Sydney were pilloried for defrauding several gentlemen with false and loaded dice at a masquerade, they stood in the Haymarket, 'facing the Opera House, the scene of their depredations'.[4] The pillory itself was meant to revolve, so that the culprit could turn to face every member of the crowd. When the attorney Edward Aylett stood for perjury by falsely claiming a legal privilege in order to escape arrest, the punishment took place in New Palace Yard, and the doors to Westminster Hall were thrown open so all the attorneys and barristers in the Hall could see. The pillory turned so that 'he was exposed to view in different situations according to the direction of the sheriffs; but the greater part of his time was allotted to afford the gentlemen in the hall a complete view of his person'.[5] Those pilloried were expected not to wear hats, 'so that [they] may be known by the people', and the nature of the offence was to be written on a paper and stuck on the pillory,[6] though the latter provision appears to have been implemented only erratically. Plate 9.1 shows Christopher Atkinson, a contractor convicted of fraudulent dealing with the Navy Victualling Board, walking around in the pillory in front of the Corn Exchange in 1783; his hat has been removed and placed on top of a central pole, around which the pillory turned.

Similarly, whipping sentences 'until her [or his] back be bloody' were individually prescribed for each offender, along routes that were often main thoroughfares. In December 1741, for example, the justices at the Middlesex Sessions sentenced a man and two women convicted of petty larceny to be whipped, respectively, as follows: from New Church in the Strand through Drury Lane to St Giles High Street; from one end of Monmouth Street in St Giles in the Fields to the other end of the same street; and from Whitechapel Bars to Whitechapel Church.[7] These routes often began or ended at or near the scene of the crime, where potential victims or acquaintances of the

Plate 9.1 Christopher Atkinson in the pillory, 1783

Source: Anon, Guildhall Library.

culprit were likely to be present. Elizabeth Bond, found guilty of stealing three pewter pint mugs from an alehouse in Leadenhall Street, was whipped over 100 yards in the same street.[8] Towards the end of this period those convicted of theft from ships and warehouses were frequently whipped on the docks and quays alongside the Thames.[9] The shaping of reputations in this way was further promoted by involving spectators in the punishment. At the pillory, the crowd was actively involved, throwing dirt, excrement, rotten eggs and vegetables, blood and guts from slaughterhouses, dead cats, and even bricks and stones. With other punishments the crowd was normally more passive: during public whippings, the most the crowd could do was shout encouragement to the whipper, and during penance the audience was expected to remain silent.

Participation in public shaming was not difficult for early modern Londoners, who were used to playing a prominent role in public street life. Indeed, popular participation in official civic and royal celebrations and processions conferred a sense of the legitimacy of public involvement in rituals and demonstrations on the streets of London.[10] And armed with such legitimacy, and the role accorded the public in apprehending suspected criminals by the judicial system, Londoners widened their role to administer punishments without judicial sanction, not only for offences which were clearly illegal (such as pickpocketing) but also of people whose actions offended social norms but who were not guilty of an illegal act (such as informers). In doing so, Londoners frequently imitated official punishments.[11] Just as crowds pelted people on the pillory, they did the same to people they encountered on the street whom they suspected of being pickpockets, sodomites and informers. In 1738, crowd hostility to the Gin Act led to frequent attacks on those who initiated prosecutions. When a mob was raised around Henry Hickson and Alice Twopenny 'by calling out informers', Hickson got away, but Twopenny 'was used in so cruel and unmerciful a manner that she was covered with mud and dirt, and lay for dead'.[12]

When Daniel Clarke, whose evidence resulted in the conviction and execution of the 'cutters' who destroyed weavers' looms during industrial protests in 1768–69, was pursued by a large mob intent on vengeance in 1771, the crowd's behaviour echoed the full range of public punishments of the time: they pelted him with mud, stones and brickbats, put a rope around his neck and threatened to hang him, and chased him through the streets and whipped him. Like some who stood in the pillory, he did not survive.[13] Although this case was clearly unusual, reports of crowd punishments involving attacks on offenders with mud, dirt and stones, or by ducking them in ponds, are scattered throughout eighteenth-century London newspapers and in the recognizances to attend Quarter Sessions issued by Justices of the Peace. Such crowd behaviour sometimes even supplemented capital punishments. On his way to be hanged at Tyburn in 1725, the notorious thief-taker Jonathan Wild was not greeted with 'those signs of pity [the spectators] generally show when common criminals are going to execution'. Instead, 'they reviled and cursed him, and pelted him with stones and dirt continually'.[14] The crowd had its own sense of justice, revealed (as we shall see) not only in its selective pelting of those who stood on the pillory, but also in the pattern of unofficial punishments administered to those who violated social norms.

II

The role of the crowd in administering punishments was undermined in the eighteenth century, however, by the changing ways in which Londoners perceived and used the city's streets. London's principal thoroughfares were increasingly differentiated from its narrower alleys and courts, with the main streets lined with symmetrical Georgian facades and paved, cleaned and cleared of obstructions. Particularly in areas of the city dominated by commercial interests, it became vital to maintain the free flow of traffic. These changes potentially undermined the practice of encouraging vast crowds to gather and observe and administer punishments in public places.[15] Crowds obstructed traffic, and the clean streets removed some of the ammunition they needed at the pillory. But these reforms of public spaces were also expressions of the changing expectations of Londoners concerning appropriate public behaviour, as the disorderly scenes at public punishments came to clash with the refined physical appearance of streetscapes. In a world where the streets were primarily conceived as both arteries of movement and as emblems of taste and regularity, orderliness, but also a certain impersonality, became an essential characteristic of the street, and it became more difficult to use the streets as places for establishing or destroying reputations. Perhaps even more importantly, changes in economic and social life caused by the decline of paternalist forms of employment (such as apprenticeship) and the growth of independent wage labour, together with high levels of migration, weakened the social ties which facilitated community-based punishments. As the communal life of the streets was undermined and public life was reconfigured, London's streets were populated by 'a new public of privatized individuals'.[16] As a result of these transformations, reputations were shaped in more private and socially selective contexts rather than on the streets, thereby undermining an essential function of traditional public punishments.[17]

It should be said that, despite the apparent incongruity between expectations of orderliness governing new public spaces and the disorder of public punishments, such punishments continued to be staged on major thoroughfares throughout the eighteenth century. The pillory was sited, and whippings occurred, all over London, in the classical spaces of the City and West End as well as in the older and less fashionable streets of the other suburbs. Atkinson, for example, stood in the pillory in front of a set of Georgian buildings (including the Corn Exchange) in Mark Lane in the City (Plate 9.1). Walter Patterson, judged a rogue and a vagabond in 1750, was sentenced to be publicly whipped at a cart's tail three times, each time in a fashionable part of the west end: Hanover Square, Pall Mall and Covent Garden Market.[18]

Nonetheless, over the course of the eighteenth and early nineteenth centuries most public punishments declined, in the sense that their use was constricted and their impact diminished. Penance disappeared, or moved into a back room of the church. In cases of fornication and bastard-bearing, the guilty party did continue to stand 'in a white sheet with a white wand in her hand and open faced with a paper of her accusation on her breast' – first at the church door 'where most of the people enter the said church', and then in front of the congregation immediately after the service ended, where he or she confessed and acknowledged the offence – but only a small number of people were convicted of this offence in the Church courts in the eighteenth century. Already at the start of our period most penances for defamation (the most common offence punished in these courts) were conducted in parish vestries, not the church itself, in the presence not of the entire congregation but of only the minister, churchwardens and the victim, as well as five or six of his or her friends, 'if they be there otherwise in their absence'.[19] By the early eighteenth century the public dimension of this punishment had thus been almost entirely removed,[20] and it was further eroded in the 1790s by the tendency of the Consistory Court to forego penance in cases of defamation if, after conviction, the parties reached a private agreement resolving their dispute. In 1831 the Royal Commission investigating the church courts found that they had 'very rarely required the performance of public penance'.[21] Private settlements had superseded public humiliation and repentance.

Whipping was the next punishment to lose some of its publicity. John Beattie has shown that the number of whippings carried out in the city declined dramatically after the introduction of transportation in 1718.[22] Within two decades, the authorities began to move some of those that still took place indoors. In the first three decades of the eighteenth century the vast majority of whippings sentenced by the justices at quarter sessions and the judges at the Old Bailey (excluding those occurring as part of the separate punishment of incarceration in a house of correction) were intended to be carried out in the traditional manner of whipping at 'a cart's tail' along a length (typically one hundred yards) of a street (as illustrated in the seventeenth-century print in Plate 9.2). But from the 1730s, sentences began to differentiate between what was sometimes referred to as 'private whipping' on the one hand and 'open' or 'public' whipping on the other.[23] A range of sentences evolved with varying degrees of publicity, including sentences carried out in prison or a house of correction, those performed at a public whipping post outside a prison or courthouse, and the traditional whipping at a cart's tail. Given the large number of visitors found in prisons

Plate 9.2 'The manner of Whipping at the Carts Tayle For petty Larceny and Offences'

Source: John Seller, *A Book of the Punishments of the Common Laws of England* (1671), n.p.

in this period, whippings there were by no means entirely private,[24] but the audiences were clearly much more restricted than those that witnessed outdoor whippings. Indeed, when the Middlesex Justices sentenced several offenders to the house of correction to be whipped before discharge in 1724 and 1725, they sought greater publicity for the sentence by ordering it 'to be published in a public newspaper for the terror of evil-disposed persons'.[25]

The abandonment of whipping through the streets for some offenders is evident in the differential fees claimed by sheriffs for carrying out the punishment, which are first evident in 1757. Whereas the sheriff claimed three pounds for whipping offenders through a specified length of street, he claimed only one pound for those for whom no place was specified; the latter were either whipped at an outdoor whipping post (there was one on Clerkenwell Green, near the Sessions House, and another outside the Old Bailey), or they were whipped in prison (this was sometimes referred to as 'private whipping'). In 1788, when the level of fees had increased, a ruling on sheriff's expenses specified that £3 was to be allowed 'for all common whipping, whether public [as at Clerkenwell Green, etc.] or private, and £6 for whipping at a cart's tail or for distance'. In 1790 whipping at a cart's tail, for which the fee claimed was identical to that paid for setting someone on the pillory, was described as an 'extraordinary whipping'.[26] This language, and the differential fees charged, indicate that those whippings for which the Sheriff claimed lower fees and/or failed to mention the location of the whipping took place either inside prison or at a whipping post, whereas those where the route is mentioned or the phrase 'at a cart's tail' is used took place in the streets.

As Table 9.1 suggests, the proportion of whippings which were recorded as taking place in public declined from between 43 per cent and 77 per cent between 1723 and 1779 to only 18 per cent in the first decade of the nineteenth century.[27] Some of the whippings for which the sheriffs did not indicate a route or specify 'at a cart's tail' may have still taken place outside rather than inside a prison, but these were never frequent. During the nine years when sheriffs listed such public stationary whipping separately, they accounted for only 14 per cent of the total number whipped. Thus mobile whippings were only to a limited extent replaced by public stationary whippings; most moved indoors. The *number* of explicitly public whippings increased until the 1780s and showed a less dramatic decline thereafter, but this was because judges and justices increasingly resorted to all forms of whipping from 1772 owing to a loss of faith in the alternative punishments

Table 9.1 Whipping sentences in London and urban Middlesex, 1723–1811 (annual averages)

	Place not specified[i]	*Public*[ii]	*Total per year*	*% public*	*Total number*
1723–29	1.4	4.9	6.3	77	44
1730–39	8.9	7.9	16.8	47	168
1746–59[iii]	15.0	11.6	26.6	44	133
1760–69	10.0	16.1	26.1	62	261
1770–79[iv]	29.0	21.7	50.7	43	456
1780–89	89.5	27.4	116.9	23	1169
1790–99	45.2	26.0	61.2	26	612
1800–11	60.2	23.0	73.2	18	878

Notes

[i] As argued in the text, such punishments occurred primarily inside a prison or house of correction, though a minority may have occurred at a whipping post outdoors.

[ii] Along a specified route and/or 'at a cart's tail', or at a whipping post on Clerkenwell Green or at the Old Bailey. Punishments at whipping posts were only separately identified in the following years: 1789–92, 1795–6, 1798 and 1809–10.

[iii] 1746, 1751, 1757–9. Cravings are missing for all other years.

[iv] Except 1773, for which cravings are missing.

Source: Sheriff's Cravings for London and Middlesex, to year ending at Michaelmas: PRO, E197/32–4, T64/262, T90/146–7, 165–9. Does not include whippings carried out in the house of correction as part of a sentence of incarceration, since such punishments were not the responsibility of the sheriff.

of transportation (which was in any case suspended between 1776 and 1787) and the death penalty.[28] Nonetheless, as a proportion of all whipping sentences, from the 1780s the courts became significantly less prone to require whippings to be carried out in public. The public whipping of women was abolished in 1817, and that of men apparently ended in the 1830s, though it was not formally abolished until 1868.[29]

The reduced use of mobile whipping was paralleled by the abolition in 1783 of the procession of capital convicts from Newgate Prison to their place of execution at Tyburn; just as some whippings were administered outside the Sessions House or the Old Bailey, after 1783 executions were carried out on a scaffold erected immediately outside Newgate Prison. Although these could still attract large crowds, new arrangements separated the crowd from those punished and expedited the process. 'Instead of taking several hours and being played out through the streets of London, the hanging took minutes and was hidden as far as was possible.'[30] Similar changes affected stationary whippings. In 1788 Sheriff Bloxam clearly felt that the whippings outside the Old Bailey were insufficiently public. *The Times* reported that on one occasion he 'was determined it should not be nominally public only [and had the 12 convicts] severally mounted upon the gallows in the Sessions Yard'.[31] In contrast, some discomfort about even stationary outdoor whipping may be evident in the plans of the Middlesex justices to erect a whipping post outside their new sessions house in 1785. Perhaps conscious of the conflict between this form of punishment and the orderly principles embodied in the design of their new building and the paved grounds surrounding it, the justices called for a post which could 'be removed occasionally'.[32]

The pillory, on the other hand, by definition could only be used in public, and it continued to be used sporadically throughout the eighteenth and early nineteenth centuries, punishing an average of about five people per year in the metropolis, with a temporary surge to more than 10 per year in the 1750s and 1760s.[33] Nonetheless, given that the total number of convictions for all criminal offences, and of course the overall population of the metropolis, were increasing significantly over this period, the importance of the pillory in the judicial repertoire of punishments was declining proportionately. More importantly, the range of offences punished was increasingly restricted, with few pilloried after 1775 for riot, seditious words or any felony. An 1816 statute restricted the use of the pillory to perjury only and it was abolished altogether in 1837.[34]

III

Although each punishment had its own chronology of change, by the early nineteenth century all the traditional public shaming punishments played a much reduced role in metropolitan sentencing practices. How do we account for these changes? Can we link new attitudes concerning the appearance and use of public streets with changing attitudes towards public punishments? The usual explanations for the decline of public corporal punishments are, first, a growing distaste for violence and, second, increasing concerns about the maintenance of public order when such punishments were carried out. Both these explanations have some merit. Along with the increasing intolerance of physical violence in other contexts (such as wife beating and duelling[35]) there is evidence among late eighteenth-century enlightened opinion of distaste for corporal punishment and a desire to seek the reformation of the offender instead. John Beattie ascribes the decline of public physical punishments to 'a fundamental rejection of punishments that were violent in themselves or that encouraged public violence', an aspect of a more general cultural intolerance of violence which emerged at this time.[36] Patrick Colquhoun was certainly keen to limit the suffering incurred by those who were whipped when he advised constables in 1803 that the punishment was solely meant 'as an example to others to abstain from criminal offences' and was 'not an act of resentment to the delinquent who suffers. This unpleasant duty should therefore be executed so as to make a proper impression on those who witness the punishment, without exercising a greater degree of severity than is necessary to obtain that object.' Similarly, echoing a parliamentary speech made by Edmund Burke in 1780, Colquhoun argued that the pillory 'is a punishment of great and lasting infamy, by the ignominious exposure of the delinquent, and not intended for personal suffering, according to the will or unrestrained licence of a turbulent populace'.[37] The idea that the pillory was not intended for personal suffering inflicted by the crowd would have seemed preposterous to most eighteenth-century Londoners, but some attitudes had changed. The few occasions on which people were killed on the pillory encouraged further concerns about crowd violence. Following the brutal treatment of two of the thief-takers from the McDaniel Gang on the pillory in 1756, an observer complained that the 'mob' had acted like animals:

> it is not so truly the greatness of the crime which inflames them, as the scent of the carnage; and now, by one murder, they have got a taste for blood, it is high time that they should be considered as dogs ... and that no more victims should be exposed to their resentment.[38]

The increasing sensitivity to the use of violence in corporal punishments is especially marked in the case of women, for whom such public punishments effectively ended long before the public whipping of women was abolished in 1817: as is evident in Table 9.2, the number of women whipped in public declined dramatically from the 1770s (while that of men increased into the 1780s), and the same is true of the pillory. No women were sentenced to either punishment in London after 1798. The explanation for this shift is probably the same as that offered by V.A.C. Gatrell for the abolition

Table 9.2 Sex of convicts whipped by location of whipping[i]

	Place not specified (annual averages)			*Public (annual averages)*			*% of all women whipped publicly*
	M	*F*	*%F*	*M*	*F*	*%F*	
1730–39	4.6	4.3	48	5.6	2.2	28	34
1746–59[ii]	3.8	11.2	75	6.2	5.4	47	33
1760–69	3.9	6.1	61	9.4	6.7	42	52
1770–79[iii]	13.2	15.7	54	19.4	2.2	10	12
1780–89	53.4	35.9	40	25.5	1.9	7	5
1790–99	40.1	5.0	11	15.5	0.4	3	7
1800–11	50.4	9.5	16	13.0	0	–	–

Notes
[i] Table excludes those few defendants whose sex is not known.
[ii] 1746, 1751, 1757–59. Cravings are missing for all other years.
[iii] Except 1773, for which the cravings are missing.

Source: As for Table 9.1.

of the practice of burning the bodies of women hanged for coining or murdering their husbands in 1790: women, even convicts, were increasingly seen as victims of their weaker natures and therefore as deserving of sympathy, while male judges sought to display 'their potency, benevolence, and chivalric selves' by exercising mercy.[39]

Support for whipping as a punishment for men continued well into the nineteenth century, not just among the lower classes, but also in some sections of the upper classes. As Peter King comments, 'the flogging culture ran deep'. Nonetheless, we have seen that most whipping sentences occurred indoors in the early nineteenth century, and whipping was apparently only targeted at the lower classes, such as the rank and file of the army.[40] As Gatrell has argued with respect to capital punishment, it was elite squeamishness about witnessing violence, rather than disapproval of violence against men *per se*, which explains why these punishments were moved indoors.[41] As one contemporary commentator wrote in 1813 following the violent pillorying of the Vere Street gang for sodomy in 1813, the offence merited death, but it should be carried out without permitting such 'disgusting spectacles', which offend 'female delicacy and manly feeling'.[42]

There were also of course serious concerns about maintaining order during public punishments, particularly at the pillory. From the start of our period, sheriff's officers and constables were routinely summoned to attend, and officers formed a ring of protection around it. The number of officers deployed seems to have fluctuated depending on the sheriff's judgement of the extent of disorder expected. In some cases, even early in the period, large numbers of extra officers were summoned. When William Fuller stood three times in the pillory in 1703 for political libel, 'a great many constables and watchmen' were present on the first day, and on the second 'sheriff's officers and others [were] laid tightly about [the pillory] for [his] defence'. When John Middleton stood in the pillory in 1723 for attempting to earn rewards by making false accusations of treasonable practices, such was the popular hostility against him that the high constable summoned 20 constables and 104 assistants to protect him, though even this number could not prevent the crowd from smothering him to death with dirt. As this suggests, the officers occasionally misjudged the number of guards required: when Henry Groves stood on the pillory for defrauding tradesmen of thousands of pounds in 1755, 'the constables were obliged, in order to save themselves, to leave him to the resentment of the populace'.[43] In some cases where the officers were content to see the offender attacked by the crowd, one suspects their efforts at protection were minimal. After a sheriff's officer, Mr Watson, placed Middleton in the pillory (incorrectly, as it turned out), he went to the tavern to drink a pint of wine. Watson later confessed 'he was acquainted with the persons against whom Middleton had sworn falsely … and that he had said to Middleton now he had got him he hoped he should have his True, meaning his Due'.[44] In contrast, when they wanted to, the authorities could sometimes maintain perfect order. Ruth Paley argues that the reason two of the thief-takers pilloried in 1756, McDaniel and Berry, were well-protected, while two others were violently attacked, was that the former possessed damaging information which the authorities did not want released.[45]

Sollom Emlyn claimed in 1730 that officers could 'effectually' protect men on the pillory when they 'find an advantage in it'.[46] Indeed, the sheriff (or, in the city, the City Marshall) could manipulate the system of claiming expenses for extra officers to his own advantage. When Aylett stood in the pillory outside Westminster Hall in 1786 for perjury, the sheriff took 'uncommon pains … to preserve the peace, there being every reason to believe that but for the precaution used the prisoner's life would have been taken by the mob'. This included the hiring of 34 sheriff's officers and about 550 petty constables, as well as paying the scavenger to clean Palace Yard in advance to prevent the crowd from having anything to throw. Why Aylett was afforded such intense protection, which meant that no one was allowed even to attempt to throw anything at him, is unclear. (In a cryptic comment, *The Times* suggested that Aylett's wealth protected him.[47]) But the Sheriff clearly tried to turn the occasion to his financial advantage, claiming a total of £105 in expenses, including coffee for the officers and dinner and drinks at a local tavern. The Treasury allowed only £51 1s., less than half the sum claimed.[48] Similarly, in 1813 the Committee for Letting the City's Lands investigated the costs of hiring extra constables for attending the pillory and on other occasions and discovered there were inadequate controls over the costs claimed by the City Marshall.[49]

Some historians have claimed that the problem of maintaining order at the pillory increased during the eighteenth century. James Cockburn refers to 'the escalation of violence at the gallows and pillory', without providing much evidence of the latter, alleging that 'after mid-century, the mob in London and other towns openly controlled the pillory'.[50] It is of course difficult to measure disorder over time, for the evidence is limited and perceptions of violence are subjective. When William Holdbrook stood in the pillory in Bloomsbury Market in 1719 for attempted sodomy, *The Original Weekly Journal* reported that 'the mob had certainly murdered him could they have got him in their power, for a hackney coach was tore to pieces that took him up to carry him to Newgate'. B.R. Burg, however, points out that 'the tormentors were more entertained than enraged by the would-be sodomite', for he was pelted with rotten eggs and cucumbers, 'hardly projectiles that would be chosen by a man determined to maim or kill'.[51] Despite the limitations of the evidence, it is worth noting that the number of deaths and near-deaths on the pillory in London reported in a sample of the printed sources did not increase over the century (Table 9.3). There were two cases in the first quarter of the century, four each in the second and third quarters, and only two in the final quarter. It is true that the number of cases (in addition to those just mentioned) in which reports state that the offender was 'severely' pelted was highest in the third quarter, but this reflected the increased number of people who stood in the pillory at that time and was not repeated in the fourth quarter. The lack of greater disorder at the end of our period was partly the result of more systematic policing, but it is important to note that the pillory was policed, and crowds were capable of inflicting brutal violence, *throughout* this period. When Middleton stood in 1723, several constables claimed they attempted to prevent the crowd from throwing *any* dirt at him. That he died in the pillory was due both to the vigorous efforts of an angry crowd and the neglect or

Table 9.3 Responses of crowds to those placed on the pillory in eighteenth-century London

	Applauded by crowd	*Condemned (total) by crowd*	*Deaths caused by crowd*	*Near deaths caused by crowd*	*Severely pelted*
1700–24	6	6	1	1	2
1725–49	3	9	2	2	2
1750–74	6	18	2	2	8
1775–99	0	6	2	0	2

Note on sources: This table is not meant to be comprehensive, but it is based on a wide-ranging survey, including all relevant secondary sources, the *Gentleman's Magazine* (using the index), relevent pamphlet literature; Knapp and Baldwin, *The Newgate Calendar*, and a sample of London newspapers, comprising complete runs for approximately one year in every ten: *Weekly Journal: or British Gazeteer* (1721), *London Journal* (1725, 1731), *London Evening Post* (1741, 1751, 1761), *General Evening Post* (1771, 1781); *The Daily Universal Register* (1785), *The Times* (1795).

complicity of the sheriff's officers. The accounts of his death, as well as those of the crowd's treatment of William Fuller in 1703 and John Waller in 1732, are every bit as gruesome as are those of the Vere Street gang in 1810.[52]

What seems clear is that *sensitivity* to disorder on the pillory increased over time. When William Smith died on the pillory in Southwark in 1780, the *Gentleman's Magazine* ascribed this to 'the severity of the mob', and Edmund Burke raised the case in the House of Commons. He complained that the pillory had become 'an instrument of death', blamed the death on the 'mob', and asked that the punishment be abolished. But it appears that the true cause of Smith's death was the fact that, as was possibly the case with Middleton, the pillory was improperly set up, with 'the hole for his neck too high, and only his toes touched the stand'. As his widow complained, 'his was absolutely hung in the pillory'.[53] Evidence of a lowering threshold of disorder also comes from manuals for constables, which, after failing to mention anything about officers' duties to maintain order at the pillory for most of the eighteenth century, instruct the constable attending the pillory in 1790 and 1803 'to do his utmost to preserve the peace, and to prevent all outrage or violence towards the offender from taking place'.[54]

A related concern regarding crowd behaviour at the pillory was the fear that, instead of reviling and attacking the convict, the crowd would subvert judicial intentions and applaud him or her and donate refreshments and money. There are many famous examples of this, from Daniel Defoe, who was pelted with flowers in 1703 (Plate 9.3), to John Williams, who republished the famous 45th issue of John Wilkes's *North Briton* in 1765 and was given 200 guineas which had been collected from the crowd, and Daniel Eaton, who stood in 1812 for publishing the third part of Thomas Paine's *Age of Reason* and was applauded, presented with refreshments, had the sweat wiped from his face, and generally 'received every possible mark of compassion and of applause' from the between 12–20,000 spectators present.[55] Such subversions of the judicial process naturally caused concern and not just at the end of our period. In 1756 a correspondent in the *Gentleman's Magazine* called attention to the inconsistency that 'butchers' drovers' and the like should determine the extent of punishment for those standing in the pillory, 'when the most substantial master butcher in England is by our laws deemed incapable of serving as a juror in matters of life and death'.[56] The favourable treatment received by Eaton in 1812 contributed to other pressure a few years later for the abolition of the pillory. Yet, paradoxically, incidents in which crowds praised rather than pelted people on the pillory became very rare from the 1770s (and, as is evident in Table 9.3, did not occur at all in the last quarter of the century), largely because judges stopped sentencing those found guilty of sedition to the pillory.[57] William Cobbett claimed that Eaton's was 'the first instance within the memory of persons fifty years of age, of anyone being applauded in the pillory of England', and indeed the latest previous example I have identified in London was John

Plate 9.3 Daniel Defoe on the pillory (c. 1730–50)
Source: Eyre Crave, Guildhall Library.

Williams in 1765.[58] In 1793 the radical John Frost was convicted of seditious words, imprisoned, and sentenced to stand on the pillory, but concerns about how the crowd would behave led the judges to remit the pillory portion of his sentence. This was a wise judgement, for according to Francis Place when Frost was released from prison 'the crowd pulled his coach through the streets'.[59]

Nonetheless, concerns about the crowd subverting court-imposed sentences were uppermost during the debate in the 1810s that led to the restriction of the pillory to perjurers in 1816. The immediate precipitant was the sentencing of Thomas Lord Cochrane, convicted of a stock exchange fraud, to the pillory in 1814, a sentence which was seen as unjust and likely to lead to public disorder. Paradoxically, although there was apparently considerable public sympathy for Cochrane (which suggests he would have been well-treated on the pillory), the controversy the sentence aroused was used to highlight the dangers of disorder. It was argued, notably in a pamphlet by Thomas Talfourd, that the pillorying of a gentleman constituted an unequal punishment since he would suffer more disgrace than 'a hardened villain' would. Among the reasons advanced for the abolition of the pillory – it did not offer the offender the possibility of reformation; the extent of the punishment was determined by the mob rather than the judges – Talfourd noted the dangers of disorder: 'those whom you suffer to riot on the side of the laws may soon learn to oppose them with similar outrages ... we educate them for revolution and carnage'. As Greg Smith has argued, contemporaries were worried that public punishments 'threatened to undermine social order because they were themselves lawless, disorderly, and anarchic'.[60]

IV

Changing attitudes towards violence and new expectations concerning public order certainly help explain the decline of public punishments in London in the 'long' eighteenth century. But these issues should not be overemphasized given the continued use of violence in private, and the apparent lack of increase in either disorder or crowd sympathy for those punished. Moreover, these factors cannot explain changes in penance, where issues of violence and crowd disorder do not arise. It is possible that in this case the crucial factor was the declining interest of the potential audience (the congregation), and this highlights the point that the missing factor in the analysis so far has been the views of the crowd itself concerning the merits of these punishments. It is my contention that the changing attitudes of those who traversed London's streets contributed to the demise of public punishments. In a word, many Londoners were losing interest. Although they may have continued to join crowds, they became less willing to become subsumed into the crowd, and to actively join in communal punishments, unless they specifically identified with the views expressed. These changes are evident in an apparent decline in the number of extra-judicial street punishments inflicted by groups of Londoners, such as mobs which pelted suspected miscreants with dirt, water and excrement, or spat at them. The number of such incidents recorded on recognizances issued by the Middlesex justices of the peace to attend quarter sessions declined dramatically. Sample evidence indicates that they averaged around 11 per year in the first half of the eighteenth century, compared to less than two per year after 1750. Concurrently, the total number of recognizances issued for participating in mobs and tumults declined by over three-quarters.[61] As Martin Ingram has argued, the link between popular and official shaming punishments was broken in the eighteenth century, and this evidence suggests that it was the unofficial punishments that declined first.[62]

Another indicator that suggests declining communal interest in public punishment is the changing language with which crowds participating in or observing punishments were described in the press. Most commonly referred to as mobs or the 'rabble' early in the century, a new word, 'populace', became common from the 1760s. Although often used as a synonym for 'mob', 'populace' had slightly different connotations, in that it was a more passive term: unlike mob, it could not easily take the form of a verb. A description of the crowd when a man was pilloried for attempted sodomy in October 1761 illustrates this semantic difference. 'For the first half hour', the report begins, 'he received very little injury from the populace, the pillory being surrounded with a great number of peace and sheriff's officers, but at length the mob overpowered them, and drove most of them away'. The report continues with a description of the violent attacks committed by the 'mob' on the man, that left him 'the most miserable object imaginable'.[63]

The increasing use of the term 'populace' may have only been used ironically by a press which sought higher standards of behaviour on London's streets, but it may also reflect real changes in the composition and behaviour of some crowds attending public punishments. Increasingly after 1750, crowds are described in newspapers as composed of specific occupational or other groups. Instead of being described as the 'mob' or 'populace', rioters were reported, for example, to be sailors, butchers, butcher boys or prostitutes.[64] If this change in labelling reflects real changes in the composition of the crowd (and not just more detailed journalism), it suggests that Londoners may have become less willing to join undifferentiated crowds which gathered in the streets, whether in order to inflict informal punishments, to observe whippings, or to attack men or women standing in the pillory. They continued to participate in crowds, but only when it served their own sectional interests or they could directly identify with the other members of the crowd. It was alleged, for example, that the violent treatment of the Vere Street Gang in the Haymarket in 1810 was caused by a mob that had been organized for that purpose.[65] Otherwise, Londoners ignored the punishment.

There is not much evidence documenting crowd responses to public whipping, making it difficult to detect any changes over time. Witnesses of course experienced little opportunity to participate in this punishment directly, though it is possible that the severity with which the executioner wielded his whip depended on how loud the observers shouted. That the punishment was not always fully implemented is suggested by the fact that one whipping sentence from the Middlesex court, of an incorrigible rogue, particularly specified that 'the person who whips him is required to do his duty'. Emlyn complained in 1730 that it was 'in the power of the common hangman to make ... whipping as severe or as favourable as he pleases'.[66] It seems likely, therefore, that the court depended on the spectators to egg the whipper/executioner on. There is, however, some evidence that audiences did not always behave the way the authorities expected. Peter King notes that when petty thieves were publicly whipped crowds were often sympathetic to the offender and 'hooted at or jostled' the whipper. Yet the punishment could destroy reputations, and crowds even joined in the punishment. In 1768 William Crammer petitioned the Middlesex court for remission of his sentence, 'not only with regard to himself (who is of a very weakly constitution) but also for the great scandal that will [be inflicted] on his honest and creditable relations and friends that reside thereabout, besides the danger of being murdered by the populace'.[67] Yet such concerns may have been exaggerated in petitions like this in the hope of securing sympathy from the justices. In 1786, *The Times* complained that the punishment of whipping was 'so trifling, as to be only a matter of merriment, even to the persons on whom it is inflicted'. Although the paper goes on to comment that 'the ceremony generally collects four or five hundred blackguards, and journeymen mechanics, who wait for hours in the Sessions House Yard, thereby losing the best part of their day in idleness', the implication is that these spectators viewed the occasion primarily as a means of avoiding work.[68] It is an intriguing possibility (though impossible to prove) that whippings were moved to stationary positions or indoors not simply because they attracted the wrong sort of attention, but rather because they attracted very little attention at all from passers-by.

With the pillory, whose impact as a punishment depended fundamentally on the crowd playing its allotted role in shaming the convict, there were legal doubts about its effectiveness from the start of our period. During the tenure of Chief Justice John Holt there was much discussion about whether standing in the pillory automatically disqualified someone from testifying as a witness in court, and in 1700 the court ruled that it did not: 'it is not the nature of the punishment, but the nature of the crime and conviction, that creates the infamy'.[69] In 1729 the damage to one's reputation incurred by standing in the pillory was deemed an insufficient punishment for the crime of forgery.[70] The fact that the judges at the Old Bailey ceased to sentence convicted felons to the pillory after 1779 further supports the view that audience-imposed shame was no longer seen as effective as it once was.[71] There is in fact more direct evidence of audience disinterest in the pillory during the second half of the eighteenth century. In a few recorded cases Londoners appear to have ignored the punishment when they encountered it as they were going about the streets. When the McDaniel gang of thief-takers stood on the pillory in 1756, newspaper reports document a porter attempting to carry some wire *through* the crowd (he lost the wire) and some drovers chasing a bullock nearby (they 'overdrove' it and it charged into the crowd).[72] When John Stephens, a tailor, was 'going through Russell Street' one morning 30 years later, he encountered a crowd attending someone standing in the pillory. Rather than join the crowd, he described it as an obstruction that prevented him from continuing on his way. While trying to make it through the crowd, he had his pocket picked.[73] The principal actors in all these cases showed little interest in the punishment taking place and simply sought to carry on with their business.

Observers also noted changes in the character of the crowd. In 1829 Francis Place claimed that, over the previous decades, a change had occurred in its behaviour: while 'formerly there were always on these occasions a sufficiently large number to keep one another in countenance and encourage the more debased "to keep up the game" ... latterly the pelting was confined to what were considered the most atrocious offences only'. Those who tried to attack 'men whose crimes were almost venial, or those whose imputed offences were political, were restrained by the better portion of the spectators, and the constables, and pelting at length was almost wholly limited to men convicted of attempts to commit unnatural crimes'.[74] This suggests that at least some members of the crowd had internalized more restrained codes of behaviour. An anonymous anti-monarchical tract published around 1820, which noted that both good and bad men could be found on the throne as well as in the pillory, commented with respect to the pillory, 'how little real disgrace attaches to this exposure', and notes that even when 'the surrounding populace' sought to condemn the offender, they know 'that even in that case, *the law permits not a hand to be raised against him,* [and] will be satisfied with confirming the justice of his sentence with hisses and groans'.[75] In contrast to many written contemporary accounts, late eighteenth-century illustrations of the pillory do not depict the crowd throwing things; the spectators generally appear passive, as is evident in Plate 9.1. In contrast, depictions of Defoe in the pillory (Plate 9.3) present a much more chaotic scene.[76] Whether this change was due to decreasing crowd interest or higher standards of public behaviour is unclear.

With the increased policing of the pillory, also depicted in the prints, the role of the crowd was in any case downgraded; we have seen how limited a role was accorded to the spectators when Aylett stood there in 1783. With improved cleansing of the streets there was less material immediately available to throw – in sharp contrast to 1723, when the crowd found so much dirt and mire raked up on the streets to throw at Middleton that they left a pile two feet deep underneath him.[77] Later in the century the crowd had to be sufficiently organized to bring its own weapons, or purchase rotten refuse from hucksters who had identified a marketing opportunity. Moreover, with the pillory surrounded by a large cordon of officers there was little left for the spectators to do. Francis Place describes how at Charing Cross the constables 'permitted a number of women to pass between them, into the open space around the pillory'. Only these women, as moral agents of the community, were able to pelt the offender, supplied with materials handed to them by other spectators.[78] Reports in *The Times* in the 1790s of people standing in the pillory include no mention of crowd hostility, despite potentially provocative behaviour by those supposedly being punished. A man standing in 1796 for attempted rapes on two children, a crime which normally attracted severe crowd hostility, laughed at and scorned the spectators, while in 1797 an attorney, Crosley, treated the punishment lightly, wearing a black suit and his 'natural-curled wig'.[79] Either these men relied on crowd apathy, or they were confident the constables would protect them from the crowd. There is also some evidence that the intended communal nature of pillory punishments was disrupted by particular groups of people dominating the crowd. When Tousant Urvoy stood in the pillory at the Old Bailey for perjury in 1761, 'some of the mob began to pelt him, according to their usual custom, but were soon prevented by a party of butchers, who drove them off'.[80] For all these reasons, the role of the ordinary Londoner became marginalized. This is not to deny that there continued to be times when crowds inflicted considerable harm on those standing in the pillory. But such occasions were far from typical and, indeed, could only occur when the offence both attracted particular opprobrium *and* the authorities lost control of the crowd. At other times, there was little left for the crowd to do.

However, the biggest threat undermining the impact of the pillory as a communal punishment may have been the changing ways in which reputations were shaped in the metropolis, in particular the growing influence of the printed word. As oral public insults declined, Londoners in the late eighteenth century resorted to printed insults (and apologies) as means of influencing reputations.[81] Similarly, printed publications were used to shape the views of crowds attending public punishments. Pamphlets and handbills were published, to be handed out before or at the pillory, encouraging the crowd to pelt (or not) the offender. One broadside, apparently distributed just before a man convicted of sodomy was killed in the pillory, depicted such a man standing in the pillory with mostly female spectators preparing to pelt and flog him. It included a ballad condemning 'a race so detested, of honour divested' and inviting 'the daughters of Britain ... to well flog'em with birch'.[82] Before Defoe stood in the pillory, at least three pamphlets were published encouraging the crowd to attack him. One broadside (now vanished) included a print showing Defoe's face disfigured by pelting and included the lines:

> Who this should be I do not know
> Unless a Whig? I guess he's so,
> – If I am right, pray take a throw.[83]

But most commonly in the eighteenth century printed handbills were used to state the case for the defendant, winning the crowd's sympathy and negating the intention of the punishment. Defoe himself wrote a 'Hymn to the Pillory', distributed while he was there, in which he claims the pillory will have no impact on him, for the shame and pain inflicted by the crowd could not affect the virtuous: 'Thou art no shame to truth or honesty / Nor is the character of such defaced by thee ...'. The real shame, Defoe argues, is on the authorities who placed him there.[84] Similarly, Edmund Curll, who anticipated harsh treatment when he stood in the pillory at Charing Cross in 1728 for political libel, distributed a broadsheet justifying his conduct, arguing that Queen Anne had licensed the books he published.[85]

Attempts like this to influence the crowd could be effective. The *British Spy; or Derby Post-Man* reported that, when Curll stood in the pillory, 'he was treated with great civility by the populace, which is thought to be chiefly owing to the insinuating paper his agents dispensed round about the pillory'. According to another account, the crowd 'smiled and grumbled at governmental stupidities, and either waited to cheer at the end of the hour or went their several ways'. Afterwards, the crowd carried him off 'as it were in triumph' to a neighbouring tavern.[86] Similarly, when John Sweetman and Thomas Howard stood in 1771 for compounding a penal statute, the *General Evening Post* reported that 'at first, the populace, who were very numerous, began to pelt them, but handbills being dispersed, signifying that they were drawn into the affair by another person, who made off with the best part of the cash, the pelting ceased, and they stood quietly the rest of the time'.[87] Print, of course, did not shape the opinions only of those who gathered at the pillory. Distributed in advance, such handbills could serve to attract a friendly audience, who could provide protection from any who remained hostile. Moreover, publications defending the reputations of those who had been pilloried could remain in circulation and counteract the long-term damage to their reputations they incurred by having been so punished. As popular culture became more dependent on written rather than oral communication for the transmission of news and information, the visual spectacle of the pillory (which relied on word-of-mouth reports of the event for its efficacy) lost some of its power to shape reputations.[88]

V

The growing importance of print in shaping audience responses to the pillory reflects the fact that shame works differently in the modern city. It is not simply that the printed word began to supplant oral communication as a means of shaping reputations, but that reputations came to be established by more narrowly defined reference groups. In a rapidly changing metropolis where most of the people one encountered in public were strangers and acquaintances between neighbours became increasingly superficial, judgements concerning character and reputation based on appearances, or on hearsay from neighbours or the diverse range of people one encountered on the streets, became increasingly unreliable. Consequently, by the end of the eighteenth century reputations were no longer primarily established by events and spectacles in public places. Attempts to shame people, whether through official punishments, popular imitations of such punishments or public insults, lost their effectiveness. Rather, reputations were established and defended either in the world of print, or within the narrower contexts of one's work, voluntary society or church. Moreover, the role of individual conscience and self-identity became increasingly important.[89] The older system of communally shaped reputations persisted in the narrow courts and alleys of the metropolis inhabited primarily by the lower class.[90] But these new ways of establishing reputations meant that London's main streets, their functions now dominated by traffic and architectural display, became inappropriate places to establish and destroy reputations.

This evidence places the reform of the penal system in the eighteenth and early nineteenth centuries in a new light. It suggests that the abandonment of public punishments was not simply the result of the adoption of increasingly enlightened (but also frightened) attitudes by those who established the penal laws and issued sentences, but was also the product of changing elite – and popular – understandings of what the streets were for. Elites sought to control and discipline the crowd, but Londoners of all social classes were simultaneously losing interest in public punishments, not simply due to changing attitudes towards violence or because their participation was circumscribed by official policing, but also because reputations were shaped in new ways, in which what happened on the street became less important. In explaining why public punishments declined in this period, we need to pay more attention to the attitudes and behaviour of those who were expected to take part, and to contextualize these in the distinctive social dynamics of modern urban life.

Notes

1 LMA (London Metropolitan Archive) MJ/SP/1725/Jan/36.
2 BL Add. MSS., 27826, fo. 172.
3 *The Proceedings on the King's Commission of the Peace, Oyer and Terminer, and Gaol Delivery for the City of London, and County of Middlesex, held at Justice Hall in the Old Bailey* [hereafter, *Old Bailey Proceedings*], Dec. 1717.
4 A. Knapp and W. Baldwin, *The New Newgate Calendar* (London, [1819]), ii, 83–5.
5 *Morning Chronicle, and London Advertiser*, no. 5468, 22 Nov. 1786.
6 *The Life of Infamous Actions of that Perjur'd Villain John Waller* (London, 1732), 28.
7 LMA MJ/SBP/14 (Dec. 1741).
8 *Old Bailey Proceedings*, Jan. 1768.
9 See, for example, the sentence carried out on Robert Raw in 1797: PRO T90/168.
10 R.B. Shoemaker, 'The London "mob" in the early eighteenth century', *JBS*, 26 (1987) 286–94; N. Rogers, *Crowds, Culture and Politics in Georgian Britain* (Oxford, 1998), 23–6, 274.
11 For earlier examples, see M. Ingram, 'Juridical folklore in England illustrated by rough music', in C. Brooks and M. Lobban, eds, *Communities and Courts in Britain, 1150–1900* (London and Rio Grande, 1997), 61–82.
12 *London Evening Post*, 8–11 April 1738. See also 3–5 Jan. 1738.
13 LMA OB.SP/1771/10d.
14 J. Mountague, *The Old Bailey Chronicle* (4 vols, London, 1786), I, 376.
15 P.J. Corfield, 'Walking the city streets: the urban odyssey in eighteenth-century England', *Journal of Urban History*, xvi (1990), 148; G.T. Smith, 'Civilised people don't want to see that kind of thing: the decline of public physical punishment in

London, 1760–1840', in C. Strange, ed., *Qualities of Mercy* (Vancouver, 1996), 41–4; J.M. Beattie, *Policing and Punishment in London 1660–1750* (Oxford, 2001), 447.

16 M. Ogborn, *Spaces of Modernity: London's Geographies, 1680–1780* (New York, 1998), chap. 3, esp. 79, 114.

17 R.B. Shoemaker, 'The decline of public insult in London, 1660–1800', *P&P*, clxix (2000), 126–7.

18 LMA MJ/SBB/1075, 49 (July 1750).

19 GL MSS 9,180; 9,846; 11,168; Orders of Penance 1720–24, 1727–30, 1763–1805; BL Add. MSS. 38715, fos 1–24 (Certificates of Penance).

20 For such punishments a century earlier, see M. Ingram, *Church Courts, Sex and Marriage in England, 1570–1640* (Cambridge, 1987), 294.

21 LMA DL/C/118, f. 15^{v} (*McManus* v. *McManus*), fo. 55 (*White* v. *Bower*); *Parliamentary Papers* 199 (xxiv) (1831–32), 'Report of the Royal Commission to Enquire into the Practice and Jurisdiction of the Ecclesiastical Courts', 63.

22 Beattie, *Policing and Punishment*, 444–7.

23 LMA MJ/SBB/728–956 (1715–38) and MJ/SBP/14 (January–December 1741), *passim*. The first example of the phrase 'private whipping' which I have found in the sessions records occurred in 1733: MJ/SBB/912, 71 (Oct. 1733). For the use of this distinction in the City of London in 1734, see Beattie, *Policing and Punishment*, 444. The distinction first emerges in the *Old Bailey Proceedings* around 1757. For similar developments in other counties, see J.M. Beattie, *Crime and the Courts in England, 1660–1800* (Princeton, 1986), 461; J.S. Cockburn, 'Punishment and brutalization in the English Enlightenment', *Law and History Review*, xii (1994), 172; P. King, *Crime, Justice and Discretion in England, 1740–1820* (Oxford, 2000), 273. Although there was initially some uncertainty about the legality of this punishment for felons, it was given statutory approval in 1779: Cockburn, 'Punishment and brutalization', 172; Beattie, *Crime and the Courts*, 544–5.

24 See, for example, Ned Ward's description of a whipping in Bridewell, *The London Spy*, ed. P. Hyland (1698–99; East Lansing Michigan, 1993), 110.

25 LMA MJ/SBB/827, p. 50; 829, pp. 59–61.

26 PRO Sheriff's Cravings for London and Middlesex, T64/262 (1757) T90/166 (1788) and 167 (1790).

27 For the decline of public whipping in Essex, see King, *Crime, Justice and Discretion*, 272–3, and in Surrey and Sussex, Beattie, *Crime and the Courts*, 614.

28 Beattie, *Crime and the Courts*, 543–8; J.R. Dinwiddy, 'The early nineteenth-century campaign against flogging in the army', *EHR*, xcvii (1982), 319.

29 57Geo. III c.75; C. Emsley, *Crime and Society in England, 1750–1900* (2nd edn, 1996), 249.

30 P. Rawlings, *Crime and Power: A History of Criminal Justice 1688–1988* (1999), 53; V.A.C. Gatrell, *The Hanging Tree. Execution and the English People, 1770–1868* (Oxford, 1994), 53–4, 57. On the 1783 move to Newgate, see also S. Wilf, 'Imagining justice: aesthetics and public executions in late eigtheenth-century England', *Yale Journal of Law and the Humanities*, v (1993–94) 51–70; S. Devereaux, 'Convicts and the State: The Administration of Criminal Justice in Great Britain During the Reign of George III' (PhD dissertation, University of Toronto, 1997), 240–8.

31 *The Times* (8 March 1788), 3d.

32 LMA MJ/OC/III, f. 160. In 1790, the Sheriff charged £6 to set up the whipping posts in Clerkenwell Green: PRO T90/167. Similarly, in 1759 the permanent gallows at Tyburn were replaced by temporary structures erected on each hanging day: Rawlings, *Crime and Power*, 51.

33 PRO E197/32–4; T64/262; T90/146–7, 165–9.

34 T.R. Forbes, 'A study of Old Bailey sentences between 1729 and 1800', *Guildhall Studies in London History*, v (1981) 33; 56 Geo. III, c. 138 (1816); 1 Vict., c. 23 (1837).
35 J.M. Beattie, 'Violence and society in early-modern England', in A.N. Doob and E.L. Greenspan, eds, *Perspectives in Criminal Law* (Aurora, Ontario, 1985), 50–1; D.T. Andrew, 'The code of honour and its critics: the opposition to duelling in England, 1700–1850', *SH*, v (1980), 409–34.
36 Beattie, *Crime and the Courts*, 138, 616. See also R. McGowen, 'Punishing violence, sentencing crime', in N. Armstrong and L. Tennenhouse, eds, *The Violence of Representation* (London, 1989), 140–56; J. Sharpe, 'Civility, civilizing processes, and the end of public punishment in England', in P. Burke *et al.*, eds, *Civil Histories: Essays Presented to Sir Keith Thomas* (Oxford, 2000), 215–30; G.T. Smith, 'The State and the Culture of Violence in London, 1760–1840' (PhD dissertation, University of Toronto, 1999), chap. 7.
37 P. Colquhoun, *A Treatise on the Functions and Duties of a Constable* (1803), 18; *Parliamentary History* 21 (London, 1814), col. 389.
38 *Gentleman's Magazine*, xxvi (1756) 166.
39 Gatrell, *Hanging Tree*, 336–8; King, *Crime, Justice and Discretion*, 286.
40 Cockburn, 'Punishment and brutalization', 177–8; King, *Crime, Justice and Discretion*, 273; L. Radzinowicz and R. Hood, *The Emergence of Penal Policy in Victorian and Edwardian England* (Oxford, 1990), 689–711; Dinwiddy, 'Campaign against flogging', 319–20.
41 Gatrell, *Hanging Tree*, 595–7.
42 [R. Holloway], *The Phoenix of Sodom, or the Vere Street Coterie* (1813), newspaper clipping pasted in front of BL copy (shelfmark: Cup. 364, p. 12).
43 *Mr William Fuller's Trip to Bridewell, With a True Account of His Barbarous Usage in the Pillory* (1703), 2–4; PRO SP35/44, 30 July–3 August 1723; *London Evening Post*, 27–29 May 1755.
44 PRO SP35/44, 30 July–3 August 1723; 44/290, p. 56.
45 R. Paley, 'Thief-takers in London in the Age of the McDaniel Gang, *c*. 1745–1754', in D. Hay and F. Snyder eds, *Policing and Prosecution in Britain 1750–1850* (Oxford, 1989), 335.
46 [S. Emlyn, ed.], *A Complete Collection of State Trials* (6 vols, 1730), i, p. xi.
47 *The Daily Universal Register* (*The Times*), 28 Nov. 1786, 2c.
48 PRO T90/165 (London and Middlesex, 1787); *General Advertiser*, 22 Nov. 1786.
49 CLRO PAR Book 4, pp. 459ff.
50 Cockburn, 'Punishment and brutalization', 171–2.
51 *The Original Weekly Journal*, 25 July 1719; B. R. Burg, *Sodomy and the Perception of Evil: English Sea Rovers in the Seventeenth-Century Caribbean* (New York and London, 1983), 35–6. According to the *Weekly Journal, or Saturday's Post* (25 July 1719), he was also pelted with cats.
52 PRO SP35/44, 30 July–3 August 1723; *Mr William Fuller's Trip to Bridewell*, 1–7; *The Life of Infamous Actions of that Perjur'd Villain John Waller*, 29; *Phoenix of Sodom*; and A.W. Simpson, 'Masculinity and Control: The Prosecution of Sex Offences in Eighteenth-Century London' (PhD, New York University, 1984), 732–59 and appendix iv; *The Times*, 28 Sept. 1810.
53 *Gentleman's Magazine*, L (1780), 243; LI (1781), 61; PRO T1/556/390; Smith, 'Decline of Public Physical Punishment', 33.
54 Colquhoun, *Treatise*, 18. See also *The Duty of Constables* (Gloucester, 1790), 35.
55 P.R. Backsheider, *Daniel Defoe, His Life* (Baltimore and London, 1989), 118; *Gentleman's Magazine*, XXXV (1765), 96; W. Cobbett, *Weekly Political Register*, xxi, no. 24 (13 June 1812), 748.

56 *Gentleman's Magazine*, XXVI (1756), 166.
57 BL Add. MSS 27826, p. 180.
58 Cobbett, *Weekly Political Register*, 750.
59 BL Add. MSS. 27826, 179. Frost's ill-health was used to justify this decision: PRO T90/168 (1793); *The Times*, 6 and 19 Dec. 1793; J. Epstein, 'Spatial practices/democratic vistas', *SH*, XXIV (1999), 300.
60 [T. Talfourd], 'Brief Observations on the Punishment of the Pillory' (1814), in *The Pamphleteer: Respectfully Dedicated to Both Houses of Parliament*, (London 1814), iv, 534, 538, 548; Smith, 'Decline of Public Physical Punishment', 34–7.
61 These calculations are based on an 4 per cent sample of the hundreds of thousands of recognizances in the Middlesex sessions rolls over the period from 1701 to 1779 which identified 516 incidents of defendants accused of raising or participating in mobs and tumults. The sample consisted of one meeting of the court every other year (the court met twelve times a year, including meetings of the Westminster sessions). This calculation does not include the smaller jurisdictions of the City of London and Southwark. The trends identified are thus only indicative, and cannot be assumed to represent a precise indication of patterns of change. LMA MJ/SR/1972-3376.
62 Ingram, 'Juridical folklore', 81–2.
63 *London Evening Post*, 15–17 October 1761.
64 *London Evening Post*, 28 April and 3 November 1761; *General Evening Post*, 12 Feb. 1771.
65 Simpson, 'Masculinity and Control', 732.
66 Beattie, *Crime and the Courts*, 463; LMA MJ/SBB/1058, 49–50 (Dec. 1748); *Complete Collection of State Trials*, i, xi.
67 LMA WJ/SP/1768/10/35. See also MJ/SP/1749/07/17; MJ/SP/1751/01/19; MJ/SP/1760/10, bundle six (petition of George Steed).
68 King, *Crime, Justice and Discretion*, 351; *The Daily Universal Register* (*The Times*), 7 June 1786.
69 *R.* v. *Ford*, 2 Salk. 390, in *The English Reports* (178 vols; London and Edinburgh, 1900–32), xci, 595. In 1755 the same principle was extended to those punished by whipping: *Pendock* v. *MacKender*, 2 Wils. 18, *English Reports*, xcv, 662.
70 R. McGowen, 'From pillory to gallows: the punishment of forgery in the age of the financial revolution', *P&P*, clxv (1999), 123, 135.
71 Forbes, 'Study of Old Bailey Sentences', 33.
72 *London Evening Post*, 4–6 March 1756.
73 LMA OB/SP/Oct. 1786, no. 64.
74 BL Add MSS. 27826, fos 172–3.
75 *Exaltation! The Throne. The Pillory* [1820?], BL 1850.c.6 (98) (emphasis in original).
76 For late eighteenth-century depictions of the pillory, see the Guildhall Library image database, at http://collage.nhil.com/, especially image numbers 18297, 18842, 18849–51; and 'The Pillory at Charing Cross' by Rowlandson and Pugin (1809), LMA SC/PZ/WE/02/167.
77 PRO SP35/44, 30 July–3 August 1723.
78 BL Add MSS. 27826, fo. 174.
79 *The Times*, 27 July 1796, 3c and 6 July 1797, 3a.
80 *London Evening Post*, 27 Oct. 1761.
81 Shoemaker, 'Decline of public insult'; D.T. Andrew, 'The press and public apologies in eighteenth-century London', in N. Landau, ed., *Law, Crime and English Society* (Cambridge, 2002), 208–29.

82 *This is not the Thing: or, Molly Exalted* (1763?] (LMA SC/PZ/MUSIC/UNCAT); R. Norton, *Mother Clap's Molly House: The Gay Subculture in England, 1700–1830* (1992), 130.

83 J.R. Moore, *Defoe in the Pillory and Other Studies* (Indiana University Publications, Bloomington, 1939), 5; E.H.W. Meyerstein, 'Daniel, the pope and the devil. A caricaturist's portrait of the true Defoe', *Times Literary Supplement*, 15 Feb. 1936, 134. See also *The Scribbler's Doom* (1703); *The True-Born Huguenot* (1703). For another example of a broadside designed to encourage the crowd to mistreat someone on the pillory, see *Trincalo Sainted; or the Exaltation of the Jesuit's Implement and Printer General, the Notorious Nathaniel Thompson, on the Present 5th of July 1682. The Day of his ... Enthroning on the Pillory* (1682).

84 D. Defoe, *A Hymm to the Pillory* (1703), 4.

85 R. Straus, *The Unspeakable Curll: Being Some Account of Edmund Curll, Bookeseller; to Which is Added a Full List of His Books* (1927), 120–1. I am indebted to Karen Harvey for this reference.

86 *Ibid.; The Curll Papers. Stray Notes on the Life and Publications of Edmund Curll. From Notes and Queries* (privately printed, 1879), 68 [BL shelfmark 10827.aa.32]; L. Jewitt, 'The pillory, and who they put in it', *The Reliquary*, I (1860–61), 222.

87 *General Evening Post*, 18 July 1771.

88 Of course, the printed word had been used to shape political reputations for more than a century, but what was new in the late eighteenth century was the use of print to defend and attack the reputations of ordinary people. See A. Fox, *Oral and Literate Culture in England, 1500–1700* (Oxford, 2000).

89 Shoemaker, 'Decline of public insult', 126–30; C. Muldrew, *The Economy of Obligation: The Culture of Credit and Social Relations in Early Modern England* (Basingstoke, 1998), 156, 329–30; M. Mascuch, *Origins of the Individualist Self. Autobiography and Self Identity in England, 1591–1791* (Cambridge, 1997).

90 M. Tebbut, *Women's Talk: A Social History of 'Gossip' in Working-Class Neighbourhoods, 1880–1960* (Aldershot, 1995); J. Walkowitz, 'Male vice and feminist virtue: feminism and the politics of prostitution in nineteenth-century Britain', *HWJ*, xiii (1982), 86.

10
Peel, Pardon and Punishment: The Recorder's Report Revisited

*Simon Devereaux**

Few English statesmen have been subjected to as substantial a shift in historical reputation in recent years as Sir Robert Peel. Only two years after Norman Gash completed his massive two-volume biography, Derek Beales struck the first blow at Peel's status, amongst other things as the great reformer of English criminal law during his two terms at the Home Office during the 1820s, arguing that the real changes were made by the Whig ministries of 1830 and beyond.[1] Boyd Hilton has demonstrated that, in economic matters as well as his personal penal philosophy, Peel was more often dogmatic than flexible, clinging to the established ways of doing things until the last possible moment.[2] The latest and most forceful blow has come in V.A.C. Gatrell's *The Hanging Tree* (1994), which concludes with an extended portrait of Peel's seemingly unremitting severity in enforcing the letter of England's still extensive capital code down to 1830 at least.[3]

This chapter, while endorsing many of the points that have been raised concerning Peel's Home Secretaryship, argues that he is still largely deserving of his reputation as a reformer of the criminal law's practice as well as its letter. It does so through a study of the unique pardon procedure which, from the 1690s until 1837, prevailed in the largest of England's criminal jurisdictions: metropolitan London, comprising of the City of London and the county of Middlesex.[4] This procedure, known as 'the Recorder's Report',

* I am grateful to the Centre for Critical and Cultural Studies at the University of Queensland for a Faculty Research Fellowship during which this article was completed. Earlier research for it was supported by an Izaak Walton Killam Postdoctoral Fellowship and research grants from the University of Queensland. A short version was presented to the 1998 meeting of the North American Conference on British Studies, held in Colorado Springs. For their comments and suggestions on the first full-length draft, I owe thanks to Jerry Bannister, John Beattie, Paul Crook, Paul Griffiths, Philip Harling, Joanna Innes, Randall McGowen, Andrea McKenzie, Allyson N. May, Robert Shoemaker and Greg T. Smith. And I owe special thanks to Vic Gatrell for generously enduring the earlier version and calling my attention to errors in my reading of his work.

consisted of a private meeting of the monarch, the senior members of cabinet, the judicial bench, and the chief sentencing officer of the Old Bailey, an official known as the Recorder of London.[5] 'In no other context', it has been suggested, 'was the power of life and death wielded with such remote and capricious disdain'.[6] In fact, close scrutiny of the available evidence suggests that the conduct of the Report during Peel's tenure of the Home Office (1822–27, 1828–30) was more restrained and more closely-considered than in the years immediately preceding his Home Secretaryship. Moreover, although Peel had no qualms about sending people to the gallows where he thought it warranted, he appears to have been far more sensible of – and responsive to – the increasingly obvious moral and practical limits of England's 'bloody code' than were many of his other Tory colleagues. That sensitivity can be discerned through both a closer analysis of his role in the workings of the gallows in London during the 1820s and in an effort to locate Peel's views on hanging in the wider context of his other reform initiatives, not only in the wider realms of punishment, but also that of police reform.

I

Much of what follows takes issue with the last two chapters of Gatrell's *Hanging Tree*, so let us begin with a core proposition of that book. Gatrell begins by arguing that a statistical survey of the application of England's criminal law over the long term suggests something fundamental about the ultimate reasons for its decisive rolling back in the early nineteenth century. By that time, England's burgeoning population, coupled with a number of legal changes during the previous half-century designed to reduce the costs of prosecuting accused offenders, produced an unprecedented surge in the rate of capital convictions. However, 'It was understood that there was a threshold beyond which the number of executions could not safely pass' without bringing the criminal law into disrepute. In an effort to avoid exceeding that threshold, the proportion of condemned offenders actually put to death soon shrank to so small a scale as to render the system patently ineffective as a deterrent to criminals. The will of England's rulers to enforce the 'bloody code' did not therefore simply retreat in the face of new mentalities regarding the morality or efficacy of capital punishment. Of crucial importance, too, was the sheer pressure of numbers being brought to bear upon these new mentalities. 'The bloody code [therefore] might fairly be said to have collapsed under pressure of the criminal law's mounting prosecutory effectiveness.' The causes of its reform therefore 'were multiple, and only rash historians would privilege material, or political, or cultural causes without interrelating all three'.[7]

The process by which this critical 'pressure upon structures' was felt, however, was neither as steadily linear nor so largely ignored (and even aggressively resisted) by officials as the relevant passages of *The Hanging Tree* seem to suggest. Far greater pressures of this sort, for instance, were both encountered and surmounted by officialdom during the 1780s than in the 1820s.[8] Above all, for present purposes, it is inaccurate to assert that Robert Peel 'let more people hang in the 1820s than any predecessor in office, and he meant to go on killing them'.[9] It must be understood from the outset that we can only really speak of Peel having an immediate hand in the hanging of Old Bailey convicts. Outside London, the circuit judges sent letters to the Home Secretary listing all the convicts at each assizes whom they believed should be pardoned and on what terms, and from 1728 those recommendations, which comprised the vast majority of all pardons granted outside London (as opposed to those subsequently solicited through individual petitions), had been accepted unquestioningly by government.[10] So well-understood had this routine become that in 1823 a law was passed (4 Geo. IV, c 48) that eliminated the increasingly pointless formality of pronouncing sentence of death upon assize convicts whom the judges intended to pardon in their circuit letters.

This legislation did not apply to the convicts of the Old Bailey, however, and it was with them that the Home Secretary's hand was most regularly and heavily felt amongst the thousands of people pardoned in early nineteenth-century England. In their case, Peel was by no means the most bloody-minded of Home Secretaries. Only three of the thirteen men who served in that office before him did so for comparable periods of time. Two of these three, Lord Sydney (1782, 1783–89) and Viscount Sidmouth (1812–22), hanged far more Old Bailey convicts than he did: about 333 and 224 respectively, compared with Peel's 142. And the third, the Duke of Portland (1794–1801), ran him close at about 135 in only seven years compared with Peel's eight. Indeed, in both 1785 and 1787, Sydney managed to hang fully two-thirds as many Old Bailey convicts (97 and 92) as did Peel during his entire eight-year tenure as Home Secretary. We might further note that the annual average of London executions under three other previous Home Secretaries – Lord North (36), William Grenville (21) and Henry Dundas (20) – also exceeded Peel's figure of about 17. Nor did the figure of 14 Londoners hanged during the eight months in 1827 that Peel was out of office depart in the slightest from his annual average.[11]

In the shorter term, however, it can be argued that Peel's sense of mercy seemed distinctly lacking by comparison with at least some of his predecessors. His time at the Home Office was in fact characterized by markedly higher execution levels in London, in both absolute and relative terms, than those which had prevailed during the first decade of the nineteenth century, when the annual number of Old Bailey executions rose no higher than 14 (in 1807) and fell as low as five (in 1803). Indeed, so striking is the change between this decade and the years following the Napoleonic Wars that we should probably speak in terms of there having been something of a 'revival' in the application of the capital code in London in the face of the intense social disorders of that era.

Yet there is another and more immediately relevant yardstick by which Peel might be measured. Execution levels during his Home Secretaryship in fact constituted a significant retreat from the appalling new high-points achieved during the final years of his immediate predecessor, Viscount Sidmouth. We would be wrong to overlook the significance of Lord Chancellor Eldon's remark to Peel in November 1822 that 'Times are gone by when so many Persons can be executed at once as were so dealt with twenty years ago'.[12] Following the executions of that month, there was a marked decline in execution levels in London by comparison with Sidmouth's last two years in office (Table 10.1).

Table 10.1 Capital punishment at the Old Bailey (excluding murder), 1813–37

Year	*Condemned*	*Hanged*	*(% of condemned)*
1813	145	12	(8.3)
1814	139	15	(10.8)
1815	130	8	(6.2)
1816	232	18	(7.8)
1817	201	13	(6.5)
1818	206	20	(9.7)
1819	175	20	(11.4)
1820	197	37	(18.8)
1821	170	30	(17.6)
1822	133	22	(16.5)
1823	127	17	(13.4)
1824	149	11	(7.4)
1825	154	15	(9.7)
1826	196	17	(8.7)
1827	212	17	(8.0)
1828	171	21	(12.3)
1829	147	26	(17.7)
1830	120	3	(2.5)
1831	151	2	(1.3)
1832	127	2	(1.6)
1833	99	1	(1.0)
1834	75	–	–
1835	76	2	(2.6)
1836	67	–	–
1837	55	–	–

Notes: All annual totals in Tables 10.1 and 10.2 express the London mayoral year (that is, November through October) rather than the calendar year. I have excluded those convicted of murder because that crime remained a hanging offence for more than a century after 1830 and therefore does not constitute a reasonable measure of Tory severity. I have also excluded the highly unusual Cato Street Conspirators of 1820. The figures for 1828 include one condemned forger who committed suicide in Newgate the night before his execution.

Sources: Old Bailey Sessions Paper (OBSP); *The Times* of London.

The retreat that took place under Peel's tenure becomes even more apparent when execution rates are expressed not in terms of numbers hanged per year, but rather the number hanged on any given execution day (Table 10.2). Whereas the Recorder's Report under Sidmouth never hanged fewer than three people at a time and averaged between five and six, under Peel it generally hanged no more than three and seldom more than four. In this connection, it is worth emphasizing that the number of people hanged at any given time was the more important element for men of government in calculating the maximum extent to which the capital code could be imposed without provoking public discontent. This calculation had to be made Report-by-Report, six to eight times per year, and our common resort to parliamentary data for annual execution levels will afford us only a crude sense of changing official perspectives on acceptable execution levels.

Averages can be deceptive, too, so we are obliged to suggest reasons why, on five occasions, Peel's Reports hanged more than four people at once. One factor was a purely structural one. Both cases of six people being hanged at once, as well as two others when five people were executed, clearly stemmed in part from the conjunction of two sessions in one Report. If the two Reports had been held separately, the more normal execution day average of two or three might have prevailed. The main explanation for occasional departures from that rule, however, appears to be an even simpler one: some crimes had multiple perpetrators, whose guilt could not be sufficiently distinguished to pardon one without pardoning the others. Of the six people hanged together in November 1822, two had been jointly convicted of sodomy and two others of a burglary. Of the six hanged together three months later, fully four had been convicted of a single burglary. Such cases

Table 10.2 Numbers executed on individual hanging days at the Old Bailey, 1820–30

Year	*One*	*Two*	*Three*	*Four*	*Five*	*Six*	*Seven*	*Eight*	*Avg*
1820	–	–	–	1	2	2	–	1	5–6
1821	–	–	2	2	1	1	–	1	4–5
1822	1	4	1	–	–	1	–	–	2–3
1823	1	–	2	1	–	1	–	–	3–4
1824	2	1	2	–	–	–	–	–	2
1825	1	1	3	1	–	–	–	–	2–3
1826	1	3	–	1	–	1	–	–	2–3
1827	1	2	–	3	–	–	–	–	2–3
1828	1	3	–	1	2	–	–	–	3
1829	1	2	3	3	–	–	–	–	2–3
1830	3	–	–	–	–	–	–	–	1

Note: Again, this table excludes murderers, in this case because, from 1752 until 1832, they were individually hanged on separate days – and the Cato Street conspirators are again excluded.

Sources: As for Table 10.1.

also played the decisive role in putting five men on the gallows together on two occasions in 1828, and even on those four occasions when Peel's Reports sent four men to their deaths.[13]

The kind of reasoning underlying such a practice might undoubtedly seem awful to modern sensibilities, but it is certainly comprehensible. It also reinforces an important point: punishment, for the sake of example, was imposed not so much upon the individual criminals as upon the crime they had committed, and in the absence of any compelling reason to the contrary, consistency demanded that the former had all to pay equally for the latter. Where it is possible to tell from surviving documents, the crimes involved were unusually serious ones. The case of three men (of five) jointly hanged in May 1828 for a single housebreaking incident was deemed to be a 'Bad' one because they had threatened their victims with pistols and tied them up.[14] The Report of July 1829 was thought to be 'the heaviest... ever known', involving 'more cases for serious consideration than [had] occurred for some time'.[15] The seven people it left to hang went to the gallows on two separate days, possibly by deliberate contrivance: four the first day and three others five days' later. Once again, multiple offenders were a factor. Two of the men had been convicted of the same robbery, two others of the same forgery. Peel's departure from Sidmouth's practice of hanging so many people at once could therefore be rendered fragile by circumstances outside his control. A single 'unpardonable' crime, committed by multiple offenders, could drastically alter the practice on a given occasion.

In general, then, it appears that after Peel's arrival at the Home Office in 1822, the Report was consistently conducted in light of an understanding that it had best put no more than three or four people on the gallows at once. The determination to ensure this could sometimes produce some inconsistencies in decision-making which, to a modern sensibility, might well seem bizarre and horrifying. 'I do not like Recorder's reports', the second Lord Ellenborough confided to his diary in June 1828:

> I am shocked by the inequality of punishment. At one time a man is hanged for a crime, which may be as two, because there are few to be hanged, and it is some time since an example has been made of capital punishment for his particular offence. At another time a man escapes for the same crime, having the proportion of five to two to the other, because it is a heavy calendar, and there are many to be executed. The actual delinquency of the individual is comparatively little taken into consideration. Extraneous circumstances determine his fate.

Again, later that same year: '[M]en are punished not with reference to the extent of their own crimes, unless they be very great, but with reference to the number and circumstances of similar crimes committed by others at the same time.'[16] But Ellenborough was surely mistaken if he regarded the conducting of the Report, first, so as to punish serious crimes at times when they seemed to be at unacceptably high levels, and second, to do so in a manner that did not provoke contempt for the criminal law, as entirely wrong-minded. Such considerations were not 'extraneous circumstances'; they were, as we have recently been reminded, of the essence in that 'rich and finely tuned field of discretionary justice' which England's criminal law comprised until the reforms of the late 1820s and after.[17]

In any case, before we take Ellenborough to be an advocate of a modern emphasis on consistency in punishment, it should be borne in mind that his real object in lamenting the conduct of the Report appears to have been a belief that it should be hanging *more* offenders, not less. 'There were at least ten cases in which the punishment of death ought to have been inflicted', he said of the Report held on 7 May 1828, but 'We chose [only] six'.[18] The Duke of Wellington, too, once deemed 'six only' to be a poor showing for a Report that had reviewed so 'many… atrocious cases… .[19] Parliamentary critics of the capital code thought that a law which prescribed death for an offence but whose administrators seldom or never imposed it was self-defeating as a deterrent, but most Tory ministers were determined to retain the option of hanging for those times when the crime in question might again assume dangerous proportions, and many of them would clearly have been glad to hang more than the Report under Peel usually allowed. And indeed, although Ellenborough thought the Report 'a very difficult and painful duty' of government and one that he wished did not fall to their lot, he finally concluded that he and his colleagues carried it out 'most conscientiously'.[20] If Ellenborough seemed of two minds about the competing claims of certainty and proportion in punishment by comparison with the need to keep hangings to an acceptable level, it is surely because by the 1820s many other English people were similarly confused, as we will see in the last part of this chapter.

Any bald assertion that Peel 'meant to go on killing' people faces a final objection, at least so far as the London context is concerned. From 1830 onwards, execution levels in the Old Bailey, especially when murder is discounted, were vastly reduced by comparison with the prevailing practices of the 1820s (Table 10.1). Historians critical of Peel have noted that a sharp distinction should be made between Tory governments and their post-1830 Whig successors so far as their respective determination to impose capital punishment was concerned.[21] In the case of London, however, they have missed where another significant line might be drawn. The election prompted by George IV's death on 26 June 1830 returned a Tory majority, albeit a fragile and fractious one, and the government did not fall until November, by which time all the Recorder's Reports for that year had been held. Thus, it was in fact Peel and not his Whig successors who initiated (however late in the day) the decisive pre-abolition rolling back from 1830 onwards. The Whigs' subsequent conduct of the capital code at the Old Bailey was not a renunciation of Peel's legacy, but the clear continuation of its final form. How this significant transformation came about, and Peel's role in it, are subjects that bear closer consideration, but first let us see if we cannot move beyond the bare statistical patterns enumerated here and consider some of the indirect indications of the nature of the Recorder's Report.

II

None of what has been said so far does much to mitigate the fact that Peel and his fellow ministers were more than comfortable with imposing the law's ultimate sanction in a manner that modern legal and humane sensibilities, with their emphasis on consistency of principle and (for most of the Western world) abhorrence of the death penalty, will easily find repellent. We must simply accept the fact that none of these men appear to have questioned their right to impose death on a wide range of criminal activities. Omission to impose that sentence in one instance was a mercy for which a convict might hope, but it was not a right upon which they could presume. The real question is, what quality of decision-making actually prevailed in the Recorder's Reports of the 1820s? In the absence either of formal minutes or the actual documents prepared by the Recorder himself, this is a topic that remains almost entirely shrouded in mystery. Outside the bare legal records of convict lists and petitions, we are almost entirely confined to a tiny handful of peripheral participants' observations, and these observations, as we have seen, are none too promising as testimony to the Report's quality in terms of consistency. The main object here is to consider the significant body of peripheral and circumstantial evidence which suggests that the quality of decision-making that prevailed at the Recorder's Report may actually have been considerably better than has recently been suggested.[22]

In the first place we must try to identify how decisions were made at the Report and whose voice carried the greatest weight. One attendee reported in 1829 that the council's final decisions sometimes went 'to the vote, and [were] decided by the voices of the majority', but the context of this quote suggests that this practice was in fact uncommon.[23] By comparison, the importance of the Lord Chancellor's advice is repeatedly made clear in correspondence regarding the scheduling of the Report; there are many occasions on which it had to be arranged in light of his attendance in Chancery or the House of Lords.[24] Moreover, Lord Eldon, who was Lord Chancellor almost continuously from 1801 to 1827, frequently remarked to Peel and others on how often he had gone over the evidence of each case prior to the meeting of the Report.[25] Indeed, Eldon may have had some hand in the moderated execution levels of the 1820s. We have already noted his 1822 remark to Peel on the need to keep those levels in check. He also commented on many occasions about how much more often than his colleagues he tended towards mercy in the Report, and his remark that the Recorder of London, Newman Knowlys, 'is much more bloody minded than I am' (a view corroborated by others) suggests that the effort to keep numbers down was primarily the work of Eldon and Peel.[26] It may in fact have been the case that Peel's most important contribution to the Report came *after* its meetings, when it fell solely to him to defend its decisions against further petitioning and critical scrutiny.[27] On the other hand, if Eldon played a role in initiating the relative restraint of the 1820s, he must presumably have also been instrumental in the much harsher gallows discipline of the first years of that decade, and his departure after 1827 did not signal any obvious alteration the Report's conduct during the last year's of Tory governance. The general impression, that the Lord Chancellor, the Recorder and the Home Secretary exercised the preeminent influence in shaping the conduct of the Report, is further reinforced when it is noted that the Report's major resource for accounts of the cases they heard (other than the written report read by the Recorder himself), the printed account of trials known as the Old Bailey Sessions Paper, was not generally made available to anyone else in the cabinet until 1829.[28]

Correspondence relating to the Lord Chancellor's activity prior to its meeting suggests that the Report itself was a far more comprehensive and considered process than previous accounts have suggested. One might assume, from the large number of cases that came before each meeting (from one to three dozen for each sessions), that each convict received short shrift. In fact, pre-Report correspondence between the Recorder, the Lord Chancellor and Peel reveal that it was invariably understood that most cases did not involve 'serious' crimes, would not lead to execution, and therefore did not need to be discussed at all at the Report. Only a handful of cases needed to be considered for execution, and the Report could therefore concentrate all its time and attention upon these problematic decisions. '[T]here are thirteen Cases', Peel was informed of the forthcoming Report of the July sessions for 1824, 'of which not more than three would be read – one of Burglary – one of Horsestealing, and the other of forging a Banker's Cheque under Circumstances of great distress'.[29] The convicts in question were unusually lucky: none of them was hanged. Again, in January 1826, Eldon reported to Peel that in the forthcoming Report 'I don't read one Case in which the Law should take its Course', and indeed, once again, no-one was hanged from the sessions in question.[30] On the other hand, the Report of 36 condemned convicts for September 1822 had to be postponed because 'The Recorder himself will not be ready for a fortnight...and as the Report is a very heavy one, it will take some time to peruse and consider all the documents relating to it.'[31] Seven of these people were hanged. Four years later, Eldon sent a letter regarding another forthcoming Report which is suggestive of the care and attention to detail which might sometimes be taken there:

> The Report must, I think, be a very long one, if the Case of the last Report of the Convict for the Bethnal Green Robbery, and also the Report of the

> present Session of [James] Bishop for a Bethnal Green Robbery, is read at length. Read at length it must be, I think, for Bishop is convicted upon Mr Fuller's Oath as to the Identity of his Person, when three Persons are acquitted, equally sworn by him, as to whom (the whole three) the Jury thought him mistaken. Bishop, and the Convict of the last Session must, I think, have a Right to have the whole Evidence read as to the three acquitted, in order to see whether the King can safely act as to those persons upon the Verdicts against them, produced by Fuller's Evidence the others are acquitted.[32]

Bishop was left to die at the Report but subsequently pardoned. Other instances may be cited indicating that government officials did not expect the Report to be rushed in any way. Many letters stress the likelihood of its being prolonged by the number of serious cases requiring close attention, and most Reports seem to have lasted several hours.[33] Even then, there are numerous instances of certain cases being held over for consideration at the next Report, either because more evidence was required or because there simply was not enough time to review the evidence already in hand before making a decision as to life or death.[34]

It should be noted, moreover, that the devotion of such lengths of time to the close consideration of so few cases appears to have been a relatively recent development. It was certainly a vast improvement over the practice which had prevailed only 40 years earlier. The contrast between the conduct of the Reports of the 1780s and those of the 1820s is particularly significant because the former decade was the last time prior to the latter in which comparably large numbers of cases came before each sitting of the Report. That which was held on 22 August 1783, which reviewed the cases of 13 men and resolved to hang eight of them, kept King George III and his ministers occupied for only 75 minutes (and one newspaper of the time reckoned this to be 'an unusual length of time'). Another held in October of the same year was disposed of more swiftly still. On that occasion, a bare hour was deemed sufficient time in which to decide to hang 10 of 12 capital convicts.[35] Such expedience should not be surprising in light of a policy, implemented for a time from September 1782 onwards, of hanging without exception all those convicted of robbery. But not everyone whose case was considered at these Reports had committed that crime, and such exceptions to that rule as soon were made must presumably have been decided upon after at least some measure of discussion and consideration.[36] Moreover, the duration of these Reports is perfectly congruent with one of 1775 which reviewed 15 cases and resolved within the space of one hour to hang six people.[37] By comparison with examples such as these, the conduct of the Report under Peel (or even Sidmouth for that matter), in which it was routinely understood long before the council gathered that most of the capital convicts would not face the noose, thus leaving several hours for the Report to review in detail a handful of more problematic cases, looks a model of scrupulous care.

III

Whatever else one might want to say about George III and his readiness to let so many of his subjects be hanged, he at least seems to have regarded the business of Recorder's Reports as being serious enough to warrant his remaining awake throughout their – in his case, admittedly, usually brief – duration. His successor, confronted with a far more detailed and time-consuming procedure, was not so scrupulous. Those who want to see the Report in the worst possible light have evoked a vision of George IV dozing indifferently while the fates of his less fortunate subjects were decided. It is of course by no means clear that even so indolent and self-indulgent a monarch as 'Prinny' fell asleep during each and every Report. Sadly, however, his having done so on at least three separate occasions is only too well-documented.[38] But the image of a dozing monarch need not be taken as a reflection of the dismal quality of decision-making at the Report. Enough has been said already about both the length of Reports and the attention to detail which they involved to provide a more than adequate explanation as to why a man of George IV's character might soon have found himself bored to the point of somnolence.[39] The more interesting question surely is why none of his ministers seem to have thought it necessary to bother to wake him.

The simple answer to this question is that, by the 1820s, the need to ensure the presence of the king at the Report was more often a problem than a benefit. I am not thinking here of the troubles caused by the king's occasional, half-hearted efforts to secure pardons for convicted criminals. Those few instances in which George IV roused himself to a show of concern for the fate of Old Bailey convicts almost always arose only after the Report had been held, when it was expected that only the appearance of compelling new evidence should warrant reconsideration of any case. During the Report itself, so far as we can tell, the king seems to have remained largely silent (when awake).[40] Getting him there in the first place, however, often proved a taxing chore for his ministers.

The king delayed and prevaricated over the scheduling of Reports on many occasions, routinely pleading the vicissitudes of the royal health, an excuse which his ministers sometimes viewed with scepticism. 'Is it ascertained that the Royal Gout has so far left him that *he* can attend?' Eldon once asked of Peel.[41] On one occasion the king underscored both the purported frailties of his constitution and the undue strain which he believed the Report to impose upon it by stating his intention to 'receive the Council in his Frocks'.[42] On yet another, his physician informed Peel that the Report had to be scheduled to suit the royal convenience so far as the king's determination to 'visit all of the Theatres' one week and to depart for Brighton the next were concerned.[43] The low point in this sorry saga of monarchical obstreperousness came near the end of the king's life, when he allowed his personal detestation of the Common Serjeant, obliged to deliver the Report because the Recorder himself was ill, to forbid his attending him because the man in question, Sir Thomas Denman, had spoken against the king during the proceedings against Queen Caroline in 1820 (and despite Denman's having offered, and the king's having accepted, the former's 'humble apology' for doing so only the year before).[44] The Report in question, already three weeks overdue, was a particularly pressing necessity, as it encompassed not only the cases of the October sessions just past but also six others from the previous September for which there had not been sufficient time to arrive at a satisfactory decision during the last Report.[45] Yet still the king stood on his pride, petulantly expressing to Wellington his 'extreme surprise' that he should be expected 'to submit to the indignity of receiving the Common Serjeant ... when you cannot fail to know the insult which I have received from that individual, and you ought to know the firmness of my character in not bearing an insult from any human being with impunity'.[46] The king preferred to receive the Report from the Deputy Recorder, stamping and storming before Wellington, who in vain emphasized the need for three men awaiting report to be hanged for the sake of example. Eventually the king got his way; the Report was not heard until Christmas Eve.[47] '[R]eally', remarked an appalled outsider at the time, 'if [such] personal exclusions are to be allowed, and personal caprice to weigh ... and the King is humoured in these things, we might as well be living in Algiers'.[48]

Such delays were not merely personally irritating or offensive to Peel and his colleagues, though on more than one occasion the king clearly meant them to be particularly annoying to Peel, whom he loathed.[49] Routine sittings of the Recorder's Report were essential in an era when, with 20 to 40 capital convictions at each Old Bailey sessions, there were serious risks of disease and disorder in a now routinely overcrowded Newgate prison.[50] More importantly, they threatened to erode or altogether to destroy the lesson in social discipline which was the principal rationale for public execution. It was established practice for the Report of the convicts of each Old Bailey sessions to be held immediately before the following sessions had concluded. (Trials were held eight times yearly until the jurisdiction of the court was reorganized in November 1834, after which they were held monthly.) For example, the Report for the January 1823 sessions was held on Friday, 21 February, two days after the February sessions had commenced, and the resultant executions were held the following Wednesday the 26th, the day before those sessions ended.[51] On this occasion, when one of the king's attacks of gout threatened to jeopardize the scheduling of the Report, Peel was careful to emphasize to the royal physician that 'as the Sessions at the Old Bailey, being the Third [to be held without a Report], will Commence next week, it is as well that you should be apprized of it, and perhaps should mention the Circumstance to His Majesty, whenever you think that He can without Pain undertake the Journey' to London.[52] Although I have found no comment on this strategy amongst the manuscripts of contemporaries, its object seems clear enough: to establish, and regularly to reiterate, a clear connection in the public's minds-eye between the processes of trial and execution. A survey of contemporary periodicals reveals that this pattern of scheduling was established from the accession of George III in 1760, and it appears to have been well-known to contemporaries by the end of the eighteenth century.[53] By comparison, during the reign of George II (1727–60) when the Report was often heard by a small body of ministers known as the Lords Justices during the monarch's frequent and prolonged absences in his Hanoverian homeland, it was generally the case that two and sometimes three sessions were allowed to accumulate before a single Report was held to hear all their cases at one sitting.[54]

This move away from the practice of allowing successive sessions to accumulate for a single Report probably did not reflect a more tender official regard for the mental and emotional agonies that a condemned offender, uncertain of his or her ultimate fate, might have to endure for months rather than weeks – surely a fine distinction at best for anyone at the time who might actually have responded to such considerations. Rather it was probably intended to enhance and sustain the theatrical potency of the execution ritual in London. In the first place, it was important that Reports and their consequent executions be held near enough to the sessions from whence they arose in order that the public might remember the specific names and crimes of those sent to the gallows. Thus, when the sessions for December 1816 and January 1817 had been allowed to go unreported before the onset of those for February 1817, a grand jury investigating the state of Newgate Prison complained 'that there are 101 male and female convicts under sentence of death, and that the congregating such a number increases their depravity, *besides the ends of justice being defeated, so far as regards example, by the particulars of each case being forgotten*' by the public at large.[55] Secondly, it seems to have been hoped that the moral lessons of the capital code would be further reinforced by holding the Report of each sessions immediately before or during the next, so that everyone – the general public, as well as the condemned and other criminals of the current sessions – would witness the salutary example of a hanging either during or soon after the current trials. (This was surely why the ministry allowed the two sessions just mentioned to continue unreported until three days into the next sessions.) Since the middle of the eighteenth century, then, it appears to have been an article of faith amongst officials that temporal concentration was vital to the social and psychological efficacy of the capital code in London.[56]

If we are correct in contending that Peel was sensitive to the need to maintain a reasonably coherent and 'acceptable' numerical distribution of executions, then by the 1820s there must surely have been a third important consideration demanding a timely turnover in Reports. If two or more Reports were allowed to accumulate, Peel and his fellow ministers would be confronted with an extremely serious difficulty, namely that strict adherence to prevailing practice might oblige the Report to execute far fewer convicts than either principles of consistency or the prevalence of particular crimes might otherwise demand. It was exactly this sort of confluence, of two sessions comprising 53 convicts, that prompted Eldon's caution to Peel against hanging too many people.[57] That Report may have been deliberately delayed further to preclude the resultant executions taking place during the same week as the Lord Mayor's Day celebrations in the City of London. '[P]erhaps', Peel's under-secretary suggested to him, 'you would wish to avoid the display of Executions and festivities so near together'.[58]

All such vital calculations regarding the public impact and acceptability of the Newgate execution ritual were fundamentally jeopardized every time the monarch failed to produce himself for the Report in timely fashion, but George IV seems seldom to have paid such subtle considerations of governance any heed, even from the outset of his reign. 'The King [remains] still at Brighton', wrote one well-informed observer in March 1820,

> and deaf to the entreaties of his ministers that he would return to town where three Recorder's Reports are waiting... It is a sad thing in these times, when the personal character of the Sovereign might do so much towards tranquilizing the country, that nothing can persuade him to attend to business and cease to make himself ridiculous at his years.

Near the end of his reign, this same observer used the occasion of another shocking royal delay in hearing the Report to pronounce an epitaph on his reign: 'The fact is that he is a spoiled, selfish, odious beast, and has no idea of doing anything but what is agreeable to himself, or of there being any duties attached to the office he holds.'[59] By comparison, George's younger brother, William IV, seemed a blessed relief, readily agreeing to his Lord Chancellor's suggestion in November 1834 that the Reports 'ought to be made to him more frequently' (as indeed they would need to be under the recently-passed Central Criminal Court Act) and without reference to his 'personal convenience'. 'Was that not well done by our Billy', remarked an official of the time, compared to his brother 'the *Tourist*'?[60]

Why then did Peel and his colleagues persist in a system so easily threatened, and sometimes thwarted, by an uncooperative monarch? Why not simply remove the king altogether from the decision-making process in London, just as he had been almost entirely removed from that of the assizes almost a century beforehand? The fact of the matter was that no one knew precisely why the practice of the Recorder's Report before king and council had arisen in the first place, so the Tories were uncertain if they were empowered to discontinue it. The issue was canvassed among themselves in

February 1828, when there were 'already two [Reports] waiting for [the king], and a third coming in a short time, while Newgate is full, and the prisoners in a state of disorder', a situation which had provoked questions in the House of Commons. At that time, some statesmen seem to have believed that the Report stemmed from an obligation on the monarch personally to decide pardons for the jurisdiction in which he resided, and thus that the Report could not be held at Windsor as the king desired.[61] This posed an interesting question as to whether he might be obliged to determine pardons for any other part of the nation in which he might happen to be residing at assizes time. (Once, when George IV was passing through Gloucester, one of the presiding judges presumed this to be the case. 'What'! the horrified king was said to have cried, 'am I to be followed all over the country with the Recorder's report'?[62]) One senior Tory wondered 'whether the King's intervention was necessary at all, as his Secretary of State might do in the London and Middlesex cases as in those of the Circuits'.[63] In the event, however, the remaining Reports of the reign were held at Windsor to suit the ailing king's convenience and at what must have been considerable trouble for busy government ministers based in London. It was only in late June 1830, when George IV was on his death-bed, that Peel finally set his under-secretary the task of seeking out the origins of the Report. That effort came to nothing, however, the under secretary concluding simply (and vaguely) that it appeared 'to be one of the early Privileges of the City of London, of which the origin is lost in obscure antiquity'.[64]

It fell to the Whigs, during the seven years left to the Report, to make more aggressive attempts to bring its practice to an end, specifically on the grounds that allowing so obvious a variation in procedure to London convicts violated the principles of growing centralization and uniformity of practice in legal administration. Twice in 1832 they tabled legislation that would have applied to Old Bailey convicts the Act of 1823 which enabled judges to forbear pronouncing sentence of death in those cases where it was understood the death penalty would not ultimately be applied – a measure which would simply have formalized in law the practice that had long prevailed of acknowledging, before the Report met, which cases were not actually going to end in hanging.[65] This was resisted by the Tories in the House of Lords as an invasion of royal prerogative, but the Whigs returned to the question two years later in an abortive clause of the Central Criminal Court Act of 1834, and yet again during the final months of William IV's reign when, in the Second Report of the Commission on Municipal Corporations, it was asserted that 'We cannot discover any peculiar advantage in the practice of reporting the capital convictions at the Old Bailey to [His] Majesty in Council, if such a practice is not thought necessary in respect of capital convictions in any other part of the Kingdom.'[66] It may well have been the case, as Lord Ellenborough insisted years later, that the Report was finally abolished at Queen Victoria's accession two months later (by 1 Vict., c77) because the 'penalty of death ... [still] attached to certain ... crimes, which it was then deemed improper to bring under the notice of a youthful Queen'.[67] Moreover substantive reforms to the capital code made that same year effectively reduced the number of cases to be heard at the Report to so small a number that persistence in the procedure may have seemed not only indecent but ludicrously archaic.[68] We would be wrong, however, to neglect the Whigs' powerful attraction to an opportunity of smashing one element, however reduced in practical scope it had become by 1830, of the power and prestige of the nation's preeminent corporate power. (And Ellenborough, after all, was a Tory and liable to put the best possible face on such a diminution of the royal prerogative.) But we have moved well-ahead of ourselves, in cultural if not temporal distance. Suffice it to say that the slumbers of King George IV do not necessarily suggest the poor quality of decision-making which might have prevailed at the Report. Rather, they were probably induced in him precisely by the time-consuming care and detail with which the Report was being conducted by the 1820s. They were surely also indicative, most fundamentally, of the increasing irrelevance of the monarch to its processes.

IV

The constant theme of all considerations surrounding the Recorder's Report was the central importance that Peel and his colleagues attached to hanging as a means to deter serious criminality. We cannot understand the competing claims they entertained upon the lives or deaths of Old Bailey convicts without acknowledging this fact. Some Tories, like Ellenborough and Wellington, believed unquestioningly in the deterrent value of hanging and would gladly have sent more people to the gallows than the Reports of the 1820s finally allowed. 'Twenty-six magistrates at Canterbury sentenced to three days' imprisonment threshing machine breakers who pleaded guilty'! snorted Ellenborough in October 1829. 'Such has been the terror struck into them'![69] Others, like Peel and Eldon, seem clearly to have recognized the need to maximize the deterrent message of execution by minimizing the numbers put to it in an effort to avoid triggering public outcries against the cruelty or apparent pointlessness of such displays. In the end, this was a balancing act in which the Tories were on the losing side, and no member of government appears to have been more conscious of this fact than Peel himself.

Within a year of assuming the Home Secretaryship, Peel had become persuaded of the urgent necessity to enhance the deterrent force of the criminal law at every level. 'I propose to bring in a Bill empowering the crown to send a Convict Ship to any of the Foreign Settlements, and thus to unite Transportation, Hard Labour, and the Discipline of the Hulks', he informed the attorney general in February 1823. 'I think this would be considered a more severe Punishment next to Death, than any that is at present employed.'[70]

Peel's intention that transportation and the hulks be made more imposing punishments was soon implemented. The search for places 'more oppressive and more effectual in subduing the refractory or turbulent spirits' amongst convicts sent to New South Wales had already been instigated by the colonial Office in 1820, and by 1825 new penal settlements were opened at sub-tropical Moreton Bay as well as Norfolk Island.[71] In 1824 an even more oppressive new hulks establishment was opened in Bermuda.[72] Peel similarly hoped that ending the pronouncement of death sentence upon convicts whom the judges intended to pardon would 'make the passing of that Sentence on offenders whom it is intended to execute Much More Solemn and impressive'.[73] In the early 1820s, then, Peel clearly believed deterrence to be the most important of penal purposes at every level of the penal order, not just hanging.

Most surprisingly, perhaps, this appears to have been true even of imprisonment, a measure with which Peel's name is often closely associated given that he presided over the passage of the first acts extensively to prescribe uniform standards for all English gaols (4 Geo. IV, c 64). In fact, as even his biographer noted, this measure had been inherited by Peel from his predecessor, and '[i]n placing it on the statute book Peel had acted more as a midwife than as parent'.[74] He seems indeed to have been far less sympathetic to the penal value of confinement than was the supposedly more brutal-minded Sidmouth. Peel had little or no time for the notion that criminals might be reformed. His comment to Elizabeth Fry, following a visit to the women's ward at Newgate in the spring of 1823, is shot through with careful reserve and qualification:

> I witnessed with great pleasure the very decorous behaviour of those who attended prayers, and I had every evidence which exterior Deportment could afford during a short visit, that a great and awful impression had been made on the minds of probably very depraved Characters, by the habit of daily attendance on Divine Worship, and by feelings of gratitude for [your] unremitting and disinterested kindness.[75]

With a close colleague, Chancellor of the Exchequer, he was more forthright. 'I am not enamoured of the Penitentiary system', he wrote Henry Goulburn, '[t]he Penitents are, at best, generally speaking Idle hypocrites'.[76] Peel's detailed inquiries at this time as to the effects of the treadmill, and the vast amount of material on that subject that has survived amongst his papers, are surely indicative of a determination on his part that imprisonment, too, should carry with it a more awesome deterrent value.[77] On this score, then, Vic Gatrell is absolutely right when he asserts that Peel sought to make the criminal law 'more efficient, even more punitive – more of a terror, not less'.[78]

It would be misleading, however, to concentrate solely upon Peel's punitive frame of mind, because Peel himself came to abandon his faith in the effectiveness (though not, admittedly, the deservedness) of all penal measures. By March 1826, he had concluded that all his efforts to reduce crime by enhanced deterrent measures had failed. '[T]he whole subject of what is called secondary punishment is full of difficulty', he confided to Sydney Smith. All the new transportation, hulks and imprisonment measures did not seem to detract 'from the vast harvest of transportable crime that is reaped at every assize', nor could he imagine any others that might. 'The real truth is that the number of convicts is too overwhelming for the means of proper and effectual punishment. I despair of any remedy but that which I wish I could hope for – a great reduction in the amount of crime'.[79] By the end of that same year, Peel was beginning to make plans for a measure that did indeed aim largely to bypass the whole vexed and futile question of effective punishments: the creation of a preventative police force in London, which he viewed as a 'decisive measure' for the reduction of crime there. 'Forty-six [capital] Convictions at one Sessions', he concluded in first announcing his new strategy to a colleague, 'What further proof can be requisite that the present system is defective?'[80] This referred to the Old Bailey sessions of September 1826, the final occasion on which he allowed six people to be executed together. From this time onwards, his attention was focused primarily upon preventing crime in the first instance rather than seeking to deter it by new, more closely calibrated impositions of the death penalty and harsher secondary penal regimes, and it is surely no coincidence that the pressure on the Old Bailey's gallows was released, as we have seen, in 1830 (Table 10.1), the first full year in which his New Police were at work on the streets of the metropolis.[81]

It might be argued that Peel's apparent awareness of the increasing futility of the capital code by the mid-1820s makes his persistence in imposing the death penalty thereafter the more shocking and contemptible. Securing passage of the new police bill was not to be an easy matter politically, however, and even after three years of careful groundwork, his ultimate success therein still owed as much to a lucky confluence of circumstances as to his political skill.[82] Yet there can be no escaping the fact that Peel had no compunction about sending people to their deaths, and undoubtably Gatrell and Hilton are correct to believe that he simply did not see anything immoral in this. He was indeed an 'ethical pessimist'.[83] By the same token, however, it might fairly be pointed out that the desire to retain the letter, if not the strict practice, of the capital code, if only for the most exemplary instances of certain crimes, was not confined to the Tories of the 1820s. In 1840 such prominent Whigs as Sir James Graham and even Earl Grey himself 'deprecated the [1837] alteration in the penal code, which diminished the number of crimes punished capitally', and four decades later still, Sir James Fitzjames Stephen was still making the same case. '[W]e have gone too far in laying [the punishment of death] aside', he argued in his *History of the Criminal Law of England* (1883), suggesting that hanging should be revived for some 'political offences', in 'cases which outrage the moral feelings of the community to a great degree', and for carefully-selected 'receivers of stolen goods, habitual cheats, and ingenious forgers'.[84] By these lights, Peel's caution in reducing the effective criminal code of the 1820s, coupled with his measure of restraint in its enforcement, especially by 1830, does not look so extraordinary or cruel as readers of more recent work might be led to believe.

It would be a mistake in any case to conclude from his continued enforcement of a faltering capital code that Peel was largely indifferent to public opinion. On the contrary, he seems to have been only too painfully aware of its increasingly insistent power and the limitations it might impose. In overriding the king's urge for a pardon in the controversial case of a forger of 1828, Peel insisted 'that it would be very difficult hereafter to enforce the capital sentence of the law in any case of forgery, if mercy be extended in this case'.[85] This does not sound like somebody who thinks that he can hang men with impunity; it sounds like someone who knows that the credibility and public acceptability of the system he is upholding is hanging by an increasingly frayed thread.

We must not forget that, in contemporary minds, the movement for reform of the English criminal law was part of a larger and increasingly widespread belief that the whole of English public life and its institutions needed reform. 'The first law which it becomes a Reformer to propose and support, at the approach of a period of great political change', wrote the poet Percy Shelley in 1814, 'is the punishment of death'. Shelley viewed the death penalty as the principal plank in a decrepit aristocratic order.[86] Randall McGowen has shown that a similarly dichotomous world-view was expressed in the early nineteenth-century parliamentary debates on the capital code. Defenders portrayed the prevailing system as one in which paternalistic judges, acting under a discretionary capital code, would best ensure certainty and proportion in the assignment of punishments. Critics advocated an ideal of impartial, precisely-prescribed legal codes which would minimize the application of a capital sentence that was seldom if ever to be imposed anyway.[87] This sense of irreducible division in every dimension of the late-Hanoverian public order is often apparent in other contemporary observations. 'What I want to see the State do', wrote Sydney Smith in 1819, 'is to lessen in these sad times some of their numerous enemies. Why not do something for the Catholics and scratch them off the list? Then come the Protestant Dissenters. Then of measures, – a mitigation of the game-laws – commutation of tithes – granting to such towns as Birmingham and Manchester the seats in Parliament taken from the rottenness of Cornwall – *revision of the Penal Code* – sale of the Crown lands – sacrifice of the Droits of Admiralty against a new war; – anything that would show the Government to the people in some other attitude than that of taxing, punishing, and restraining.'[88]

The following year, another observer noted that 'Roman Catholic Claims, Parliamentary Reform, Amendment of Criminal Law, and all other matters which are not of pressing urgency, have, for the time, been merged in the interest that has been excited by the Queen's [i.e., Caroline's]' cause.[89] Two years after that, the Duke of Wellington, contemplating the readmission of George Canning to the cabinet, admitted the attendant political risks in a letter to the king: 'Mr. Canning has taken a line upon the Criminal Laws, & is known to entertain opinions on the Catholic question, quite different from some of your other Servants' in government.[90] To see the issue of criminal law placed before that of Catholic Emancipation in weighing the dangers of Canning is powerfully indicative of the prominence and weight that the former issue possessed as a divisive element in public and political life by the early 1820s. Many historians have commented on the larger, common identity amongst the great reforms of the late 1820s and 1830s, emphasizing how the word 'reform' came to embody a wider and deeper hope for a better society than any one of these measures could ever have delivered either singularly or even collectively.[91] Reform of the criminal law ought to be added to the wider list of associated reforms in religious liberties, municipal reform and overhaul of the poor laws than has generally been the case in recent years, when many historians seem to be impressed more by continuities than departures.[92]

Peel understood the growing force of this dichotomous vision of public life only too well, and far better than many of his colleagues, even if he perhaps felt little more sympathy with it than they did. He expressed both his recognition of and distaste for the phenomenon in a famous, much-quoted letter of 1820:

> Do not you think that the tone of England – of that great compound of folly, weakness, prejudice, wrong feeling, right feeling, obstinacy and newspaper paragraphs, which is called public opinion – is more liberal – to use an odious but intelligible phrase – than the policy of Government? Do not you think that there is a feeling, becoming daily more general and more confirmed ... in favour of some undefined change in the mode of governing the country?[93]

Peel sometimes sought the measure of public opinion in considering petitions for mercy from outside London. In evaluating one such controversial case, he asked his under-secretary to determine if 'the prevailing feeling in London, among those whose opinion is worth having, is in favor of the remission of the Capital Sentence'?[94] He made an even more sublimely significant yet ambivalent statement after sending an investigator named Stafford to gather extra evidence for deciding whether or not to let a Warwickshire man be hanged for rape. 'I attach less importance to the public feeling and opinion in the Town with respect to the character of the parties, and guilt of the accused, than to the opinion which Stafford himself has formed – but the public opinion and feeling are not to be disregarded.'[95]

In these sorts of statements, Peel betrayed a deep-set ambivalence about the extent to which public opinion was to be followed and the extent to which it ought to be set aside.

He clearly believed it to be important, however, and this was one critically important manner in which Peel seemed increasingly to diverge from his more severe-minded colleagues during the 1820s. If his conduct of the capital code in London occasionally provoked disapproving observations from men like Wellington and Ellenborough, Peel's moderation regarding Whig adjustments to his Forgery Act of 1830 laid bare their differences of attitude regarding public opinion. 'Peel thinks', Ellenborough observed disapprovingly, 'that after the vote of the House of Commons [for the bill] no verdicts will be obtained' against accused forgers. '[B]ut may not a contrary vote of the House of Lords turn public opinion into its former course? I think it may.' Later, when the Lords voted down the Commons' more radical amendments, he noted with satisfaction that 'Peel would have given it up. Now, I think one large majority will set public opinion right again'.[96] Peel was not so confident of being able to direct the course of public opinion as were many of his colleagues. In this, as on several other accounts, he appears to have been becoming markedly more 'liberal' during the 1820s than were most of his ministerial colleagues.[97]

V

So we must dispense with any image we may entertain of Peel as a humanitarian reformer. It is worth noting, however, that the two most prominent advocates of Peel's status as a 'great reformer', Leon Radzinowicz and Norman Gash, never made any such claims for him in the first place. If there is a hero in Radzinowicz's account of 'The Movement for Reform' of the English criminal law, it is not Peel but Sir Samuel Romilly, a man who

> took upon himself the ungrateful task of forcing the subject of criminal law reform upon the attention of Parliament at a period notoriously unpropitious to any change… [Whose] high sense of public duty and deep conviction made him persevere even when the hopelessness of his endeavours became obvious… [and who] succeeded in rousing public opinion and… bequeathed a programme to fight for and an example to follow.

By comparison, 'on the crucial issue of the severity of criminal law, and particularly the restriction of the death penalty, Peel was much behind the predominant opinion of the day'.[98] For his part, Gash, states that 'Peel was disinclined to go as far [in law reform] as the Whig reformers and indeed much of the educated public would have liked. His tenure of the Home Office did in fact see a considerable drop in the [overall] number of executions. But he preferred to combine a relative strict code with a flexible use of judicial reprieve until the effects of his legal reforms were clear.'[99] The conclusion of this essay must therefore be a somewhat ironical one. To some extent it has simply filled in details of a broader picture first sketched out by Radzinowicz and Gash, and once we recognize the real character of this picture, it does not seem to be at odds with the 'ethical pessimist' delineated in more recent studies of Peel. These studies do not so much reveal a new figure as cast light into some of the darker corners of the long-established portrait. Once we accept that Peel – and not only Peel, but many other people of the 1820s and beyond, Whig as well as Tory – still thought it acceptable to put people to death, not only for murder but also for strikingly aggravated forms of crime against property, as well as rape, sodomy and sheep-stealing, our principal concern must then be to measure as best we can the quality, logic and outcome of the procedures by which servants of the state reached their decisions as to who should live and who should die.[100]

By both these standards, the decision-making process that appears to have been applied to the vast majority of London's capital convicts during Peel's Home Secretaryship seems far better than recent work might lead us to believe. In terms of its outcomes, it was markedly more restrained in simple numerical terms than was the regime of Sidmouth's last years, although as we have noted it does not compare as well with the years immediately preceding Sidmouth. More significantly, the care with which decisions appear to have been made at the Recorder's Report seems to have been far superior to that taken during the late eighteenth century. This in itself is surely suggestive, not only of the growing technical complexity of the criminal law (though to some extent it must have reflected this), but also of a general sense amongst those responsible for exercising the prerogative of mercy that their decisions now operated within the context of a declining public acceptance – and in some places, indeed, an openly aggressive critique – of capital punishment in both general terms as well as in its application to particular offences. And this latter was a circumstance to which Sir Robert Peel appears to have been markedly more sensitive than most of his Tory colleagues, even if ultimately he had little more compunction than them about leaving men to hang. There is still room to acknowledge the conscientiousness of the man, even if we cannot endorse some of the principles his conscience embraced.

Notes

1 Norman Gash, *Mr Secretary Peel: The Life of Sir Robert Peel to 1830* (1961); *id.*, *Sir Robert Peel: The Life of Sir Robert Peel after 1830* (1972); Derek Beales, 'Peel, Russell and Reform', *HJ*, 17 (1974), 873–82.

2 Boyd Hilton, 'Peel: A Reappraisal', *HJ*, 22 (1979), 585–614; *id.*, 'The Ripening of Robert Peel', in Michael Bentley ed., *Public and Private: Essays in British History presented to*

Maurice Cowling (Cambridge,1993), 63–84. An excellent, up-to-date survey of Peel's life and legacy is provided in T.A. Jenkins, *Sir Robert Peel* (Basingstoke, 1999).

3 V.A.C. Gatrell, *The Hanging Tree: Execution and the English People, 1770–1868* (Oxford, 1994; revised paperback edn, 1996). Attempts to evaluate Gatrell's approach and conclusions include Boyd Hilton, 'The Gallows and Mr Peel', in T.C.W. Blanning and David Cannadine eds, *History and Biography: Essays in Honour of Derek Beales* (Cambridge, 1996), 88–112; Sara Sun Beale and Paul H. Haagen, 'Revenge for the Condemned', *Michigan Law Review*, 94 (1996), 1622–59; and Randall McGowen, 'Revisiting the Hanging Tree: Gatrell on Emotion and History', *British Journal of Criminology*, 40 (2000), 1–13.

4 By the Central Criminal Court Act of 1834 (4&5 Will. IV, c36), those areas of the counties of Kent, Surrey and Essex into which the metropolitan conurbation had extended by that time were added to the Old Bailey's jurisdiction, as well as the Admiralty Sessions which previously had been tried there under separate commission.

5 For an earlier account of the Recorder's Report during this era, see A. Aspinall, 'The Grand Cabinet, 1800–1837', *Politica*, 3 (1938), 333–44. Its origins after 1689 are analysed in J.M. Beattie, *Policing and Punishment in London, 1660–1750: Urban Crime and the Limits of Terror* (Oxford, 2001), 346–62. Throughout this article I use 'Report' to signify the meeting, as opposed to the actual document which the Recorder of London produced and read at that meeting, no copies of which appear to have survived for the early nineteenth century.

6 Gatrell, *Hanging Tree*, 543 (and see chap. 20 in general).

7 *Ibid.*, 19–21, 25.

8 See my forthcoming *Convicts and the State: Criminal Justice and English Governance, 1750–1810*, chap. 4, to be published by Palgrave Press Like Randall McGowen ('Revisiting the Hanging Tree', esp. 3–4), I am also uncertain that Gatrell's emphasis on material factors goes as far as he appears to believe towards devaluing cultural considerations in explaining the reforms of the early nineteenth century. After all, two hundred years earlier, the far higher execution levels of Tudor and early Stuart England did not have a similar effect in so comprehensively de-legitimating the already comprehensive capital code of that era (see Philip Jenkins, 'From Gallows to Prison? The Execution Rate in Early Modern England', *Criminal Justice History*, 7 (1986), 51–71).

9 Gatrell, *Hanging Tree*, 585.

10 J.M. Beattie, *Crime and the Courts in England, 1660–1800* (Princeton, NJ, 1986), 431–2. On the Home Circuit, for instance, individual cases referred to judges numbered only 2 as against 86 convicts covered by the circuit pardon in 1815, 1 against 98 at one assizes in 1820, 3 against 60 at another assizes of 1825, and 2 against 56 at yet another of 1830 (count derived from records in PRO HO 6, HO 13, HO 47, and PC 1).

11 Some of these figures are more accurate than others. For 1810 through 1837, I have compared the list of condemned prisoners in the Old Bailey Sessions Paper with newspaper notices of Recorder's Reports and Old Bailey executions. Before 1810 I have had to rely on the same source most other historians use, the figures given in House of Commons reports on the criminal law. But the latter are sometimes reported differently (compare the summary figures at 1819 (62) XVII, 295–300 – on which I rely here – with the more detailed breakdown at 1819 (585) VIII, 152–63), and the numbers reported to have been executed in one year often include persons convicted the year before, rendering accurate statistical

calculations impossible without the closer scrutiny afforded by comparing the Sessions Paper and newspapers.

12 BL Add MS 40315, fos 63–4. Cf. Gatrell, *Hanging Tree*, 543–5.

13 It might also be worth noting that Peel was Home Secretary on only one of the three occasions in 1827 when four men were executed at once.

14 PRO HO 6/13, handwritten notes of Recorder Newman Knowlys on cases for Report of January 1828 sessions.

15 Lytton Strachey and Roger Fulford eds, *The Greville Memoirs, 1814–1860* (8 vols, London: Macmillan, 1938), I, 304; PRO HO 6/14, Recorder of London to Robert Peel, 5 July 1829.

16 Lord Colchester ed., *A Political Diary, 1828–1830, by Edward Law, Lord Ellenborough* (2 vols, London: Richard Bentley, 1881), I, 154–5, 267–8. Compare the reading of these quotes and their significance in Gatrell, *Hanging Tree*, 547–50.

17 Peter King, *Crime, Justice, and Discretion in England, 1740–1820* (Oxford: Oxford University Press, 2000), 355 and *passim*. See also Beattie, *Crime and the Courts*, chap. 8.

18 Colchester, *Political Diary*, I, 101. And in the end, one more of those six was spared.

19 Francis Bamford and the Duke of Wellington eds, *The Journal of Mrs. Arbuthnot, 1820–1832* (2 vols, London: Macmillan, 1950), II, 59.

20 Colchester, *Political Diary*, I, 268.

21 Beales, 'Peel, Russell and Reform', 879–80; Gatrell, *Hanging Tree*, 570, 579–82.

22 Gatrell, *Hanging Tree*, chap. 20.

23 Strachey and Fulford, *Greville Memoirs*, I, 304–5.

24 BL Add MS 40299, fos 63–4, 313–4; Add MS 40315, fos 276–7; Add MS 40352, fos 119–21; Add MS 43067, fos 196–7.

25 BL Add MS 40315, fos 63–4; [T.C. Hansard ed.,] *The Parliamentary Debates, from the Year 1803 to the Present Time* (hereafter *Hansard*), 3/13 (1832), col. 987.

26 BL Add MS 40315, fos 63–4; Horace Twiss ed., *The Public and Private Life of Lord Chancellor Eldon* (3 vols, London: John Murray, 1844), I, 398–9; Strachey and Fulford, *Greville Memoirs*, I, 304.

27 Indeed, Gatrell's general contempt for the practices of the Report seems to derive primarily from Peel's tough-mindedness in this respect in particular (*Hanging Tree*, 556–63).

28 Colchester, *Ellenborough Diary*, I, 294, 295. Although its proper title was *The Whole Proceedings on the King's Commission of the Peace, Oyer and Terminer, and Gaol-Delivery for the City of London; and also the Gaol-Delivery for the County of Middlesex; Held at Justice-Hall in the Old-Bailey, etc.* contemporaries invariably used the name 'Sessions Paper', and the convenient short form OBSP is widely-used amongst historians. The uses of the Sessions Paper in the Report during the eighteenth century are discussed in Beattie, *Policing and Punishment*, 451–2, and Simon Devereaux, 'The City and the Sessions Paper: 'Public Justice' in London, 1770–180', *JBS*, 35 (1996), 469–82.

29 BL Add MS 40367, fo. 184.

30 BL Add MS 40315, fos 237–8.

31 BL Add MS 40351, fos 236–7.

32 BL Add MS 40315, fos 276–7.

33 Bamford and Wellington eds, *Journal of Mrs Arbuthnot*, II, 168; Devon Record Office, 152M, C1819/OH, Sidmouth to Sir Benjamin Bloomfield, 19 Nov 1819; BL Add MS 40299, fo. 132.

34 This happened with convicts of the sessions for February 1823, October 1824, February 1826, April 1826, September 1826, September 1827, September 1829 and January 1830 (PRO HO 6/6–15).

35 *The Morning Chronicle, and London Advertiser*, 23 August 1783, 23 October 1783; *The Morning Post, and Daily Advertiser*, 23 August 1783 (source of quote); *The London Packet; or, New Lloyd's Evening Post*, 22–24 October 1783.

36 Both the conduct of the Recorder's Report and the rapid shifts in the character and scale of capital punishment in London during the 1780s are discussed in my *Convicts and the State*, chaps 4 and 6.

37 *Morning Chronicle*, 7 Oct. 1775, 13 Oct. 1775.

38 Bamford and Wellington eds., *Journal of Mrs Arbuthnot*, II, 59; Colchester, *Ellenborough Diary*, I, 47; II, 36.

39 E.A. Smith, *George IV* (New Haven, CT, 1999) is a recent, largely unpersuasive effort to rehabilitate its subject.

40 For an example of the king exerting pressure during a Report, see the account from 1820 in Arthur Aspinall ed., *The Diary of Henry Hobhouse (1820–1827)* (1947), 17.

41 BL Add MS 40315, fo. 112 (emphasis in original).

42 BL Add MS 40358, fo. 51.

43 BL Add MS 40299, fos 262–3.

44 Bamford and Wellington, *Journal of Mrs Arbuthnot*, II, 314.

45 PRO HO 6/14, Recorder's 'List of Capital Convicts to be Reported to His Majesty in Council', 24 Dec. 1829 (amended from 10 Nov. 1829).

46 Sir Joseph Arnould, *Memoir of Thomas, First Lord Denman, formerly Lord Chief Justice of England* (2 vols, 1873), I, 436.

47 Strachey and Fulford, *Greville Memoirs*, I, 238, 332–3, 338–40, 342; Bamford and Wellington, *Journal of Mrs Arbuthnot*, II, 314.

48 Henry Brougham, quoted in Arnould, *Memoir of Denman*, I, 309.

49 A. Aspinall ed., *The Letters of King George IV, 1812–1830* (3 vols, Cambridge, 1938), III, 116–17; *id.*, ed., *The Correspondence of George, Prince of Wales, 1770–1812* (8 vols; 1963–71), VIII, 472.

50 A point that had been made forcefully to the king by Sidmouth in April 1820 (Devon Record Office, 152M, C1820/OH, Sidmouth to Bloomfield, 4 April 1830).

51 Dates derived from *The Times* of London.

52 BL Add MS 40299, fos 159–60.

53 'The Recorder will probably make his Report on Wednesday next', one man wrote to William Wilberforce regarding their efforts on behalf of a condemned convict in Newgate in January 1803, adding that 'The Execution is usually the Wednesday following the Report' (Bodleian Library (Oxford), MS Wilberforce d.17, fos 127–8).

54 This pattern is easily detected in a survey of the notices of Old Bailey sessions, Recorder's Reports and Tyburn executions given in *The Gentleman's Magazine* and *The London Magazine* during these years. The practice of the Report at this time is discussed in Beattie, *Policing and Punishment*, 448–62.

55 *The Times* of London, 25 Feb 1817 (my emphases).

56 For a more detailed discussion of the various changes proposed and implemented in the public presentation of criminal justice in London during the 1780s, see my forthcoming article 'Recasting the Theatre of Public Justice in London: The End of the Tyburn Procession in Its Contexts'.

57 BL Add MS 43015, fos 63–4.

58 BL Add MS 40352, fos 119–21.

59 Bamford and Wellington, *Journal of Mrs Arbuthnot*, I, 10, 333.

60 John Gore ed., *Creevey's Life and Times: A Further Selection from the Correspondence of Thomas Creevey* (1934), 392 (emphasis in original).
61 Colchester, *Ellenborough Diary*, I, 19, 29–30 (quote); *id.*, ed., *The Diary and Correspondence of Charles Abbot, Lord Colchester, Speaker of the House of Commons, 1802–1817* (3 vols, 1861), III, 548–9, 551; B.L., Add MS 40300, fos 219–20.
62 Viscount Esher ed., *The Girlhood of Queen Victoria: A Selection from Her Majesty's Diaries Between the Years 1832 and 1840* (2 vols, 1912), I, 285.
63 Colchester, *Colchester Diary*, III, 548.
64 BL Add MS 40400, fos 200–1. For the Report's actual origins during the reign of William and Mary, see note 5 above.
65 Commons Parliamentary Papers, 1831–32 (294) IV, 197–8; Lords Parliamentary Papers, 1832 (102) CCXCVI, 687–90.
66 *Hansard*, 3/11 (1832), cols 1274–5; 3/13 (1832), cols 543–4; 3/24 (1834), cols 1004–5; 'Second Report of the Commissioners Appointed to Inquire into the Municipal Corporations in England and Wales: London and Southwark; London Companies' (25 April 1837), Commons Parliamentary Papers, 1837 (M.C. 1) XXV, 1–592 (quote at 14).
67 *Hansard*, 3/174 (1864), col. 1484. Such crimes included, of course, rape and buggery, the latter of which sent two men to the gallows at Newgate as late as November 1835.
68 Gatrell, *Hanging Tree*, 564–5.
69 Colchester, *Ellenborough Diary*, II, 398.
70 PRO HO 44/13, no. 14.
71 A.G.L. Shaw, *Convicts and the Colonies* (1966), 188–90.
72 Charles Campbell, *The Intolerable Hulks: British Shipboard Confinement, 1776–1857* (3rd edn, Tucson, 2001), chap. 11.
73 PRO HO 44/13, no. 13.
74 Gash, *Mr Secretary Peel*, 315. See also BL, Add MS 40315, fos 85–6.
75 BL Add MS 40355, fo. 195.
76 Surrey History Centre, Acc 319 (Goulburn Papers), Box 39, Peel to Goulburn, n.d. [1828?].
77 BL Add MS 40360–2 *passim*; PRO HO 44/14, fos 2–32.
78 Gatrell, *Hanging Tree*, 568.
79 Charles Stuart Parker ed., *Sir Robert Peel from His Private Papers* (3 vols, 1891–99), I, 401–2.
80 BL Add MS 40390, fos 190–2. The text of this letter, minus the final sentence which I have quoted, is printed in Parker, *Sir Robert Peel*, I, 432–3. Peel's desire to pursue police reform seems to have existed almost from the moment he assumed office; see Leon Radzinowicz, *A History of English Criminal Law and Its Administration from 1750 – Volume One: The Movement for Reform* (1948), 587–8, and Gash, *Mr Secretary Peel*, 309–14.
81 Thus, in October 1829 and February 1830 respectively, Peel rejected suggestions for new transportation measures and further refinements to imprisonment alike on the grounds of expense (PRO HO 43/37, 479–82; HO 43/38, 185–7).
82 Elaine A. Reynolds, *Before the Bobbies: The Night Watch and Police Reform in Metropolitan London, 1720–1830* (Basingstoke, 1998), chap. 8.
83 Gatrell, *Hanging Tree*, 576–85; Hilton, 'Gallows and Mr Peel', 94.
84 Lady Dorchester ed., *Recollections of a Long Life, by Lord Broughton (John Cam Hobhouse) with Additional Extracts from His Private Diaries* (6 vols, 1910–11), V, 273; J.F. Stephen, *History of the Criminal Law of England* (3 vols, 1883), I , 478–9.

85 Aspinall, *Letters of George IV*, III, 449.
86 'On the Punishment of Death: A Fragment' (*c*.1814); in Roger Ingpen and Walter E. Peck eds, *The Complete Works of Percy Bysshe Shelley* (10 vols, 1965; reprint of 1926–30 edn), VI, 185.
87 Randall McGowen, 'The Image of Justice and Reform of the Criminal Law in Early Nineteenth-Century England', *Buffalo Law Review*, 32 (1983), 89–125.
88 Nowell C. Smith ed., *The Letters of Sydney Smith* (2 vols, Oxford, 1953), I, 341 (my emphasis).
89 Colchester, *Colchester Diary*, III, 145–6. For the initial effectiveness of the Caroline agitation as a focus for radical politics in general, see Thomas W. Laqueur, 'The Queen Caroline Affair: Politics as Art in the Reign of George IV', *Journal of Modern History*, 54 (1982), 417–66.
90 Bamford and Wellington, *Journal of Mrs Arbuthnot*, I, 189.
91 John Cannon, 'New Lamps for Old: The End of Hanoverian England', in Cannon ed., *The Whig Ascendancy: Colloquies on Hanoverian England* (1981), 100–24; Derek Beales, 'The Idea of Reform in British Politics, 1829–1850', *Proceedings of the British Academy*, 100 (1999), 159–74.
92 A recent, vigorously-argued case for continuity is Richard Price, *British Society, 1680–1880: Dynamism, Containment and Change* (Cambridge, 1999), esp. chaps 7–8. For some significant doubts, see David Eastwood, 'The Age of Uncertainty: Britain in the Early-Nineteenth Century', *Transactions of the Royal Historical Society*, 6th Series, 8 (1998), 91–115.
93 Louis J. Jennings ed., *The Croker Papers: The Correspondence and Diaries of the Late Honourable John Wilson Croker* (2nd edn, revised; 3 vols, 1885), I, 170.
94 BL Add MS 40360, fos 68–71.
95 PRO HO 47/68, Peel to G.R. Dawson, 31 Aug 1825.
96 Colchester, *Ellenborough Diary*, II, 271, 294.
97 Hilton, 'Ripening of Peel', 63–84; *id*., 'Gallows and Mr Peel', 110–12; Jenkins, *Sir Robert Peel*, chap. 2.
98 Radzinowicz, *History of English Criminal Law*, I, 525, 606.
99 Norman Gash, *Aristocracy and People: Britain, 1815–1865* (1979), 118.
100 Of the seven people who were hanged by the Grey and Melbourne ministries from 1831 and 1837 for crimes other than murder, one was a sheep-stealer and two had been convicted of sodomy (from notices in *The Times*).

11
'I Could Hang Anything You Can Bring Before Me': England's Willing Executioners in 1883

*Greg T. Smith**

I

Five years before the haunting image of 'Jack the Ripper' would infect the psyche of Victorian society, the English public was captivated by another killer who, incidentally, also went by the trade name of 'Jack'. Yet unlike the mysterious, sadistic and elusive London murderer, this other Jack – himself a killer of sorts – was well-known to the Metropolitan police, to the local authorities, and even to the Home Office: in fact, he was on their payroll. This other Jack, known popularly as 'Jack Ketch', was none other than the common hangman whose real name was William Marwood. A shoemaker and leather craftsman by trade, Marwood had served as London's executioner since 1874. But when he died on 4 September 1883, word spread quickly that a rather unsavoury job vacancy had emerged.

Hanging was the established method of executing felons in Britain until 1969 when the death penalty was abolished altogether for murder. Prior to 1868, hangings had been carried out in public before large crowds at various select sites in London and around the country. From the late Middle Ages until 1783, London's executions were carried out at Tyburn, until the eighteenth century an isolated spot on the western outskirts of the metropolis, near present-day Marble Arch. Executions in London, or 'hanging days', happened about every two months, following the regular sessions of the metropolitan courts. It was then that the condemned men and women

* This research was supported by the Social Sciences and Humanities Research Council of Canada. Earlier versions of this article were presented to audiences in Toronto and Winnipeg. I would like to thank Peter Bailey, John Beattie, Mark Gabbert, Stephen Heathorn and the editors of this collection for their many helpful comments and suggestions.

were taken from their cells in Newgate prison, London's principal gaol, and paraded through the city streets via a regular route to the permanent gallows constructed at Tyburn. Other cities and towns around the country had their familiar execution sites too, usually located on the outskirts of populated areas. In 1783, under pressure from the Sheriffs of London and Middlesex to clamp down on the mischief and general disorder caused by the Tyburn crowds, and coupled with petitions from the men and women of self-styled 'quality and distinction' who were buying up property in the increasingly fashionable area surrounding Tyburn, the procession was abolished.[1] Executions were still to be carried out in public, but in London at least, from 1783–1868, they were carried out on scaffolds erected in the street just outside the walls of Newgate prison.

Until the mid-nineteenth century, executions remained public and often grisly events. Well into the nineteenth century, death by hanging was an even more unpleasant sight because the techniques of inflicting death were still crude. At Tyburn and many other places, the condemned prisoner was strangled to death because of the method of hanging. The condemned experienced no significant drop since, in most cases, the victim was attached to the noose while standing on a cart or ladder. Once the noose was fastened, the hangman would simply pull the cart or wrench the ladder away, leaving victims – as the contemporary cant put it – to 'dance the Tyburn jig'; in other words, to kick, writhe and buck as they slowly strangled to death. Though this method of execution often included a short drop, the only technical improvement after 1783 in the executions carried out in front of Newgate on temporary scaffolds was the installation of a trap-door below the victim. It was the early nineteenth-century hangman William Calcraft who applied 'science' to the method of execution and began testing the effects on the rope of various longer-length drops, using sandbags as dummy victims. But even Calcraft's improvements, which also consisted of an improved trap door and a leather harness for the wrists, were not entirely perfected during his long period of service from 1828–74. He still had to pull on the legs of many condemned men in order to hasten death and limit suffering.[2]

One aspect of the public's curiosity at public executions, and one of the concerns raised when it was first suggested that executions be removed from public view, was the desire to see that the hangman did his job properly. As the final agent in the grand machinery of English justice, the hangman embodied the ultimate reality of how the state would deal with its most heinous offenders. As an extension of state power, the hangman was expected to carry out his duties to the best of his ability, in a calm and dignified, even mechanical manner. He was certainly not to show any emotion towards the condemned, nor to the crowd who watched. Often this was a difficult task. The state's executioner had never been an admired figure. The crowds at public executions in the seventeenth and eighteenth centuries almost universally derided the executioner, and there are many examples of the depth of popular fear and loathing for the common hangman from England, Germany, France, Holland and other countries.[3] The execution mob came not only to condemn or cheer the unfortunate victims; they were also there to judge the work of the hangman and to ascertain, through him, the mercy or justice of the state. When things went poorly and the hanging was somehow botched, the crowds could turn riotous. In April 1821, when the intoxicated hangman at York was unable to carry out his duties without the assistance of the gaoler and one of the Sheriff's officers, the crowd turned nasty. After finally dispatching the condemned man, the executioner was verbally assaulted by the mob, with several people calling out 'Hang him – hang Jack Ketch – he's drunk![4] Similar scenes had played out in the eighteenth century and for this very reason in London, and elsewhere, armed and mounted constables were frequently on hand at public executions to maintain some degree of order amidst the larger chaos.[5]

Two of the nineteenth century's most prominent hangmen did their best to rehabilitate the executioner's equivocal image. Rather than accepting the hangman's lot as social pariah, William Calcraft and his successor took pride in their part-time profession. Calcraft kept his favourite ropes in a canvas bag and was willing to show them to the curious, thereby bridging the awkward social distance between executioner and public. In 1874, Calcraft was urged into retirement at the age of 74, and was replaced by William Marwood. He was selected because he had acted as an assistant to Calcraft at a hanging in Lincoln gaol in 1871. Contemporaries and historians have since characterized Marwood as something of a humanitarian because of his improvements on Calcraft's methods. In a letter to the authorities at Scotland Yard, written shortly before he died, Marwood deplored the 'very ugly slow process, simply strangulation' employed by his predecessor. To his mind, Calcraft's methods caused 'great lingering suffering and much unnecessary pain to the Culprit' and for this reason Marwood experimented with the 'long drop' method of execution – much longer drops than Calcraft had attempted. This improvement, boasted Marwood, allowed him to discharge his duties 'with promptitude and with humanity' and 'apparently without the slightest pain'.[6] The innovations he introduced and the modicum of humanity those changes brought to the task earned him some small degree of respect not often shown to men in his position. Regardless of what others thought of him, Marwood saw himself as an important government official, not as a social pariah as many of his predecessors had felt themselves. He preferred to call himself 'executioner' rather than 'hangman' to lend some degree of professionalism to the job, and he did his best to present himself as a proficient functionary, at least when he was on the job.

When he was first hired to carry out various executions, Marwood endeavoured to maintain the traditional anonymity of the position and hid the fact of his alternate occupation from his neighbours in his hometown of Horncastle.[7] When that fact was revealed, 'his presence in the little town ... was not at all appreciated, and he was continually hooted at and hissed'. Over his 12 years of service, though, such overt derision from his neighbours gradually receded; and when he was at home in Horncastle, and not 'on circuit' as Marwood called it, he 'went in and out as an ordinary mortal' and tended to business at his cobbler's shop.[8] Nevertheless, despite the fact that Marwood had largely blended into the community by the time of his death the residents of Horncastle were not at all keen to see his successor appointed from their small town. As one reporter writing from Horncastle upon Marwood's death put it, thankfully nothing was known there of a potential successor, and given that Marwood had neither a son nor a known assistant, 'the inhabitants unanimously hope he will not reside here'.[9]

Marwood himself saw nothing wicked or unethical in his position. He regarded himself as 'a fellow-labourer with the judge, and not a bit more concerned in the culprit's death',[10] an opinion which, judging by the number of serious applications to replace him, was more widely shared than some might have suspected. What sullied Marwood's reputation, and what raised public anxieties about the place for a common hangman in a civilized society, was his perceived lack of decorum and discretion when he circulated in public. Marwood, like Calcraft, came to relish the public attention and macabre curiosity that drew people towards the hangman. And since Marwood had the gift of the gab, he was often willing to talk about his experiences to reporters after a hanging over a drink in a local pub. He cultivated that notoriety further by displaying his ropes and some of the personal effects of notorious criminals he had executed in a makeshift museum in his Horncastle cobbler's shop. It was because of this 'morbid vanity', as one reporter called it, that Marwood styled himself the holder of a 'Crown Office' and painted the same over his shop door.[11] This behaviour contributed to the popular misconception that Marwood was indeed the holder of some permanent, government post.

So, even though executions had been removed from the public gaze for nearly seven years by the time of Marwood's appointment, he was still a relatively well-known figure. In his hometown many locals knew him by name or by sight, but the wider public gained some knowledge of him because of the presence of witnesses, notably newspaper reporters, at the hangings now carried out behind the prison walls. A few witnesses were required to be present at executions according to statute, while the relatives of the prisoner or any person the Sheriff or local justices of the peace thought proper to admit were also allowed.[12] Newspaper reporters were frequently invited as witnesses and played a key role in presenting a public version of what had become a closed judicial ceremony. Despite the intimacy of the event itself after 1868, newspapers were able to provide a new kind of experience of public justice for an audience much larger and more diverse than was ever achieved when hangings were held in the open.[13] For 20 years reporters enjoyed this privileged vantage from which to describe and critique the hangman's work until the press was formally excluded from the witness list by a Home Office that was growing ever more anxious about the effect of the detailed newspaper accounts of hangings upon public morals.[14] The presence of reporters was at the sheriff's discretion, but one source suggests that Marwood frequently requested that they be excluded from executions 'for no other reason but that he disliked them'.[15] It is more likely, however, that Marwood resented the formal scrutiny that reporters offered, including the revelation of specific details about the event such as the precise length of the drop, the thickness of the rope, or the complaints from the victim about the tightness of the noose.[16] Marwood wanted to avoid the harsh criticism that could follow if he bungled the hanging or if the victim was made to suffer or was, as sometimes happened, decapitated through a miscalculation of the drop. Such incidents, which exposed the grisly realities of death by hanging, were more easily hushed up by prison officials when reporters were kept safely beyond the prison walls.

Marwood's moves to professionalize the post of hangman also came as a consequence of legal and social changes in Victorian England that would have a direct impact on the need for his services. By the 1860s, capital punishment had been removed from virtually all of the offences to which it had formerly applied. At the end of the eighteenth century there were well over 200 capital offences on the books, but the second quarter of the nineteenth century witnessed a vigorous campaign of legal reform which, by 1861, saw the number of capital offences reduced to only four: murder, treason, piracy with violence, and arson committed on royal ships or dockyards, or in arsenals. In practice, only murder was punished capitally with any kind of regularity. By the 1860s the most serious acts of violence had grown exceptionally rare, with rates of violent crime in decline; thus, fewer people were coming to trial on capital murder charges and fewer still were convicted and sentenced to death.[17] Thus the reduction in the number of capital offences and the decline in the incidence of murder over the course of the nineteenth century made the hangman's duty increasingly sporadic. Second, with improved rail service to most parts of the country by the 1870s, it was no longer necessary for each county or town to employ its own hangman. Indeed, as the hangman was less frequently required, and as his increasingly rare performances fell under greater scrutiny from the press, it may have seemed preferable to local authorities simply to employ the man with the most experience when the need arose. Marwood had acquired a reputation as a skilful practitioner of his craft, as a man who could put the condemned to death 'neatly'.[18] As a consequence, he was regularly employed outside of London to the extent that by the early 1880s, through common practice, the duties of the common hangman had devolved largely to one person. For these reasons most people assumed, mistakenly, that there was only one public executioner employed by the Home Secretary to carry out the law's dark business. Thus when Marwood died on 4 September 1883, following a short illness, many were quick to presume that the authorities would seek out a successor to fill the vacant post.

Marwood's death, and the vacancy that it created – though neither a permanent government post, nor a royal appointment – nonetheless initiated a discussion within official circles over what kind of man should replace him. Meanwhile, in the press, it sparked a wider debate over the method of execution and even the necessity of maintaining the death penalty at all. One critic suggested a return to the early-modern practice of appointing another convict to do the job. In compensation for a reduced sentence and 'certain indulgences' in the form of meals or leisure time, 'some ruffian' under sentence of penal servitude might be trained by 'a skilled orthopraxist ... a practitioner experienced in all matters connected with the spine and the extremities ... to perform his duties properly'.[19] Others argued that it was hanging itself that was the problem. The *Observer* advised that 'if the present form of capital punishment is to be retained the death sentence must be carried out in a less bungling fashion than it now too often is'.[20] Marwood's occasional bungling and the grisly mishaps that sometimes accompanied hangings (specifically, decapitation) led certain critics to suggest the time had come to substitute an alternate, 'scientific' form of inflicting death for hanging, such as electrocution. However, as the *Western Daily Press* reminded its readers, regarding the

> suggestions now freely and not unnaturally made that some other mode of inflicting death should be resorted to, it should be remembered that the sentence of the law expressly defines the way in which death shall be inflicted, and presumably an Act of Parliament would be necessary in order to abolish the hangman and substitute the electrician.[21]

Moreover, such innovations undermined one of the chief functions of the death penalty – that is, the ignoble death of the offender at the hands of the state's hangman. Such a grim end for offenders was still considered part of the 'deterrent efficacy' of capital punishment. To substitute the hangman, concluded the *Observer*, would only give 'intending murderers' the knowledge that rather than a particularly indignant death at the hands of the common hangman, 'they were to be politely bowed out of the world by a man of science armed with an electric battery'.[22]

Others argued, even more contentiously, the necessity of abolishing the death penalty altogether. Abolitionists – always on the political margins – had been pushing the issue upon successive governments from the late eighteenth century but had always remained a tiny, if vocal minority. As V.A.C. Gatrell has recently explained, the concessions made to penal reform for capital offences came slowly and piece meal before 1840. Over the course of the 1860s, as publicity gradually eclipsed necessity as the key issue in the death penalty debates, and after the capital offences were pared down to just four, abolitionists were isolated still further.[23] Even those who had called for the removal of the death penalty from property offences could still justify its retention in the case of murder. The end of public hanging in 1868, Gatrell argues, effectively silenced the abolitionist cause for a century by forcing a compromise of a massively reduced capital code and the abolition of public executions, while retaining the death penalty itself.[24] By this compromise, conservative supporters of hanging were guaranteed that the public terror of the gallows would not be suppressed entirely. Indeed, with the successful infiltration of newspapermen as witnesses at many executions, such proceedings although now out of sight, were far from out of mind.

II

That ordinary citizens were quick to take up pen and paper upon Marwood's demise to promote themselves as possible hangmen was not, in itself, unique. In 1851, Charles Dickens' weekly journal *Household Word* reprinted a number of letters written to the High Sheriff of Suffolk from people seeking to fill in for Calcraft, who was unable to carry out a scheduled hanging in Ipswich due to a previous engagement.[25] What was exceptional about the public response to the vacancy caused by Marwood's death, however, was the overwhelming number of applicants. Though replacements for Marwood's position were never solicited, hundreds of people volunteered their names as possible candidates for his job. Within 24 hours' notice of Marwood's death, the offices of both the Home Secretary, Sir William Harcourt, and the Sheriffs of London and Middlesex were flooded with letters inquiring about the job and requesting their consideration as Marwood's replacement. The enthusiastic interest in the post shocked even the most hardened newspaper editors. The *Bristol Mercury and Daily Post* stated 'the old proverb that there is no accounting for tastes is illustrated by a statement published yesterday [that is, 7 September, three days after Marwood's death and just two days after it had been reported in the papers] to the effect that a great number of applications have been addressed to the Home Secretary for the vacant post of hangman'.[26] Within three days of Marwood's death, the Home Secretary had received 362 letters of application, and the sheriffs of London and Middlesex received at least a further one hundred.[27] By the third week of September, it was being reported in reputable papers and journals that 'upwards of 1,200 applications' had been received by the Home Secretary, and forwarded to the London authorities.[28] A number of people applied directly to the Lord Mayor of London or to the metropolitan sheriffs, as well as to the central government authorities, just to be sure. The Home Office tried to stem the tide of letters by disowning the common hangman as an official of the central government, despite Marwood's self-styling as the holder of a 'Crown Office'. A notice appeared in *The Times* for 10 September stating that 'it is neither the right nor the duty of the Secretary of State to make any such appointment. There is no such office as that of public executioner appointed by the

Government. It is the right and the duty of the Sheriff to employ and to pay a fitting person to carry out the sentence of the law.'[29] This only encouraged more applications to the London and Middlesex sheriffs, including a number of applicants who had previously applied only to the Secretary of State.

The Home Office was technically correct in their statement, though the general public and the applicants among them for the hangman's job could be excused for the confusion. Marwood's popularity and self-promotion had helped create the impression that Marwood was the nation's hangman. However, strictly speaking, he was hired on each occasion merely as an assistant to the Sheriffs of the various counties on account of his particular skill and experience. Further confusion may have arisen from the recent proclamation of the New Prison Act, which renamed the county jail 'Her Majesty's Prison', and which would have so named Newgate and Holloway prisons in London. Since Marwood was frequently under contract with the Sheriffs of London and Middlesex, many could have assumed that the new Act made all associated prison functionaries government officials.[30] But this was not the case and local sheriffs retained, theoretically, the role of hangman. In practice, they simply contracted-out that most unpleasant responsibility of actually extinguishing the lives of the condemned to a man willing to do the job for a fee.[31] That cold fact may have contributed to the popular opprobrium for the common hangman, but it did not deter a good many from seeking the job anyway. Indeed, it appears that Victorian England had its fair share of willing executioners.

In all, it seems that more than 1400 unsolicited letters were received in the roughly three-week period following Marwood's death.[32] Some among the press dubbed it a 'very ghastly' fact that England was full of so many nascent hangmen. Nothing could be more 'revoltingly indecent', declared the *Illustrated London News*, than 'the number and importunity of the applications made to the Home Office from all parts of the country for the "post" or "appointment" supposed to have been left vacant by the deceased hangman'.[33] The 'brisk competition for the hideous office' did little 'to increase our admiration for human nature', said the *Observer*.[34] Other commentators, though, focused more on the ambivalent place for the hangman in society. One journalist conceded 'there is a certain sense in which it is gratifying to find that a task which must naturally be repugnant to thousands has yet a curious fascination for plenty of persons who could no doubt soon obtain skill if they do not already possess it'.[35]

Nearly all of the letters sent to the London authorities survive in the records of the Corporation of London, since those received at the Home Office were forwarded to the Sheriffs of London and Middlesex.[36] Though apparently a complete list of all applicants was not kept, and some letters must have gone missing, analysis of those that remain permits some insight into the popular view of the hangman's job, as well as into attitudes towards the task of capital punishment in late Victorian England. As unsolicited texts crafted for a particular purpose in unusual circumstances, it is not surprising that the letters expose a wide range of ideas, opinions and information. Some letters are merely inquiries about the position, many more offer personal testimonials – from the mundane to the disturbingly enthusiastic – while a few take the opportunity to expound on the law, on the death penalty, and on the hangman's place in a civilized society. As the Home Secretary Sir William Harcourt noted himself, 'a certain portion of them are likely to be hoaxes'.[37] One letter in particular clearly was sent as a lark; a group of friends got another drunk and got him to sign a letter unknowingly. When he sobered up, his mates must have told him what they had done because a few days later, the man, Henry Senior, wrote to the Home Secretary to beg that his application be withdrawn. His letter reads:

> Sir, You must not take any notice of the letter you have received with my name attached to it asking for the situation as hangman as I was drunk when they got me to signe my name to it. I am very sorry indeed that anything of this sort should have occurred it would be a disgrace for me to have to hang any one as I am learning Manufacture with my Father and am only a young man.

Senior's friends might have been having him on all along as the man's letter bears the notation from the Home Office that 'his application has not yet been received'.[38] But Senior was enough scared for his reputation that, just to be sure, he sought to rescind the letter. Even presumably serious applicants had later reservations about what they had done. R.A. Matthews had second thoughts only hours after posting his initial letter of application. In a subsequent letter to the Secretary of State posted later the same day, he admits that his application 'was written without due consideration & I would beg that your lordship will treat my application as though it had not been made'.[39]

Requests for anonymity mark a common feature among many of the letters. Some did not want to be identified even as applicants, much less as successful applicants. Others feared that even if they were ultimately unsuccessful, if the mere fact of their application became common knowledge, it would reflect poorly upon them, possibly damaging their reputation and social standing within their communities. As a result, a few applied anonymously, or under pseudonyms, while others offered to supply their real names upon appointment.[40] J.R. Poole begged to be excused for writing for such an important office on 'Note Paper' explaining 'I have sent it like a private letter, so that there should be no suspicion among the Hartlepool folks, as if it was found out that I applied for the appointment, and not get it, I think it would be constantly thrown up to me'.[41] Similarly, Henry Turpil of St Andrews, Scotland wrote 'i wish this letter to be strictly Private if i get the situation it would not matter so much but if i was not to get it and it became known it would ruin me for i am also a married man'.[42] Ironically, both of these letters suggest that some of the dishonour attached to the position of public hangman might eventually be alleviated if one later secured the post. One 'T.M.' asked that if the appointment had already been made upon receiving his letter, that the Home Secretary would 'please throw this into the fire as if you had never received it'.[43] Some asked that, if letters of recommendation be solicited on their behalves, the nature of the job be concealed from their referees. As one man employed in 'a rather large firm' on the Isle of Wight said, 'should this applycation leak out one might have to go by an unpleasant name'. Still, he was willing to take further steps to maintain his anonymity should he be accepted for the position. The man assured the Home Secretary that 'should you do me the honour of appointing me to the office I would remove to where I am not known and my constant endeavour will [be] to keep myself unknown to the public'.[44] Another cunning applicant, named Robert Downie, suggested that if he were selected his name 'should be written backwards. I then would appear as Mr Einwod.'[45] Still others were more creative in their plans to avoid detection. One John Smith of Stoke Newington stated 'it would be my object to keep my incognito wherever I might be sent – and I would use such disguises That my own family Circle would fail to recognize me'.[46]

Though the bulk of the letters offer little more than matter-of-fact details about the individual applicants, a good many are interesting in their revelations of ambivalent attitudes towards the death penalty, and towards those human beings who actually did the law's dirty work at this point in the late nineteenth century. Though many supported the ultimate sanction of the law, there was still considerable reluctance to be counted among the hangman's close friends or family, even by artificial association. One anonymous letter from Scotland, not specifically applying for the position, asks that the name of the successful applicant be kept confidential to avoid damaging others with the same name. The person writes:

> In appointing another hangman may I suggest that his name be not divulged. Within these last 20 years two good family names have been spoiled. The Calcrafts a good old Dorsetshire family and the Marwoods on the borders of Devon and Somerset are instances. Let him be some criminal and always styled the common hangman.[47]

Yet another man who applied for the job, only to later write back asking that his name be withdrawn, told the Home Secretary that after applying, 'I mentioned it to day to my wife and it has made her very ill, and she will separate from me if I accept the post, and that means disaster to me therefore Gentlemen if you will take my name off the list I shall feel deeply grateful to you'.[48] A lawyer from Great Yarmouth also asked that his name be withdrawn when, after conferring with a colleague about his application, he was advised 'not to accept the appointment on any account as being degrading to the legal profession', fearing too that he 'should incur the risk of being struck off the Rolls'.[49]

The publicity that both Calcraft and Marwood had cultivated as hangmen evidently aroused some measure of disapproval, again an obvious signal that, for some, the business of execution, though a necessary evil, was one best transacted out of public view. The *Graphic* hoped that whoever replaced Marwood would emulate his 'professional ways', but 'trusted that he will talk less to newspaper reporters' than his predecessor.[50] Another suggested that the name and identity of the common hangman be kept strictly secret, and that the successful applicant

> should adopt a '*nom de guerre*'; say 'Nemesis' [and should] assume various disguises when travelling on duty; now appearing as a soldier, next as a sailor, anon as a policeman, then as a handcuffed prisoner on his way to gaol, &c &c, and when officiating should don a costume concealing his face & person, so that even prison warders should be unable to recognise him.

In this applicant's view, such precautions would help to recapture some of the awe and mystery associated with the execution of felons and help to enhance the 'dreadful solemnity of such occasions', which, presumably, had been lost due to Marwood's bungling and contemptible public behaviour.[51]

Most of the honest applicants, however, were simply putting themselves forward as men possessed of what they considered the requisite qualifications for an unpleasant but necessary job. Frank Tracy applied 'not on any morbid fancifil grounds but as a duty'. Stephen Anscomb saw the job as a 'national obligation', and Thomas Stott offered himself for the situation, as he said, 'to do my duty to my country and fellow men and to carry out the law of the land'.[52] Most applicants tried to highlight what they construed as their particular qualifications for the job including brute strength, previous experience with police work, or a facility with knots, though what the authorities sought in an ideal candidate was never spelled out in detail. Henry Kelly claimed that along with his 'strength and ability' he had been 'a practical rope tyer for upwards of 10 years'.[53] Another had been a bell hanger, while a smith from Liverpool deemed himself 'a good judge of weights'.[54] Others still suggested that their trades as butchers, abattoir workers, surgeons, military men or police officers had hardened them to death. As a pig slaughterer, Joseph Whitehouse could claim he was fit for the job since 'my nerves are like iron', while John Porter of Lancashire claimed he was 'capable of anything as my courage is good'.[55] Some sent photographs or business cards, others included testimonials from friends, neighbours, clergymen and employers to support their applications.[56] Many, including Bartholomew Binns, who was eventually selected for the post, were succinct in their initial letters, informing the Home Secretary or Sheriffs of only basic physical and mental characteristics. Binns' brief letter reads:

> Hon Sir, Learning by this days paper that the public executioner (Marwood) is dead I beg most respectfully to apply for the situation. I am 43 years of age 5 feet eleven inches high and weigh about 12 stone can furnish you with first class references as to character & etc.
> Hoping to hear from you at an early date.
> I am Yours obediently,
> Bartholomew Binns[57]

Such comparatively pedestrian letters are, of course, interesting in themselves, as they also allude to many of the central aspects of the masculine ideal – duty, respect, physical prowess, character – that other applicants elaborate on in greater detail. In this way, the letters provide a unique insight into largely working-class conceptions of masculinity not often revealed in such explicit terms.[58] They reveal, for example, how working-class masculinities were not as closely linked to particular work as middle-class notions of it. Many were willing to tolerate the less salubrious aspects of the job, if the compensation for it would assist them in fulfilling their expected roles as providers for the family. John Adamson from Manchester was willing to take the job 'if the selery Will keep a Wife And to Children'. Similarly, an Irishman named James Smith living on his 7s. per week pension from the Royal Artillery stated how, being 'out of Employment … would gladly do any thing in Honesty' to support his six daughters, since his three sons were of 'no help to me'.[59]

Some of the applicants revealed a long fascination with the hangman and nothing short of a burning desire to take up the position. If anything, C.H. Thompson, a bill-poster in Essex, was honest in his letter: 'all I can offer in my behalf is a love of seeing executions and a firm belief in my own nerve and capability for the vacant office'.[60] Others pointed to their strength of mind and body as reasons for being selected. A Liverpool man proffered as his qualifications his youth, 'I am 20 years of Age', his strength, and his willingness 'to hang 10 persons Daily', the phrase being triple underlined in his letter.[61] Still other more enthusiastic applicants claimed that they were made of sufficient stuff to be able to execute anyone. On the possibility of assuming the office of hangman, Philip Hamond related how he 'always had an idea [he] should like to do so', adding 'I feel I could hang any thing you can bring before me'.[62] Joseph Dixon was more specific and confirmed that, 'As regards to execution enny releation that would Never Bother Me.'[63] Another stated 'I am willing to hang Father Mother Sister Brother if required',[64] and a number of other applicants expressed similar assurances.[65] James Billington, a hairdresser from Bolton, was willing to 'Hange any one the Law require'. His enthusiasm and personal interest in the job are both striking and chilling for their sincerity: 'I may Say it is a Post I have wanted ever since I was a boy and have practised the same with dummies many a time & believe that I could improve the present system'.[66] Billington's enthusiasm would be rewarded in 1891, when he was asked to take up the post following James Berry's resignation.[67]

One man tried to put himself forward as the cost-efficient choice, stating that he was willing to 'Hang For 3 Month For Nothing'.[68] Thomas Swanson, apparently a local preacher in Northumberland, was also willing to offer his services 'without a selery', considering himself 'a public benefactor'. What was more, he said he had 'experimented on almost every domestic animal extant and can prove to your satisfaction my ability to satisfy you in a scientific manner without resorting to the long drop which is so obnoxious to the general public'. Swanson apologized for his style, fearing that 'perhaps my writing may not give you the most favourable impression'. He puts this down to being self-taught, stating that 'all I've learned I got since I reach maturity'. Despite his poor schooling, he thought himself fit for the post and could produce references since he was 'well know [*sic*] in Northumberland as the Hartley Poet or the Happy preacher'.[69]

Another enthusiastic amateur named George Deakin, from Ireland, wrote that he had made hanging his special hobby 'for some time passed'; indeed, to the detriment of his livelihood. 'I had held good jobs in my time', he laments, 'but have lost em through pain too much attention to the hangin business'. To prove his readiness to take the post, he claimed that he was ready 'to hang anibody on the spot on receiving your words'.[70] And there were many others who indicated that they had given the matter considerable 'scientific' attention; or who included sketches of their plans for new drops or details of their improved devices.[71] One demonstrated his proficiency with knots by including three small pieces of rope, tied in various knots and attached to the bottom of his letter. But one of the most bizarre letters, which yet seems genuine, comes from a London man named Frederick Whiting, and reads as follows:

> Rt. Honourable Sir, Owing to Mr Marwoods death having occurred, and the Office being left vacant, I beg to offer my services and bring under your notice a few of my qualifications for so important a situation.
> 1) I am of a suitable Age (25).
> 2) I am good at tying knots, and understand the manipulation of Ropes.
> 3) I am possessed of a vast quantity of muscular power.
> 4) I am very steady, being almost a Teetotaller.
> 5) It will be a labour of love, which will increase as years roll on, I at the present time having an intense aversion of every human being.
> 6th & last) I am not known or easily recognized, am entirely dependent on my own resources, and should you kindly favor me with this Office I promise on my part to leave no Rope unturned to temper Justice with Humanity.

> I hope that you will not think this haste on my part untimely, but owing to the excessive competition of the times, I am reluctantly compelled to smother my sympathy with the bereaved Family through my desire to secure the situation.
>
> I remain your humble & respectful servant,

Although this letter may well have been sent as a hoax, it does allude to many of the same concerns about anonymity, humanity and personal qualities (being 'almost' a teetotaller) that the ostensibly serious applicants highlighted too.[72] And again, whether constructed in jest or in good faith, the letter also draws upon broadly shared ideas about masculinity – common to many of the letters – to construct an image of the ideal applicant. Both youth and physical strength are mentioned here, as in a large proportion of the letters, suggesting an image of the powerful, masculine state, whose hired muscle would always remain dutifully bound, if need be, to wrestle recalcitrant offenders to their legally determined and morally justified end. Men were also apt to mention their workmanlike skills and independent means. In still another letter – again possibly a hoax – the author or authors reveal the same shared cultural assumptions about the qualities collectively imagined to be necessary in a hangman. Ten people signed their names to support an applicant named John Smith. The testators claim that that Smith was a man fit for the post, 'as he Posesses both nerve and power. In fact', they continue, 'He is the Son of a Man who once faught and Vanquished a russian Bear.' In a postscript to the letter, the authors also reveal an overt note of contemporary anti-Irish prejudices, adding 'we are sure if you would appoint Him you would not regret it as He cannot abide to look at an Irishman without wishing for revenge'.[73] The implication of course was that as the nation's hangman, he was bound to come face to face with many Irish men (and women) as they were presumed to be responsible for much of the crime in nineteenth-century Britain.

Strength of body and nerve were assumed to be necessary traits by many applicants, suggesting the popular conception of what attributes someone presumably man enough for such a job must have. But in fact, by the late nineteenth century with the 'long drop' now in common use, the art of hanging had been substantially developed and the hangman's physical strength and brutal nature were no longer necessary to finish victims who were seen to be suffering. Since public executions were abolished, there was less concern over the need to subdue or mollify anxious victims who might disrupt the state-imposed solemnity of the event, or even try a last minute escape. The crowd's immediate reaction to such indecorous scaffold scenes, which nevertheless continued after 1868, was now eliminated. Once removed behind prison walls, the hangman was able to test the scaffold, the trap door, and his ropes at his leisure before the actual event, without criticism and pressure from the crowds. Furthermore, the brutal tasks formerly assigned to the common hangman – beheading, public burning of women, whipping of petty offenders through the streets – had long been abolished by the late nineteenth century, and hangmen had been urged for nearly a century to minimize the pain and suffering of the condemned in carrying out their task. Modern executions were supposed to be, ironically, civilized affairs.[74] In keeping with the spirit of the age, the authorities sought a man of good character and reasonable physical condition (not ill, too old, or mentally disturbed) and, most importantly, one who was capable of carrying out his duties in an efficient and humane manner. A tailor from Notting Hill in London seemed attuned to these contemporary attitudes concerning the death penalty. In a supplementary letter to his initial application, he adds that he could 'suggest a Means of rendering Death by Hanging Certain and instantaneous', which he felt was necessary given that 'public opinion seems in favour of the instantaneous Death of the condemned ones'.[75]

The final selection process was difficult because of the volume and mixed quality of the applicants. The authorities in the central government and in London were clearly taken aback by the flood of letters that followed Marwood's death. The London sheriffs and Home Office undersecretaries who first vetted the letters must have shuddered (or chuckled) to think of some of the applicants as potential fellow civil servants. Indeed more than a few applicants must have seemed no better than the people the hangman was expected to deal with.[76] The final decision, however, rested with the Sheriffs of London. That point had been established in the summer of 1883 when Marwood petitioned the Home Office for a fixed salary. In a letter to the Home Office, Edward Read, the Clerk of the Central Criminal Court explained that although Calcraft, Marwood's predecessor, had been a paid official of Newgate prison, 'Marwood has never had any such definite appointment' and was not a permanent official of the state.[77] Thus it was not in the Home Secretary's power to determine the hangman's pay. Still, this did not deter him from making suggestions to the Sheriffs about how Marwood's successor should be treated. Though admitting he had 'no power to give them directions, or to interfere with their discretion' in selecting a replacement for Marwood, the Home Secretary recommended to the Sheriffs that 'similar action should be taken now as in the case of Calcraft' and a permanent employee should be created.[78] It was assumed that county sheriffs would continue to hire the London hangman for jobs in their districts.

On the afternoon of 24 September, the Sheriffs of London and Middlesex (Alderman Polydore de Keyser and Alderman Joseph Savory) interviewed 17 men whom they had selected from the hundreds of applicants. According to a report in the *Lincoln Gazette*, James Berry and a builder named Richard Taylor from Lincoln were the final two choices. Taylor had been chosen by Marwood in August to study as his assistant and the Home Office had agreed to pay for his training. But in the end neither was offered the job. Instead the sheriffs decided upon an unremarkable, 43-year-old Dewsbury man named

Bartholomew Binns.[79] Binns, formerly a foreman platelayer on the Lancashire and Yorkshire Railway, was made an employee of the Corporation of London 'with a general retaining fee … acceded to by the Court of Aldermen' shortly after his appointment.[80] But, unfortunately, Binns' incompetence was soon revealed. He bungled the second and fourth hangings he was hired to perform and arrived too drunk to perform the fifth. In December 1883, at the coroner's inquest following the execution of Henry Dutton at Kirkdale Prison, Liverpool (Binns' third job), the prison's governor Major Leggett testified that in his opinion the hanging was 'clumsily, inefficiently performed'. When asked specifically whether he thought Binns was sober, Leggett demurred, 'well, I should not like to say'.[81] Early the next year, Binns was replaced by James Berry who served as executioner until 1892.

Reading these letters raises the obvious question: why would so many people genuinely want this job? To answer that, it is necessary to situate the job of common hangman within the larger social, cultural and especially economic context of the time, given the working-class backgrounds of many applicants. For nearly six decades after the defeat of Napoleon in 1815, Britain had enjoyed an unprecedented trend of upward economic growth. In the early 1870s, however, competition from other nations began to challenge Britain's traditional dominance in the production of raw materials like coal, tin and iron, and finished goods such as steel and textiles, while butchers and meat producers were beginning to be threatened by frozen imports from Argentina, Australia and New Zealand. [82] Predictably, then, a number of the applicants appear to have been from among the working poor within these specific trades, or at least working-class men who had been displaced by the economic decline of the 1870s and 1880s. There are many colliers, joiners and railwaymen among the applicants, some explicitly mentioning their difficulty in finding work or in making ends meet. It is not surprising to see how applicants indicated that they saw the position as just another job, a service to be provided to the community for a price. John Gitson said that he was applying 'for the simple reason that my present employment is not sufficiently remunerative to enable me to live comfortably'. T.W. Winbrush, a Worcestershire pork butcher and provisions dealer, said he was motivated to apply because he 'did not have enough trade to keep [him] fully employed'.[83] Joseph Richards wrote to the Secretary of State indicating that after a 20-year career as a ship's carpenter, he had little luck in finding steady employment since settling in Oxford. His honesty regarding the perceived applicability of his skills comes through in his letter: 'I am fully acquainted with almost every knot that is tied & if necessary could build a scaffold. I am aware Sir of the unpleasant duties of the office I wish to undertake but privation & hard times are much worse.'[84] Whether or not this straightforward, rational approach in their letters worked to the applicant's favour in the eyes of the metropolitan sheriffs is hard to determine. Henry Hall noted in his letter that he had 'been accustomed for some years to Police & Railway work', which elicited a marginal check mark from at least one official who vetted his letter. Hall also stated that he was 'at present out of employment', a point that was also underlined, though whether favourably or unfavourably is unclear.[85] We do know that he was not offered the position. It should go without saying why a Stortford man's claim that though he had 'failed in business as a Ropemaker... [I] think I could carry out the duties of the office in a satisfactory manner' drew no further action from the Sheriffs.[86] James Berry, a boot salesman who applied to replace Marwood, and who eventually replaced Binns, claimed in his memoirs that his initial application for the post was made out of necessity: 'I was simply driven to it by the poverty-stricken condition of my family, which I was unable to keep in reasonable comfort upon my earnings.'[87]

But not all of the applicants were from the ranks of the working poor, or unemployed. William Cawthorn wrote that he could supply references from the 'leading Gentlemen of the parish to which I have the honour to belong'.[88] Another man named Goscombe indicated he was willing to do the necessary work for travel costs only, and of course the self-proclaimed sociopath, Frederick Whiting, noted that he was 'entirely dependent on my own resources'. Applications came too from military pensioners, active or retired police officers as well as from various tradesmen who were looking to supplement their incomes.[89] But only a small number identified themselves as 'white-collar' workers, such as the lawyer who later withdrew his name. Other respectable members of middle-class society, those more likely to share abolitionist sympathies, tried to dissuade other men from applying for the position. When James Billington asked a minister to support his application, the minister confided to the sheriffs that he had learned of the nature of Billington's application 'with regret & have tried to dissuade him from applying but as he insists upon doing so I cannot refuse to testify at this request to his good character'.[90]

How remunerative was the hangman's job? We know what the late hangman was paid because in July of 1883, a little more than a month before his death, Marwood appealed to the authorities at Scotland Yard for an increase in his compensation. At that point he was receiving a flat fee of £10 plus travelling expenses for a single job, and an additional £5 for multiple hangings. Marwood, however, wanted to draw a regular, fixed salary of £100 per year from the central government along with an £8 fee per job, with travelling expenses to be paid by the contracting Sheriff. Marwood suggests that in some instances, as when a prisoner had been granted a reprieve while he was en route to the job, his retainer was not paid and he was unable to recover his out-of-pocket expenses.[91] But there appears to have been little support for his request. Some may have found Marwood's request for a fixed salary for an intermittent task rather presumptuous. The average 'moderate family' defined by Charles Booth, lived on an income of £18 21*s*. per week.[92] Wages for a rural labourer in 1883 ranged between £14 19*s*. per week or, at best, around £50 annually. A slate miner in the north earned only £5 more than that annually, while closer to the mark, the average rate of pay for county and city police officers was around £69 and £74 respectively. Even the most highly skilled manual labourers in England and Wales could only command an annual income of £73.[93] When Calcraft resigned his office in June of 1874, he was retired on a weekly pension of 25*s*., equivalent to his last salary.[94] Marwood's salary request would therefore have put him solidly within the ranks of the middle class, a possibility which was likely to rankle the sensibilities of more than a few civil servants who may have heard of this.[95] Even if he were asked to perform eight hangings a year – roughly half the annual average number of executions in England and Wales between 1879–89 – at £10 per hanging, the executioner would still pull in a supplemental income more than equivalent to the best paid skilled labourer.[96] For an unwaged working man, then, the job must have had at least its pecuniary attractions, even if it proved only a supplemental and inconsistent income.

Financial compensation alone might explain the desire of some men to fill the vacant position. Still, we should probably not be too quick to dismiss the real sense of duty and necessity that surely motivated a number of applicants to put their names forward for the job. As the letters themselves reveal, the applicants are generally working-class or lower-middle-class men, who had largely internalized the concepts of hard work, law and order, and duty to queen and country. Their familiarity with the rough edges of Victorian society had prepared them for the harsh realities of life. And if they could be of service to their country while drawing a salary or commission that seemed to compensate handsomely for relatively limited work, and if they saw themselves as being made of the right stuff for such a particularly unpleasant job, then why not apply?

Many believed that the public criticism and social revulsion against the person of the executioner was partly brought on by the public persona cultivated by men like Calcraft and Marwood. But if the conduct and identity of the executioner could be concealed, like the executions themselves, the public image of the hangman might be rehabilitated; and the person carrying out the job could perhaps satisfy his own conscience that he was merely an agent of larger forces, simply carrying out an unpleasant task. The candid use of words and phrases in the letters that hint at duty, order, and custom suggest a deep belief in the justness of the death penalty. In the eyes of the largely working-class applicants, the death penalty constitutes a necessity, a fundamental pillar of justice and the law in a modern civilized society. Though some may well have been simply writing in words they thought their potential employer wanted to hear, the brevity of most letters and the unsophisticated and often phonetic style in which they are written suggests a more honest, unself-conscious use of such language. If they were constructing themselves for this particular job, these would-be hangmen were doing so by drawing upon the language and shared cultural assumptions that they themselves had internalised and understood, and expressed those beliefs in the words and syntax that came naturally to them.

Although the volume of applications attests to a certain degree of support for the death penalty, a handful of letters are explicit in approving of its use. One Charles Carden wrote, 'I approve of our criminal code as it now stands and have strong views in favour of the present system of capital punishment, which I consider the most humane, effective & impressive possible system.'[97] There were many other applicants who expressed or implied their general approval of the death penalty, and its important role in maintaining order, deterring potential offenders, and suitably punishing the most serious offences. That many of the applicants comment directly on, or at least allude to, the larger place of the executioner in society suggests, too, a degree of acceptance of the death penalty and an implied expectation that such a penalty would remain a central aspect of the state's power. People would not likely apply in good conscience for a job they abhorred, or that they believed was about to be abolished. Still, others were more equivocal about the need for the death penalty and the means of execution, whereby one man was hired by the state specifically to kill others. Speaking of the job of hangman, Augustum Bond wrote that 'though the vocation is not a[n] honourable one ... it is manifestly essential in all civilised countries'.[98] Another wrote that, though the hangman's duties may be regarded as 'of the most repulsive character', it was yet important to recall that 'they involve the necessary fulfilment of the law, discharged in the name of the law as a punishment for outrages on Society, and as a deterrent against future evil doing'.[99]

Such ambivalence about the hangman pointed to deeper concerns about the death penalty. In vetting these letters, government officials were forced to come face to face with the often-camouflaged reality that the state killed people. The vacancy caused by Marwood's death reminded state officials of the uneasy truth that the putting to death of its members was not in fact the distant, disconnected event that centuries of ritual, and volumes of legal and moral justification had constructed it to be. Even its removal from public view twenty years earlier could still only be hailed a partial victory for civilized society. Regardless of the complex cultural artifice that surrounded the idea of the death penalty, the mechanics of its execution were brutally straightforward: one human being was hired and ordered to kill another. The method of the killing was fixed in precedent as hanging. But to minimize the opportunities for errors and consequently undue pain and suffering on the part of the condemned person – all potential consequences of the chosen method of killing – which was now unacceptable to the civilized Victorians, the authorities tended to seek a skilled practitioner to carry out the task. As the Clerk to the Central Criminal Court explained, 'the Hangman is simply there as an Assistant to relieve the Sheriff of the painful task which would otherwise be imposed upon him of personally hanging the Culprit'.[100] The technical act of killing another person is thus rendered the quintessentially menial task, full of unpleasantness, and one that would be avoided entirely if people behaved in an orderly, civilized manner and obeyed the law. Considered in this light then, it is less surprising that men accustomed to other unpleasant and unpopular jobs would see themselves as eminently qualified for the job of common hangman. For such men, financial compensation alone may well have been enough to encourage an application. James Berry estimated there were roughly 20 executions annually in Great Britain by the time of his tenure, netting him perhaps £200 per year if he was hired to carry out all of the jobs. Though it could constitute a healthy if occasional supplement to an otherwise meagre income, as Berry himself pointed out, this was 'an uncertain commission' and not a fixed, guaranteed wage.[101] When murder rates fluctuated down, the number of capital offences committed diminished, and executions grew more infrequent. And still, sheriffs outside of London were not obliged to hire the City's hangman.

In light of the interest in the position, what can be said about the role of the hangman in nineteenth-century English society? The overwhelming response to Marwood's death in the late summer of 1883 and the presumably honest desire by hundreds of men to take up the position suggests the need to reassess our understanding of the place of capital punishment in nineteenth-century society. Perhaps middle-class sensibilities have been overemphasized in the discussion of penal reform and popular attitudes towards the death penalty. Was there still widespread support for capital punishment among a broader section of society than previously assumed? Despite support for abolitionist campaigns, there were still many who were in favour of the death penalty as a suitable punishment for certain crimes, with more than 1,000 people seriously willing to carry out the deed. These letters provide further evidence that the concerns about the death penalty were largely class-based. Beyond the moral and philosophical objections to the death penalty raised by educated middle-class abolitionists, or more cynically their affected squeamishness, there was considerably wider support among Britain's labouring class for capital punishment. At least these letters establish a certain degree of acceptance that there had to be a man who was willing to carry out the act itself. But even a cursory reading of these letters demonstrates that this is perhaps an overly liberal and presentist reading of these texts, one that is too heavily laden with post-abolitionist baggage. For, indeed, the sheer volume of letters at this point in Victoria's reign indicates that there was no shortage of willing executioners among her majesty's civilized subjects. And in an age before more antiseptic, technological innovations were devised for putting people to death, the job of common hangman would likely fall to no more and no less than a common man, who was willing to hang men.

Notes

1 V.A.C. Gatrell, *The Hanging Tree: Execution and the English People, 1770–1868* (Oxford, 1994), 602–3.

2 G. Abbott, *Lords of the Scaffold: A History of the Executioner* (1991), 135–6.

3 G.D. Robin, 'The Executioner: his place in English society' *British Journal of Sociology*, 15 (1964), 234–53; T.W. Laqueur, 'Crowds, carnival and the state in English executions, 1604–1868', in A.L. Beier *et al.* eds, *The First Modern Society: Essays in English History in Honour of Lawrence Stone* (Cambridge, 1989), 322; Gatrell, *Hanging Tree*, 99–100; P. Spierenburg, *The Spectacle of Suffering* (Cambridge,1984), 13–18; R. Van Dülmen, *Theatre of Horror: Crime and Punishment in Early Modern Germany*, trans. E. Neu (Oxford, 1990); R. Evans, *Rituals of Retribution: Capital Punishment in Germany, 1600–1987* (Oxford, 1996), 53–64.
4 *Maidstone Journal and Kentish Advertiser*, 1 May 1821.
5 Gatrell, *Hanging Tree*, 604; J.M. Beattie, *Policing and Punishment in London, 1660–1750* (Oxford, 2001), 129–30, 155–6.
6 PRO HO 144/18/46327/126. On Marwood as a 'man of science', see H. Engel, *Lord High Executioner: An Unashamed Look at Hangmen, Headsmen, and their Kind* (Toronto: Key Porter, 1996), chap. 4.
7 *Bristol Evening News*, 5 September 1883, 4.
8 *York Herald*, 5 September 1883, 5.
9 *Bristol Evening News*, 5 September 1883, 4.
10 *Bristol Evening News*, 19 September 1883, 2.
11 *Illustrated London News*, 15 September 1883, 251.
12 31 & 32 Vict., c. 24, (1868), s. 3.
13 For an examination of this reconfiguration of the 'public' in the expression of justice through newspaper reports of hangings, see S. Devereaux, '"Public justice" and nineteenth-century newspapers', paper delivered at American Society of Legal History conference, Toronto, October 1999.
14 D. Cooper, *The Lesson of the Scaffold* (1974), 174n; H. Bleackley, *The Hangmen of England* (1929), 51.
15 *The Graphic*, 8 September 1883, 239.
16 See for example the report of the execution of Charles Peace in *The Times*, 26 February, 1879, 10.
17 V.A.C. Gatrell, 'The decline of theft and violence in Victorian and Edwardian England', in V.A.C. Gatrell, B. Lenman and G. Parker eds, *Crime and the Law: The Social History of Crime in Western Europe since 1500* (1980), 286–9; T.R. Gurr, 'Historical trends in violent crime: a critical review of the evidence', *Crime & Justice: An Annual Review of Research*, 3 (1981), 310–11.
18 *The Graphic*, 8 September 1883, 239. In a letter to the Home Office dated 16 August 1883, Edward Read, Clerk to the Central Criminal Court, surmised that Marwood was 'always employed to the exclusion of other Candidates' because of the 'natural desire of those responsible for the execution to secure the services of a skilful and experienced person' (PRO HO 144/118/28103/5).
19 *Illustrated London News*, 15 September 1883, 251.
20 *The Observer*, 9 September 1883, 5.
21 *Western Daily Press*, 10 September 1883, 5.
22 *The Observer*, 9 September 1883, 5.
23 Gatrell, *Hanging Tree*; R. McGowen, 'Civilizing punishment: the end of the public execution in England', *JBS*, 33 (1994), 262, 274–5.
24 Gatrell, *Hanging Tree*, 23.
25 'The Finishing Schoolmaster,' *Household Words*, III (May, 1851), 169–71.
26 *Bristol Mercury and Daily Post*, 8 September 1883, 5.
27 Harcourt cites the figure in a letter to his permanent under-secretary, A.F.O. Liddell, (PRO HO 144/18/46327/178).
28 *The Law Times*, 22 September 1883, 357.

29 *Times*, 10 September 1883, 4.
30 *Illustrated London News*, 15 September 1883, 251.
31 This point was spelled out in a Home Office memo written 11 August 1883, when the issue of paying for Marwood's assistant was under discussion (PRO HO 144/118/A28103/3).
32 James Berry, *My Experiences as an Executioner*, ed. H. Snowden Ward (1972), 18.
33 *Illustrated London News*, 15 September 1883, 251.
34 *The Observer*, 9 September 1883, 5.
35 *Bristol Evening News*, 19 September 1883, 2.
36 The surviving letters (roughly 800 in number) are located in the Corporation of London Record Office (CLRO) under 'Officers: Executioner'. They are filed in three boxes, but are unsorted and are not indexed. I will refer to them here by sender's name and the letter's date.
37 PRO HO 144/18/46327/178.
38 Letter from Henry Senior, 7 September 1883.
39 Letter from R.A. Matthews, 11 September 1883.
40 For example 'Joe Grimm', Letter from Joe Grimm (Nomme de Geurre), 18 September 1883.
41 Letter from J.R. Poole, 10 September 1883.
42 Letter from Henry Turpil, 11 September 1883.
43 Letter from 'T.M.', 8 September 1883.
44 Letter from F. Woodford, 15 September 1883.
45 Letter from Robert Downie, 10 September 1883.
46 Letter from John Smith, 11 September 1883.
47 Anonymous letter, 5 September 1883.
48 Letter from J. Husband, 8 September 1883.
49 Letter from William Sayer, 8 September 1883.
50 *The Graphic*, 8 September 1883, 239.
51 Letter from J. Hart, 7 September 1883. John H. Duckworth of Lancashire also noted in his letter 'unlike Marwood I am no bragger' (6 September 1883).
52 Letters from Frank Tracy, 8 September 1983; Stephen Anscomb, 5 September 1983; Thomas Stott, 6 September 1883.
53 Letter from Henry Kelly, 4 September 1883.
54 Letter from Thomas Williams, 10 September 1883.
55 Letters from Joseph Whitehouse, 5 September 1983; John Porter, 6 September 1883.
56 Among those who included photos were W. Knight, Edward Musson and Horatio C. Smith.
57 Letter from Bartholomew Binns, 5 September 1883.
58 On British masculinities, see M. Roper and J. Tosh, eds, *Manful Assertions: Masculinities in Britain since 1800* (1991); J. Tosh, 'What should historians do with masculinity? Reflections on nineteenth century Britain,' *HWJ*, 38 (1994), 179–202.
59 Letters from John Adamson, 5 September 1883; James Smith, 15 September 1883. On the significance of 'dignified' work to middle-class masculinity, see Tosh, 'What should historians do with masculinity?', 185–6.
60 Letter from C.H. Thompson, 5 September 1883.
61 Letter from S. Calderwood, 5 September 1883.
62 Letter from Philip Hamond, 11 September 1883.
63 Letter from Joseph Dixon, 16 September 1883.
64 Letter from Martin McGerney, 5 September 1883.
65 Letters from Benjamin Devey, 6 September 1883; John Coggan, 9 September 1883.

66 Letter from James Billington, [?] September 1883.
67 Engel, *Lord High Executioner*, 81, 84.
68 Letter from James Hookway, 8 September 1883.
69 Letter from Thomas Swanson, 9 September 1883.
70 Letter from George Deakin, 5 September 1883.
71 William Payman's letter (10 September 1883) includes a sketch of the drop he would use and claims 'I count my plan the quicker plan on record'. Frederick Ralph suggests in his letter of 10 September, replacing the cross beam of the scaffold with a roller 'similar to a well windlass' as well as an extra harness to be used to support 'Culprits of the Fainting Order' which would eliminate the need for extra warders on the scaffold.
72 Letter from Frederick Whiting, 5 September 1883. The 1881 census records show that a 23-year-old Frederick Whiting did reside in Chatsworth Road, London.
73 Letter from John Smith, 6 September 1883.
74 McGowen, 'Civilizing punishment', 280; G.T. Smith, 'Civilized people don't want to see that kind of thing: the decline of public physical punishment in London, 1760–1840', in C. Strange ed., *Qualities of Mercy: Justice, Punishment, and Discretion* (Vancouver, 1996), 28–9.
75 Letter from W.T. Greening, 10 September 1883.
76 *The Graphic* stated that 'no doubt the reading of the letters must have shot light horrors through the pulses of the officials entrusted with the disagreeable duty of selection' (8 September 1883, 239).
77 PRO HO 144/118/A28103/5.
78 PRO HO 144/18/46327/177.
79 *Lincoln Gazette*, 6 October 1883, 7; PRO HO 144/118/A28103/3.
80 PRO HO 144/18/46327/188.
81 *The Times*, 4 December 1883, 12.
82 Sir R. Ensor, *England 1870–1914* (Oxford, 1936), 105–10; D. Beales, *From Castlereagh to Gladstone, 1815–1885* (1969), 232–7; D. Read, *The Age of Urban Democracy: England 1868–1914* revised ed. (1994), 215, 228.
83 Letters from John Gitson, 5 September 1983; T.W. Winbush, 6 September 1883.
84 Letter from Joseph Richards, 5 September 1883.
85 Letter from Henry Hall, 5 September 1883.
86 Letter from R.P. Franklin, 11 September 1883.
87 Berry, *My Experiences as an Executioner*, 17.
88 Letter from William Cawthorn, 6 September 1883.
89 Letters from James Smith, retired from royal artillery; Edwin Lucas, former seaman and pensioned police officer; George Wooder, butcher; W.T. Greening, tailor.
90 Letter from Rev. D.L. Prosser, [?] September 1883.
91 PRO HO 144/18/46327/126, Letter from Marwood to Home Secretary, 5 July 1883.
92 J.F.C. Harrison, *Late Victorian Britain 1875–1901* (1990), 187.
93 For wages for skilled labour, see K.T. Hoppen, *The Mid-Victorian Generation, 1846–1886* (Oxford, 1998), 21, 63 (table 3.1). For other wages cited, see *Return of Rates of Wages in the Mines and Quarries in the United Kingdom* (1891), Cmd. 6445, xxxiii; *Return of Rates of Wages Paid by Local Authorities and Private Companies to Police* (1892), Cmd. 6715, ix. The report notes that 'the minimum rate for constables remains about the same as in 1886, but the maximum has advanced 5s. per week' (xv).
94 CLRO Gaol Committee (Aldermen) minutes, September 1873–November 1874, 94–5.

95 Hoppen notes that even by the early twentieth century, 'only 2.0 per cent of all employees and professional persons in Britain were earning as much as £200 a year' (*Mid-Victorian Generation*, 34).

96 There were 165 executions carried out in the period 1879–89 in England and Wales, an average of 15 per year. The years 1881 and 1889 had the lowest number at 11, while 1888 had the highest number at 22 (Parliamentary Papers. House of Commons. Judicial Statistics for England and Wales 1879–89).

97 Letter from Charles Carden, 5 September 1883.

98 Letter from Augustum Bond, 4 September 1883.

99 Letter from J. Hart, 7 September 1883.

100 PRO HO 144/118/A21803/5.

101 Berry, *My Experiences as an Executioner*, 120.

Index

Note: particular 'Acts of Parliaments', 'Courts', 'Offences', 'Officials' and modes of 'Punishments' are indexed under those headings.